HOW THE WORLDS BECAME

How the Worlds Became

Philosophy and the Oldest Stories

STEPHEN R.L. CLARK

Angelico Press

First published in the USA
by Angelico Press 2023
Copyright © Stephen R.L. Clark 2023

All rights reserved:
No part of this book may be reproduced or transmitted,
in any form or by any means, without permission

For information, address:
Angelico Press, Ltd.
169 Monitor St.
Brooklyn, NY 11222
www.angelicopress.com

Ppr   978-1-62138-935-4
Cloth 978-1-62138-936-1

Book and cover design
by Michael Schrauzer

CONTENTS

Acknowledgments ix

1 Introduction 1
2 How the Worlds Become 19
  The One that Became a Million 20 / *What Are Gods?* 30 / *Catastrophe and Creation* 45
3 Astronomy 51
  Heavenly Bodies and Their Cycles 51 / *Planetary Influences* 60 / *Here Comes the Sun* 73
4 Powers and Personalities 82
  Allegory and Art 82 / *Levels of Being* 89 / *Possession* 99 / *Principles and Persons* 109
5 Families and Dysfunctional Divinities 123
  War in Heaven 123 / *Genesis* 135 / *Sub-Creation* 144 / *Might-Have-Beens That Maybe Are* 153
6 Ritual and Belief 160
  Faith without Belief 160 / *Sounds and Music* 167 / *Silence and Self-Contradiction* 173
7 Monotheisms 186
  Modern Derogations of Monotheism 186 / *Akhenaten and After* 192 / *The Hebrew Story* 198
8 How to Escape 205
  Time and the Transient 205 / *Make Maths, not War* 215 / *Fairyland* 217 / *In the Beginning* 227
9 Other Identities 237
  Surviving Life 237 / *Dreaming the World Alive* 247
10 Talking of the End 253
  Might the Monsters Win? 253 / *Malice or Indifference?* 259 / *Apocalypse and the End of Days* 264
11 New Beginnings 273
  Stories Old and New 273 / *The Birth of the Son of God* 280
12 Conclusion 289

Related Works by Stephen R.L. Clark 295
Bibliography 297
Index 318

ACKNOWLEDGMENTS

MY THANKS AS ALWAYS TO MY FAMILY, FRIENDS, and colleagues for their inspiration and correction over many years, especially Hilary Armstrong, Gary Chartier, Gillian Clark, Douglas Hedley, Michael McGhee, Mervat Nasser, and Panayiota Vassilopoulou. My thanks also to the Universities of Liverpool and Bristol for providing me with library resources, and virtual habitations, as Emeritus Professor of Philosophy and Honorary Research Fellow in Theology and Religious Studies.

The still greater debt is to the long line of mythmakers, Egyptologists, philosophers, and mythologists, from Homer to Hermes Trismegistus, Parmenides to Plotinus, Snorri Sturluson to Olaf Stapledon — or even Lucretius to Lovecraft. Those named individuals would themselves also acknowledge the long lines of anonymous authors who spoke for and to the common mass of humankind. We have often forgotten how to listen to the stories that even philosophers tell because we no longer take the commoner stories as seriously as we should. "The lover of myth is in a way a lover of wisdom, for the myth is composed of wonders."[1] Conversely, those who seek out wisdom will usually find a myth. Once upon a time that was enough, or almost enough, to know.

---

[1] Aristotle, *Metaphysics* 1.982b17.

~1~
Introduction

The kings [of Egypt] were appointed from the priests or from the military class, since the military class had eminence and honour because of valour, and the priests because of wisdom. But he who was appointed from the military class was at once made one of the priests and a participant in their philosophy, which, for the most part, is veiled in myths and in words containing dim reflexions and adumbrations of the truth, as they themselves intimate beyond question by appropriately placing sphinxes before their shrines to indicate that their religious teaching has in it an enigmatical sort of wisdom. In Saïs the statue of Athena, whom they believe to be Isis, bore the inscription: "I am all that has been, and is, and shall be, and my robe no mortal has yet uncovered."[1]

THIS STUDY BEGAN—LIKE MANY OTHERS OF MY works—in a fit of mild exasperation. The notion is now widespread that Abrahamic monotheism, in all its manifold versions, is merely a "Bronze Age Myth," an arbitrary explanation for our and the world's existence with no better standing than "Spaghetti Monster" or the Great Pumpkin. Those who endlessly recirculated this meme or mental microbe were firmly ignorant of monotheistic philosophy over the last three thousand years, invincibly persuaded that the supposed beginnings of the story must somehow be an argument against its present, complex reality. A reasonable first response, it seemed to me, was to observe that there was another and much more common Bronze Age Myth remarkably like a current cosmological theory, and that perhaps revealed an underlying predisposition in much human

---

[1] Plutarch, "Isis and Osiris," ch. 5, in *Moralia* 5:24–25; see Assmann, *Moses the Egyptian*, 83.

thought: namely, that Everything began from Nothing. That story will be the first that I examine.

As usual, the project expanded around me. On the one hand, what do these many stories show about our human predispositions (or even our human prehistory), and how might we learn a little about the universe and ourselves by reconsidering them, with imaginative sympathy? On the other, what do they conceal from us about the universe and ourselves?

Does it seem absurd to spend any time or energy in examining or developing apparently fantastic stories, whether old or new? Philosophers, it is popularly supposed, must argue from clearly correct premises by inexorably logical steps to their often surprising conclusions, following "the argument" where it alone might lead.[2] They must have shed their personal or cultural prejudices, and only accept "objective" propositions of a kind that require no special moral or religious virtue, nor any long apprenticeship or cultural context, to discern. That this claim itself has a special history, and rests on largely unargued premises, is usually forgotten. Nor is it acknowledged that such an intellectual parsimony leaves us necessarily ignorant of almost everything we once thought we knew. Descartes at least acknowledged that for all practical purposes he would rely on "received wisdom" in the absence of incontrovertible proof of any substantive thesis.[3] Oddly, later philosophers have simultaneously argued against Descartes' own belief that he could indeed establish some incontrovertible truths (namely that he did himself exist and think, and that there was an infinite reality, identified as God, against which all his thoughts were measured), and failed to admit that their own convictions were grounded only

---

2 The common definition of a "paradox" as "an argument from incontestable premises to an unacceptable conclusion via an impeccable rule of inference" (Sorensen, "Philosophical Implications of Logical Paradoxes," 138) is weighted against acceptance of the conclusion: the better course is often to suspect both premises and the rule. Sorensen's alternative definition is less constrained: "a 'paradox' is a set of individually plausible but jointly inconsistent propositions" (ibid., 140).
3 Descartes, *Discourse on Method* [1637], 3.22, in *Philosophical Writings*, 122: "For I had begun at this time to count my own opinions as worthless, because I wanted to examine them all, and didn't see how I could do better than in the meantime to follow those of the most sensible men."

Introduction

in just the sort of "received wisdom" that they also wish to mock. Chesterton, in an early, popular essay, listed four deeply rooted — and unprovable — beliefs:[4]

> 1. Every sane man believes that the world around him and the people in it are real, and not his own delusion or dream. No man starts burning London in the belief that his servant will soon wake him for breakfast. But that I, at any given moment, am not in a dream, is unproved and unprovable. That anything exists except myself is unproved and unprovable.
>
> 2. All sane men believe that this world not only exists, but matters. Every man believes there is a sort of obligation on us to interest ourselves in this vision or panorama of life. He would think a man wrong who said, "I did not ask for this farce and it bores me. I am aware that an old lady is being murdered downstairs, but I am going to sleep." That there is any such duty to improve the things we did not make is a thing unproved and unprovable.
>
> 3. All sane men believe that there is such a thing as a self, or ego, which is continuous. There is no inch of my brain matter the same as it was ten years ago. But if I have saved a man in battle ten years ago, I am proud; if I have run away, I am ashamed. That there is such a paramount "I" is unproved and unprovable. But it is more than unproved and unprovable; it is definitely disputed by many metaphysicians.
>
> 4. Lastly, most sane men believe, and all sane men in practice assume, that they have a power of choice and responsibility for action.

These were articles of faith, and ones that Chesterton continued to affirm, both as being true and as being, exactly, articles of faith. "There are no rationalists. We all believe fairy-tales, and live in them.... Some hold the undemonstrable dogma of the existence

---

4 "Philosophy for the Schoolroom," in *Daily News*, June 22, 1907, reprinted in Maycock, *The Man Who Was Orthodox*, 92ff. See also Chesterton, *Orthodoxy*, 26: "[I]f a man began to burn down London and say that his housekeeper would soon call him to breakfast, we should take him and put him with other logicians."

of God; some the equally undemonstrable dogma of the existence of the man next door."5 But it should also be clear that he felt the opposite temptations, and might sometimes almost have agreed to them. Of the ending of *Midsummer Night's Dream*, he says:

> One touch is added which makes the play colossal. Theseus and his train retire with a crashing finale, full of humour and wisdom and things set right, and silence falls on the house. Then there comes a faint sound of little feet, and for a moment, as it were, the elves look into the house, asking which is the reality. "Suppose we are the realities and they the shadows." If that ending were acted properly any modern man would feel shaken to his marrow if he had to walk home from the theatre through a country lane.6

It is that balance of the mundane and the mysterious that makes Chesterton, for all his faults, a valuable resource — and the same may be said for Philosophy in general (as I shall seek to show).

The late antique philosopher Plotinus accepted both that we often had no alternative but to rely on traditional images and metaphors to gesture toward the mystery of things, and that those images could indeed — sometimes — be really reliable evidence.

> The wise men of Egypt, I think, also understood this, either by scientific (*akribes*) or innate (*sumphute*) knowledge, and when they wished to signify something wisely, did not use the forms of letters which follow the order of words and propositions (*logoi* and *protaseis*) and imitate sounds and the enunciations of philosophical statements (*prophoras axiomaton*), but by drawing images and inscribing in their temples one particular image of each particular thing, they manifested the non-discursiveness of the intelligible world, that is, that every image is a kind of knowledge and wisdom and is a subject of statements, all together in one, and not discourse (*dianoesis*) or deliberation (*bouleusis*).7

---

5   Chesterton, *Heretics*, 123.
6   *Good Words*, vol. 45 (September–October 1904), 621–26; see http://www.gkc.org.uk/gkc/books/midsummer_nights_dream.html (accessed Jan. 17, 2023).
7   *Enneads* V.8 [31].6 (all passages from the *Enneads* are drawn from Hilary Armstrong's translation, with occasional corrections); see also *Ennead* IV.3 [27].11; *Asclepius* 37. See also Hornung, *Conceptions of God*, 258: "The language in which

Introduction

I shall return to the larger and more important implications of Plotinian heuristic thought. As to the supposed necessity of describing the world "objectively," consider at least the early beginnings of that creed.

> The poets of old to make all things look more venerable than they were devised a thousand false Chimaeras; on every Field, River, Grove and Cave they bestowed a Fantasm of their own making: With these they amazed the world.... And in the modern Ages these Fantastical Forms were reviv'd and possessed Christendom.... All which abuses if those acute Philosophers did not promote, yet they were never able to overcome; nay, not even so much as King Oberon and his invisible Army. But from the time in which the Real Philosophy has appear'd there is scarce any whisper remaining of such horrors.... The cours of things goes quietly along, in its own true channel of Natural Causes and Effects. For this we are beholden to Experiments; which though they have not yet completed the discovery of the true world, yet they have already vanquished those wild inhabitants of the false world, that us'd to astonish the minds of men.[8]

Ridding the world of spectres was a *theological* decision, and Sprat here echoes the words of Athanasius in the fourth century AD, in his essay on the Incarnation:

> In former times every place was full of the fraud of oracles, and the utterances of those at Delphi and Dodona and in Boeotia and Lycia and Libya and Egypt and those of the Kabiri and the Pythoness were considered marvellous by the minds of men. But now since Christ has been proclaimed everywhere, their madness too has ceased, and there is no one left among them to give oracles at all. Then, too, daimones used to deceive men's minds by taking up their abode in springs or rivers or trees or stones and imposing upon simple people by their frauds. But now, since the Divine appearing of the Word, all this

---

we speak of the world will never be entirely contained in mathematical formulas, nor will it be contained entirely in words. So long as there is content that cannot be expressed in a univalent form, at every stage of consciousness language will turn to images as an adequate descriptive medium.'
8 Sprat, *History of the Royal Society*, 340.

fantasy has ceased, for by the sign of the cross, if a man will but use it, he drives out their deceits.[9]

There is a difference between Sprat and Athanasius, despite the similarity of their rhetoric. Sprat believed that there were never any fairies, spirits, or other such Chimaeras, and the change he describes is epistemological: that is, we are no longer to project our fancies into the outer world, nor "anthropomorphise" beasts or trees or streams by imagining their purposes or point of view. The proper route to knowledge is the "real," experimental method. Athanasius, on the other hand, was making an *ontological* claim: the daimones, the demons, were really being exorcised, and so left springs, rivers, trees and the rest to be themselves. It was still open to him to believe that those natural beings were alive and—possibly—well-disposed. The Athanasian project is compatible with the sort of imaginative insight that I shall be describing. Sprat's less so.

For to rid the world of all spectres, in the end, is also to rid it of souls, and goals. If all things are confined to their "true channel" of cause and effect then it is unnecessary, even unhelpful, to consider any animal's point of view—or even any human's. How anything *feels* to another, or what it is like to *be* them, becomes irrelevant, and so do any purposes they might seem to have or serve. We should, it seems, attempt to exclude any feelings of sympathy or concern or symbolic association from our assessment of the "brute facts." The same must be true—though it is impossible really to believe it—of our own selves and purposes. I may think (or rather, the words might somehow emerge on screen or paper) that I am writing to enlighten myself and others about how best to think and feel: in objective fact, it seems, there are only material motions that result in transient alterations in an unmeaning, boundless array. C. S. Lewis attempted to describe the mental condition of a philosopher deeply persuaded of this notion:

---

9 Athanasius, *On the Incarnation*, ch. 8, par. 47. See also Origen, *Contra Celsum*, 54 [1.60]: "It is probable that at the birth of Jesus when, as Luke records and as I believe, 'a multitude of the heavenly host praised God and said, Glory to God in the highest, and on earth peace, goodwill among men,' the effect of this was that the daemons lost their strength and became weak; their sorcery was confuted and their power overthrown; they were not only overthrown by the angels who visited the earthly region on account of the birth of Jesus, but also by the soul of Jesus and the divine power in him."

Introduction

> For many years he had theoretically believed that all which appears in the mind as motive or intention is merely a by-product of what the body is doing... Increasingly, his actions had been without motive. He did this and that, he said thus and thus, and did not know why. His mind was a mere spectator. He could not understand why that spectator should exist at all.... There was no tolerating such an illusion! There were not, and must not be, such things as men.[10]

The fully disengaged account of things is not one that *we* can actually believe, whatever philosophers may sometimes claim. Other sorts of creature, maybe, could seemingly endorse it—but of course they too would not be "believing" it, since they could have no point of view at all, nor any real existence beyond their material being. Consider Lafferty's Programmed People, who insist (to the resurrected Thomas More) that they are not themselves conscious:

> "You are not conscious?" Thomas gasped. "That is the most amazing thing I have ever heard. You walk and talk and argue and kill and subvert and lay out plans over the centuries, and you say you are not conscious?"
>
> "Of course we aren't, Thomas. We are machines. How would we be conscious? But we believe that men are not conscious either, that there is no such thing as consciousness. It is an illusion in counting, a feeling that one is two. It is a word without meaning."[11]

Their claim to "believe" these things is itself merely a line in the program, without real meaning or intent.

For better or worse, we must acknowledge our own conscious being, and tell stories to ourselves and others about our beliefs and purposes: we must live in a richly imagined world, and realize that not all our beliefs are grounded merely in abstract axioms or simple deductive logic, nor are they automatic responses to immediate sensory stimulation. Does it matter even if a story is

---

10 Lewis, *That Hideous Strength*, 444.
11 Lafferty, *Past Master*, 149. See also Peter Watts, *Blindsight*, for a more careful—but still self-contradictory—attempt to outline what various sorts of nonconscious intelligence might be like, even (as it were) from "the inside"; see also my own "Selfless Civilizations."

not "literally" true? Does it matter if a story *couldn't* be true—at least to the best of our current knowledge? There need be no one universal answer. Philo of Alexandria, despite devoting his energies to unravelling the allegorical significance of early Hebrew history, also insisted that the merely *historical* story was true (a story, remember, that is already more than a merely material account)—and indeed that its truth mattered for its allegorical significance. The People of Israel really had escaped from Egypt, and this was why they should and could reinforce that story at Passover every year. If they had not so escaped in merely historical fact—a fact entailing more even than an observation that some past clutch of people once crossed the Red Sea, pursued by horsemen and chariots—there would be less force in the injunction to remember both that they were now free and that they owed fellow-feeling and respect to any people escaped from similar degradation. The moral and political injunction was not a personal choice, but one enjoined by the Lord who had rescued them, and who was still present in their experience. When Hebrew prophets rebuked the people for backsliding, they could call on historical, "literal" convictions about the perils of apostasy: "This was the iniquity of your sister Sodom: she and her daughters had pride of wealth and food in plenty, comfort and ease, and yet she never helped the poor and wretched."[12]

An alternative, "realistic," history could instead have validated all manner of tyrannical and exploitative behaviour. We may now prefer to believe that Sodom's destruction was, as it were, "accidental," having no connection with its residents' particular wickedness: there are even theological reasons to avoid such moralistic interpretations of disaster.[13] In that case we can perhaps take the stories as simply allegorical, but it may still be important that, in some strict sense, there "really was" a disaster, and it really was disastrous (as it would not have been if there was no one to experience it). There really was a Flood (or probably many floods) in the ancient Middle East (as we in "the West" now call it), and folk memory of the event, and of the surviving

---

12 Ezekiel 16.49.
13 Luke 13.1-5; John 9.1-3.

remnant, was both conditioned by, and reinforced, moral and political insights—to which topic I shall return.

This story itself—of why I began the work—is one that I shall elaborate below, in an attempt to make imaginative storytelling philosophically respectable, and to learn what I can from the oldest stories on hand. Our ancestors and predecessors told stories about the world and their relations, addressing in imaginative ways questions that we now consider "philosophical" or "scientific." As Allen has put the point (though still conceding more to the Greeks' originality than is strictly justified):

> It is a persistent, if no longer intentional, bias of Western thought that "serious" philosophy began with the Greeks. In the sense of philosophy as a science—a system of intellectual principles developed according to fixed rules of investigation—this is true. But in the broader sense of philosophy as a system of human thought it is, of course, erroneous. All human beings ponder, speculate, and attempt to communicate abstract concepts to others, and the pre-Hellenic peoples of the Near East were no exception. What renders their thinking less than "philosophical" to us are two limitations of Western—not ancient—thought. We have divorced philosophy, as a discipline, from religion. In the former we appreciate reality objectively, as something capable of study; in the latter we understand it subjectively, as something that can only be experienced. This dichotomy did not govern ancient Near Eastern thought. To it, all appreciation of reality was subjective—"I-Thou" rather than "I-It." The results of ancient speculation are therefore communicated in the context of religion rather than science. This may render them less immediately appreciable to us as valid attempts to understand the universe, but it does not diminish their value as records of human thought. Once alerted to the difference, however, we have little difficulty in recognizing that validity. It is far more difficult for us to appreciate the concepts themselves—not because they are necessarily alien to our own experience of the world, but because of the images through which the ancients have communicated them to us. To minds accustomed to abstractions like energy and matter, the image of a

creator producing the first beings through masturbation seems to have little value in the overall history of human attempts to explain the origins of the universe. This is a matter of form, not content. The biological imagery provided the ancient Egyptian with a means of visualizing and communicating basic concepts that are more familiar to us as abstract principles or the terms of an equation. To appreciate the true intellectual content of ancient thought, we have to look behind the images for the concepts those images are meant to convey.[14]

Or maybe we should retain the images, without imagining that there are definite "concepts" which it would be better to consider, especially when those concepts ("energy" or "matter" or "causation") are themselves rather more obscure than the original images.

"The more unencumbered [*monotes*] I am, the more I have come to love myths," said Aristotle in his late life, unsurprisingly:[15] "philosophy begins from wonder... and a man who is puzzled and wonders thinks himself ignorant. Hence even the lover of myth is in a sense a lover of wisdom, for the myth is composed of wonders."[16] And it is those who know their own ignorance that can hope to achieve wisdom.

My project is to explore stories drawn from across the world (though chiefly from the ancient Near or Middle East), with proper regard for scholarly judgement about their meaning and their sources. Abstract and imaginative thought can both contribute to this enterprise: both "left-brain" and "right-brain" thought,

---

14 Allen, *Genesis in Egypt*, 9.
15 Aristotle, fr. 609 Rose (*Pseudepigraphus*, 596 [*Letter to Philip*, 14]), cited—a little patronisingly—by Jaeger, *Aristotle*, 321 (the passage is frequently misidentified as fr. 668 Rose). I doubt the usual translation of "*monotes*" as "solitary." This might be an appropriate reference to Aristotle's exile from Athens and his school, he having fled Athens when Alexander's death was reported "lest the Athenians sin twice against philosophy" (Origen *Contra Celsum*, 60 [1.65]: see Natali, *Aristotle*, 63, 168 for the late and doubtful sources of this popular anecdote). I prefer to reckon that "focused" or "single-minded" or (as here) "unencumbered" is closer to the likely intention—as it also is in the notorious phrase of Plotinus, recommending "a flight of the alone (*monos*) to the Alone": *Ennead* VI.9 [9].11, 51. But the fragment lacks sufficient context for any certain conclusion.
16 Aristotle, *Metaphysics* 1.982b17. The wonder that Aristotle here identifies may be taken simply as puzzlement, but there is another and perhaps a better beginning, in the feeling of awe: see Plato, *Theaetetus* 155d.

in the terms made popular in recent neurophilosophical enquiry. Or to put it another way: "If the heart is to perceive the Word of God resounding in itself, and if it is to intensify its own spiritual instinct, it must open what Ibn 'Arabi calls its 'two eyes'—the eye of reason and the eye of imagination, or discursive thought and mythic vision."[17]

This is not a new endeavour, but it is one that is now neglected. Militant atheists are generally well-persuaded that they have read the Hebrew and Christian scriptures more attentively than have believers, and are eager to point out the contradictions, follies, and appalling wickedness that they apparently contain.[18] More sympathetic readings of the scriptures, employing whatever tools of allegory and literary discrimination, are regarded as merely hypocritical. Here as in other matters there is sometimes a strange alliance between those militants and scriptural fundamentalists, both persuaded that there is no other way of reading scripture than the "literal" or "historical" (which usually means only that they stick to their own first reading). "Liberal" or "progressive" readers are considered heretics or hypocrites.

But militants are not, of course, the only people to have worried about the Scriptures. Chesterton gives the following words to his Father Brown, in "The Sign of the Broken Sword":

> Sir Arthur St. Clare was a man who read his Bible. That was what was the matter with him. When will people understand that it is useless for a man to read his Bible unless he also reads everybody else's Bible? A printer reads a Bible for misprints. A Mormon reads his Bible, and finds polygamy; a Christian Scientist reads his, and finds we have no arms and legs. St. Clare was an old Anglo-Indian Protestant soldier.... Of course, he found in the Old Testament anything that he wanted—lust, tyranny, treason. Oh, I dare say he was honest, as you call it. But what is the good of a man being honest in his worship of dishonesty?[19]

---

17 Chittick, *Science of the Cosmos*, 71.
18 The following few paragraphs are drawn, with some corrections, from my earlier work *Understanding Faith*, 61–63.
19 G. K. Chesterton, *The Innocence of Father Brown* (1911), reprinted in Chesterton, *Father Brown Stories*, 266–67.

The scriptures of whatever creed need to be interpreted as a whole, and within an appropriate oral tradition. Indeed, they take their identity from the relevant oral tradition: the works which now make up "the Bible," for example, were not even collected together for several centuries after the Christian Churches—or the Rabbinic Synagogues—were established, and it has always been a matter for common judgement which texts are to be included, and with what authority.[20] "If one may not delve into the sayings of Scripture and the Fathers with a speculative mind, the whole Bible falls apart, Old and New Testament alike."[21] Without that context, taken *out* of context, particular passages are often peculiar, absurd, or wicked. The same is true for the work of pagan poets, and Egyptian priests.

> If, then, you listen to the stories about the gods in this way, accepting them from those who interpret the story reverently and philosophically, and if you always perform and observe the established rites of worship, and believe that no sacrifice that you can offer, no deed that you may do will be more likely to find favour with the gods than your belief in their true nature, you may avoid superstition which is no less an evil than atheism.[22]

This is not to say that nothing can be learnt from a relatively straightforward reading, nor to insist always on "allegorical" as against "literal" meanings. Nor is it to say that the allegorical meanings are advanced simply to cover up moral or factual absurdities in the "literal" text: "ancient allegorical interpretation was in its very first germs positive, not defensive in its aim; that is to say, it was practiced in order to make more explicit the doctrines which the students of the poets [notably Heraclitus, Pherecydes, and Parmenides] believed to be actually contained in the poets' [that is, Homer's and Hesiod's] words, and not simply to defend the poets against censure."[23]

---

20 See Barton, *A History of the Bible*.
21 Maximus the Confessor at his trial (in AD 654) in response to the suggestion that we should do no more than read the "simple words of Scripture": *Patrologia Graeca* 90:149a, cited by von Balthasar, *Cosmic Liturgy*, 53.
22 Plutarch, "Isis and Osiris," 11, in *Moralia*, 5:31.
23 Tate, "History of Allegorism," 107, cited in Dawson, *Allegorical Readers*, 251; see also Naddaf, "Allegory and the Origins of Philosophy."

Introduction

The very meaning of "literal" and "allegorical" is often not entirely clear. Someone who says, for example, that he was "literally over the moon when he heard the news" does not expect to be asked how many miles over, what escape velocity he had achieved, or what fuel was used. "Literally" here means "emphatically" or some such, not "non-metaphorically." It may well be true that he was over the moon, in the sense he meant, even if pedants (and philosophers) snigger. Similarly, I suggest, someone who says she believes that the Bible is "literally true" almost certainly does not mean that every sentence of the Bible has a clear "historical" implication (let alone a "moral" one), but rather that the Bible is "not mistaken," that its "truth" is certain however difficult it may sometimes be to disentangle what truth that is. What genre any particular passage of "the Bible" belongs to is contested, even within the mainstream Christian tradition. Certainly not every passage is offered as "historical truth." *The Song of Songs*, for example, is not a historical document recording the thoughts and actions of a particular woman and her man, even if—which is possible but unproven—this was the original intention of the poet who wrote it.[24] Its significance, as part of Scripture, is for the faith community which put the texts together to determine.[25] The early chapters of *Genesis* have been understood anagogically from very early, and their usefulness in the tradition is as such.

> If the Manichees were willing to discuss the hidden meaning of these words [the opening chapter of *Genesis*] in a spirit of reverent inquiry rather than of captious fault-finding, then they would of course not be Manichees, but as they asked it would be given them, and as they sought they would find, as they knocked it would be opened up to them. The fact is, as you see, people who have a genuine religious interest in learning put far more

---

24 No love poem, even if inspired by and addressed to a particular beloved, speaks only of and to that particular beloved: any such *merely* private verses would not be worth remembering.
25 See Pike, *Mystic Union*, 66ff.; Shuve, *Song of Songs*. Shuve argues, plausibly, that Christian commentators who (as we say) "allegorized" the work did not do so to cover up the supposedly salacious "real meaning": they took the obvious, "commonsensical" reading to be about the relations of Christ and His Church, as Rabbinic commentators likewise took it to be about the relations of God and His people (ibid., 4–13).

questions about this text than these irreligious wretches; but the difference between them is that the former seek in order to find, while the latter are at no pains at all to do anything except not find what they are seeking.[26]

Augustine goes on to say that though there is nothing necessarily wrong in interpreting the text "literally" and "historically," there is also an "anagogical" significance, here and elsewhere, which is often paramount.

> If there is no other way of reaching an understanding of what is written that is religious and worthy of God, except by supposing that it has all been set before us in a figurative sense and in riddles, we have the authority of the apostles for doing this, seeing that they solved so many riddles in the books of the Old Testament in this manner.

The Emperor Julian had the same approach to the great "pagan" poets:

> The more paradoxical and prodigious the riddle is the more it seems to warn us not to believe simply the bare words but rather to study diligently the hidden truth, and not to relax our efforts until under the guidance of the gods those hidden things become plain, and so initiate or rather perfect our intelligence or whatever we possess that is more sublime than intelligence, I mean that small particle of the One and the Good which contains the whole indivisibly.[27]

Even those who insist that some particular biblical account is indeed "historical" need not suppose that the event would have been easily and equally apprehensible, in the recorded terms, to "just anyone." The story of the Flood,[28] for another example, is a story about someone's daring to do what his neighbours think absurd, and being vindicated; a story about the survival of a remnant through catastrophe; a story about something that contains and preserves the seeds of everything;

---

26 Augustine, *On Genesis: A Refutation of the Manichees* (AD 388/389), Bk. 2, 2.3, in Augustine, *On Genesis*, 72.
27 Julian, *Speeches*, 2:105 [*Oratio* 7].
28 Genesis 6–9. See Cohn, *Noah's Flood*.

Introduction

a story about being born again, after baptism; a story that offers some reason for our being allowed to eat some animal-flesh;[29] a story asserting that all humankind is closely related, but that some peoples ("the children of Ham") should nonetheless be servants.[30] Of course, it might also have a historical implication, and many commentators amused themselves in seeking to work out how to house and feed the different animals, or wondering how *global* the cataclysm was. Perhaps the most significant moral of the story, when that was taken as one founded, at least, on historical fact, was that there had been worlds, or world-ages, before our own, and that our world also could be swept aside. "As it was in the days of Noah, so will it be at the coming of the Son of Man. For in the days before the flood, people were eating and drinking, marrying and giving in marriage, up to the day Noah entered the ark."[31] To that catastrophe ("the world turned upside down") I shall return. But historical fact was probably not the original point, nor even the reason why the story still speaks even to those who doubt its geological veracity. At the least, we should be very sceptical of the sort of modern atheist who claims to know all about the Scriptures and their supposed absurdities:

> But perhaps after hearing the claim I know them all from some vulgar blockheads who were unaware of their own ignorance, he [that is, Celsus] imagined that after he had been taught by such teachers he knew everything. He seems to me to have done something of this sort: he is like a man who went to stay in Egypt, where the Egyptian wise men who have studied their traditional writings give profound philosophical interpretations of what they regard as divine, while the common people hear certain myths of which they are proud, although

---

29 Though, properly understood, the concession does *not* permit the actual killing of animals for food: "this bond doth give thee here no jot of blood," as Portia points out to Shylock (*The Merchant of Venice*, Act IV, Scene 1, line 302).
30 Genesis 9.20-27. The identity and destiny of those children has been misjudged over the centuries, to dreadful effect: in the beginning they were the very nations that the children of Israel found in possession of political and military power (Amalekites, Babylonians, Egyptians, Philistines and the like: Genesis 10.7-20). That they—the obvious imperial masters—would in the end bow down before the very peoples they conquered was a promise or prophecy, not an excuse for oppression.
31 Matthew 24.37-38.

they do not understand the meaning; and he imagined that he knew all the doctrines of the Egyptians after learning from their common people without having had conversation with any of the priests or having learnt from any of them the secret teachings of the Egyptians. What I have said about the Egyptian wise men and common people can also be seen in the case of the Persians; among them there are mysteries which are explained rationally by the learned men among them, but which are taken in their external significance by rather superficial minds and by the common people among them. The same may be said of the Syrians and Indians, and of all who have both myths and interpretative writings.[32]

We do need to be cautious in our allegorical readings, in case we miss what was once the real point. In similar style even modern fantasies may too easily be read as simple metaphors: vampire fictions must "really" be about divergent sexual experience; extraterrestrials, as well as fairies, must "really" represent ordinarily foreign tribes. If the stories purport to describe a wider world than the familiar, this is an illusion: "really" they are about *our* world, about familiar problems, of tribal or familial identities, adult responsibilities, sex, friendship, death and hatred. Even stories which, superficially, seem to be meant as *explanations* of some current fact or fashion turn out rather to be *recommendations* or warnings. Stories, like rituals, may often be intended as *inspirations* rather than *explanations*. This may indeed be a good way of reading and understanding some stories, but it may also distract attention from yet other layers of meaning. The stories may be genuinely "metaphysical" rather than only or merely "moral," even when they are not "literal": attempts to describe or attend upon a supposed reality "beyond the fields we know" and having only an ambiguous relationship to present social facts. They may even have a fully "material" or "natural" significance, and be intended to preserve the memory of matters beyond immediate memory:

---

32 Origen, *Contra Celsum*, 15 [1.12]. Origen himself is usually scornful of the Egyptians' worship (as he supposes) of "irrational creatures," though he seems to accept Celsus's report that the Egyptians "teach that such worship is respect to invisible ideas and not, as most people think, to ephemeral animals" (ibid., 139 [3.18]).

Introduction

> Simply, before writing, myths had to serve as transmission systems for information deemed important; but because we — now that we have writing — have forgotten how nonliterate people stored and transmitted information and why it was done that way, we have lost track of how to decode the information often densely compressed into these stories, and they appear to us as mostly gibberish. And so we often dismiss them as silly or try to reinterpret them with psychobabble.[33]

But despite that warning I shall usually be pressing the *allegorical* or sometimes the *anagogical* interpretation of the stories, rather than the merely literal or moral. More matters may be important than merely material events, or even moral example. According to ancient hermeneutical advice, there are literal, moral, allegorical, and anagogical readings of scripture or pagan myth. *Lettera gesta docet, quid credas allegoria, moralis quid agas, quo tendas anagogia.*[34] Quite what these terms mean may emerge in my discussion. Here at the start it may be enough to say that "allegorical" interpretation, in all its various kinds, is not meant to be a merely abstract exercise: the unravelling of an arbitrary code to reveal an obsolete secret. We should at least entertain the possibility that the stories are meant to change us: to *form* us and not simply to inform. And to do so, in part, precisely by opening our eyes to a much larger world. It is a topic I have addressed before, examining the myths and metaphors that Plotinus used.[35] These were never simply coded descriptions of the cosmos as he envisaged it (though they were indeed intended to be veridical), but tools to structure his students' morals and imagination, so as to *feel* the truth of his account. And the same must be true here: my enterprise is not simply to understand new or old stories

---

33 Barber and Barber, *When They Severed Earth from Sky*, 2. Barber and Barber, while acknowledging the astronomical associations identified by Santillana and Von Dechend (see below), usually treat stories of disasters as dramatic narratives about volcanic eruptions and the like. In *Celtic Gods*, Baillie and McCafferty, though acknowledging the impact of volcanos on our history, prefer to suggest that the stories record the passage of comets and associated meteorites. Both notions may be partly true, without exhausting the meanings.
34 Augustine of Dacia (d. 1282), *Rotulus pugillaris*, I, ed. Angelus Walz (Pont. Inst. Angelicum, 1929); see De Lubac, *Four Senses of Scripture*, 1–9, 271–77.
35 Clark, *Plotinus: Myth, Metaphor, and Philosophical Practice*.

and promote an *imaginative* approach to abstract philosophical questions, but to locate my own escape from exile. Being (relatively) unencumbered (because retired from paid employment), and yet still confined in an ageing world and body, I love myths more, and do not care if this love seems "escapist"!

> Why should a man be scorned, if, finding himself in prison, he tries to get out and go home? Or if, when he cannot do so, he thinks and talks about other topics than jailers and prison-walls? The world outside has not become less real because the prisoner cannot see it.[36]

We should entertain the thought that these old stories were, from their beginnings, *serious*: late antique philosophers who made their allegorical significance explicit were not merely "saving mythology" from its moralistic critics by arbitrary reinterpretation[37]—as some modern critic might laboriously allegorize or psychoanalyse a popular romantic comedy or action movie—but (at least in their intention, and perhaps in fact) unveiling the original meaning of the stories. And those stories may still have an important metaphysical meaning, precisely because they were also meant as morals.

---

36 Tolkien, *Monsters and the Critics*, 148.
37 See Dawson, *Allegorical Readers*; Brisson, *How Philosophers Saved Myths*.

∽2∾
How the Worlds Become

> Late one night, for no particular reason, something stirred
> in the black mud at the bottom of Berkeley's Creek.[1]

ANCIENT EGYPTIAN STORIES, TO BEGIN AT THE beginning, tell how the First Thing emerged from Nothing, and gradually became "the million things," including personal beings of a larger and longer-lasting sort than human or other animals. Similar stories, around the Mediterranean and elsewhere, give narrative and imaginative form to speculations about the cosmos that may—as Aristotle supposed—have been well-developed theories in earlier ages, before the catastrophes that divide our human history. As cosmogonical speculations they resemble modern cosmological theories, and raise similar questions about the possibility of there ever being (?) Nothing, or the equal oddity of things having been "forever." It may be supposed instead that their original sense and importance were less as "theories" about the world, or even about human society, than as transformative resources for humane living. Their "religious" significance is both to remind us that we are ourselves not gods (or not yet gods), and to provide ways of enlivening our spirits. The old stories speak of floods, plagues, fire and volcanic eruption, when the gods are bored with humankind, or offended by the noise of our constant quarrels. But the cosmogonical aspects should not be neglected, nor misunderstood. Our predecessors wondered both how all things came to be, and also how best to live. Their stories are congruent, at least, with ours, and take their beginning from similarly speculative thought. We don't know what earlier cultures achieved, and whether myths and proverbs might not be the remnants and mementos of an

---

1 Wagner and Brooks, *Bunyip of Berkeley's Creek*, 1.

earlier developed philosophy.² That is at least a better starting point than the widespread belief that our predecessors were all childish, stupid, or superstitious. It is also worth considering that our own cosmological stories may themselves have a moral or anagogical significance, and rely far more for their appeal on our imagination than on rational observation or calculation.

THE ONE THAT BECAME A MILLION

Once upon a long ago Something came to be: the primeval atom which contained all things as possibilities, the singularity in which, were the flow of time to be reversed, all matter, mind and energy would once again coincide. "Before" that Something there was no time, no place, no distance. We may speak of that "before" as Nothingness or as Darkness, but neither term quite fits: there was nothing there to be dark or empty, until there was a place to fill or a light to create shadows.

That Something, the primeval atom, somehow blossomed, exploded, sneezed, spat, ejaculated, laughed, or shouted. And then there were the First Somewhats to have distinct and definite natures (wet and dry, up and down), and the first to be entangled in each other's being. From these in turn came Earth and Heaven, and all the Million Things, the changing complex of the cosmos that we inhabit, like grubs within a tree which stretches everywhere, and accommodates all things that are.³ We ourselves, we shortlived animals, are late comers in the blossoming, and can only imagine what things came before—unless, perhaps, some of the earlier beings have chosen to tell us stories. Those earlier beings, we may say, were wonderful, and possibly they are around us still. They may be visible aloft, in ordered companies: sun, moon, "fixed" and "wandering" stars. They may be visible down here: rocks, mountains, rivers. We might call them "gods," as long as we recall that they are only older creatures,

---

2 This is not to endorse any particular current fables about a "lost Atlantis" and the like: our pre-historical ancestors may not have built great cities, nor mounted imperial campaigns against their neighbours (as Plato's Atlanteans did). They may still—like many indigenous tribes in Australia and the Americas—have managed the land in rather less urban ways, and thought carefully about their situation: see Gammage, *Biggest Estate on Earth*.
3 *Ennead* IV.3 [27].4, 26–30.

How the Worlds Become

born from the same beginnings, and—unlike Greek *theoi*—they too are mortal.[4]

The story I have sketched is the Egyptian "Heliopolitan" cosmogony, though I have deliberately framed it to be almost the same as recent cosmological speculations about the Singularity from which all things began in what is vulgarly called "the Big Bang," rather as the Egyptians sometimes called it Atum's ejaculation (a metaphor that has no special erotic resonance, as shown by the equivalent metaphors of spitting, crying, or shouting). Similar stories were told across Bronze Age Eurasia. Even in Egypt there were variants: the Hermopolitan Ogdoad, describing the primeval nothing in terms of associated pairs of "gods" representing its "inert," "dark," infinite, and unknowable nature,[5] or the Memphite emphasis on Ptah's creative word.[6]

What seems common to all the stories is the notion that Being came to be from Nothing (or at least *after* Nothing), and that this "Nothing" is not even, despite the struggling descriptions, dark or empty. Having no properties of its own neither has it any power of generation or construction. It doesn't *exist* at all! Ordinary absences, of the cat from the basket or the once-living from their former home, or even of merely imagined creatures from anywhere in the fully realized cosmos, are familiar enough. But what can the *absolutely non-existent* "be"?[7] Nor can anything "come into being from non-being," as Anaxagoras was to recognize[8] as well as Parmenides, who declared the way of "non-being" both impossible and mistaken.[9] There is no such thing as Nothing! As the American philosopher Jonathan Edwards was to insist many centuries later, "if any man thinks that he can think well enough how there should be nothing, I'll engage that what he means by 'nothing' is as much something as anything that ever [he] thought

---

4 Hornung, *Conceptions of God*, 143.
5 Allen, *Genesis in Egypt*, 201.
6 Allen, *Genesis in Egypt*, 46.
7 See Hornung, *Conceptions of God*, 172–73, citing the "negative confession" from *The Book of the Dead*, ch. 125: "I do not know the non-existent" (Wallis-Budge, *Egyptian Book of the Dead*, 365–71).
8 Waterfield, *First Philosophers*, 126 [DK59A52].
9 "The way that it is not and that it must not be: this, as I show you, is an altogether misguided route. For you may not know what-is-not—there is no end to it—nor may you tell of it" (Waterfield, *First Philosophers*, 58 [DK28B5]).

of in his life; and I believe that if he knew what nothing was it would be intuitively evident to him that it could not be."[10] Edwards went on to suggest that the Something that must be, eternally and undeniably, was both "Space" and "the Mind of God," perhaps recalling the Rabbinic tradition that God was to be called "the Place" (*hamaqom*) "because the universe is located in Him, not He in the universe."[11] The Egyptian version, however, spoke of that primeval darkness in obvious metaphor rather as an ocean, Nun, or as the eternal serpent, Apopis, which will one day engulf all things once again.[12] "After the 'millions of years' of differentiated creation the mayhem before creation [or rather, the primeval 'darkness' rather than 'confusion'] will return; only the primeval god (Atum) and Osiris will remain 'in one place'—no longer separated in space and time."[13] So Atum, in *The Book of the Dead*, informs a hopeful candidate for almost-eternal life:

> You shall be for millions on millions of years, a lifetime of millions of years. I will despatch the Elders and destroy all that I have made; the earth shall return to the Primordial Water, to the surging flood, as in its original state. But I will remain with Osiris. I will transform myself into something else, namely a serpent, without men knowing or the gods seeing.[14]

Stoic philosophers had a similar expectation of a time "when the world is dissolved and the gods have been blended together into one, when nature comes to a stop for a while."[15] They spoke of that conclusion as a "conflagration" rather than a flood, but expected the same absence of all distinctions.

---

10   Edwards, *Works*, 203.
11   Midrash Genesis R. 68, in Maccoby, *Philosophy of the Talmud*, 24; see also Copenhaver, *Hermetica*, 9 (2.4): "Place is incorporeal, but the incorporeal is either divine or else it is god"; so also Philo, *On Dreams* 11.63, in *Collected Works*, 5:329: "God Himself is called a place, by reason of His containing things, and being contained by nothing whatever, and being a place for all to flee into, and because He is Himself the space which holds Him; for He is that which He Himself has occupied, and naught encloses Him but Himself."
12   Hornung, *Conceptions of God*, 158–59.
13   Hornung, 163, citing the *Coffin Texts* 7.467e–468b.
14   Tyldesley, *Myths and Legends*, 172, quoting *Book of the Dead*, spell 175 (which is not included in Romer, *Book of the Dead*).
15   Seneca, *Letters* 9.16, in Long and Sedley, *Hellenistic Philosophers*, 1:277 [460].

Plotinus chose instead to emphasise the nullity of existence (so to speak) without any distinctions. As he put it, "before soul it was a dead body, earth and water, or rather the darkness of matter and non-existence, and 'what the gods hate.'"[16] That "matter" is in a way the principle or the beginning (*arche*) of all evil—but only in the sense that evil involves dissolution, death, decay, and the loss of substantial being: what is "material" can lose its own being, and be dissolved or eaten up into some other things. "Mere" matter is nowhere apprehensible, hidden by golden chains.[17] Unlike Edwards's God, neither Plotinian Matter nor the older Egyptian "Nun" has any power or purpose or identity—though the very fact of there possibly being something that arises from or in it perhaps begins to suggest that it does after all have a real *potential* (and is therefore already something actual, even if that actuality is indefinable).[18] So "Nothing" is gradually turned into "Something"—but the strict doctrine remains that Nothing is indeed nothing whatever at all! The Creator, when Creation is considered, does not have to work with any preexistent somewhat:

> In the case of matter, absence of illumination is the result of deficiency and want of limitation due not to a superabundance of power but to a lack [of it]. And indeed Egyptian tradition also says the same about [matter]. At any rate, the divine Iamblichus reported that Hermes too wants materiality to be derived from substantiality. And in fact it is even likely, [he adds,] that Plato gets this kind of view of matter from [Hermes] as well. In the first instance, then, it is from the above-mentioned principles [sc. the One, Unlimitedness, and One Being] that matter derives its existence.[19]

---

16 Ennead V.1 [10].2, 22–28. On Plotinus's Egyptian roots, see MacCoull, "Plotinus the Egyptian?"
17 Ennead I.8 [51].15.
18 Thus Hornung comments on the sun's daily immersion in darkness that "regeneration is impossible in the ordered and defined world. It can happen only if what is old and worn becomes immersed in the boundless regions that surround creation—in the healing and dissolving powers of the primeval ocean Nun": *Conceptions of God in Ancient Egypt*, 161. See also Schweizer, *Sungod's Journey through the Netherworld*, 10.
19 Proclus, *Commentary on Plato's Timaeus*, I.386.5-15, pp. 25–26; see also *Ennead* IV.3 [27].9, 23–26.

Myths have a narrative form, laying out unchanging and eternal relationships as if they were episodes in a timebound story.[20] Since there was no time — no period or rate of change — "before" Atum, there were no empty and changeless ages "before" creation,[21] but it might still be true that there have been only a finite, definite number of events or moments *since* Atum began to be, or began to procreate, and only a finite, definite number of distinguishable places (assuming that neither time nor space is *infinitely* divisible). In that sense the cosmos might have a finite span, in space as well as time, even though the acres of dusty eternity "surrounding" it are merely fictions. Maybe Atum will rise "again," and the embalmed dead with him/her/it.[22] Is this simply to affirm its eternal unchanging being, as later fictions have suggested? Must the cosmos always be exactly as it is, whether we think of it as endlessly repeated, or as simply "being" from the primordial singularity to its eventual collapse? Or might there instead be many versions of the cosmos, as though Atum, like the Sun himself, were endlessly reborn each "morning" of the world? That is, perhaps, the story truer to the Egyptian hope, as it also was to Plotinus, who jokingly (?) suggests that we might get better parts next time![23] "Each performance of the play is different, with different actors and different settings."[24] There is no definite answer to these questions, either in Egyptian tradition or in present philosophical analysis, despite the attraction even physicists feel to the notion of an ever-repeating cosmos. But the melancholy hope for at least a temporary return to some happy state is perennial.

---

20 *Ennead* III.5 [50].9, 24–29. It may be significant that Egyptian gods don't seem to have *narratives* till late: they are presented first as images, and the stories are added later (see Quirke, *Exploring Religion*, 35, 113–15).
21 As Augustine knew: *Confessions* 11.12. See also Mersini-Houghton, *Before the Big Bang*, 25: "Time stops at this singularity — there is no 'before'; clocks freeze. Space stops there — there is no beyond. According to Hawking and Penrose, nature forbids scientists to explore the moment of creation, let alone look past it, because nothing, absolutely nothing, existed before creation."
22 Quirke, *Exploring Religion*, 145, citing *Book of the Dead*, ch. 175.
23 *Ennead* III.2 [47].17, 47–49. This is not the place for a lengthy examination of Plotinus's approach either to determinism or to the Stoic notion of an endlessly repeating cycle of events or circular passage of time.
24 Allen, *Genesis in Egypt*, 27.

How the Worlds Become

A destined time shall come when it is decreed that Areimanius, engaged in bringing on pestilence and famine, shall by these be utterly annihilated and shall disappear; and then shall the earth become a level plain, and there shall be one manner of life and one form of government for a blessed people who shall all speak one tongue. Theopompus [of Chios; c. 380–315 BC] says that, according to the sages, one god is to overpower, and the other to be overpowered, each in turn for the space of three thousand years, and afterward for another three thousand years they shall fight and war, and the one shall undo the works of the other, and finally Hades shall pass away ; then shall the people be happy, and neither shall they need to have food nor shall they cast any shadow. And the god, who has contrived to bring about all these things, shall then have quiet and shall repose for a time, no long time indeed, but for the god as much as would be a moderate time for a man to sleep.[25]

That ethical implication or social use of the story—though maybe more significant to its first tellers—is of less importance for the moment than the strictly cosmogonical. Atum itself must be conceived at once as Something and as Nothing-in-particular. "Atum is the god who 'in the beginning was everything', complete in the sense of being an undifferentiated unity and at the same time nonexistent, because existence is impossible before his work of creation."[26] As Plotinus put it, the One "is not one of all things, but is before all things."[27] On the Heliopolitan story preserved in the Coffin Texts[28] the real beginning of things comes only when Atum, somehow, procreates: sneezes, spits or ejaculates Shu and Tefnut (the dry and the moist). These latter in turn engender Geb and Nut, who are the earth and sky, or else the down below and the up above. The vulgarity of the metaphors, apparently founded on puns, should not surprise us: our own notion of "the Big Bang," after all, has often been found

---

25 Plutarch, "Isis and Osiris," 47, in *Moralia*, 5:116–17, summarizing Zoroastrian myth.
26 Hornung, *Conceptions of God*, 67.
27 *Ennead* III.8 [30].9, 54–55.
28 See Allen, *Middle Egyptian*, 175–78.

both misleading and a little crude.[29] The converse absurdity that things have always been very much as they are now, and that we are therefore always already completing a countdown without beginning,[30] did appeal to other Mediterranean minds, as it also appeals to many moderns. The ancient dream that Everything will be dissolved, and then be formed anew, still has enormous power. So strong is it indeed that even speculative cosmologists, compelled to recognize that this whole cosmos is at once decaying and expanding, fruitlessly, forever, instinctively propose that *this* world is only one of indefinitely many in an imagined multiverse. They may even hope that creatures very much like us will appear again, indefinitely many times, even though we (they) can never learn from the experience. If that were so we need no further timebound explanation for any current feature, including the existence of living things, and minds.[31] All things, on these terms, have always existed more or less as they now are — except that catastrophes must also sweep things clean for new and ignorant beginnings. Which might explain the congruence of the ancient stories and the modern cosmological. Proverbs and folkstories are "the remnants of philosophy that perished in the great disasters that have befallen mankind, and were recorded for their brevity and wit."[32] Everything, so Aristotle said, has already been discovered, and forgotten, an infinite — or at least an indefinitely large — number of times.[33]

---

29 See Kragh, "Big Bang: The Etymology of a Name" for an account of the gradual triumph of the term, as well as the associated theory.
30 See Craig, *Kalam Cosmological Argument* for a discussion of the oddities involved in supposing that things have really been "forever"; see also Jaki, *Science and Creation*, for arguments — starting with an analysis of Olbers' Paradox — that over infinite ages accumulated light and heat would (infinitely long ago) have burnt up the universe entirely.
31 See Hoyle, *Black Cloud*, 162.
32 Aristotle, *On Philosophy*, fr. 8 Rose, in Ross, *Fragments*, 77 [fr.10].
33 *De Caelo* 270b19-20, *Meteorologica* 339b27-28, *Politics* 7.1329b25-26. See also Ecclesiastes 1.10: "Is there anything of which one can say, 'Look this is new'? No, it has already existed, long ago before our time. The men of old are not remembered, and those who follow will not be remembered, by those who follow them." On the other hand, "each leaf, of oak and ash and thorn, is a unique embodiment of the pattern, and for some this very year may be the embodiment, the first ever seen and recognised, though oaks have put forth leaves for countless generations of men" (Tolkien "On Fairy Stories," in *Tree and Leaf*, 57; see Macleod and Smol, "A Single Leaf").

I shall return to the story of repeated catastrophe, but first consider again the implications of Atum's first emergence (or Ra's, Amun's, or Ptah's). What is the relation between Atum Itself and the Million Things it engenders or becomes? Is the procreation a real *creation*? Is there a plan as well as a pattern? In the later Memphite cosmogony it seems indeed that Ptah *intended* that the cosmos should exist and have the forms it does. And in Hermopolis "Thoth acquired a leading role in the drama of creation itself as a demiurge who called things into being merely by the sound of his voice."[34] Something existed "before" or "behind" or "above" nature. But in the Heliopolitan there seems no sign of any foresight, any more than in the cosmogony described some centuries later by Hesiod:

> First of all Chaos came into being, then broad-breasted Earth, the ever-safe foundation of all the deathless ones, who live on the peaks of snowy Olympos, and shadowy Tartaros in a hiding place of the earth with its wide ways, and Eros, who is the most beautiful of all the deathless gods, who relaxes the limbs and overwhelms the mind and wise counsel in the breasts of all the gods and men. From Chaos came Darkness and black Night, and from Night came Brightness and Day, whom Night conceived and bore by uniting in love with Darkness. Earth bore starry Sky first, like to her in size, so that he covered her all around, everywhere, so that there might always be a secure seat for the blessed gods. And Earth gave birth to the blessed Mountains, the pleasant halls of the gods, the nymphs who live in the wooded hills. She bore the barren waters, raging with its swell, Sea, without making delightful love. But then, uniting with Sky, Earth bore deep-swirling Ocean, and Koios, Kreios, Hyperion, Iapetos, Theia, Rhea, Themis, Mnemosynê, golden-crowned Phoibê, and beloved Tethys. After them was born crooked-counselled Kronos, the youngest and most terrible of these children, who hated his powerful father.[35]

An older Phoenician version of the story attributed to one Sanchuniathon of Berytus (supposedly writing around the time

---

34 Fowden, *Egyptian Hermes*, 23.
35 Hesiod, *Poems*, 36–37 [*Theogony*, 116–38].

of the Trojan War) was preserved by Philo of Byblos, a Hellenized Phoenician, living c. AD 70–c. 160.[36]

> The first principle of the universe [Sanchuniathon] supposes to have been air dark with cloud and wind, or rather a blast of cloudy air, and a turbid chaos dark as Erebus; and these were boundless and for long ages had no limit. But when the wind, says he, became enamoured of its own parents, and a mixture took place, that connexion was called Desire. This was the beginning of the creation of all things: but the wind itself had no knowledge of its own creation. From its connexion Mot was produced, which some say is mud, and others a putrescence of watery compound; and out of this came every germ of creation, and the generation of the universe. So there were certain animals which had no sensation, and out of them grew intelligent animals, and were called "Zophasemin," that is "observers of heaven"; and they were formed like the shape of an egg. Also Mot burst forth into light, and sun, and moon, and stars, and the great constellations.[37]

In this story what was (in some sense) before there were any ordered things is described as "chaos" in our modern sense (of confusion), rather than the ancient Greek (for which "chaos" is a yawning gap).[38] So also in the Mesopotamian story recounted in the *Enuma Elish*, which is perhaps the origin of both Greek and Hittite stories:

> Firm ground below had not been called by name,
> Naught but primordial Apsu, their begetter,
> (And) Mummu-Tiamat, she who bore them all,
> Their waters commingling as a single body;
> No reed hut had been matted, no marsh land had
>   appeared,
> When no gods whatever had been brought into being,

---

36 Gruen, *Rethinking the Other*, 342; see Baumgarten, *Phoenician History*, 3–6; Fishbane, *Biblical Myth*, 112–13.
37 Eusebius, *Praeparatio* 1.10, p. 15.
38 So also in Sturluson, *Prose Edda*, 16 ("Beguiling of Gylfi," ch. 4): "As is told in Voluspa: First was the age when nothing was: Nor sand nor sea, nor chilling stream-waves; Earth was not found, nor Ether-Heaven,—A Yawning Gap, but grass was none."

Uncalled by name, their destinies undetermined—
Then it was that the gods were formed within them.[39]

The Hesiodic or Hittite account differs also from the Egyptian in postulating several "first things" (Earth, Tartaros, Eros) rather than the singular Atum. But perhaps this is only to say that they replace Atum by "Chaos." The very next things, or principles, are usually what we would now call abstractions or at least impersonal realities (like wet and dry, darkness and light, or earth and heaven). So also Anaximander, following ancient precedent, proposed that fundamental polarities emerged from "the indefinite" (*apeiron*).[40] When Mot "burst forth into light" is the moment when there were sentient beings to see it: before there was "soul," remember, there was only "darkness."[41] The later unheralded appearance of something more like "personal" beings, with purposes and family relationships, culminates in murder and betrayal—but also in the promise of a decent peace, in the re-creation of Osiris or the triumph of Zeus over his Titanic kin. The dysfunctional families of these early "persons," in many different traditions, will concern me later.

---

39 *Enuma Elish* 1.1–10, in Pritchard, *Ancient Near Eastern Texts*, 61. "The description presents the beginnings of the world as a watery chaos in which the powers of the fresh waters underground, Apsu, and the powers in the salt waters of the sea, Ti'amat, mingled" (Jacobsen, *Treasures*, 168). Jacobsen, and other commentators, take "Mummu" here to mean "the matrix," as an epithet of Tiamat, though Mummu appears a little later as Apsu's "vizier" (ibid., 170).
40 Waterfield, *First Philosophers*, 14 [T15; DK 12A9, B1]: 'Anaximander said that the first principle and element of existing things was the boundless (*to apeiron*); it was he who originally introduced this name for the first principle. He says that it is not water or any of the other so-called elements, but something different from them, something boundless by nature, which is the source of all the heavens and the worlds in them. And he says that the original sources of existing things are also what existing things die back into 'according to necessity; for they give justice and reparation to one another for their injustice in accordance with the ordinance of Time', as he puts it, in these somewhat poetic terms. It is clear that, having noticed how the four elements change into one another, he decided not to make any of them the underlying thing, but something else beside them; and so he has creation take place not as a result of any of the elements undergoing qualitative change, but as a result of the opposites being separated off by means of motion, which is eternal" (Theophrastus fr. 226a, cited by Simplicius, *Commentary on Aristotle's 'Physics,'* CAG IX, 24.14–25 Diels). This is not, *pace* Rovelli's *Anaximander*, a radically new idea.
41 *Ennead* V.1 [10].2, 24–27.

WHAT ARE GODS?

What might make these early stories different from modern cosmological speculations? One complacent answer would be that the ancients were only speculating, whereas nowadays the stories are to be checked against detailed observations and mathematical calculations. The "Big Bang" is to be endorsed because that story fits astronomical data better than the main alternative ("Steady State"): we can observe — or at least acknowledged experts can observe — the whisper of the very beginnings, and the "red-shifted" radiation of distant stars and galaxies (which suggests that they are travelling away from us and from each other). Calculations can convincingly reveal the way original symmetries were broken to reveal electromagnetic radiation, "weak force," "strong force" and gravity. Strangely (perhaps) even immensely distant parts of the visible cosmos — so widely distant that they cannot now affect each other — act according to the very same laws, and follow the same fortune, as all retaining the natures they shared at their beginning. The relative strengths of these distinct forces seem, so far, to be merely what they happen to be, or else to be precisely what they *need* to be if any living and sentient organisms are to have a chance of existing. Those cosmological arguments, as well as the grounds for supposing that the mathematical arts are of any use in assessing them, are of considerable interest, and the associated disputes between different metaphysical theorists, but it can be admitted that most people who endorse these differing theories, of a unique "Big Bang" or a succession of such Bangs or a simultaneous proliferation of infinitely many universes each with their own ratio of powers, do so without any clear understanding of the cosmological or mathematical calculations. They are merely accepting some particular vision or tradition, as easily as the ancients. Indeed, this last observation may apply even to the expert cosmologists who propound the distinct theories far in advance of any definitive mathematical or astronomical resolution of the disputes.[42] That the universe of our experience

---

[42] See Ćirković, *Astrobiological Landscape* for a wider, imaginative exploration of possible universes stemming from variations in the original conditions. The applicability of mathematics to worlds far away and very long ago is an unresolved mystery for any but unapologetic Platonists: see Wigner, "The

is "expanding" and was once, many billions of years ago, more closely packed, appears to be supported by present observations. That it was ever packed into an incomprehensible point (which would, by *present* natural law, be an inescapable "black hole") is an imaginative extrapolation, accepted—if it is—because it means we are all One! If there ever was such a "singularity" it was, in a way, "supernatural," beyond the reach of present regularities.

One frequent response to the question, "why is there anything?," is to observe that, by hypothesis, there can be no explanation: anything that might be proposed as *causing* the existence of whatever there now is must itself be something that is already "in existence." There may have been (the best ancient and modern theories all agree that there was) a "First Thing" or an "Initial Order," but there can be no *explanation* for that thing or order: it is only what it is. Something stirred, as my epigraph has it, "in the black mud of Nothing," for no particular reason, and might as well be a Bunyip. But there are problems with this easy abandonment of explanation. If the Bunyip, as it were, can have emerged from Nothing once, why may it not again? Why may not anything at all "just happen," for no particular reason and at any time? This is not a world we'd readily accept, in which the murder weapon merely "materializes" on the library floor, or monsters snap into being without any possible warning. We can suggest—Hesiod himself suggested—that Earth and Heaven have stopped procreating now, and all the things there are must now proceed according to fixed patterns, expectably. But this too is only to *report* a fact or fancy, without any credible reason. The next response is to assume that the laws which now describe the world can also, *pace* Wittgenstein,[43] *explain* its existence. For some cosmologists (most notably, Leonard Krauss[44]) this amounts to giving a definite description of the original Nothingness, now conceived as potent rather than merely potential: the cosmos emerges from a sea of virtual particles very much as advocates

---

Unreasonable Effectiveness of Mathematics in the Natural Sciences."
43 Cf. Wittgenstein, *Tractatus*, p. 85 (6.371): "the whole modern conception of the world is founded on the illusion that the so-called laws of nature are the explanations of natural phenomena."
44 Krauss, *Universe from Nothing*.

of the "steady state" cosmology imagined that new particles were always emerging from the happy nothing (again, for no further reason than that they always do). But this is only to declare that the world has always existed, in the order we now acknowledge, and—once again—abandons any further attempt at explanation, with the same unwelcome implications.

Maybe there is only one possible way for the world to be, despite there being no obvious reason for the ratios of the original forces? But this too is an inadequate response. "Even if there is only one possible unified theory, it is just a set of rules and equations. What is it that breathes fire into the equations and makes a universe for them to describe?"[45] Even if this were the only world there *could* be, that mere fact would not explain why there is any world at all—unless the rules and equations had a "supernatural" existence distinct from and prior to the realization of a world that observed them: that is, if Plato's *Nous* is really real. For how else can mere "laws" exist than in the Intellect? And what power do they have except as some agent wills? Or in Egyptian terms, as the Word of Ptah?

Or should I allow another distinction between the ancient and modern stories to have more force (as is perhaps already implied in my mention of Ptah)? The story of the Big Bang and the forces crystallised, as it were, from the primordial event, is offered merely as a would-be factual account of things, with no special moral implications, or incentive to offer "worship" (whatever that may be) to the original things. What that difference amounts to is worth further thought. And it may be, once again, that we are not so different from the ancients as at first we think. Consider what it means, imaginatively and morally, to recognize that the Bang did not happen far away, and that it was and is more like an unfolding, a blossoming, than an explosion. It did not occur in an already existing space, nor push outward against already existing obstacles. All things—including space, time, and matter—are being

---

[45] Hawking, *Brief History of Time*, 174. The later Hawking seems to have concluded, without visible argument or explanation, that the "laws" themselves *can* somehow compel the existence of the stuff whose motion they describe: see Hawking and Mlodinow, *The Grand Design*. Hawking there declared (ibid., 14) that "philosophy is dead," again without visible argument.

created in that ongoing event. In its later stages the particular stuff of which we ourselves are made is apparently star-stuff, formed in the first generation of stars, to be spread across the cosmos like dandelion seeds by exploding stars. There is a poetry of cosmology and astronomy at least as moving as the ancient tales of Atum and its offspring, even if most of it is as yet unwritten. We are not yet fully acclimatised even to a heliocentric cosmology, let alone a cosmos whose centre is everywhere.[46]

> It would be an interesting speculation to imagine whether the world will ever develop a Copernican poetry and a Copernican habit of fancy; whether we shall ever speak of "early earth-turn" instead of "early sunrise," and speak indifferently of looking up at the daisies, or looking down on the stars. But if we ever do, there are really a large number of big and fantastic facts awaiting us, worthy to make a new mythology. Mr. Wardlaw Scott, for example, with genuine, if unconscious, imagination, says that according to astronomers, "the sea is a vast mountain of water miles high." To have discovered that mountain of moving crystal, in which the fishes build like birds, is like discovering Atlantis: it is enough to make the old world young again. In the new poetry which we contemplate, athletic young men will set out sturdily to climb up the face of the sea. If we once realize all this earth as it is, we should find ourselves in a land of miracles: we shall discover a new planet at the moment that we discover our own. Among all the strange things that men have forgotten, the most universal and catastrophic lapse of memory is that by which they have forgotten that they are living on a star.[47]

---

46 As is said of God (a sphere whose centre is everywhere, and whose circumference nowhere): the first known use of the phrase is in the twelfth century: see Hudry, *Liber 24 Philosophorum*. The text may be a Latin translation of an Alexandrian handbook, and its assumed association with Hermetic sources may not be mistaken. See also Borges, "Pascal's Sphere." Borges concludes his essay with the comment "perhaps universal history is the history of the diverse intonation of a few metaphors."

47 Chesterton, "In Defence of Planets," *The Defendant* (www.gutenberg.org/files/12245/12245-h/12245-h.htm#A_DEFENCE_OF_PLANETS, accessed October 2, 2022). This was in response to Wardlaw Scott's *Terra Firma*, in favour of a Flat Earth — a notion, it must repeatedly be emphasised, that was *not* the standard belief of medieval Europe.

In the same essay, Chesterton expressed surprise that poets had not picked up other marvellous implications of twentieth-century science.

> To what towering heights of poetic imagery might we not have risen if only the poetizing of natural history had continued and man's fancy had played with the planets as naturally as it once played with the flowers! We might have had a planetary patriotism, in which the green leaf should be like a cockade, and the sea an everlasting dance of drums. We might have been proud of what our star has wrought, and worn its heraldry haughtily in the blind tournament of the spheres. All this, indeed, we may surely do yet; for with all the multiplicity of knowledge there is one thing happily that no man knows: whether the world is old or young.

To return for the moment to the ancients and their stories: "the Egyptians lived in a universe composed not of things, but of beings."[48] There was, so to speak, a soul in all things, whether it was a distinct subject or simply (?) the Egyptians' own imaginative identification with whatever they encountered. There is, in a phrase shared by Sprigge and Nagel, "something it is like to be"[49] a beast, a tree, a river or a star. So how are any of these beings, from Atum to Osiris, "gods"? The Egyptian term *ntr* is equated with *theos* in the Rosetta Stone,[50] and such entities are offered thanks and worship in the Egyptian cult, but they do not seem to have the distinctive, world-transforming, natures that the Olympians have, especially in Otto's evocation.[51] When the Greeks sought to equate Zeus with Amon-Ra, Hermes with Thoth, or Demeter with Isis, this may be as misleading or even blasphemous as the equation of Dionysos and the Hebrew YHWH.[52] Maybe it is also

---

48 Allen, *Genesis in Egypt*, 8.
49 Sprigge, "Final Causes"; Nagel, "What Is It Like to Be a Bat?"
50 See Hornung, *Conceptions of God*, 43.
51 Hornung, *Conceptions of God*, 256, commenting on Otto, *Homeric Gods*.
52 See Amzallag, "Was Yahweh Worshiped in the Aegean?," after Plutarch, *Quaestiones Conviviales* 4.6.1–2. Tacitus, being prejudiced against the Jews, dismisses the suggestion: "from the fact that their priests used to chant to the music of flutes and cymbals, and to wear garlands of ivy, and that a golden vine was found in the temple, some have thought that they worshipped Father Liber, the conqueror of the East, though their institutions do not by any means

misleading to equate *ntr* and *theos*? The further question, whether there was any sense that there was a *single* source of godhood, the One God behind or above all gods, may have no stable answer: even Atum, "the One that became a Million," is not therefore a single consistent agency at work in all that is. At least we should not assume that either *theos* or *ntr*, when the terms are used without any particular specification of *which* "god" is meant, refers to any such monarchical principle. Even if some "god" is named as the sole creator or sustainer in particular hymns or spells it does not follow that even that god's worshippers meant to exclude or demote all other gods — at least until Akhenaten's revolution. Nor is it clear that these "gods" are quite what are imagined in a modern or even a later Mediterranean sensibility. Might the cosmogonies I have described be as bereft of really religious significance as modern stories of Big Bangs, Dark Matter and Dark Energy (all liable, no doubt, to be transformed to myth after some coming cataclysm, and already having some emotional resonance), even if they all have the same chance of poetic or aesthetic elaboration as the modern stories? Maybe so — but there is some reason to think otherwise: indeed, to think the reverse.

That there are powers in the world which far transcend the human is obvious: earthquakes, tornadoes, volcanic eruptions, meteor strikes and even summer heats and winter frosts are not at our command. These powers are not just "facts": they also inspire awe, identified by Jacobsen with a "sense of the numinous."

> It is understandable that numinous experience in situations connected with basic life-sustaining activities would assume special significance and call for special allegiance. Thus the earliest form of Mesopotamian religion was worship of powers of fertility and yield, of the powers in nature ensuring human survival.[53]

Or threatening it.

It is also naïve to suppose that we can much better control *internal* passions: lust, anger, envy, indolence. The very first lesson

---

harmonize with the theory; for Liber established a festive and cheerful worship, while the Jewish religion is tasteless and mean" (*Histories* 5.5). It seems fair to say that he misunderstood the stories.
53 Jacobsen, *Treasures*, 26.

of anything we might call "religion" or even "common sense" is that we ourselves aren't now "gods," and need to recognize, with Ptahhotep [25th and 24th century BC], that "man's plans are never fulfilled; what happens is what god commands."[54] Gods (or whatever else we call them) are the "great and powerful ones who make a mockery of human pretensions."[55] Volcanic eruption or tsunami, plagues and madness sweep our world away. Zeus and YHWH alike send "lying spirits" to corrupt our common sense — or at any rate our senses are corrupted in all-too-familiar ways.[56] But these gods and spirits are not necessarily wholly indifferent or malevolent powers. The Egyptians associated them with their enlivening effects. "The queen regnant [Hatshepsut] shows herself to be 'divine' through her divine aroma and the golden radiance, both of which emanate from the gods."[57] In the very beginning, it seems, gods were produced from the creator's sweat, and humans from his tears![58] And this too has later echoes: "a shadow's dream is man, but when (a) god sheds a brightness, shining light is on earth and life is as sweet as honey."[59]

Burkert has proposed that the root of the term *theos* means "amazing," "wonderful."[60] The story fits Egyptian experience.

> The larger theology of "*The Hymn to the Aten*" and Psalm 104 is one that celebrates, in Breasted's words, "the universal presence of God in nature" and the "mystic conviction of

---

54 Hornung, *Conceptions of God*, 211–12.
55 Hornung, *Conceptions of God*, 207.
56 Homer, *Iliad* 2, 1–30; I Kings 22.19-23; see also Exodus 9.12 on God's "hardening Pharoah's heart."
57 Hornung, *Conceptions of God*, 64; cf. ibid., 133: Amun when begetting Hatshepsut is shown as *ntr* by his aroma.
58 Hornung, *Conceptions of God*, 149–50.
59 Pindar [522–443 BC], *Pythian* 8.95-97. The ode was composed in honour of a young wrestler, Aristomenes of Aegina, in 446 BC. Oddly, to our sensibility, it is full of reminders of inevitable defeat, only sometimes relieved by well-deserved but transient victories. The shadow is presumably a shade: the dead dreaming of a life once-lived. Pindar most likely thought that there were many such gods to brighten our day, but he may have meant to speak here of "the divine" rather than any particular god. And 'divinity" need not be considered merely an abstract quality, but rather the eternal being manifested in the many gods.
60 Burkert, "From Epiphany to Cult Statue"; cf. Herodotus, who declares that the original inhabitants of Greece called them "*theoi*, disposers, because they had disposed and arranged everything in due order": *Histories*, 117 [2.520].

the recognition of that presence by all creatures." If one may speak of the experience that gave rise to these two poems, which is, in turn, the experience they convey, it is what Abraham Joshua Heschel calls "radical amazement." "Awareness of the divine begins with wonder," Heschel writes, and "wonder or radical amazement, the state of maladjustment to words and notions, is therefore a prerequisite for an authentic awareness of that which is."[61]

This wonder — which may be aroused by volcanic eruptions, tsunamis, tigers and tyrannosaurs as well as by woods in spring or the song of birds — is not simply "nature worship." As Levenson puts it, "nature is but the all-encompassing evidence of [God's] supernatural wisdom and the medium by which people come to suspect it."[62] Nor is it a scholastic "argument from design," but the brute recognition of something awesome in the very fact of existence (and nothing is to be gained, for the moment, by analysis of the term "supernatural," which does not seem — any more than "natural" — to have any clear Egyptian cognate). Monotheists are not the only people to feel such awe — indeed the recognition of more particular gods may be commoner: the presence of Aphrodite, Hermes, even Ares, is made known in the elevation of our spirits, the discovery of greater possibilities than we can ordinarily encompass — and of course the associated depression of our spirits when the gods retire (or send a lying spirit).

> A god may be sensed and seen not only in his attributes of fragrance, radiance and power, but also and more forcefully in the way he affects men's hearts — in the love, fear, terror, respectful awe, and other feelings that his presence evokes.[63]

The god, we may suspect, actually *is* that effect. Aristotle's god is himself *theoria*,[64] and it is not clear that Aristotle supposed that there was any further "entity" with the mere property, even the essential property, of always "theorising" (which is to say,

---

61 Levenson, *Creation and the Persistence of Evil*, 62, citing Breasted, *Dawn of Conscience*, 292 and Heschel, *God in Search of Man*, 46.
62 Levenson, *Creation and the Persistence of Evil*, 64.
63 Hornung, *Conceptions of God*, 134.
64 Aristotle, *Metaphysics* 12.1072b13-28; see *Nicomachean Ethics* 10.1177b28-34.

enjoying only and always itself, uniting subject and object).⁶⁵ That very activity, desired by all things in the world, is itself the god, and we may—intermittently and inadequately—share that life. It is said that the citizens of Lampsacus, on the death of Anaxagoras in 428 BC, "erected an altar to *nous kai aletheia*, mind and truth, because they had gathered that these were his gods (or that this was his god)."⁶⁶ They were not obviously mistaken.

In ancient Egypt this elevation of the spirits was conveyed rather through images, as Plotinus recognized in a passage cited earlier:

> One must not then suppose that the gods and the "exceedingly blessed spectators" in the higher world contemplate propositions (*axiomata*), but all the Forms we speak about are beautiful images in that world, of the kind which someone imagined to exist in the soul of the wise man, images not painted but real. This is why the ancients said that the Ideas were realities and substances. The wise men of Egypt, I think, also understood this, either by scientific (*akribes*) or innate (*sumphute*) knowledge, and when they wished to signify something wisely, did not use the forms of letters which follow the order of words and propositions (*logoi* and *protaseis*) and imitate sounds and the enunciations of philosophical statements (*prophoras axiomaton*), but by drawing images and inscribing in their temples one particular image of each particular thing, they manifested the non-discursiveness of the intelligible world, that is, that every image is a kind of knowledge and wisdom and is a subject of statements, all together in one, and not discourse (*dianoesis*) or deliberation (*bouleusis*).⁶⁷

Classicists tend to insist that Plotinus misunderstood the purpose of Egyptian images and hieroglyphs. Egyptologists are more supportive of his interpretation:

---

65 Aristotle, *Metaphysics* 12.1074b35-36. Plotinus, and other Platonists, disagreed: the unknowable One transcends both being and knowledge—and this too has its parallel, at least, in Egyptian thought: "Amun is one, concealing himself.... He is hidden from the gods, and his aspect is unknown. He is farther than the sky, he is deeper than the Duat.... He is too great to investigate, too powerful to know" (Allen, *Genesis in Egypt*, 1, citing hymn to Amun).
66 Anscombe, *Faith in a Hard Ground*, 56 (after Diogenes Laertius, *Lives* 2.3.10).
67 *Ennead* V.8 [31].5,20-6,9; citing Plato, *Symposium* 215b; see also IV.3 [27].11.

How the Worlds Become

The mixed form of their [the Egyptians'] gods is nothing other than a hieroglyph, a way of "writing" not the name but the nature and function of the deity in question. The Egyptians do not hesitate to call hieroglyphs "gods," and even to equate individual signs in the script with particular gods; it is quite in keeping with their views to see images of the gods as signs in a metalanguage. As is true of every Egyptian hieroglyph, they are more than just ciphers or lifeless symbols; the god can inhabit them, his cult image will normally be in the same form, and his priests may assume his role by wearing animal masks.[68]

The sculpted or painted images are coded statements—or rather invocations. "The wise men of old... made temples and statues in the wish that the gods should be present to them."[69] Conversely, hieroglyphs are images. And both may make the god, the presence, visible. Hornung goes on to say that none of these images give any information about "the true form of a deity": "every image is an imperfect means of making a god visible" and "scarcely any important deity is restricted to a single form and manifestation."[70] As indicated in the *Corpus Hermeticum*, "the very quality of the speech and the sound of Egyptian words have in themselves the energy of the objects they speak of"[71]—and for that very reason their force is not well conveyed in Greek (or English) paraphrase (though those languages too allow for similar effects).

> Now all the World knows that the Græcians, treated of the greatest Human Persons and Things in their Prose, but that Poetry was a Language which they reserv'd for their Gods, and for the Things which related to them. And I am apt to believe, that Poetry from hence was called, the Language of the Gods, because when ever the Græcians in the Poetical times, introduc'd their God's Speaking, they were sure to speak in Verse.[72]

---

68 Hornung, *Conceptions of God*, 124.
69 *Enneads* IV.3 [27].11.
70 Hornung, *Conceptions of God*, 125.
71 Copenhaver, *Hermetica*, 58 [16.1]. See Fowden, *Egyptian Hermes*, 37–38; Hanegraaff, *Hermetic Spirituality*, 116.
72 Dennis [1658–1734], "The Grounds of Criticism in Poetry" [1704], in *Critical Works*, 339. See also Origen, *Contra Celsum*, 25 [1.25]: "experts in the use of charms relate that a man who pronounces a given spell in its native language

For the same reason it is probably an error to describe the stories as anything that the ancient Egyptians "believed" or sought to offer as simply "factual" hypotheses, to be considered, corrected, rebutted or replaced. The point is rather to make a god visible, in image, story or ritual: that is, to elicit worship. Momentarily we can relax, relieved of any need to pursue elusive goals: wealth, health, and later victory. It is enough simply to be here, "at the still point of the turning world," where we may find

> The inner freedom from the practical desire,
> The release from action and suffering, release from the inner
> And the outer compulsion.[73]

Even professed materialistic atheists may feel such awe, delight, and freedom: the difference is that, strictly speaking, they must think that such things are no better than occasional, enforced relaxation.

And what is the point of "making a god visible"?

> For the Egyptians an image is not "merely" an image; it constitutes a reality and a physical presence. The temple is a "sky" on earth, which contains the efficacious image of the god and may serve as an abode for the god himself.... One, and by no means the least, of the aims of the cult is to make the earth an attractive place for the gods to live, to create in the temple a worthy residence for the god's image and a likeness of the sky, and to tend the cult image so well that it is happy to live among men.[74]

---

can bring about the effect that the spell is claimed to do. But if the same spell is translated into any other language whatever, it can be seen to be weak and ineffective. Thus it is not the significance of the things which the words describe that has a certain power to do this or that, but it is the qualities and characteristics of the sound.'

73 Eliot, 'Burnt Norton,' 2.16–26, in *Four Quartets*, p. 5.
74 Hornung, *Conceptions of God*, 229; see Plotinus, *Ennead* IV.3 [27].11: 'the wise men of old... made temples and statues in the wish that the gods should be present to them." Armstrong (*Enneads* vol. 4, pp. 70–71) suggests that this alludes to 'the ancient Egyptian practice of ritually animating statues,' as if they were expected to get up and walk (on which see Johnston, 'Animating Statues"; Uždavinys, "Animation of Statues in Ancient Civilizations'). This seems to me an unduly literalistic reading both of Plotinus and the Egyptians, but cf. Hanegraaff, *Hermetic Spirituality*, 68–72, arguing that the combination of expectations, sounds and (potentially) hallucinogenic incense can explain how devotees really did see statues moving.

This may also be the inner meaning of the most famous of Egyptian buildings, the pyramids:

> Just as the "primeval hill" of solid land once emerged from the dark waters to establish earth and sky firmly against dissolution and chaos, so this reproduction of the primeval hill made in stone — namely, the pyramid — was supposed to oppose the powers of chaos and death. May the buried king and the life of the people entrusted to him be protected, and may he share in the world's created order forever! Even more: the king was buried in the desert, symbolically at the edge of this world, close to the dangerous abyss, since only here, so near to chaos, could life be renewed. In ancient Egypt, the monuments constructed according to cultural values were in the service of the miraculous regeneration of life at the edge of dissolution and death.[75]

Not tombs for the dead, but would-be wombs. So also in Mesopotamia:

> The temple, no less than the ritual drama and the cult image, was a representation of the form of the power that was meant to fill it. Like a human dwelling, the temple was the place where the owner could be found. Its presence among the houses of the human community was visible assurance that the god was present and available, that he — as the hymn to the moon god expressed it — "among the (creatures) in whom is breath of life has settled down in a holy abode."[76]

That sense of sacred presence has played a significant role in religious and political history. Centuries later the envoys of Vladimir of Kiev, visiting the great church of Hagia Sophia in Constantinople, reported: "we were led into a place where they serve their God, and we did not know where we were, on heaven or on earth; and do not know how to tell about this. All we know is that God lives there with people and their service is better than in any other country. We cannot forget that beauty."[77] And in Western Christendom Abbot Suger, architect and builder of

---

75 Schweizer, *Sungod's Journey through the Netherworld*, 6.
76 Jacobsen, *Treasures*, 16.
77 See Foltz, *Noetics of Nature*, 78, 126.

the abbey church of St. Denis, said that he saw himself, when in the church, "dwelling in some strange region of the universe which neither exists entirely in the slime of earth nor entirely in the purity of heaven, and that by the grace of God, [he could] be transported from this inferior to that higher world in an anagogical manner."[78] Ancient Egypt, perhaps, had less disdain for "the slime of earth." The cosmos itself is such a temple. We are lucky to be involved in the material world!

> Man is therefore a great miracle, a being to be admired and honoured. He passes into the nature of a god as if he is a god himself. He knows the nature of the daimons inasmuch as he recognizes himself to have come from the same source. He looks down on [*despicit*] the part of him that is human, because he has put his trust in the divinity of the other part. O, how much luckier a mixture human nature is! He is joined to the gods by a kindred divinity while looking down on the part in himself that is no more than terrestrial. All other beings, to whom he knows to be connected by heavenly disposition, he draws close to him in a bond of affection while raising his gaze to heaven. Thus he is placed in the happier state of a middle position: he values [*diligat*] what is below him and is valued by what is above him. He takes care of the earth, quickly mingles with the elements, and plumbs the depths of the sea with the sharpness of his mind. All things are open to him. Heaven does not seem too high, for he measures it as if from nearby with his soul's sagacity. No misty air troubles the directedness of his soul, no dense earth obstructs his work, no depth of water impairs his view. He is everything and everywhere at the same time.[79]

A temple may be a place where our spirits are elevated by a sense of beauty, and also of historical connections. Correspondingly, in speaking of the whole cosmos, or at least of the world as we experience and enjoy it, as something like a temple, an ordered whole where the Sun rides daily across the sky for the good of mortals, we may find a better role than as grubs within

---

78 Panofsky, *Abbot Suger*, 21, 65.
79 *Asclepius* 6, as quoted by Hanegraaff, *Hermetic Spirituality*, 59; cf. Copenhaver, *Hermetica*, 69–70.

a rotting tree, or as slaves to inhuman powers (as Babylonian myths had it, and as some moderns expect).

> It is very much the same as if anyone were to place a man, a Greek or a barbarian, in some mystic shrine of extraordinary beauty and size to be initiated, where he would see many mystic sights and hear many mystic voices, where light and darkness would appear to him alternately, and a thousand other things would occur; and further, if it should be just as in the rite called enthronement, where the inducting priests are wont to seat the novices and then dance round and round them—pray, is it likely that the man in this situation would be no whit moved in his mind and would not suspect that all which was taking place was the result of a more than wise intention and preparation, even if he belonged to the most remote and nameless barbarians and had no guide and interpreter at his side—provided, of course, that he had the mind of a human being? Or rather, is this not impossible? Impossible too that the whole human race, which is receiving the complete and truly perfect initiation, not in a little building erected by the Athenians for the reception of a small company, but in this universe, a varied and cunningly wrought creation, in which countless marvels appear at every moment, and where, furthermore, the rites are being performed, not by human beings who are of no higher order than the initiates themselves, but by immortal gods who are initiating mortal men, and night and day both in sunlight and under the stars are—if we may dare to use the term—literally dancing around them forever—is it possible to suppose, I repeat, that of all these things his senses told him nothing, or that he gained no faintest inkling of them, and especially when the leader of the choir was in charge of the whole spectacle and directing the entire heaven and universe, even as a skilful pilot commands a ship that has been perfectly furnished and lacks nothing?[80]

---

80 Dio Chrysostom, "Man's First Conception of God," *Discourses* 35–37 (12.31–34). The "leader of the choir" (*koruphaios*) is most likely the musician sitting at the centre of a choral dance, in the place of Apollo (who is the god "who sits in the centre, on the navel of the earth, and is the interpreter of religion to all mankind": Plato, *Republic* 4.427c).

Hornung suggested that the emergence of more openly anthropomorphic images for the powers that govern the world in the early third millennium showed that humans were then "achieving new self-awareness," no longer wholly "the plaything of incomprehensible powers."[81] As significant players in the game of life humans themselves could be all be "images" of a god: "even a criminal condemned to death is one of the 'sacred herd' of god."[82]

> For the teacher Ani [that is, the author or compiler of *The Book of the Dead*] at the end of the 18th Dynasty "men are the equals of god because of their custom of listening to a man who brings a plea. Not only the wise man is his equal, as if the rest were so many cattle."

"I made every man like his fellow," say the Coffin Texts. "I brought into being the four gods from my sweat while men are the tears of my eye."[83] Men—that is, humans—are born, it seems, as emblems or avatars of the god's sorrow and compassion. Even so, it was the reigning king who was the principal divine image, and potentially the source of revelation. *Pace* both Assmann and Hornung we should not read too much universal or exclusive humanism back into the record, as though it were *obvious* that such humanism is a truth which all reasonable people must accept, and *obvious* that it would constitute an expectable advance.[84] This notion has often infected classical scholars faced

---

81 Hornung, *Conceptions of God*, 105.
82 Hornung, *Conceptions of God*, 138, citing the Westcar Papyrus.
83 Pritchard, *Ancient Near Eastern Texts*, 8.
84 So also Jacobsen, *Treasures*, 9: "The situationally determined, nonhuman, forms that we have observed here are all original or old forms or—as in the hymn to the moon god—survivals into a later age. They appear to have had their floruit in Protoliterate or earlier periods, that is to say, during the fourth millennium BC. Even then, however, the human form would seem to have been an alternative, or perhaps a competing, possibility; and with the beginning of the third millennium, from Early Dynastic onward, the human form came to dominate almost completely, leaving to the older forms the somewhat ambiguous role of divine 'emblems' only. This victory of the human over the nonhuman forms was won slowly and with difficulty. To the latest time the older forms retain a curious vitality, seeming to lurk under the human exterior ready to break through it to reveal the true essence of the divine power and will: rays pierce through the human body of the sun god from within, ears of grain grow out through the human shoulders of the grain goddess, serpent heads through those of Ningishzida, and when Gudea sees the god Ningirsu in a dream the god still has the wings of his old form, the thunderbird

by the passages in Homer's works where some god "takes the form" of a bird: this has seemed so offensive that the passages have to be read as merely similes, rather than transformations.[85] There seems to me no good reason for this prejudice, even if later poets and critics chose to despise more obviously theriomorphic representations (on which more below). The sculpted images continued to combine zoomorphic codes, and it was axiomatic in later centuries that the Egyptians must still be thinking themselves subject to "every kind of monstrous god and barking Anubis too."[86] In other words, they remained conscious, on the one hand, of the material and symbolic contribution that the nonhuman made and makes to the cosmos we enjoy, and on the other still found profit in conceiving a single visible human image in which the many strands of life could be partly reconciled. "Man is a lumpe where all beasts kneaded be. Wisdom makes him an ark where all agree."[87]

CATASTROPHE AND CREATION

Once upon a time we knew, perhaps, our place!

> Since man, as the Sumerians saw him, was weak and could achieve no success in anything without divine assistance, it was fortunate that all these human workers in and outside the temple could invigorate themselves with divine power. Each group of human toilers had human overseers; but above these there were divine officials to direct the work and infuse success into human efforts.[88]

Maybe people did begin to feel more confident in the early years of the third millennium, and (conversely) had been less confident before. Maybe—as Plato declared that the Egyptian priests told Solon—they were still recovering from catastrophe.

Imdugud. He retains those wings in Assyria in representations carved as late as the first millennium. Also—and importantly—on crucial occasions it was in their old forms as 'emblems' that the gods elected to be present to follow and guide the army to victory, or to be brought out to witness and guarantee the making of oaths.'
85 See Buxton, *Forms of Transformation*, 31–37.
86 Virgil, *Aeneid* 8.698.
87 Donne, *Complete Verse and Selected Prose*, 163.
88 Jacobsen, *Treasures*, 81.

> Like the rest of mankind you have suffered from convulsions of nature, which are chiefly brought about by the two great agencies of fire and water.... The memorials which your own and other nations have once had of the famous actions of mankind perish in the waters at certain periods; and the rude survivors in the mountains begin again, knowing nothing of the world before the flood.[89]

Xenophanes of Colophon (570–478 BC) cited evidence for the suggestion: "shells are found inland and in the mountains, in the quarries at Syracuse the impression of a fish and seaweeds has been found;... on Malta there are slabs of rock made up of all kinds of sea-creatures. He says [so Hippolytus declared] that these came about a long time ago, when everything was covered with mud, and that the impression became dried in the mud. He claims that the human race is wiped out whenever the earth is carried down into the sea and becomes mud, that then there is a fresh creation."[90] Or perhaps there has always been a remnant saved from ruin, from which the world was repopulated, indefinitely many times. Aristotle may even have supposed that all other creatures were literally descended from those surviving human remnants: an idea also present in Olaf Stapledon's future history.[91] We are in no better position than Diodorus to answer

---

89 Plato, *Timaeus* 22B.
90 Waterfield, *First Philosophers*, 29 [21A33DK], a text cited in Hippolytus, *Refutation of All Heresies* 1.14.5–6, ed. Marcovich.
91 Aristotle, *De Partibus Animalium* 4.686a25–687a2: see Clark, *Aristotle's Man*, 28–30; Stapledon, *Last and First Men*, 255: "Two hundred million years after the solar collision innumerable species of sub-human grazers with long sheep-like muzzles, ample molars, and almost ruminant digestive systems, were competing with one another on the polar continent [of Neptune]. Upon these preyed the sub-human carnivora, of whom some were built for speed in the chase, others for stalking and a sudden spring. But since jumping was no easy matter on Neptune, the cat-like types were all minute. They preyed upon man's more rabbit-like and rat-like descendants, or on the carrion of the larger mammals, or on the lusty worms and beetles. These had sprung originally from vermin which had been transported accidentally from Venus. For of all the ancient Venerian fauna only man himself, a few insects and other invertebrates, and many kinds of micro-organisms, succeeded in colonizing Neptune. Of plants, many types had been artificially bred for the new world, and from these eventually arose a host of grasses, flowering plants, thick-trunked bushes, and novel seaweeds. On this marine flora fed certain highly developed marine worms; and of these last, some in time became vertebrate, predatory, swift and fish-like. On these in turn man's own marine descendants preyed, whether as sub-human seals,

the question on a *cosmic* scale, even if we can now be fairly sure that humankind did, sometime, have a beginning—though long before our recorded history.

> One group, which takes the position that the universe did not come into being and will not decay, has declared that the race of men also has existed from eternity, there having never been a time when men were first begotten; the other group, however, which hold that the universe came into being and will decay, has declared that, like it, men had their first origin at a definite time.[92]

We may like to believe that what we call "prehistory" was populated only by tribes of nomadic savages. Actually we do not know what societies developed long ago, within our species or another, nor what the "uncivilized"—those without abiding cities—knew that we have forgotten. Graeber and Wengrow are probably right to suggest that our ancestors tried out many ways of living together.

> If human beings, through most of our history, have moved back and forth fluidly between different social arrangements, assembling and dismantling hierarchies on a regular basis, maybe the real question should be "how did we get stuck?" How did we end up in one single mode? How did we lose that political self-consciousness, once so typical of our species? How did we come to treat eminence and subservience not as temporary expedients, or even the pomp and circumstance of some kind of grand seasonal theatre, but as inescapable elements of the human condition? If we started out just playing games, at what point did we forget that we were playing?[93]

After our own future (likely) collapse, most easily readable traces of our passage will soon have vanished—and we may be correspondingly entirely ignorant of earlier passages.[94]

---

or still more specialized sub-human porpoises. Perhaps most remarkable of these developments of the ancient human stock was that which led, through a small insectivorous bat-like glider, to a great diversity of true flying mammals, scarcely larger than hummingbirds, but in some cases agile as swallows."
92 Diodorus, *Library* 1.6.3.
93 Graeber and Wengrow, *Dawn of Everything*, 115.
94 See Schmidt and Frank, "The Silurian Hypothesis."

On one cosmological story there is an absolute catastrophe to come, mirroring the absolute beginning, a time when everything will have happened and there will be nothing else to do. On another there are many *local* catastrophes, indistinguishable for their victims from the absolute, within an eternally existing Reality that ceaselessly remakes itself. In either case we may find a sort of joy, even an impulse to worship, in the contemplation of either the everlasting or the transient reality. We seem to want there to be cycles. Even the recurrent disasters (volcanic eruption, meteor strike or rampant evolution of toxin-producing life-forms) that have caused past mass extinctions (very roughly, every 26 million years)[95] are easily blamed on cycles: perhaps the dark star Nemesis regularly disturbs the Oort Cloud and sends comets heading towards the inner solar system (and coincidentally, us).[96] We *expect* things to go in cycles. Modern cosmologists, perturbed by the thought of a single absolute beginning in "the Big Bang," would like this to be only one of indefinitely many "bangs" as each cosmos expands and then contracts, or else engenders new cosmoi through the proliferation of black holes.[97]

But is the cosmos on either story something that anyone in any way "intended"? Are there "gods," in the sense that is now thought obvious: actual, personal, powerful creators? That question may itself lead towards a monotheistic conception: if the cosmos were the product only of many distinct intentions, each with their own goals and natures, then the whole itself must be unintended—and this is hardly enough to serve either as an explanation of all things, or a clear inspiration for our lives together. It is after all obvious that many particular features of our present world have been *intended*, if only by human beings or other intelligent creatures. "Gods," so called, would merely be an addition to the stock of locally powerful agents. It might even turn out to be true that many large-scale features of the observable cosmos have been "engineered" by earlier intelligences, and what we take to be

---

95 Raup and Sepkoski, "Periodicity of Extinctions in the Geologic Past."
96 See Muller, *Nemesis: The Death Star*. The notion was presented first in *Nature* 1984.308 (5961), pp. 713–15 and 715–17, by two sets of authors, (1) D. P. Whitmire and A. A. Jackson and (2) M. Davis, P. Hut, and R. A. Muller.
97 See Smolin, *The Life of the Cosmos*.

"natural" is only the effect of many disparate, ancient, powers.[98] Astronomers are nowadays slow to suggest that odd astronomical events ("odd" according to current physical theory) might be the result of astro-engineering or cosmic conflicts: it seems easier, to us, to seek out inanimate or mindless explanations, whereas our ancestors, familiar with the effects of life and mind on earth, saw nothing odd about imagining such causal powers elsewhere.[99]

> It seemed good to their Maker to fill all parts of the universe with living beings. He set land-animals on the earth, aquatic creatures in the seas and rivers, and in heaven the stars, each of which is said to be not a living creature only but mind of the purest kind through and through; and therefore in air also, the remaining section of the universe, living creatures exist. If they are not to be apprehended by sense, what of that? The soul too is a thing invisible.[100]

All such agencies, however, even if they have occasionally intervened in human history, are only vulgarly "godlike": they neither explain the totality, nor inspire us to any real or decent worship. The only singular cosmic purpose that might either *explain* things or rightly *inspire* devotion would be one that had no acceptable rival, and itself had no need of any further explanation.

But before we can seek out any such unified theory or single purpose in the cosmos we must attend to more local explanations and inspirations. Where might our ancestors have expected to locate such putative creators? In a world beset by unpredictable catastrophe it might most easily be the things, the beings, most likely to survive—whether as individual entities or recurrent types—that would seem most likely to be our masters and our makers. Mountains and rivers and great trees on the one hand, and the constantly returning seasons on the other, constitute the immediate context of our lives, but the most obvious and

---

98 See Scharf, "Is Physical Law an Alien Intelligence?"
99 See Loeb's *Extraterrestrial* for a (flawed but impassioned) plea that astronomers should take the likely reality of extraterrestrial life more seriously. Loeb draws especially on the peculiarities of a recent extra-solar visitor, Oumuamua, which he suggests is best understood as a solar sail, left over from some exploratory civilization.
100 Philo, *On Dreams* 22.135, in *Collected Works*, 5:369–71.

universal divinities, seemingly untouched by any catastrophe, are up aloft, in the heavens: Sun and Moon and the fixed and wandering stars.

> Now certainly the whole earth is full of living creatures and immortal beings, and everything up to the sky is full of them: why, then are not the stars, both those in the lower spheres and those in the highest, gods moving in order, circling in well-arranged beauty? Why should they not possess virtue? What hindrance prevents them from acquiring it? The causes are not present there which make people bad here below, and there is no badness of body, disturbed and disturbing. And why should they not have understanding, in their everlasting peace, and grasp in their intellect God and the intelligible gods? Shall our wisdom be greater than that of the gods there in the sky? Who, if he has not gone out of his mind, could tolerate the idea?[101]

---

[101] *Ennead* II.9 [33].8, 32–40.

～3～
Astronomy

> A tradition has been handed down by the ancient thinkers of very early times, and bequeathed to posterity in the form of a myth, to the effect that these heavenly bodies are gods, and that the Divine pervades the whole of nature.[1]

HEAVENLY BODIES AND THEIR CYCLES

Amongst the suggestions that later Christian authorities deemed most dangerously heretical is the worship of heavenly bodies, and any suggestion that we might join their number. Christians, by the emperor Justinian's decree, were not to agree that the stars themselves were living, nor that our resurrection bodies were spheres (that is to say, that we could expect to rise as stars).[2] But the story of an ascent into the visible heavens has a wider provenance and a greater influence than Justinian would have approved. And even if we could not ascend, the sidereal gods might come down.

To begin again at the beginning:

> A tradition has been handed down by the ancient thinkers of very early times, and bequeathed to posterity in the form of a myth, to the effect that these heavenly bodies are gods, and that the Divine pervades the whole of nature. The rest of their tradition has been added later in a mythological form to influence the vulgar and as a constitutional and utilitarian expedient; they say that these gods are human in shape or are like certain other animals, and make other statements consequent upon

---
1 Aristotle, *Metaphysics* 12.1074b1–15.
2 Sherwood, *Earlier Ambigua*, 77–81. Cf. Uždavinys, *Ascent to Heaven*, 145: "In early Jewish mysticism, the angels in heaven and the stars are thought to be identical. Therefore, the righteous ones ascend in order to shine as the stars in heaven (*yazhiru ke'zohar ha-raqi'a*: Daniel 12.3). The human worshipper is to be turned into the heavenly worshipper, transformed into an angel."

and similar to those which we have mentioned. Now if we separate these statements and accept only the first, that they supposed the primary substances to be gods, we must regard it as an inspired saying; and reflect that whereas every art and philosophy has probably been repeatedly developed to the utmost and has perished again, these beliefs of theirs have been preserved as a relic of former knowledge.[3]

There may have been other and better reasons to depict those original gods as human or animal than merely to engage "the vulgar," but Aristotle was probably correct to suggest that their "godliness," at first, lay simply in their permanence, their constantly recurring order, their sheer uncountable number,[4] as well as their obvious splendour. The fixed stars rose and fell with the seasons, and even the planetary, "wandering," stars had an order difficult to discern but still reliable. Human and other earthly lives were moulded and guided by the heavens: what could they be but gods?

> When the strength of the piercing sun lets up from its sweaty heat, and powerful Zeus brings the autumnal rains, and the skin of mortal men is much relieved; when the star Sirius goes over the head of humans, born to misery, a little by day, but takes up more of the night — at that time wood cut with the iron is most resistant to worms, when trees shed their leaves to the ground and cease to send out shoots. At this time, remember to cut your wood: It is the appropriate season.[5]

Hesiod gave detailed instructions not only for agricultural but also marital and civil practices, linked to the astronomical seasons,

---

[3] Aristotle, *Metaphysics* 12.1074b1-15; see Plato, *Timaeus* 40b: "the unwandering stars... are living creatures divine and eternal and abide for ever revolving uniformly in the same spot."
[4] Abraham is promised descendants "as the stars of heaven." Their number may be the chief intention, but there may be a wider implication. "The Lord said, 'Look up into heaven and count the stars, if thou canst count their sum. So shall be thy seed' (Genesis 15.5; see also Genesis 26.4). Well does the text say 'so,' not 'so many,' that is, 'of equal number to the stars.' For He wishes to suggest not number merely, but a multitude of other things, such as tend to happiness perfect and complete": Philo, "Who Is the Heir of Divine Things?," ch. 17 [86]: *Collected Works*, 4:325.
[5] Hesiod, *Poems*, 125 [*Works and Days*, 350-57].

giving Zeus and Demeter the chief credit but mentioning also such stars and constellations as Arcturus, Sirius and the Pleiades. In earlier Babylonian terms the constellations resemble writing, and so indicate (even if they do not strictly cause) the course of earthly events.

> The metaphor of the heavenly writing therefore related the constellations to cuneiform signs from which one could read and derive meaning, and thus expressed the idea that written messages were encoded in celestial phenomena. A remarkable coincidence of conception appears with explicit reference to astrology in *The Enneads* of Plotinus, in which he says "we may think of the stars as letters perpetually being inscribed on the heavens or inscribed once for all."[6]

That last cluster of stars, the Pleiades, is an intriguing case, which tends to confirm Aristotle's suggestion that we all inherit stories from very long ago.

> There are two puzzles surrounding the Pleiades, or Seven Sisters. First, why are the mythological stories surrounding them, typically involving seven young girls being chased by a man associated with the constellation Orion, so similar in vastly separated cultures, such as the Australian Aboriginal cultures and Greek mythology? Second, why do most cultures call them "Seven Sisters" even though most people with good eyesight see only six stars? Here we show that both these puzzles may be explained by a combination of the great antiquity of the stories combined with the proper motion of the stars, and that these stories may predate the departure of most modern humans out of Africa around 100,000 BC.[7]

---

[6] Rochberg, *Heavenly Writing*, 2, citing *Ennead* II.3 [52].7, 5–13. Plotinus himself rejects much of astrological theory, but allows that the "the stars cooperate towards the whole," and may therefore be "well adapted for signs" (ibid., II.3 [52].8, 6–8). Who did the writing may be disputed: maybe it was earthly astronomers who organized the stars into meaningful constellations to remind us of appropriate maxims. Or perhaps the gods themselves did it.

[7] Norris and Norris, "Why Are There Seven Sisters?"; see Tehrani, "Descent with Imagination," which offers a phylogenetic analysis of familiar folk-tales found around the world; also Nunn and Reid, "Aboriginal Memories of Inundation," showing that oral tradition amongst the First Australian population stretches back for millennia.

HOW THE WORLDS BECAME

The full significance of the story is not explained merely by the astronomical data: why did our ancestors impose such an odd story—the hunter Orion, or a gang of youths, pursuing seven sisters—on those fixed stars? Why indeed is *any* particular story told about the heavens? Such stories do in general serve a purpose, making the bright lights above us into a memorable, often because crude or creepy, tale (and may also embody manners and morals peculiar to their particular tribe and time). But the stories cannot be allowed entirely to demean or damage the stars' splendour: up aloft is the pattern of all proper earthly life. The sight of them—as also of other splendours—"takes us out of ourselves."[8]

Or to put it another way: the heavenly bodies define the world of time in which we live:

> Time came into existence along with the Heaven, to the end that having been generated together they might also be dissolved together, if ever a dissolution of them should take place; and it was made after the pattern of the Eternal Nature, to the end that it might be as like thereto as possible; for whereas the pattern is existent through all eternity, the copy, on the other hand, is through all time, continually having existed, existing, and being about to exist. Wherefore, as a consequence of this reasoning and design on the part of God, with a view to the generation of Time, the sun and moon and five other stars, which bear the appellation of "planets," came into existence for the determining and preserving of the numbers of Time.[9]

---

8 So also Immanuel Kant, *Critique of Practical Reason*, 166: "Two things fill the mind with ever new and increasing admiration and awe, the oftener and more steadily we reflect on them: the starry heavens above me and the moral law within me. I do not merely conjecture them and seek them as though obscured in darkness or in the transcendent region beyond my horizon: I see them before me, and I associate them directly with the consciousness of my own existence. The former begins at the place I occupy in the external world of sense, and it broadens the connection in which I stand into an unbounded magnitude of worlds beyond worlds and systems of systems and into the limitless times of their periodic motion, their beginning and their continuance." Kant further claims that "the former view of a countless multitude of worlds annihilates, as it were, my importance as an animal creature" (to that notion, of cosmic insignificance, I shall return).
9 Plato, *Timaeus* 38bc.

Astronomy

Days, months, and years exist because of the perpetual, cyclical dance of the sun and moon, as well as those "other stars [whose] revolutions have not been discovered by men (save for a few out of the many); wherefore they have no names for them, nor do they compute and compare their relative measurements, so that they are not aware, as a rule, that the 'wanderings' of these bodies, which are hard to calculate and of wondrous complexity, constitute Time."[10] All the stars, Plato suggested, would sometimes return to the same arrangement "when all the eight circuits, with their relative speeds, finish together and come to a head, when measured by the revolution of the Same and Similarly-moving."[11] This Great or Platonic Year has sometimes (mistakenly) been identified with the time taken for the "precession of the equinoxes" to come round to its beginning.[12] But that "Precessional Great Year" is itself of interest. Nowadays the sun rises at the Spring Equinox against the background of Aquarius (or very nearly so), and Polaris is the North Star. But this is only a transient condition: two thousand years ago it rose against the background of Pisces at the Spring Equinox, and there was no visible star to mark the northern end of the heavenly axis. There was an empty space in heaven there, and two fainter stars of Ursa Minor (Kochab and Pherkad: *Beta* and *Gamma Ursae Minoris*) were the nearest visible stars.[13] In a still earlier age, during the Egyptian Old Kingdom, the Pole Star was Thuban in the constellation Draco—and perhaps this was the dragon that Apollo defeated at the navel of the world.[14] This "precession of the equinoxes," the grand cycle that takes 25,920 years to complete, was calculated, according to our current histories, by Hipparchus of Rhodes about 140 BC.[15] The

---

10 Plato, *Timaeus* 39cd.
11 Plato, *Timaeus* 39d. This Great or Platonic Year is said—for example by Adam (*Republic*, vol. 2, pp. 202, 298–306), on the basis of arcane numerological calculations derived from Plato, *Republic* 8.546b—to amount to a span of 36,000 solar years.
12 See Heath, *Aristarchus of Samos*, 170–73.
13 See Copenhaver, *Hermetica*, 19 (5.4): "the bear that turns around itself and carries the whole cosmos with it"; see also p. 9 (2.7).
14 See Barber and Barber, *When They Severed Earth from Sky*, 208, 240.
15 Ptolemy, *Almagest* 3.1; 7.1–3. See Ulansey, *Origins of the Mithraic Mysteries*, 76–81 for further evidence that the precession was indeed Hipparchus's reasoned conclusion, and for the religious uses made of the idea thereafter.

"discovery" would have been an extrapolation from a tiny observable change—unless he had the long records of Babylonians or others to confirm the guess. He supposed, in line with our general preference for supposing *cyclical* change, that the sun and the wandering stars were working back through the zodiacal signs to complete a circuit (and not just oscillating). Proclus reckoned that the Egyptians and Chaldeans ("who even before their observations were instructed by the gods") had reached the same conclusion.[16] Possibly, but unprovably, the discovery was even earlier: Santillana and Von Dechend suggested that astronomical observations lie behind much European mythology (in particular, that stories of past and predicted "disasters" have mostly, they proposed, referred to the precession of the equinoxes, and the periodic "drowning" of constellations as the perceived axis of rotation shifts).[17] New ages dawn, perhaps, as the sun rises against different zodiacal backgrounds over millennia: the Christian Fish replaces the Ram, as the Ram two thousand years earlier had replaced the Bull, as the major influence on human life and thought.[18] Another way of describing the story of that most recent change was that the Virgin would have a son: that is, the sun rises in Virgo at the *autumn* equinox when it rises in the Fishes in the spring.[19] The story has had more obvious influence on *modern* literature and esoteric theory than is easily discerned in the ancient.[20] That

---

[16] Though Proclus himself—like Manilius, *Astronomica* 1.521-3—found it incredible that the stars should ever change (Proclus, *Commentary on Timaeus* 40AB, cited by Kidd, *Poseidonius*, 269). He was mistaken, but of course the changes I am describing here were not changes in the stars themselves, but only in the position where they seem to be.

[17] Santillana and Von Dechend, *Hamlet's Mill*; see Feyerabend, *Against Method*, 29-30.

[18] "The zodiac consists of twelve 30° segments (1 sign = 30°), named for twelve ecliptical constellations, all of which belonged to the list of stars in the path of the moon found in [the astronomical compendium] MUL.APIN. Although the names of the zodiacal signs derived from an original relation to the zodiacal constellations, once the signs were defined by longitude rather than the constellation, they ceased to have any real relation to the constellations and became a mathematical reference system, representing the 360° of the ecliptic, counted from some defined starting point" (Rochberg, *Heavenly Writing*, 128).

[19] See Virgil, *Eclogues* 4.6-7: "iam redit et Virgo, redeunt Saturnia regna; iam nova progenies caelo demittitur alto." Virgil's poem was long taken to be an unconscious prophecy of the birth of Christ.

[20] See Graves, *White Goddess*, 96, 371; Druon, *Alexander the Great*, ch. 5. Both authors give the precession an esoteric significance. Neither provides any

Astronomy

this age is truly "the dawning of the Age of Aquarius," when old men shall dream dreams and young men see visions,[21] is either premature or over-optimistic.

Whether or not ancient stories in many differing civilizations do record the relative positions and motions of the heavenly bodies over many ages (as Santillana and Von Dechend hoped to show) remains unproven but is still strangely attractive. It is even *possible*, for example, that the scandalous story of Hephaestus's trapping Ares and Aphrodite records some notable conjunction:

> None other than Homer recounts a "silly story" [*Odyssey* 8.266-366] in which Hephaistos, tipped off by Helios/ Sun, catches his wife Aphrodite/Venus in bed with Ares/ Mars. Enraged, he casts an invisible net that holds them while he appeals to Zeus/Jupiter, Hermes/Mercury, Poseidon, and Apollo to come around and laugh at them, until Poseidon gravely persuades him to let them go. If the planets are gods, this stellar event, which has to have occurred before Homer (ca. 800 BC) and after Zeus became celestial ruler (ca. 2150 BC), must encode a massing of all five visible planets.... One and only one such massing has occurred in the last 5000 years—a truly memorable event to long-time sky-watchers... It was visible just before sunrise throughout what we would call late February 1953 BC Homer carries baggage far older than the Trojan War.[22]

Similar interpretations may be offered for many other stories, but there is some risk that these readings, even if notionally correct, remain misreadings, since we forget that—on the ancient account—the planets really are gods. Whoever chose to record the conjunction so (if indeed they did) did not consider the

---

ancient source to establish that the precession was recognized or thought important. Neugebauer, "The Alleged Babylonian Discovery of the Precession of the Equinoxes," demolished the once popular argument that the discovery was made in the fourth century BC by a Babylonian astronomer. The recorded astronomical observations of that time were never secure nor accurate enough to allow a considered theory (but maybe even older observers noticed).
21 Joel 2.28.
22 Barber and Barber, *When They Severed Earth from Sky*, 190-91, after Santillana and Von Dechend, *Hamlet's Mill*, 177. Zeus became celestial ruler when "the spring equinox came from Taurus into Aries around 2150 BC" (Barber and Barber, 210).

event a merely astronomical curiosity, but at the very least an engaging, "meaningful" conjunction. A minimalist interpretation of that claim is simply that the stars mark out, even create, the time, giving both warnings and advice in their passage. But even that may not do justice to the way our ancestors would have *felt*: times and seasons create our lives together, and we celebrate the returning seasons rather than submit to a drunkard's walk through life, without rhyme or reason.[23] Exceptional but still expectable events such as planetary conjunctions remind us of the longer history in which we live. Even now there is something marvellous in the thought that we can name the stars that were once and will be again "the Pole Star." Even now, it seems to be worth acknowledging occasional conjunctions of the planetary stars. Whatever seems to have passed away—both in heaven and on the earth—will come again:

> The world's great age begins anew,
>   The golden years return,
> The earth doth like a snake renew
>   Her winter weeds outworn:
> Heaven smiles, and faiths and empires gleam
>   Like wrecks of a dissolving dream.[24]

And whatever comes again will also fail again. The story of the Four Ages endlessly repeated—Gold, Silver, Bronze and Iron—is widespread, from archaic Greece to India. By Hindu reckoning each Age has a definite period of many thousand years (and we are—as Hesiod also supposed—in the middle of the worst, the darkest, Age).[25] Hesiod, who added an Age of Heroes between the Bronze and Iron, made no guess about the length of each age, nor the whole cycle. Nor did the Egyptians, though "Thoth, the scribe

---

23 Cf. Clark, "End of the Ages."
24 Shelley, "Hellas: Chorus" (*Poetical Works*, 2:366), after Virgil, *Eclogue* 4. Shelley, more openly than Virgil, regretted that the eternal return would also involve repeated wars: "Oh cease! must hate and death return? / Cease! must men kill and die? / Cease! drain not to its dregs the urn / Of bitter prophecy. / The world is weary of the past, / Oh might it die or rest at last!"
25 The whole cycle, a single day of Brahma, takes 4,320,000,000 solar years (Zimmer, *Myths and Symbols*, 16), a period radically different in imagination from Hellenic estimates, and still much less than the nearly 14 billion years that our cosmos has apparently, on modern terms, survived.

Astronomy

and archivist of the gods and reckoner of time who 'reckons years, months, days, hours, and moments' assigns a fixed lifespan not only to people but also to the gods."[26] The Sun, they said, dies daily and is reborn, but they also spoke of Ra's senility, when Isis tricked him (or will trick him?) into revealing his real name, and so surrendering power and authority.[27] In the *Canon of Kings* merely human rulers are preceded by a succession of gods ("Ptah, Re, Shu, Geb, Osiris and so forth"), each ruling for a long but limited time before authority passes.[28] Authority will also pass in the end from Egypt—and the whole world—as the gods depart:

> A land once holy, most loving of divinity, by reason of her reverence the only land on earth where the gods settled, she who taught holiness and fidelity will be an example of utter unbelief. In their weariness the people of that time will find the world nothing to wonder at or to worship. This all—a good thing that never had nor has nor will have its better[29]—will be endangered. People will find it oppressive and scorn it. They will not cherish this entire world, a work of god beyond compare, a glorious construction, a bounty composed of images in multiform variety, a mechanism for god's will, ungrudgingly supporting his work, making a unity of everything that can be honoured, praised and finally loved by those who see it, a multiform accumulation taken as a single thing.... How mournful when the gods withdraw from mankind!... Such will be the old age of the world: irreverence, disorder, disregard for anything good.[30]

---

26 Hornung, *Conceptions of God*, 155.
27 Hornung, 153–54, 169.
28 Hornung, 154.
29 *Ennead* II.9 [33].4, 26–27: "What other fairer image of the intelligible world could there be? For what other fire could be a better image of the intelligible fire than the fire here? Or what other earth could be better than this, after the intelligible earth? And what sphere could be more exact or more dignified or better ordered in its circuit [than the sphere of this universe] after the self-enclosed circle there of the intelligible universe? And what other sun could there be which ranked after the intelligible sun and before this visible sun here?"
30 Copenhaver, *Asclepius* 25–26: *Hermetica*, 82. Compare the Norse expectation of the last days of this world: "Brothers shall strive and slaughter each other; own sisters' children shall sin together; ill days among men, many a whoredom: an axe-age, a sword-age, shields shall be cloven; a wind-age, a wolf-age, ere the world totters" (Sturluson, *Prose Edda*, 78 [*Beguiling of Gylfi*, 51]).

And the whole cosmos will one day be swallowed up in Apopis[31] (and perhaps be born again). Maybe, as Plotinus hints, we might manage better next time.[32]

PLANETARY INFLUENCES

That the heavenly bodies indicate or influence our lives through the cycles of days, months, years and aeons is easy to believe. What of the meaning of particular stars, and especially the "wandering" stars? Late antique Platonists described the ascent to "Heaven" as a progressive purging of planetary influences acquired during the soul's descent or fall to Earth.[33]

> In the *Timaeus* the God who makes the world gives "the first principle of soul," but the gods who are borne through the heavens "the terrible and inevitable passions," "angers," and desires and "pleasures and pains," and the "other kind of soul," from which comes passions of this kind. These statements bind us to the stars, from which we get our souls, and subject us to necessity when we come down here; from them we get our moral characters, our characteristic actions, and our emotions, coming from a disposition which is liable to emotion. So what is left which is "we"? Surely, just that which we really are, we to whom nature gave power to master our passions.[34]

Each planet had some character to contribute, whether or not there was any sort of "person" attached forever to that planet, or merely (?) an imagined reminder of the planet's supposed character. Our progress "upwards" can be conceived as a successive stripping away of the garments donned in the earlier descent from heaven through the planetary spheres.

> The attainment [of the good] is for those who go up to that higher world and are converted and strip off what we put on in our descent; (just as for those who go up to the celebrations of sacred rites there are purifications and strippings off of the clothes they wore before, and

---

31 Hornung, *Conceptions of God*, 158–59, 163, 178.
32 *Ennead* III.2 [47].17, 42–53.
33 See Clark, "Climbing up to Heaven."
34 *Ennead* II.3 [52].9, 7ff., after Plato, *Timaeus* 69c5ff.

Astronomy

going up naked) until passing in the ascent all that is alien to the God, one sees with one's self alone.[35]

More details about the planetary influences can be learnt from Macrobius, and from the *Hermetica*. According to the Hermetic text, *Poimandres*, in its ascent the soul "at the first zone surrender[s] the energy of increase and decrease; at the second [zone] evil machination, a device now inactive; at the third the illusion of longing, now inactive; at the fourth the ruler's arrogance, now freed of excess; at the fifth unholy presumption and daring recklessness; at the sixth the evil impulses that come from wealth, now inactive; and at the seventh zone the deceit that lies in ambush."[36] Servius the Grammarian, in his commentary on Virgil's *Aeneid* 6.714, offers a slightly different array of planetary vices, acquired in the soul's descent: "the astrologers claim that when the souls descend, they draw with them the sluggishness of Saturn, the anger of Mars, the lust of Venus, the desire for wealth of Mercury, the desire for power of Jupiter." Tadeusz Zieliński commented that it was "obvious" that the two other familiar vices, gluttony and envy, should be associated respectively with the "all-consuming Sun," and "the pale Moon."[37] The seven planetary rulers are of course a common feature of apocalyptic and "gnostic" texts: enemies of humanity and servants of a maleficent creator whom the Saviour must bypass in his descent, and we in our ascent. Whether the authors of those texts—for example the *Apocryphon of John*—intended any coherent narrative in naming and describing them we cannot now discover.[38]

---

35 *Ennead* I.6 [1].7. See also Proclus, *Elements of Theology*, proposition 209: "[The soul] ascends by putting off all those faculties tending to temporal process with which it was invested in its descent, and becoming clean and bare (*kathara kai gumne*) of all such faculties as serve the uses of the process."
36 Copenhaver, *Hermetica*, 6 [1.25]; see Scott, *Origen and the Life of the Stars*, 89; Fowden, *Egyptian Hermes*, 109.
37 Tester, *History of Western Astrology*, 119, citing Tadeusz Zieliński, *Philologus* 64.1905, 21ff.
38 See *Apocryphon of John* [second century AD] 12.12-21, in Layton, *Gnostic Scriptures*, 37. Plotinus acidly remarks that "by giving names to a multitude of intelligible realities they think they will appear to have discovered the exact truth, though by this very multiplicity they bring the intelligible nature into the likeness of the sense-world, the inferior world" (II.9 [33].6, 28-31).

This is not to say that the planets are *essentially* maleficent. Plotinus at least insisted that "the sun and other heavenly bodies...communicate no evil to the other pure soul."[39] "Even if their bodies are fiery, there is no need to fear them."[40] Even in *Poimandres* the archons of the planetary spheres are initially created as part of the cosmic order, helping souls on their way. Macrobius preferred to speak rather of capacities than vices: by his account we pick up "reason and understanding" (*logistikon* and *theoretikon*) in the sphere of Saturn, "in Jupiter's sphere, the power to act, called *praktikon*; in Mars' sphere, a bold spirit or *thymikon*; in the sun's sphere, sense-perception and imagination, *aisthetikon* and *phantastikon*; in Venus' sphere, the impulse of passion, *epithymetikon*; in Mercury's sphere, the ability to speak and interpret, *hermeneutikon*; and in the lunar sphere, the function of moulding and increasing bodies, *phytikon*."[41] Lunar influence isn't merely corporeal (as it might seem): below the Moon is the realm of the transient, the mutable, and its power allows us instability, for good as well as ill.[42]

Celsus, according to Origen, found a similar—but disordered— set in Mithraic or Persian mysteries:

> There is a ladder with seven gates and at its top an eighth gate. The first of the gates is of lead, the second of tin, the third of bronze, the fourth of iron, the fifth of an alloy, the sixth of silver, and the seventh of gold. They associate the first with Kronos (Saturn), taking lead to refer to the slowness of the star; the second with Aphrodite (Venus), comparing her with the brightness and softness of tin; the third with Zeus (Jupiter), as the gate that has a bronze base and which is firm; the fourth with Hermes (Mercury), for both iron and Hermes are reliable for all works and make money and are hardworking; the fifth with Ares (Mars), the gate which as a result of the mixture is uneven and varied in quality; the sixth with the Moon as the silver gate; and the seventh with the Sun as the golden gate, these metals resembling

---

39 *Ennead* II.3 [52].9, 35f.
40 *Ennead* II.9 [33].13, 11–12.
41 Macrobius, *Commentary*, 136 (I.12).
42 See Lewis, *Discarded Image*, 3–5, 108.

Astronomy

their colours.... He connects musical theories with the theology of the Persians which he describes. He waxes enthusiastic about these and gives a second explanation which again contains musical ideas.[43]

"The sun and other heavenly bodies... communicate no evil to the other pure soul."[44] But even Plotinus also acknowledged that their gifts are, in us, often corrupted:

> What comes from the stars will not reach the recipients in the same state in which it left them. If it is fire, for instance, the fire down here is dim, and if it is a loving disposition (*philiake diathesis*) it becomes weak in the recipient and produces a rather unpleasant kind of loving (*ou mala kalen ten philesin*); and manly spirit, when the receiver does not take it in due measure, so as to become brave, produces violent temper or spiritlessness; and that which belongs to honour in love and is concerned with beauty produces desire of what only seems to be beautiful, and the efflux of intellect produces knavery (*panourgia*); for knavery wants to be intellect, only it is unable to attain what it aims at. So all these things become evil in us, though they are not so up in heaven.[45]

Up in the heaven of the "fixed stars" our souls are freed from evils, or will be when we rejoin their company.[46] In some accounts our freedom is to be achieved by seemingly ceremonial means: "to persuade the archons to let him pass, the soul must address them by name, recite the correct formula, and show to each of them a 'symbol.'"[47] The ceremonials, presumably, must at least be *humbly* conducted, or else earn Plotinus's rebuke:

> They themselves most of all impair the inviolate purity of the higher powers in another way too. For when they write magic chants, intending to address them to those powers, not only to the soul but to those above it as well,

---

43 Origen, *Contra Celsum*, 334-35 [6.22]. I shall address some of the related "musical" themes below.
44 *Ennead* II.3 [52].9, 35f.
45 *Ennead* II.3 [52].11.
46 *Ennead* III.4 [15].6, 27-28: "when the souls are set free they come there to the star which is in harmony with the character and power which lived and worked in them."
47 Collins, "The Seven Heavens," 84.

what are they doing except making the powers obey the word and follow the lead of people who say spells and charms and conjurations, any one of us who is well skilled in the art of saying precisely the right things in the right way, songs and cries and aspirated and hissing sounds and everything else which their writings say has magic power in the higher world? But even if they do not want to say this, how are the incorporeal beings affected by sounds? So by the sort of statements with which they give an appearance of majesty to their own words, they, without realising it, take away the majesty of the higher powers.[48]

Plotinus was not, perhaps, always as dismissive of apparently nonsensical speech as he suggests. Elsewhere, after all, he acknowledges that our experience of the One lies beyond any "rational" understanding, and that our words can only be *evocative*, not descriptive.

> Our awareness of that One is not by way of reasoned knowledge (*episteme*) or of intellectual perception (*noesis*), as with other intelligible things, but by way of a presence (*parousia*) superior to knowledge.[49]

That, after all, is why the "wise men of old" employed images rather than careful propositions.[50] Sounds may be as animated as Egyptian statues: "just as a divine presence illuminates a statue in a ritual, so too the human mind, when it expresses a divine name in 'articulated sounds' reveals the hidden being of the gods."[51] The mistake is to suppose that the gods are compelled by such sounds, without our proper engagement with the ritual.

---

48 *Ennead* II.9 [33].14, 1–12. Janowitz (*Icons of Power*, 15) is, I think, mistaken in supposing that Plotinus "disdained prayers altogether": certainly the passage she cites (*Ennead* IV.4 [28].26, 1–4), carries no such implication. His complaint is only against mechanical or coercive accounts of prayer.
49 *Ennead* VI.9 [9].4, 1–4. See also *Ennead* V.5 [32].6, 23–29: "we in our travail do not know what we ought to say, and are speaking of what cannot be spoken, and give it a name because we want to indicate it to ourselves as best we can. But perhaps this name 'One' contains [only] a denial of multiplicity. This is why the Pythagoreans symbolically indicated it to each other by the name of Apollo, in negation of the multiple [that is, A—Pollon: Not Many]."
50 *Ennead* V.8 [31].5.
51 Janowitz, *Icons of Power*, 41, citing Proclus, *Platonic Theology* 1.29.123–4.

Fowden commented on such rebukes that the mass of the ordinarily "religious" in late antiquity (or other ages) would make no clear distinction between "religious" observance and would-be "magical" control.

> The magician's potential power was considered to be unlimited, certainly equivalent to that of the gods, once he had learned the formulae by which the divine powers that pervaded the universe could be bound and loosed — such was the logical corollary of the Egyptians' belief in the dynamism of words and spells. Ritual purity was essential to the magician's success, but personal, ethical purity was deemed irrelevant.[52]

Magicians of this sort held to the same creed as modern scientists: that the powers which govern the universe are morally neutral, and that no special ethical or spiritual virtue is needed to discern the truth, or control what happens.[53] But perhaps the creed is incoherent in either case. Magicians and scientists alike must, at the least, put aside their passions, and speak honestly of their achievements, being ready at all times to be proved mistaken: "Refutation is the greatest and chiefest of purifications, and he who has not been refuted, though he be the Great King himself, is in an awful state of impurity; he is uninstructed and deformed in those things in which he who would be truly blessed ought to be fairest and purest."[54]

Both the scientist and the magician are working on themselves as well as on their projects, seeking to bring about the sort of consciousness appropriate to the reality they hope to see and employ. What that reality is, and what that consciousness should be, are the truly important questions. What shall we say to each planetary demon, or each attractive supposition, as we progress to "heaven"? "Man's highest aspiration in this life, if he happens to be endowed with a kingly soul," so some astrologers thought,

---

52 Fowden, *Egyptian Hermes*, 81.
53 Cf. Lewis, *Abolition of Man*, 52–53: "For magic and applied science alike the problem is how to subdue reality to the wishes of men: the solution is a technique; and both, in the practice of this technique, are ready to do things hitherto regarded as disgusting and impious — such as digging up and mutilating the dead."
54 Plato, *Sophist* 227c. On the further history of this trope, see Boyle, "Pure of Heart"; Ross, *Metaphysical Aporia*.

"is to contemplate the stars and commune with them, separated for a time from his bodily envelope."[55] How exactly are we to consider ourselves "gods" (especially when—at the moment—we so obviously aren't), or how to become them? I shall return to the questions in a later chapter.

How much of this late antique account can be found in even more ancient sources? Ancient texts speak of the King's ascent to heaven, in ways that are "fundamental for the proper understanding of Second Temple Judaism and of early apocalyptic Christianity, whose mythologems can be traced back ultimately to Mesopotamian antiquity."[56] But according to the Pyramid Texts the King ascends, whether to the fixed stars or to the solar boat, by right of his original, divine birth and his personal (both ceremonial and moral) purity. Even if later Egyptians allowed that any of us could or would ascend (as Plato too proposed),[57] there is no mention in the Egyptian texts of any *planetary* aids or obstacles (though many other monsters). So where did the authors of the Hermetic texts find the idea? What led our ancestors to associate the planetary bodies with these faculties and their likely attendant vices? Would they have supposed—as perhaps later astrologers supposed—that the particular faculties we each acquired in the original descent would depend on exactly what planets and what planetary demons our souls encountered as they came down from the heavens into earthly bodies? "The demons on duty at the exact moment of birth, arrayed under each of the stars, take possession of each of us as we come into being and receive a soul."[58] But how

---

55 Fowden, *Egyptian Hermes*, 93.
56 Uždavinys, *Ascent to Heaven*, ix-x. See Davis, "The Ascension Myth"; Naydler, "Plato, Shamanism and Ancient Egypt." Naydler, incidentally, offers a scathing rebuke to those classical scholars who contemptuously dismiss the Greeks' own conviction that they owed something to the Egyptians, and shows that the seemingly "shamanic" element in Pythagorean and Platonic thought could as easily have been learnt from Egypt as from the North.
57 Schweizer, *Sungod's Journey through the Netherworld*, 143: "From this time on [in the New Kingdom], every deceased person, not just the pharaoh and his entourage, had to face the Judgment of the Dead and justify his or her deeds before Osiris. And with that, everyone had the possibility of becoming one of the blessed dead who accompanied Re in his sun barque."
58 Copenhaver, *Hermetica*, 60 (16.15); see Hanegraaff, *Hermetic Spirituality*, 90-91: "The world is a dangerous place full of powerful forces that seek to enslave our souls and make us forget our true divinity. As newborns we simply

Astronomy

long was the journey for any one of us from There to Here? There seems no easy way to calculate the routes and times we took: "from moment to moment [the demons] change places, not staying in position but moving by rotation."[59] Discovering what demons influenced our birth is rather a matter of uncovering their present influence in us:

> Henceforth and until the very end of our lives, they are always "lying in ambush in our muscle and marrow, in our veins and arteries, in the brain itself, reaching to our very guts," always trying to shape our souls in accordance with their own peculiar astral energies — "for the essence of a daimon is its energy."[60]

Were these planets therefore considered *gods*, as being worthy of worship? The Egyptians, at any rate, "conceived of only a few of the most important stars and constellations as deities"[61] — which is as much as to say that only some of the heavenly bodies had any cult associated with them. The sun, the moon and Sothis (Sirius) were the chief objects of worship. Sothis came to be thought a manifestation of Isis, and Osiris was found in the constellation Orion (as well as in the Underworld). The other planetary bodies were considered manifestations of Horus, but not (apparently) particularized, nor given special worship. In later periods of Egyptian history the souls of the dead were thought to reside in the multitude of the fixed stars, and called "gods," of a sort. Was this notion an expansion of an older belief, that the dead Pharaoh rose up to heaven, or did even the earlier Egyptians hope for as much for themselves? In either case, the questions remain: what explains the widespread planetary associations, and why should anyone hope or expect to be fixed stars?

---

cannot resist the powerful daimonic invasion of our bodies and souls that takes place at our moment of birth; but what we can do is free ourselves from their dominion later on in our lives. Difficult as this may be (whence the small number of practitioners), we can learn to first recognize and then resist the powerful forces of daimonic temptation that try to keep us enslaved. We can practice techniques of liberation that weaken and may finally break their dominion over our souls."

59 Ibid.
60 Hanegraaff, *Hermetic Spirituality*, 223, after CH 16.13-14 (Copenhaver, *Hermetica*, 60-61).
61 Hornung, *Conceptions of God*, 80.

Both the zodiac and the planetary associations seem to have been the invention of Babylonian astrologers, probably over many centuries.[62] "The purpose of the Babylonian horoscope document was, above all, to record positions of the seven planets (moon, sun, and five classical planets) in the zodiac on the date of a birth."[63] Some of those associations, on Brown's account, can be considered "basic": how bright or faint is the star, how coloured, how slow or — as it were — "mercurial" its motion, how close to the Sun its journey, its conjunctions and oppositions. Others are "learned" associations, founded in false etymologies, their use as symbols for enemy or friendly nations, or perhaps the occasional validation of ominous predictions. None of these associations is now convincing to most of us (though our fictions often replicate them[64]): so what can be learned from them, or from the general astrological enterprise?

Consider what is now the most famous of imagined ascents to heaven, namely Dante's *Purgatory*. He too refers to the planets' influence on our character and circumstances (without granting them any power to *fix* our fates[65]) and writes that the climb up Purgatory Peak takes him through seven ledges, each with its peculiar vice: pride, envy, anger, sloth, greed, gluttony and lust are each purged in the climb. He may have borrowed part of his

---

62 Brown, *Mesopotamian Planetary Astronomy-Astrology*, 53–103. Brown suggests that it was only in the eighth century BC that accurate predictions of eclipses and other planetary movements became possible or reliable, but the familiar associations probably long preceded this.
63 Rochberg, *Heavenly Writing*, 103.
64 There is "a wide revival of belief / in presences and beings ultra-human / pervading earth, and seen in glimpses brief / as deities once were by Greek and Roman. / In other words, through scientists' acumen. / Mars, Venus, Jove returned to mens' experience / in shapes of Martians, Jovians and Venerians": Skinner, *Return of Arthur*, 2.13.
65 *Paradise*, Canto 2.118–20 (p. 51): "The other spheres through various differences dispose the distinctions held within them to their ends and to their sowings"; cf. *Purgatory*, Canto 16.73–78 (p. 172): "You men on earth attribute everything to the spheres' influence alone, as if with some predestined plan they moved all things. If this were true, then our Free Will would be annihilated: it would not be just to render bliss for good or pain for evil. The spheres initiate your tendencies: not all of them — but even if they did, you have the light that shows you right from wrong, and your Free Will, which, though it may grow faint in its first struggles with the heavens, can still surmount all obstacles if nurtured well."

Astronomy

story from Byzantine sources: "the soul's slow ascent through the tollgates of heaven,—tested at each stage by the imprecations of demons, uncertainly dependent upon the intercession of angels or saints—became the most common Byzantine view of the afterlife."[66] The idea also appears in "Gnostic" texts: *Pistis Sophia* speaks of distinct purifications for distinctive sins, administered by successive demons, followed by forgetfulness at the hands of the Virgin of Light—but there is a gap in the text, and the pattern is unclear (though the sevenfold structure is perhaps hinted at). "Hereafter they lead it [that is, the soul] to the Virgin of Light, who judgeth the good and the evil, that she may judge it."[67]

Like Gregory Palamas, Dante rejects the possibility of non-Adamite Antipodeans by supposing that the world beyond *our* lands is only ocean[68]—except for Purgatory Peak. He was not altogether mistaken: the "other side of the world" is indeed largely occupied by the Pacific Ocean, sprinkled with coral atolls and volcanic islands. But neither Dante nor his readers have ever needed to suppose that his story is *geographically* accurate, that there is a "literal" vast pit reaching down to Earth's centre and a mountain the height of Earth's radius on the opposite side! The geography is simply a way of representing vice and virtue for the human soul: so also the moral order of the heavens. The account Dante gives of vice, by contrast with the account implicit in earlier ascents, depends rather on the scholastic story, of love perverted or misplaced.[69] The vices purged in Purgatory—as well as the slightly different collection punished "forever" in Hell—are the ones identified by Pope Gregory [540–604]:

> For pride is the root of all evil, of which it is said, as Scripture bears witness, *Pride is the beginning of all sin* [Ecclesiasticus 10.1]. But seven principal vices, as its first progeny,

---

66 Dal Santo, *Debating the Saints' Cult*, 124–25; see also ibid., 124n, for more detailed references.
67 Mead, *Pistis Sophia*, 312–14 (ch. 143–47). The present (Coptic) text of *Pistis Sophia* (dating from the fourth century) was not discovered by European scholars till 1773, but its ideas will have had a wider provenance.
68 Palamas [1296–1359], *The 150 Chapters*, 9–14, in Palmer, Sherrard, and Ware, *Philokalia*, 349–52.
69 *Purgatory* 17.91–139.

spring doubtless from this poisonous root, namely, vainglory, envy, anger, melancholy, avarice, gluttony, lust.[70]

Gregory went on to detail the way that one vice arises from another:

> The first offspring of pride is vainglory, and this, when it hath corrupted the oppressed mind, presently begets envy. Because doubtless while it is seeking the power of an empty name, it feels envy against any one else being able to obtain it. Envy also generates anger; because the more the mind is pierced by the inward wound of envy, the more also is the gentleness of tranquillity lost. And because a suffering member, as it were, is touched, the hand of opposition is therefore felt as if more heavily impressed. Melancholy also arises from anger, because the more extravagantly the agitated mind strikes itself, the more it confounds itself by condemnation; and when it has lost the sweetness of tranquillity, nothing supports it but the grief resulting from agitation. Melancholy also runs down into avarice; because, when the disturbed heart has lost the satisfaction of joy within, it seeks for sources of consolation without, and is more anxious to possess external goods, the more it has no joy on which to fall back within. But after these, there remain behind two carnal vices, gluttony and lust. But it is plain to all that lust springs from gluttony, when in the very distribution of the members, the genitals appear placed beneath the belly. And hence when the one is inordinately pampered, the other is doubtless excited to wantonness.[71]

This is also the order offered in Dante's Purgatory, with only the minor change that pride and vainglory are almost the same thing.[72] The vices are to be purged in the same order as their

---

70 Pope Gregory, *Morals on the Book of Job*, Bk. 31 (44-45).86-87: www.lectionarycentral.com/GregoryMoralia/Book31.html (*Patrologia Latina* 76.620); see Tilby, *The Seven Deadly Sins*, 23.
71 Gregory, *Morals on the Book of Job*, Bk. 31 (45).89.
72 But cf. Tilby, *Seven Deadly Sins*, 161-62, after Evagrius: "Vainglory remains a very human temptation. It is essentially conceit, it feeds off admiration and needs the good opinion of others. Vainglory is nothing without its mirrors. Pride, on the other hand, is a temptation which really only comes into its own in relation to God." Ibid., 170: "the root of pride is the refusal to be subject to God and his rule"—the refusal ever to be refuted.

production, without troubling about their origin. So what would *pagans* think the proper order of purgation, acted out in their fantasy of ascent through the planetary spheres? Does it depend on thinking that one vice leads to another?

Commentators have no difficulty interpreting Dante's work as moral and anagogical, without supposing that anyone need accept his fictional geography, but usually dismiss the *pagan* stories as being merely false, or plainly superstitious, *astronomical* accounts. This is particularly so when they warn us of malevolent archons in the heavens, "ousiarchs." But there is more substance in the stories, even if there are no archons, and even if the texts which speak most often about those archons are unintelligible, to us. Our progress "upwards" can still be conceived as a successive stripping away of the garments donned in the earlier descent from heaven. Our ancestors wrote their stories on the heavens, and acted them out in rituals.

Our essential selves—they thought—were immortal spirits, with neither real beginning nor real end. Those selves belonged "aloft" but needed to acquire additional capacities if they were to manage the physical and social worlds below. These were the lesser "parts" that Plato deduced from our experience of conflict: chiefly the "spirited" and "desirous" elements, imagined in his *Phaedrus* as horses for the soul's chariot, and in *The Republic* as lion-like or yet more monstrous beasts.[73] Plotinus, following Aristotle's suggestion, reckoned that even *intelligent reasoning* was a lesser capacity than *Nous*: something that might easily become mere "cleverness," *deinotes* or *panourgia*.[74] Hildegard of Bingen (1098–1179) also insisted that our vices conceal what once were virtues. Before Adam fell "what is now gall in him sparkled like crystal, and bore the taste of good works, and what is now melancholy in man shone in him like the dawn and contained in itself the wisdom and perfection of good works."[75] And Ps-Dionysius: "[the Angels'] anger is an image of intellectual bravery of which anger is the outermost echo; their desire is that longing felt by

---

73 Plato, *Republic* 9.588c7, 590a9; see *Ennead* I.1 [53].7, 18–21.
74 See Aristotle, *Nicomachean Ethics* 6.1144a23–27.
75 Klibansky, Panofsky, and Saxl, *Saturn and Melancholy*, 80, citing Hildegard of Bingen.

the angels in the presence of God; and indeed, to put the matter briefly, all the feelings and all the various parts of the irrational animals uplift us to immaterial conceptions and to the unifying powers of the heavenly beings."[76]

The slow corruption of original virtues is traced in the imagined descent down the planetary spheres, and their later purgation by the ascent: the way upwards and the way downwards are the same.[77] There is no precise agreement about the stations on that way, but we can discern some commonalities, especially between Macrobius and *Poimandres*. They are to be studied as philosophical psychology, or as a theory of the virtues, rather than "real" or "material" astronomy.

> As the soul transcends the dominion of the lunar sphere, it is no longer afflicted by restless change but moves into a state of peaceful stability. As it transcends the dominion of Mercury, the "machinery of corruption" (*tēn mēchanēn tōn kakōn*) loses its power so that goodness can take its place. As the soul ceases to be influenced by Venus, it can no longer be led astray by sexual desires. Leaving the sphere of the Sun behind, its addiction to power vanishes too. The reckless brutality of violence that comes from Mars gives way to the energy of peace. Leaving Jupiter's dominion, the soul is no longer addicted to material possessions either. And as it finally leaves Saturn behind too, it turns its back on deceit and embraces truth.[78]

To get rid of the demons we must first acknowledge their existence.[79]

---

76 Ps-Dionysius, *Celestial Hierarchy*, ch. 15.8 (337B), in *Complete Works*, 189; see Louth, *Denys the Areopagite*, 47. Cf. Plutarch, "Isis and Osiris" 74, in *Moralia*, 5:173: "The Egyptians also honoured the asp, the weasel, and the beetle, since they observed in them certain dim likenesses of the power of the gods, like images of the sun in drops of water."
77 Heraclitus DK22B60, in Waterfield *First Philosophers*, 39; see *Ennead* IV.8 [6].1, 12–18.
78 Hanegraaff, *Hermetic Spirituality*, 183–84.
79 "According to [Les Murray's] psychiatrist, much of the most accurate scientific writing on depression and indeed on morbid psychology in general before our own age is to be found in mediaeval demonologies" (Murray, *Killing the Black Dog*). My preference is Evagrius: see Tilby, *Seven Deadly Sins*.

Astronomy

HERE COMES THE SUN

But literal astronomy need not be wholly neglected. The regular cycle of the heavens, over days, months, years and aeons demanded careful observation and measurement to discern. Reasonably, our ancestors concluded that those cycles represented the stars' own motions, and sought to discover the pattern even of the "wandering stars" which seemed to reverse their course at intervals.[80] Nowadays we are firmly and reasonably persuaded that the visible cycles of the fixed stars are entirely the effect of the Earth's rotation, and the apparent planetary cycles are the result both of the planets' own motion around the Sun and the Earth's own rotation and circuit. The very word, "planets," now means something different from the ancient "planetary stars": Sun and Moon are no longer reckoned planets, and the Earth herself is. We are riding, as Giordano Bruno recognized,[81] upon a revolving star, whose motion is compounded of her own rotation and her orbit round the Sun, the Sun's own orbit around the Milky Way, and that whole galaxy's motion towards Andromeda and away from more distant galaxies. The "fixed stars" themselves are in motion,

---

80 Swerdlow, *Babylonian Theory of the Planets*, xiii, aptly observes that in the "collection and interpretation of celestial omens, and in the observation and calculation of celestial phenomena, the Babylonians created the methods and practices of science itself as we still understand it" (though they seem not to have developed any *experimental* check on their calculations).
81 See Crowley, *Aegypt*, 399: "the sky had only begun to pale, and the dimmest stars — or those farthest off — had disappeared, when the caravan began clambering up the path toward the summit. The great starless darknesses on either hand were not sky but mountains, coming suddenly clear as though they had just awakened and stood up. Between them in the azure there flamed the morning stars. Mercury. Venus. Wet to the knees with snow-melt, Giordano climbed toward them. Earth was a star as they were; and the bright beings who inhabited them, looking this way, saw not a cold stone but another like themselves, aflame in the sun's light. He hailed them: Brother. Sister. A strange and soundless hum seemed to be filling up his ears and his being, as though the dawn itself were to make a sound in breaking, continuous and irreversible. The star he rode was turning pell-mell toward the sun with all of them aboard it, dwarfish stolid carters, chairs, animals, and men; Bruno laughed at his impulse to fall and clutch the hurtling ball with hands and knees. Infinite. You made yourself equal to the stars by knowing your mother Earth was a star as well; you rose up through the spheres not by leaving the earth but by sailing it: by knowing that it sailed." See also Galilei, "Starry Messenger" (1610), 45: the earth is "a wandering body surpassing the moon in splendour, and not the sink of all dull refuse of the universe" (cited by Pendergrast, *Mirror Mirror*, 87).

and also change over time in ways dependent on their particular mass and constitution, or the interference of other bodies. The order of the "Solar System" (as we now call it) is itself transient: the surviving planets, dwarf planets, asteroids and dust are the product of collisions over many million years, and their orbits too have changed and probably will change again, though often — in the end — in ways that "resonate" with each other.[82] The order our ancestors thought they saw — in brief — is only an appearance, and yet there is a larger and more complicated order stretching over many billion light years. How to internalize that discovery, and what moral to draw from it for our usual lives, will concern me later. The most obvious feature of the new order is that it reveals a universe vast beyond imagining — but that is perhaps not, in essence, quite so new a discovery as we think. In the "Dream of Scipio" — a text which much influenced Christian Europe — Scipio, on his own visionary ascent through the planetary spheres, saw "stars which we never see from here below, and all the stars were vast far beyond what we have ever imagined. The least of them was that which, farthest from heaven, nearest to the earth, shone with a borrowed light. But the starry globes very far surpassed the earth in magnitude. The earth itself indeed looked to me so small as to make me ashamed of our empire, which was a mere point on its surface."[83]

And yet this Earth, for ourselves as well as for our ancestors, is — to all appearance — the unmoving centre of our lives:

> Only the Earth doth stand for ever still,
> Her rocks remove not, nor her mountains meet,
> (Although some wits enriched with Learnings skill
> Say heav'n stands firm, and that the Earth doth fleet
> And swiftly turneth underneath their feet).[84]

Or as William Blake proposed:

---

82 See Murray and Dermott, *Solar System Dynamics*, 9-14.
83 "Dream of Scipio," in Cicero, *Republic*, Bk. 6, ch. 3, trans. Andrew P. Peabody. Cicero's text was repeated and amplified by Macrobius, *Commentary on the Dream of Scipio*. Note that the shining dots in the sky that we call "stars" were recognized as *globes*.
84 John Davies, "Orchestra: or, a Poem of Dancing" [1596], stanza 51, in Gardner, *New Oxford Book of English Verse*, 175.

Astronomy

> The sky is an immortal tent built by the Sons of Los:
> And every space that a man views around his dwelling-place
> Standing on his own roof or in his garden on a mount
> Of twenty-five cubits in height, such space is his universe:
> And on its verge the sun rises and sets, the clouds bow
> To meet the flat earth and the sea in such an order'd space:
> The starry heavens reach no further, but here bend and set
> On all sides, and the two Poles turn on their valves of gold:
> And if he moves his dwelling-place, his heavens also move
> Where'er he goes, and all his neighbourhood bewail his loss.
> Such are the spaces called Earth and such its dimension.
> As to that false appearance which appears to the reasoner
> As of a globe rolling through voidness, it is a delusion of
>   Ulro.[85]

This is not to engage in any ingenious but fundamentally wrongheaded attempt to suggest that we are *really* living on a disk beneath the dome of heaven, and that "space travel and anything linked to it such as 'outer space,' universal gravitation, moon landings, the ISS, satellites, the Hubble telescope, the Webb telescope, &c. constitutes a large-scale scam (admittedly well-presented and preserved)."[86] It is rather to acknowledge that the world as we immediately experience it is local, even from hilltops or balloons: the view from Scipio's heaven, the international space station, or some yet more distant extragalactic location is one that we only imagine, even if we manage also to give intellectual or notional assent to the reasonings and observations that validate it. "Real assent" and "real apprehension," as Newman proposed, "excites and stimulates the affections and passions, by bringing facts home to them as motive causes."[87] What might awaken that assent in us, and what may be its effects? One obvious but partial answer is the view of Earth from orbit, and the records of Voyagers I and II as they travel beyond the heliopause—though determined unbelievers discount such testimony as easily as

---

85 Blake, *Milton* 28 [1804], in *Complete Works*, 516. Ulro stands for the abstract, objectifying intelligence, and its objects.
86 Wilson, "Hebrew Cosmology," 22. Wilson's essay manages to combine esoteric scholarship, mostly about the *Book of Enoch*, with an almost complete lack of common sense!
87 Newman, *Grammar of Assent*, 6.

most moderns discount accounts of fairies. And of course any such view, and every view from anywhere, will reveal a cosmos centred on the viewer.

On the one hand (as enquired before), what might we profitably learn from ancient notions about the climb back up to heaven, past the planetary demons that have infected our lives? What is the relation between the virtues, vices and capacities that were symbolized by the planets as they seemed to our ancestors? On the other, how might we now fully realize the far vaster, stranger, grimmer world around us? Is there some available balance of the sort imagined by Stapledon at the close of his fantasised cosmogony?

> How to face such an age? How to muster courage, being capable only of homely virtues? How to do this, yet preserve the mind's integrity, never to let the struggle destroy in one's own heart what one tried to serve in the world, the spirit's integrity? Two lights for guidance. The first, our little glowing atom of community, with all that it signifies. The second, the cold light of the stars, symbol of the hypercosmical reality, with its crystal ecstasy.[88]

Or did Stapledon mischaracterize both our situation and the possible responses? Is "crystal ecstasy" worth worshipping? There is at least an older way of conceiving the problem, to which I shall return:

> We have touched, it would seem, a paradoxical core in the attitude of personal religion: its tacit bridging of the cosmic world and the personal world of the individual. How—one may ask—could such a union of contradictions in one attitude come to be; all that is highest, most awesome, and terrifying approached with such easy and close familiarity: "Make haste to help me, O Lord, my salvation" or "Come to me Re-Har-akhti, that thou mayest look after me" or "I have cried to thee, (I) thy suffering, wearied, distressed servant. See me, O my lady, accept my prayers!"[89]

---

88 Stapledon, *Star Maker*, 333.
89 Jacobsen, *Treasures*, 151–52.

Astronomy

But the first step beyond our local, parochial, temporary life is to acknowledge the Sun. The Sun was the most important deity for Egyptian thought, for good and obvious reason.[90] The other stellar and planetary motions may be used as symbols for moral and spiritual influences and dangers. Their movements may mark out times and seasons for our working lives. They may even be believed—by some—to be fully causal agents in our own formation. But it is the Sun above all that is most obviously in control: the centre of all our lives even before it was taken to be the real centre of our solar system. It was already the centre of the spheres: Moon, Mercury and Venus orbit "below" the Sun; Mars, Jupiter and Saturn orbit "above" it (and no other planetary stars were visible in those days). So even for those who chose to represent accumulated faculties or vices by our descent through all the planetary spheres—in which account the Sun's sphere may be responsible for arrogance, or gluttony, or imagination—it is the Sun that also represents the centre. The Sun echoes, in the phenomenal or the material realm, the might and majesty of the One itself—and especially its appearing, or not appearing, of itself:

> But one should not enquire whence [the One] comes, for there is no "whence": for it does not really come or go away anywhere, but appears or does not appear. So one must not chase after it, but wait quietly till it appears, preparing oneself to contemplate it, as the eye awaits the rising of the sun; and the sun rising over the horizon ("from Ocean," the poets say) gives itself to the eyes to see. But from where will he of whom the sun is an image rise? What is the horizon which he will mount above when he appears? He will be above Intellect itself which contemplates him. For Intellect will be standing first to its contemplation, looking to nothing but the Beautiful, all turning and giving itself up to him, and, motionless and filled somehow with strength, it sees first of all itself become more beautiful, all glittering, because he is near. But he did not come as one expected,

---

90 Hornung, *Conceptions of God*, 54; pace Porphyry, *Letter to Anebo*, as quoted by Eusebius (*Praeparatio* 3.11,45-46, p. 115), it is not true that "the Egyptians know of no other gods but the Planets and those stars that fill up the Zodiack..., and Robust Princes, as they call them" (see Assmann, *Moses the Egyptian*, 84).

but came as one who did not come: for he was seen, not as having come, but as being there before all things, and even before Intellect came.[91]

Just as the Sun sheds his light over all the world, so also the One disperses being, without losing anything of itself.[92] By *this* image at least, the whole sidereal array (including both the fixed and planetary stars) is an expression of the Sun's light, and the Sun himself is not simply one character among many, but the central source of all. Neither Plotinus nor his biographer makes his solar worship explicit—though Plotinus himself declares that where others worship the stars, "we worship the Sun."[93] And Proclus, nearly two centuries later, made "obeisance to the rising, midday and setting sun."[94] In so doing they were both acknowledging, and internalizing, a power which could not safely be seen directly, but only in its reflections and its effects. Not only philosophers were affected. The Sun was widely worshipped (or at least honoured), by Essenes, by Apollonius of Tyana, and by the Emperor Vespasian.[95] The cult of Sol Invictus, absorbing Elagabal of Emesa as well as Sol Indigenes of Rome, was publicized under the emperor Aurelian (AD 270–275) in an effort to find a focus for imperial dreams.[96] And Julian, rejecting Constantine's appeal to the Christian churches for a similar end, attempted to reinvent a solar paganism,[97] and some solar rhetoric and celebrations were absorbed in Christian ritual and rhetoric: "thine be the glory, risen, conquering Sun (or Son)."

---

91 *Ennead* V.5 [32].8, 1–17. Which is most likely why (and not from pride) Plotinus declined to go "temple-crawling" with his friend and disciple, Amelius (Porphyry, *Life*, 10, 34–41), saying that it was for the gods to come to him, not vice versa. Or as another sage declared: "Poetry and Hums aren't things which you get, they're things which get *you*. And all you can do is to go where they can find you": Milne, *House at Pooh Corner*, 146.
92 See *Ennead* I.7 [54].1, 25–30. See Wakoff, "Awaiting the Sun."
93 *Ennead* IV.4 [28].30; cf. Copenhaver, *Hermetica*, 53 [CH 13.16]; ibid., 92 [*Asclepius* 41]. See Hanegraaff, *Hermetic Spirituality*, 232–33, 259.
94 Marinus, *Life of Proclus* 22, in Mark Edwards, *Neoplatonic Saints*, 93.
95 See Stoneman, *Palmyra*, 145–46.
96 Halsberghe, *Sol Invictus*, 132, 135–75. Azize has argued in *Phoenician Solar Theology*, with citations from Mochus of Sidon and Philo of Byblos, that solar theology is a Phoenician invention, but the sources are earlier than that.
97 Julian, *Oratio* 4: *Hymn to Helios*, in *Works* 1:353–442; see Rowland Smith, *Julian's Gods*, 139–62.

Astronomy

It is easy to assume that the bright light we see in the heavens is, straightforwardly, the Sun: that is, after all, what we point to if we are asked where the Sun is just now (at any rate in the daytime). But plainly this is false, even (or especially) on a modern, "materialistic" account: the Sun itself is not a small yellow disc, however bright, emitting light only in the range we humans see, and easily obscured by clouds.

> In the long fourth chapter of his 1704 essay "The Grounds of Criticism," John Dennis draws a distinction between "Vulgar Passion" and "Enthusiastick Passion, or Enthusiasm." In delineating the latter he uses as an example our various perceptions of the sun: "... [T]he Sun mention'd in ordinary Conversation, gives the Idea of a round flat shining Body, of about two foot diameter. But the Sun occurring to us in Meditation, gives the Idea of a vast and glorious Body, and the top of all the visible Creation, and the brightest material Image of the Divinity."[98]

The thing itself is not contained in our perception of it. And once we acknowledge that, the way is open to see things otherwise than usual:

> When the Sun rises, do you not see a round disc of fire somewhat like a Guinea? O no, no, I see an Innumerable company of the Heavenly host crying Holy, Holy, Holy is the Lord God Almighty. I question not my Corporeal or Vegetative Eye any more than I would Question a Window concerning a Sight. I look thro' it and with it.[99]

So how did the Egyptians see or conceive or imagine the real Sun? Maybe it moves across the sky as it were a ball pushed by a dung-beetle? The dung-beetle's ball is a nursery for new life, and maybe the Sun itself is the source of life for all? Or maybe this is *only* a metaphor, without much real effect or meaning (though it is of interest that they could conceive of the Sun as a ball, rather than merely a disc). By another account the Sun is swallowed up by the Sky at the western horizon, and reborn

---

98 Strickland, "John Dennis and Blake's Guinea Sun," citing Dennis [1658–1734], "The Grounds of Criticism in Poetry" [1704], in *Critical Works*, 338–39.
99 Blake, "Vision of the Last Judgement" [1810], in *Complete Writings*, 617.

from the Sky at the eastern, passing invisibly through Nut's imagined body. But the principal story, reinforced by ritual and religion, is that the Sun travels in the solar boat across the sky, and passes through the Underworld at night: each hour of the night has its own monsters to evade or conquer before the boat is launched again at dawn. The common theme requires that the world of our experience is "flat." If there is a passage underneath it, that is essentially a realm of dark and danger, to be endured by the assurance of the daily escape from darkness, the daily birth from Sky. The Sun, it seems, doesn't shine during those hours of night, whether those pass in the Underworld or in the womb of Sky, but still survives to shine again.

There is a further twist in the earlier imagined history which I shall also address later: in the beginning, Earth (Geb) and Sky (Nut) — children of Shu and Tefnut (the dry and the wet, or else the air and water) — were united in love:

> But one terrible day, just as a hungry mother pig might sometimes eat her young, Nut swallowed her star-children. Geb flew into a furious rage and the land trembled and shook with his anger. To escape Geb's wrath Nut stretched herself above her brother, her fingers and toes resting on the horizons of the north, east, south and west. And Shu knelt with arms outstretched between his beloved children, holding them apart lest they should continue their quarrel.[100]

We are all living in the world formed by such quarrels and separations, imagined in many versions:

> The birth and subsequent quarrel of the visible gods Geb and Nut from the invisible Shu and Tefnut caused the world as we know it to come into being with a sky and an earth separated by the atmosphere. An alternative version of the Heliopolitan myth tells us that Shu, disapproving of his children's love for each other, forcibly separated the two, causing Geb to weep great tears which became the oceans. A third version tells us that Geb and Nut initially lay so close together that their children could

---

100 Tyldesley, *Myths and Legends of Ancient Egypt*, 38.

Astronomy

not be born. Only when Shu forced them apart could Nut give birth.[101]

In the beginning Atum was at once the source and the light of all things, and is now represented in the Sun—but that Sun is subject to the cycle of birth and death, vigour and decay, as much as any other of the Million Things. Whether we are to sorrow for the divide between Earth and Heaven that has marooned us in the in-between, or else take heart for the daily victory, is perhaps a matter of temperament. The Egyptian story seems mostly to favour the latter. Even Atum Itself will one day be alone again, or else (equivalently) united with Osiris, or swallowed by Apophis. The Sun's daily renewal may give some strength to the expectation that Atum will arise again and separate itself into the Million Things.[102] In the meantime the Sun, passing through the twelve hours of day and night, is "literally" the source of light and warmth to Earth, and anagogically a focus for our own conscious life: identifying with the Sun we may recognize changing times and tempers as merely moments. Even apparent defeat and expectable decline does not diminish the splendour. And the Egyptians could appeal to the Sun—to Re-Amun—because the Sun himself endures the dangers too.

---

[101] Tyldesley, *Myths and Legends of Ancient Egypt*, 51. Cf. Schweizer, *Sungod's Journey through the Netherworld*, 60: "Creation is often understood as a violent act, in which a previously peaceful unity is split asunder. Thus, one of the most familiar Egyptian images of creation is the separation of the primeval parental couple, the earth god Geb and the sky goddess Nut, as they lie in the act of coitus, by their father Shu, the god of air. With his powerful arms, he raises the celestial vault on high, thus creating, in the midst of nonbeing, a realm between sky and earth, a place where all lives, both divine and human, can unfold."
[102] See *Ennead* IV.8 [6].6, 1–6: "there must not be just one alone—for then all things would have been hidden, shapeless within that one."

~4~
Powers and Personalities

> Rise up and awake out of sleep, and remember that you are a son of kings; lo, you have come under the yoke of bondage.[1]

ALLEGORY AND ART

In seeking to discover hidden "meanings" in the ancient stories I am following ancient precedent, and should also acknowledge some further arguments against the effort. Stoic philosophers offered "allegorical" interpretations of familiar Greek myths, though not all supposed that these were the *original* meanings of the stories.[2] Their suggestion that the gods are best understood as elemental forces (fire, earth, air, and water) was considered atheistical, in effect, by some of their critics.

> In his interpretation of Hesiod's *Theogony* [Balbus the Stoic] does away with the customary and received ideas of the gods altogether, for he does not reckon Jupiter, Juno, or Vesta as gods, or any being that bears a personal name, but teaches that these names have been assigned by means of a sort of allegorical interpretation to dumb and lifeless things.[3]

The Stoics might reasonably respond that the elements, even stripped of supposedly misleading "personal names" and histories, might deserve our awe as essential parts of the whole "divine" cosmos, and were not — on Stoic terms — either dumb or lifeless. Nor was it only a Stoic theory.

> A scholium to Venetus B manuscript, attributed to the Neoplatonist philosopher and philologist Porphyry (AD 234–c. 305), notes the following: "Homer's doctrine on

---

[1] "The Acts of Thomas," 109-13, in Elliott, *Apocryphal New Testament*, 489.
[2] Cornutus, *Greek Theology*; see Boys-Stones, "Stoics' Two Types of Allegory."
[3] Cicero, *Nature of Gods*, 1.36; see Dawson, *Allegorical Readers*, 53-54.

the gods usually tends to be useless and improper, for the myths he relates about the gods are offensive. In order to counter this sort of accusation, some people invoke the mode of expression (*tēs lexeōs*); they feel that all was said in an allegorical mode (*allēgoria*) and has to do with the nature of the elements, as in the case of the passage where the gods confront one another. Thus according to them, the dry clashes with the wet, the hot clashes with the cold, and the light with the heavy. In addition, water extinguishes fire, while fire evaporates water; in a similar way, there is an opposition between all the elements making up the universe; they may suffer destruction in part, but they endure eternally as a whole. In arranging these battles, Homer provides fire with the name of Apollo, Helios, or Hephaestus, he calls water Poseidon or Scamander, the moon Artemis, air Hera, and so on. In the same way, he sometimes gives names of gods to dispositions, the name Athena is given to wisdom/intelligence, Ares to folly, Aphrodite to desire, Hermes to speech, all according to what is associated with each. This kind of defence is very ancient and goes back to Theagenes of Rhegium, who was the first to write about Homer [c. 530 BC]."[4]

This may expound either the original meaning or at least a fruitful application of the stories, rather than simply being a defensive reinterpretation to avoid a scandalous suggestion of bodily strife amongst the gods — but in either case the equation of gods and elements seems likely to be one of those interpretations that would earn Socrates' scorn, as much as banal decodings of the story of Boreas and Oreithyia:

> I might give a rational explanation, that a blast of Boreas, the north wind, pushed her off the neighbouring rocks as she was playing with Pharmacea, and that when she had died in this manner she was said to have been carried off by Boreas. But I, Phaedrus, think such explanations are very pretty in general, but are the inventions of a

---

[4] Naddaf, "Allegory and the Origins of Philosophy," 108, referring to Homer *Iliad* 20.67ff., "in which the gods, with Zeus's permission, descend to the plain and battle each other for the fate of Troy. The gods line up in opposition to one another—Poseidon against Apollo, Ares against Athena, Hera against Artemis, Leto against Hermes, and Hephaestus against [the river] Scamander."

very clever and laborious and not altogether enviable man, for no other reason than because after this he must explain the forms of the Centaurs, and then that of the Chimaera, and there presses in upon him a whole crowd of such creatures, Gorgons and Pegasuses, and multitudes of strange, inconceivable, portentous natures. If anyone disbelieves in these, and with a rustic sort of wisdom, undertakes to explain each in accordance with probability, he will need a great deal of leisure. But I have no leisure for them at all.... So I dismiss these matters and accepting the customary belief about them, as I was saying just now, I investigate not these things, but myself, to know whether I am a monster more complicated and more furious than Typhon or a gentler and simpler creature, to whom a divine and quiet lot is given by nature.[5]

Was Plato dismissing any attempt to explain, or explain away, the poets' stories, in favour of a more direct examination of the human condition? Or would he, according to his own common practice, pick up the suggestion that the gods were moods, traits, or dispositions? Poets and other rhetoricians, so philosophers have often concluded, appeal only to our sentiments and sensual appetites, and their stories not only have no rational basis, but are often directly harmful: they encourage us to feel inappropriate desire, fear, rage, or pity, and to think that acting on those feelings is permitted or even required. Allegorizing the stories may remove some of those implications, but still contaminate our inner feelings, precisely by invoking "gods." So it may be safer to exile all the poets (and also other artists) from the True Republic, so as to purify the mind, shedding all inappropriate desires and fears.

This is a possible, and even popular, account. Militant atheists in the present day may also wish to banish "religion": to demolish churches, burn books and mutilate icons, or else merely satirize any overtly "religious" custom. The impulse is one shared, ironically, by fervent "religionists" who cannot bear that any other view than theirs be visible. Militant atheists, indeed, are themselves "religionists," persuaded that their view of things is the

---

5 Plato, *Phaedrus* 229c–230a.

only decent and rational one!⁶ And like other such religionists they need to guard themselves:

> How can we guard our unbelief,
> Make it bear fruit to us? — the problem here.
> Just when we are safest, there's a sunset-touch,
> A fancy from a flower-bell, some one's death,
> A chorus-ending from Euripides, —
> And that's enough for fifty hopes and fears
> As old and new at once as nature's self,
> To rap and knock and enter in our soul,
> Take hands and dance there, a fantastic ring,
> Round the ancient idol, on his base again, —
> The grand Perhaps!⁷

That they do not, in practice, often desecrate cathedrals, silence Bach, or burn pictures of the Madonna, suggests that there is some public feeling against such acts even amongst those who would themselves deny any belief in "God." People may believe instead in "beauty" or "tradition," or at least wish that we not entirely reject the past (for if we do, are we not encouraging our successors also to reject our present?). And this widespread feeling may itself be rejected by those of another faith and disposition. When the Taliban destroyed the Buddhist statues of Bamyan they maybe did so not only because they rejected *Buddhism* (so after all did almost all their critics), nor even from ethnic hatred of Bamyan civilization, but because they despised — so to call it — Western aestheticism.⁸ Such aestheticism is itself a religious form (in many variants), and one that deserves attention as an answer to a merely nihilistic atheism. One variant (which I shall address later) chooses rather to emphasise *antiquity* or *tradition* than the mere enjoyment of beauty or other sorts of artistic splendour: it would do no good merely to *replicate* the statues. In the present

---

6 See Clark, 'Atheism Considered as a Christian Sect"; Clark, *Understanding Faith*.
7 Robert Browning, "Bishop Blougram's Apology" [1855], in *Poems*, 426.
8 *The New York Times* reported (March 19, 2001) that the Taliban envoy to the US had said "that the Islamic government made its decision in a rage after a foreign delegation offered money to preserve the ancient works while a million Afghans faced starvation. 'When your children are dying in front of you, then you don't care about a piece of art'": https://www.nytimes.com/2001/03/19/world/taliban-explains-buddha-demolition.html (accessed September 21, 2022).

context aestheticism of various sorts offers a way of preserving the ancient stories distinct from Stoic or other attempts at allegorizing them all, but without allowing them any serious *moral* force. We are to enjoy the stories or the pictures or the musical compositions without thinking that they might in any way be *true*. Trying to "interpret" them, to say what they "really mean," is to evade a proper *emotional* and *aesthetic* response. Both "literal" and "allegorical" readings miss the proper point: we are not to think that (for example) Seth killed his brother Osiris in real, historical time, nor yet that this is a simple allegory for sowing—or burying—grain[9] (or whatever). We are instead to *enjoy* the story as we also enjoy *The Hound of the Baskervilles*, and class their mythical protagonists alongside Sherlock Holmes.

Chesterton's take on the topic may suggest as much:

> There is one piece of nonsense that modern people still find themselves saying, even after they are more or less awake, by which I am particularly irritated. It arose in the popularised science of the nineteenth century, especially in connection with the study of myths and religions. The fragment of gibberish to which I refer generally takes the form of saying "This god or hero really represents the sun." Or "Apollo killing the Python MEANS that the summer drives out the winter." Or "The King dying in a western battle is a SYMBOL of the sun setting in the west." Now I should really have thought that even the skeptical professors, whose skulls are as shallow as frying-pans, might have reflected that human beings never think or feel like this. Consider what is involved in this supposition. It presumes that primitive man went out for a walk and saw with great interest a big burning spot on the sky. He then said to primitive woman, "My dear, we had better keep this quiet. We mustn't let it get about. The children and the slaves are so very sharp. They might discover the sun any day, unless we are very careful. So we won't call it

---

9 Assmann, *Moses the Egyptian*, 68. It is not an impossible association: "Now the green blade riseth, from the buried grain, / Wheat that in dark earth many days has lain; / Love lives again, that with the dead has been: / Love is come again like wheat that springeth green" (John M. C. Crum [1872-1958], in Dearmer, Vaughan Williams, and Shaw, *Oxford Book of Carols*, 306-7).

Powers and Personalities

'the sun,' but I will draw a picture of a man killing a snake; and whenever I do that you will know what I mean. The sun doesn't look at all like a man killing a snake; so nobody can possibly know. It will be a little secret between us; and while the slaves and the children fancy I am quite excited with a grand tale of a writhing dragon and a wrestling demigod, I shall really MEAN this delicious little discovery, that there is a round yellow disc up in the air." One does not need to know much mythology to know that this is a myth. It is commonly called the Solar Myth. Quite plainly, of course, the case was just the other way. The god was never a symbol or hieroglyph representing the sun. The sun was a hieroglyph representing the god. Primitive man...went out with his head full of gods and heroes, because that is the chief use of having a head.[10]

Chesterton's scorn is excessive: the story, if it was allegorical, was not intended to *conceal* an astronomical observation, but rather (perhaps) to convey some more detailed information down the years in a form that would be remembered, even after catastrophe. But it is right to point to the simple pleasure and importance of making up such stories. Does that exclude the possibility that they were really meant to have additional meaning and importance? "There is preserved a work by Pherecydes of Syros [c. 540 BC], a work which begins thus: 'Zeus and Time and Earth [*Chthonie*] were from all eternity, and Earth was called Gê because Zeus gave her earth (*gê*) as guerdon (*geras*)."[11] This mixture of impersonal and personal wording both begins a story and rejects the Hesiodic (and Egyptian) cosmogony: an attempt, at least, at philosophical speculation, even if, as Pherekydes apparently acknowledged, it is founded mostly on guesswork.[12]

---

10 Chesterton, "The Priest of Spring," in *Miscellany of Men*, 53–54.
11 Diogenes Laertius, *Lives* 1:125 [1.11, 119].
12 See Pherekydes' letter (supposedly) to Thales, about his work: "The facts are not absolutely correct, nor do I claim to have discovered the truth, but merely such things as one who inquires about the gods picks up. The rest must be thought out, for mine is all guess-work (*hapanta gar ainissomai*)" (Diogenes Laertius, *Lives* 1:127 [1.11, 122]). A better version of Pherekydes' apology is "all other things one has to think about, for I hint at them all allegorically" (Laks and Most, *Early Greek Philosophy*, 205 [R31b]).

In fact, few would contend...that Pherecydes' prose theogony does not have allegorical and/or symbolical passages. As we see in his opening sentence: "Zas [Zeus] and Chronos were forever and Chthonie" (DK 7B1), all names consciously contain etymological and symbolical intimations (life, time, and underworld). And is it plausible to consider the wedding of Zas and Chthonie and the embroidering of the cloth (DK 7B2) as anything but allegory?[13]

Plato's Stranger scorns these guesses:

It seems to me that Parmenides and all who ever undertook a critical definition of the number and nature of realities have talked to us rather carelessly.... Every one of them seems to tell us a story, as if we were children. One [Pherekydes] says there are three principles, that some of them are sometimes waging a sort of war with each other, and sometimes become friends and marry and have children and bring them up; and another says there are two, wet and dry or hot and cold, which he settles together and unites in marriage. And the Eleatic sect in our region, beginning with Xenophanes and even earlier, have their story that all things, as they are called, are really one. Then some Ionian and later some Sicilian Muses reflected that it was safest to combine the two tales and to say that being is many and one, and is (or are) held together by enmity and friendship. For the more strenuous Muses say it is always simultaneously coming together and separating; but the gentler ones relaxed the strictness of the doctrine of perpetual strife; they say that the all is sometimes one and friendly, under the influence of Aphrodite, and sometimes many and at variance with itself by reason of some sort of strife.[14]

Their fault, he says, is that these cosmologists "paid too little attention and consideration to the mass of people like ourselves. For they go on to the end, each in his own way, without caring whether their arguments carry us along with them, or whether we are left behind." People like "us" need explanations for the

---

13 Naddaf, "Allegory and Origins," 111, citing Ford, *Origins of Criticism*, 69; Schibli, *Pherekydes of Syros*, 39–40.
14 Plato, *Sophist* 242c–243a; see Laks and Most, *Early Greek Philosophy*, 183.

terms the cosmologists use so freely, and "reasons" to accept them. "We" aren't content to take the stories as they come. In other words, "we" aren't content to accept what Socrates is made to say in the *Phaedrus*: apparently, after all, we are bound to worry about the stories, and neither dismiss them utterly nor simply enjoy their art.

Whether the stories will help our serious speculations can only be discovered by trying to see if they do. But the attempt may still, perhaps, be playful. Plotinus was willing to allegorize the brutal stories about Ouranos, Kronos and Zeus, but Armstrong may be correct to suggest that he didn't take them entirely seriously: is Aphrodite the child of Ouranos, or Kronos, or even perhaps of Zeus? Does Zeus or Aphrodite represent the Soul in Plotinus's own cosmology?[15] But Plotinus was more consistent than Armstrong has allowed: there are, on the one hand, two forms of Aphrodite (the Titan born of Ouranos's severed genitals,[16] and the lesser, the child of Zeus), and there is also a distinction between Soul-as-Such (which is Zeus) and all particular souls, including the World-Soul (which are each Aphrodite).[17] Plotinus may even be nudged in this direction by the stories which he thinks may probably contain an ancient wisdom. But the attempt is still, probably, playful.

LEVELS OF BEING

Demythologizing the stories in the Stoic fashion, so that they merely (?) convey some astronomical or other material truth, need not eliminate their grandeur. We may even respect them more.

> It seems to me that the grim, monstrous, and unnatural character of poetic fictions moves the listener in every way to a search for the truth, and draws him towards the secret knowledge; it does not allow him, as would be the case with something that possessed a surface probability, to remain with the thoughts placed before him. It compels him instead to enter into the interior of the myths

---

15 See *Ennead* III.5 [50].2,16, 33–34. Cf. Armstrong, *Enneads* vol. 3, p. 176.
16 Who is rightly considered a god rather than simply a daimon (*Ennead* III.5 [50].2, 26).
17 *Ennead* VI.9 [9].9, 28ff.

and to busy himself with the thought which has been concealed out of sight, by the makers of myths and to ponder what kinds of natures and what great powers they introduced into the meaning of the myths and communicated to posterity by means of such symbols as these.[18]

That Kronos castrated his father, Ouranos, and was in turn castrated by his youngest son, is a brutal beginning to the world we know, and its very violence may both reflect important features of our *human* life and help the story's survival. The unanswerable question in Greek rhetoric was "Have you stopped beating your father yet?"[19] Sons were expected often to be on bad terms with their fathers!

Witness the man who was had up for beating his father and who said in his defence, "Well, my father used to beat his father, and he used to beat his, and (pointing to his little boy) so will my son here beat me when he grows up; it runs in our family"; and the man who, when his son was throwing him out of the house, used to beg him to stop when he got to the door, "because he only used to drag his father as far as that."[20]

But it does not follow that all Greeks thought that this is what *should* happen. According to Xenophon, Socrates advised his son (who was at odds with his mother) that he ought to honour his parents above all:

"From whomsoever a man receives a favour" [said Lamprocles], "whether friend or enemy, and does not endeavour to make a return for it, he is in my opinion unjust." "If such, then, be the case," pursued Socrates, "ingratitude must be manifest injustice?" Lamprocles expressed his assent. "The greater benefits, therefore, a person has received, and makes no return, the more unjust he must be." He assented to this position also. "Whom, then," asked Socrates, "can we find receiving greater benefits from any persons than

---

18 Proclus, *Commentary on Republic* 1.85.16, as translated by Coulter, *Literary Microcosm*, 57.
19 Diogenes Laertius, *Lives* 1:267 [2.135], where the question is posed to Menedemus, who rejects the game.
20 Aristotle, *Nicomachean Ethics* 7.1149b8-13; see Slater, *Glory of Hera* for further discussion of this trope.

children receive from their parents? children whom their parents have brought from non-existence into existence, to view so many beautiful objects, and to share in so many blessings, as the gods grant to men."[21]

Plato's Euthyphro does indeed use the stories to defend his attempt to bring his father to trial:

> Men believe that Zeus is the best and most just of the gods, and they acknowledge that he put his father in bonds because he wickedly devoured his children, and he in turn had mutilated his father for similar reasons; but they are incensed against me because I proceed against my father when he has done wrong, and so they are inconsistent in what they say about the gods and about me.[22]

The metaphysical interpretation of the story by late antique philosophers is more respectable and more suggestive than the moral, at least to those of a speculative mind: Ouranos stands for the One beyond all classes, Kronos for the intelligible forms eternally generated by that One, and Zeus for the Life that animates the world of time and place which mirrors intelligible reality.[23] That thesis may provide more material for philosophical analysis, without the horrid implication that sons must and should judge and — if necessary — punish their fathers, or arrange for them to be punished. Euthyphro's own claim that the traditional stories are really true, and that he himself understands them well, is explained by other Platonic testimony. He is said to have offered much the same sort of allegorized interpretation of these stories as were later endorsed by Plotinus and others: Kronos is the pure mind, created by "looking up" to the heavens.[24] So for Euthyphro at least the moral implications of the story are invoked to show his critics' inconsistency, while he himself prefers a more

---

21 Xenophon, *Memorabilia* 2.2.2–3.
22 Plato, *Euthyphro* 6a: I have proposed elsewhere ("Therapy and Theory Reconstructed") that Euthyphro is very badly treated in much modern commentary: he is doing exactly what Plato's Socrates advised (*Gorgias* 480b) in the case of a family member's wrongdoing (his father left a servant — and Euthyphro's own dependant — who killed another in a drunken brawl to die of his wounds in a ditch).
23 See Hadot, "Ouranos, Kronos and Zeus."
24 Plato, *Cratylus* 396d.

anagogical interpretation of the dealings of gods with each other. Existence, Reality, is progenitive in its essence, and to procreate is essentially to release.

> If, then, there must not be just one alone—for then all things would have been hidden, shapeless within that one, and not a single real being would have existed if that one had stayed still in itself, nor would there have been the multiplicity of these real beings which are generated from the One, if the things after them had not taken their way out which have received the rank of souls—in the same way there must not be just souls alone either, without the manifestation of the things produced through them, if this is in every nature, to produce what comes after it and to unfold itself as a seed does.[25]

But this very example hints that "demythologizing" the stories is not the same as "depersonalising" them. "The Egyptians lived in a universe composed not of things, but of beings,"[26] and so did (and do) others whom we casually consider "primitive" or "superstitious." Discovering (perhaps) the *metaphysical* meaning of the seemingly brutal stories is not necessarily to reveal them only as coded accounts of merely material and unmeaning forces.

> Primitive mentality does not indulge in poetic "personifications." It rather conceives causality altogether in terms of "persons," due to the fact that the empirical observation has not yet been able to observe the actual causal process of inanimate nature, having been restricted to focusing upon the final product only. In this respect the warning issued by the Frankforts is correct: "This does not mean (as is so often thought) that primitive man, in order to explain natural phenomena, imparts human characteristics to an inanimate world. Primitive man simply does not know an inanimate world. For this very reason he does not 'personify' inanimate phenomena nor does he fill an empty world with the ghosts of the dead, as 'animism' would have us believe."[27]

---

25 *Ennead* IV.8 [6].6, 1–9.
26 Allen, *Genesis in Egypt*, 8.
27 Peccorini, "Divinity and Immortality," 221, citing Frankfort and Frankfort, *Before Philosophy*, 14.

Powers and Personalities

Peccorini's explanation for this (supposed) error—"that the empirical observation has not yet been able to observe the actual causal process of inanimate nature"—is itself unduly dogmatic. How, after all, have *we* "observed the actual causal process of inanimate nature"? Our observations are always of what *appears* to us, contaminated (or not) by whatever "theories" we hold about the underlying nature.[28] Mere observation of natural regularities, and exceptions to those regular events, shows us nothing about what "causes" them, or how we should understand their real and inner being. As far as "observation" goes we are in no better state than the prisoners in Plato's Cave, condemned to making guesses about what will happen next on the mere memory of what patterns we have perceived so far, but with no understanding of *how* or *why* particular chains of event occur. The prisoners in the Cave would praise "the man who is quickest to make out the shadows as they pass and best able to remember their customary precedences, sequences and co-existences, and so most successful in guessing at what was to come."[29] The next stage in understanding depends on our realising that appearances depend on something closer to "the real":

> These sparks that paint the sky, since they are decorations on a visible surface, we must regard, to be sure, as the fairest and most exact of such things but we must recognize that they fall far short of the truth, the movements, namely, of real speed and real slowness in true number and in all true figures both in relation to one another and as vehicles of the things they carry and contain. These can be apprehended only by reason and thought, but not by sight.... We must use the blazonry of the heavens as patterns to aid in the study of those realities, just as one would do who chanced upon diagrams drawn with special care and elaboration by Daedalus or some other craftsman or painter. For anyone acquainted with geometry who saw such designs would admit the beauty of the workmanship, but would think it absurd

---

28 It is perhaps significant that we may easily speak of an "underlying" nature where the ancients rather think of the real world as being *above* the apparent world.
29 Plato, *Republic* 7.516cd.

to examine them seriously in the expectation of finding in them the absolute truth.³⁰

Early astronomers, it may be, had no more than their personal and cultural memory to assist them in determining when this or that bright spot of light would move across the sky. They were helped, eventually, by imagining that these bright spots were "really" moving bodies, or rather *represented* those bodies, bound together in a complex system. One of the most surprising, serendipitous, discoveries of recent years has been the Antikythera Mechanism — in effect a sophisticated astrolabe, of many interlocking wheels, by which astronomers were able to predict eclipses (dating from about 100 BC). It may even be that the use of epicyclic spheres to explain planetary motion was extrapolated from the interlocking gears of such devices:

> In other words, epicycles were not a philosophical innovation but a mechanical one. Once Greek astronomers realized how well epicyclic gearing in devices such as the Antikythera mechanism replicated the cyclic variations of celestial bodies, they could have incorporated the concept into their own geometrical models of the cosmos.³¹

The material (geocentric, Ptolemaic) model of the "fixed" and "planetary" stars served well for centuries, but the question always arose as to *why* the stars followed their roughly circular or epicyclic paths through heaven. Only after the Copernican Revolution (and Kepler's recognition that the planetary stars — now not including either the Sun or the Moon — were themselves moving in elliptical rather than circular orbits) did the beginnings of an answer emerge, in terms of Newtonian mechanics. The mathematization of the cosmos, expected long before by Plato and

---

30 Plato, *Republic* 7.529. The assumption (in http://data.perseus.org/citations/urn:cts:greekLit:tlg0059.tlg030.perseus-eng1:7.529) that those lights in the sky are strictly "material" things is in error: the phenomena themselves are not material, even though they reflect or represent "material" bodies. See Clark, "Platonists and Participation," after a presentation at Notre Dame in 2014: my thanks to the participants, especially Douglas Hedley and Gretchen Reydam-Schils, for clarifying my ideas.
31 Merchant, "Ancient Astronomy: Mechanical Inspiration." See also Merchant, *Decoding the Heavens*, for a full account of the mechanism's discovery and interpretation.

Pythagoras, became a slight possibility. The phenomenal world (that is, what creatures like ourselves can see, or hear, or feel) somehow reflects or represents the material. The material world (we find) somehow reflects or represents the mathematical. Each is an *eikon* of the higher world.[32] To discover what is *really* going on we increasingly had recourse to mathematical idealizations rather than merely material models. We can *expect* the world to be homogeneous because it is everywhere, as it were, a hall of mirrors, reflecting the True World of numbers.[33] In times past the numbers that were reckoned most important were the familiar, "natural" numbers: five, seven, twelve, and so forth. Even ratios were not clearly equated with (rational) numbers. And the cosmological speculations which relied on them seem now merely "numerological." *Our* significant numbers, so to speak, are often very much stranger (especially to a Classical sensibility): π [3.1415926535...], e [2.718281828459...], ϕ [1.6180...], $\sqrt{2}$, $\sqrt{-1}$, and aleph-null. Some of these strange numbers cannot be given any definite final expansion;[34] others have no material image (there are only a finite number even of quarks within our cosmos). And the numbers which do directly affect the material world often seem as arbitrary as the ancients' use of small and simple numbers: Avogadro's Constant, Boltzmann's Constant, Planck's Constant, the Gravitational Constant and the like. Neither the world of "pure mathematics" nor the mathematics "underpinning" the material world can be given a complete and final rationale: there remain, and must always remain, unsolved puzzles and unproven theorems, often wholly incomprehensible to the untutored. It might be easy to believe that mathematics was simply something we made up—except that it provably hangs together and allows precise predictions and achievements far beyond what we could ever sensibly have expected.

So the mathematical reality—the epitome of reason itself— remains, as Plato suggested, dependent on something that we cannot now expound in clearly rational ways. The source of its

---

32 See Ennead V.1 [10].3.8, V.1 [10].7.1-2.
33 See Tegmark, *Our Mathematical Universe*, 254-70.
34 See Plato, *Theaetetus* 147-48 on the discovery and partial systematizing of incommensurable square roots.

power, the "real reality," may still be apprehensible, but never rationalized. We can begin the task of apprehension, so Plotinus tells us, by the use of guided imagination:

> Let us then apprehend in our thought this visible universe, with each of its parts remaining what it is without confusion, gathering all of them together into one as far as we can, so that when any one part appears first, for instance the outside heavenly sphere, the imagination of the sun and, with it, the other heavenly bodies follows immediately, and the earth and sea and all the living creatures are seen, as they could in fact all be seen inside a transparent sphere. Let there be, then, in the soul a shining imagination of a sphere, having everything within it, either moving or standing still. Keep this, and apprehend in your mind another, taking away the mass (*aphelon ton onkon*): take away also the places, and the mental picture of matter in yourself, and do not try to apprehend another sphere smaller in mass than the original one, but calling on the god who made that of which you have the mental picture (*to phantasma*), pray him to come. And may he come, bringing his own universe with him, with all the gods within him, he who is one and all, and each god is all the gods coming together into one.35

Translating that passage down into a clumsier but perhaps more immediately helpful mode: we nowadays conceive the "real" material world as an array of bodies—or better, a network of distinguishable forces—spread out in different dates and locations. We think things are "far away" from each other. But the story is an illusion. The phenomena themselves, of course, are not far away from us at all: they are modes of our own sensory being, and "distance" is simply one factor in the picture, as virtual as the perspective in a *trompe l'oeil* painting. When we move to consider the reality "behind" our various viewings we carry that illusion with us. But nothing is essentially "far away": even bodily beings are not. "Nothing is a long way off or far from anything else."36

---

35 *Ennead* V.8 [31].9.
36 *Ennead* IV.3 [27].11, 22–23. Cf. Hanegraaff, *Hermetic Spirituality*, 216: "the ability 'to make far off things present' through the imagination was an important aspect of *nous* since as far back as Homer." The first century guru Apollonius

Everything, for itself, is *here*: nothing ever goes away. Consider a story from another tradition.

> When Great Master Ba (709-788 AD) and Hyakujô were walking together, they saw a wild duck fly past. Master Ba said, "What's that?" Hyakujô said, "A wild duck." Master Ba said, "Where did it go?" Hyakujô said, "It flew away." Master Ba twisted Hyakujô's nose. Hyakujô cried out in pain. Master Ba said, "Where has it ever flown away?"[37]

A similar thought is hovering on the edge of modern cosmology: neither distance nor size has any fundamental reality.[38] Every photon, for itself, is simultaneously present at every moment of its "travels." Every particle is entangled with others at whatever distance, so that their properties are mutually dependent.

The sphere that Plotinus imagines — urging us to remove all bulk, all distance from the image — appears elsewhere in his writings:

> If one likens it [that is, everything] to a living richly varied sphere, or imagines it as a thing all faces, shining with living faces, or as all the pure souls running together into the same place, with no deficiencies but having all that is their own, and universal Intellect seated on their summits so that the region is illuminated by intellectual light — if one imagined it like this one would be seeing it somehow as one sees another from outside; but one must become that, and make oneself the contemplation.[39]

The real world is not, as moderns sometimes suggest, the object of a "view from nowhere," but rather the view from *everywhere*. We are already participants in the dance that makes reality, and know — from the inside — what it is like "inside."

---

declared that imagination (*phantasia*) was "supremely philosophical," and "a more skilful artist than Imitation. Imitation will create what it knows, but Imagination will also create what it does not know, conceiving it with reference to the real": Philostratus, *Life of Apollonius*, vol. 2, p. 155 [6.19].

37 Case 53 from the *Blue Cliff Record*, the *Hekiganroku* (a collection of Ch'an koans compiled in China by Yuanwu Kegin [1063-1135]). The recognition of this truth is mostly, for most of us, merely "notional"; "real assent," real recognition, is a sudden illumination.

38 See Mack, *End of Everything*, 198-99.

39 *Ennead* VI.7 [38].15, 25-16, 3. See Sabo, "Nous: a globe of faces."

HOW THE WORLDS BECAME

We can "know" things "from the inside," because we are ourselves "inside." There are at least two implications, a metaphysical and an epistemological. Metaphysically, the Platonic claim is that reality is essentially a "minded" affair — rather than imagining an array of atomic or more familiar bodies, with no more than "primary" or "objective" properties (that seem to dissolve into merely nominal attributions), we are to conceive that colours, topologies, virtues, principalities and powers are real elements of an eternal Intellect. These are in turn reflected or refracted in our phenomenal worlds: rather than supposing that there are first distinct individuals, from which we abstract some conception of universals, we are to acknowledge that the *first* discriminable realities are "noetic," related to each other not by their disposition in a preexisting "space" but by their rational associations. Platonic Forms are not — as too many critics still suppose — "abstract universals," though it was only in the later development of Platonism that they were explicitly understood as active presences: "Proclus took the divine ideas of Plotinus and made them into gods that can not only be known (as in Plotinus) but can also know. Dionysius makes them into angels. Thus it is that the Forms of Plato become the Angels of Christendom."[40] But actually Plotinus also supposed that the Ideas, the Forms, the Rational Realities, were themselves inseparable from the Intellects that knew them: they were already the angels of Christendom (and of other related creeds). If they were not thus united their reality would always be wholly separate from any recognition of their being: even God would never truly *know* that His conception of them was the truth![41] Theirs is "the real and original world" that we now see only as they are reflected in — as it were — the water of material existence, Nun.[42] And so the myths are vindicated.

> As Brisson observes, *Metaphysics* 12.1074b1–14 shows that for Aristotle the initial or pre-anthropomorphic notion of the divinity that was handed down in the form of

---

40 Barfield, *Ancient Quarrel*, 97.
41 *Ennead* V.5 [32].1, 51–69; see Clark, "Plotinian Account of Intellect."
42 See *Ennead* I.6 [1].8, 9: we might thereby sink down into Hades and consort with shadows; see also III.6 [26].7, 41–2 on "falling into falsity, like things in a dream or water or a mirror."

myth and that identified the primary natural forces or substances with gods, must have been divinely inspired for it constitutes the germ that culminated in his own philosophical theology. More important, Aristotle (*Movement of Animals* 699b35ff.), as so many others, provides with his own notion of the Unmoved Mover an allegorical exegesis of the famous scene in Homer's *Iliad* 7 in which Zeus describes his formidable power in the form of suspending all the other gods, and thus the entire universe, from a golden chain. This is akin to Plato's contention in the *Theaetetus* (152b) that Heraclitus's famous *panta rei* was borrowed from Homer. The contention was to come full circle when the Alexandrine scholar Ammonius (second century BC) wrote a work entitled "Plato's Debt to Homer."[43]

POSSESSION

But let me return yet again from the cosmological level to the psychological (so far as they are distinguished). Let us consider the gods, the demons, the angels as actively present in the living soul. Augustine, in a sermon in AD 404, gave voice to a learned defender of pagan worship: "When I worship Mercury," we are to suppose his saying, "I worship talent. Talent cannot be seen; it is something invisible."[44] Augustine allowed the gloss, contenting himself with inquiring what it was that the "talent" in question did: "perhaps they err greatly who think that talent is to be worshipped using an image of Mercury [the god of thieves, tricksters, and traders]." This is not, or need not be, simply a Stoic allegory. It is not that Mercury is a convenient image for "Talent," but that Talent—the indefinable somewhat that enables action—is a real, occasional presence. In exercising a talent we may find ourselves doing more, more easily, and with greater grace, as something not quite ourselves acts through us.[45] This is an experience any artist

---

43 Naddaf, "Allegory and Origins," 119, citing Brisson, *How Philosophers Saved Myths*, 38.
44 Augustine, *Sermon* 26.24, cited by Ando, *Matter of the Gods*, 41.
45 Nor is this to "personify" an abstraction, as Samuel Butler suggested his Erewhonians were doing: "they personify hope, fear, love, and so forth, giving them temples and priests, and carving likenesses of them in stone, which they verily believe to be faithful representations of living beings who are only not human in being more than human" (Butler, *Erewhon*, 221). There is no need to suppose that the ancients thought that the gods "looked like" their statues.

or athlete or even academic may acknowledge, and also admit, with Augustine, that it may sometimes have a bad end. On the other hand, we do also need to plan ahead! "A proverb expresses it neatly: 'When you plan ahead your god is yours, when you do not plan ahead your god is not yours.' Here the god is clearly a power for effective thinking, planning, and inspiration, and this is the central element in the concept."[46]

There are other moods and modes of being, of a sort already described in my discussion of planetary demons: rage, greed, lust, ambition, and despair may act in us so as to push aside any considered personal choice. Or else (equivalently) create that choice. Afterwards we may wonder who or what it was that acted, whether for good or ill. We may, sometimes, knowingly give up our agency to some such master spirit. And sometimes we may find it difficult to locate any real abiding selfhood within the chaos. Philosophical discussions of personal identity have usually begun from the assumption that any reasonable theory of what is involved in such identity must confirm common judgments: called upon to prove my own identity I produce my birth certificate, passport, driving license. If there are any doubts about the authenticity of these documents, I appeal to friends and family, to medical and dental records, perhaps to traces of DNA. Commonsensically, I am an identifiable physical organism, with a unique and bounded history, however little I remember of past years, and however changed, in disposition, beliefs, and character from what I was before. People do also, sometimes, speak as if I could indeed be "a different person" (just in that my disposition, beliefs, and character have changed), or observe that I am "a different person" at home and at work, in public display and in private (it would indeed be peculiar if I weren't). But such changes don't usually amount to much. Legally and morally I am the very same person as committed whatever follies I would now like to disown: the very fact that I would now like to disown them, even forget them, is proof that they are mine! But "common sense" may not be the last word.

---

46 Jacobsen, *Treasures*, 156, citing Lambert, *Babylonian Wisdom Literature*, 227, lines 23–26.

> "Know Yourself" is said to those who because of their selves' multiplicity have the business of counting themselves up and learning that they do not know all the numbers and kinds of things they are, or do not know any one of them, nor what their ruling principle is, or by what they are themselves.[47]

Those who seek to follow that Delphic instruction—so St. Hesychios was to say—find themselves, as it were, gazing into a mirror and sighting the dark faces of the demons peering over their shoulders.[48] "We can infer from the object appearing in the mind which demon is close at hand, suggesting that object to us.... All thoughts producing anger or desire in a way that is contrary to reason [or the Spirit] are caused by demons."[49]

Is that so far from our modern experience? Any serious attempt to attend to the thoughts and feelings we experience reveals how incoherent, and often how repellent, those thoughts and feelings are.

> It is a hard matter to bring to a standstill the soul's changing movements. Their irresistible stream is such that we could sooner stem the rush of a torrent, for thoughts after thoughts in countless numbers pour on like a huge breaker and drive and whirl and upset its whole being with their violence.... A man's thoughts are sometimes not due to himself but come without his will.[50]

The thoughts, feelings, images that sweep across our consciousness, and that may briefly absorb us are not the same as the self, considered simply as that consciousness. Our error is to *identify* with the passing thoughts and feelings. Our release is to draw ourselves back from them, even from those with which we are most tempted to identify. Billy Milligan, whom the American courts—briefly—excused for rape and assault on the plea that he suffered from Multiple Personality Disorder, described the process whereby different personae moved out into control of

---

47 *Ennead* VI 7 [38]. 41, 22-25.
48 Palmer et al., *Philokalia*, 123. The original Delphic command to "know yourself" may have only required us to acknowledge our own weakness and mortality: "know that you are *not* (or at least not yet) a god."
49 Evagrios Pontikos [345-399], in Palmer et al., *Philokalia*, 39.
50 Philo, *On the Change of Names*, 239f., in *Collected Works*, 5:265f.

their shared body as one of stepping into the light of a spotlight from the corners of a dark room.[51] One interpretation of the metaphor is that it is that light itself that is the self. At least that does to some extent match the implications of meditative practice in many traditions. If "the mind" is a complex of mental microbes,[52] then we need another expression (say "the Self") for the light or space within which these complexes take shape. In Colin Wilson's words: "I speak of 'my mind' as I speak of 'my back garden.' But in what sense is my back garden really 'mine'? It is full of worms and insects who do not ask my permission to live there. It will continue to exist after I am dead."[53] C. S. Lewis may have been right to suspect—as so many of our predecessors did—that these "microbes" are rather "macrobes," demons under another name, a thought that Wilson and other science fiction writers have quite frequently developed.[54] Maybe the Ophites anticipated these later fantasies![55]

If such demons are real distinctive presences with histories of their own—rather than misleading names for similar experiences—then perhaps we can really talk to them—and this is not so far from actual therapeutic practice. "What are known as *externalizing conversations* can flush the presence and operations of anorexia/bulimia [the abusive voice] into the open":[56] in other words, demanding a response from the "disease entity" itself, the possessing demon or personality state, and so treating it as an agent with its own destructive purposes and customary techniques. And who is the "original" self: the alert, courteous and intelligent self that many anorexics display in public, or the anxious and self-hating self that cooperates with the disease?

---

51 Crabtree, *Multiple Man*, 82, after Keyes, *Minds of Billy Milligan*. MPD is now more often called "dissociative identity disorder"; see my "Personal Identity and Identity Disorders."
52 The earlier label, coined by Ritchie, *Darwinism and Politics*, 22, for what have more recently been called "memes."
53 Colin Wilson, *Mind Parasites*, 40; see my "Mind Parasites."
54 C. S. Lewis, *That Hideous Strength*, 315-16.
55 Origen, *Contra Celsum*, 346-47 [6.30]: their seven "archontic demons" are named as Michael, Suriel, Raphael, Gabriel, Thauthabaoth, Erathaoth, and Onoel or Thartharaoth—a mixture of Hebraic angelic names and gibberish.
56 Maisel et al., *Biting the Hand That Starves You*, 81. See also Allione, *Feeding Your Demons*.

Or neither? Crabtree,[57] without endorsing any strong belief in possession, reports that there are at least therapeutic advantages in accepting that hypothesis while dealing with multiples — and almost everyone involved in the care and management of anorexic or depressive patients (whether therapists, nurses, doctors, caregivers, or the victims) will end up speaking of "the disease" as exactly such an intrusive demon.[58]

The dominant interpretation of such cases of "dissociation" or "multiplicity" is that "DID clients are individual people who experience their minds as consisting of separate personalities that are able to function autonomously. Yet they are single persons."[59] But as Hacking also observes,[60] "some clients ... experience these parts as spiritual entities that are separate from themselves." And this latter judgment is truer to the accounts originally given by multiples and psychologists in the nineteenth and early twentieth centuries. "Multiple Personality Disorder" is early associated with theories of possession.[61] And it is Possession that is the commoner, worldwide, theory.

Bourguignon compares two accounts: one, by Lasky, of a multiple, "Mrs. G."; the other, by Pressel, of a case of spirit possession in Brazil. The authors, a therapist and an anthropologist respectively, have different methods, and different fundamental assumptions:

> Their reactions to the alternate personalities are correspondingly different. Lasky notes that, in spite of earlier hints of Candy's existence, he "had not lent credence" to Mrs. G.'s "second, separate personality." When Candy does appear, he is surprised and responds cautiously, telling her that he "would like to learn ... which part of Mrs. G. she represented." This statement of disbelief in her existence infuriates Candy, who replies that "she did not *represent* anything, she was herself" [Lasky, 370, italics in original]. Candy insists that she is a separate person, sharing a body with Mrs. G., who essentially agrees. She, the core

---

57 Crabtree, *Multiple Man*.
58 See, for example, Schaefer and Rutledge, *Life without Ed*; Murray, *Killing the Black Dog*.
59 Hacking, *Rewriting the Soul*, 134.
60 Hacking, 19.
61 See Crabtree, *Multiple Man*; Spanos, *Multiple Identities and False Memories*.

personality, tells Lasky that Candy "usually seemed to be someone else who knew her very well and seemed almost 'to sit on my shoulder, like a little bird'" [Lasky, 364]. This perception of Candy as separate and alien is confirmed when Mrs. G. says that though she may be embarrassed at Candy's actions, she does not feel any guilt for them. That is, she does not feel responsible for Candy's behavior. The therapist, however, does not entertain such a possibility. To him, Candy is a split off part of Mrs. G. herself, "resulting from a developmental defect of the ego." For comparison we turn not to Pressel's views on Margarida but to those of Joaõ and his fellow Umbandistas. They do not consider Margarida as a split-off part of Joaõ's own principal personality, but as a separate being. She is one of several spirits that "possess" him at intervals. In local parlance, he is her *cavalho* or "horse" whom she "mounts." She does so by temporarily displacing his personality and taking over his body. What happens on these occasions is her responsibility, not his. Margarida is believed to be a "disincarnate" spirit, that is, the spirit of a deceased person (after Pressel).... In other words, the alters of Mrs. G. and of Joaõ — who live in different cultural settings, and who seek help from different types of healers — have different ontological status: for the American psychotherapist, it is possible, although unusual, for persons to suffer from defective ego development, to use dissociation, or "splitting" rather than repression as a principal ego defense mechanism, and as a result to develop "multiple personalities." For Umbandistas, the world is peopled by disincarnate as well as incarnate spirits. Having unfinished business in the world, they seek out persons with mediumistic capacities.[62]

The robust metaphysical response to this could simply be to deny that there are or even could be noncorporeal entities of this sort. Even this claim might not finally settle the matter: viral infections don't only affect our *bodies*. Some of them affect our minds: temperament, desires and maybe even beliefs. Cat-lovers may have been infected with the same virus that, apparently,

---

[62] Bourguignon, "Multiple Personality, Possession Trance, and the Psychic Unity of Mankind," 374–76, citing Lasky, "Psychoanalytic Treatment" and Pressel, "Negative Spirit Possession."

renders mice susceptible to feline charm! Only a few years ago stomach ulcers were routinely explained as a psychosomatic response to stress: the discovery that they are bacterial in origin, and cured by antibiotics, has relieved many victims, and embarrassed older doctors. It may be that future psychologists will also be embarrassed at the discovery of simple bacterial or viral causes of the mental disorders whose victims they now patronize — and also of the mental disorders that are now usually admired (egoism, ambition, extreme self-confidence, anthropocentrism, scientism)! Or maybe there are no simple physical correlates of the infection or contagion: maybe instead we should indeed consider these possessive spirits as "mental microbes." Our ordinary mind itself is compounded of mental microbes, voices advising us to purchase this or that, to swoon over celebrities and punish deviants. Perhaps they are more than fashions. Perhaps they are indeed devils. And maybe some are angels.

Ralph Allison, a therapist notorious for his use of literal exorcism to displace what he had come to suspect were genuinely invasive spirits (whether of the deceased, or of more diabolical origin), draws attention to the phenomenon of the "inner self helper," a voice and character which distinguishes itself from the patient and seeks to assist her.[63] One odd story — this from a study of eating disorders — recounts how one abused girl prayed desperately for spiritual support, and promptly encountered a frog willing to sit on her hand. "It occurred to her that she could bring the spirit of the frog inside of her and carry this spirit with her. This arrangement seemed agreeable to the frog, and henceforth Margaret and her frog became inseparable."[64] From such encounters, cultural practices grow. They also draw attention to a traditional pattern. Not all the voices that seem to come from outside merely dispossess the "host." Nor are they all indifferent to the host's being and welfare. In older terms they may be 'guardian angels," "*daimones*" rather than demons: at once superior in power and knowledge to the ordinary self, and also in some way serving as a "higher" self with whom the host must one day identify.

---

63 Allison, "MPD, DID and Internalized Imaginary Companions," and *Mind in Many Pieces*.
64 Maisel, *Biting the Hand that Starves You*, 231.

> If a man is able to follow the spirit (*daimon*) which is above him, he comes to be himself above, living that spirit's life, and giving the pre-eminence to that better part of himself to which he is being led; and after that spirit he rises to another, until he reaches the heights. For the soul is many things, and all things, both the things above and the things below down to the limits of all life, and we are each one of us an intelligible universe, making contact with this lower world by the powers of soul below, but with the intelligible world by its powers above.[65]

Here-now, we may find ourselves advised and even bullied by our *daimon*—as "Sally" bullied "Miss Beauchamp" according to Morton Prince's account[66]—but if all goes well we shall find ourselves awakening to that "higher" self, and find yet another guiding star above us. This traditional account is at odds in one respect with the commonest modern hope: the dominant goal of therapy is usually "integration" (*aka* silencing the conversation), though there are occasional voices advising that it may be enough to achieve a reasonably stable and cooperative family of personalities. Even Prince, who decided to drive Sally away (for no better reason, it seems, than that he found her intolerably perky), imagined that she was merely retreating to "the unconscious," where she belonged, and where her talents and wit could be utilized by the newly dominant personality, "the real Miss Beauchamp." "After successful integration," so Ross reports,[67] "MPD patients function much better than before, and can be released from the mental health system." But older traditions—as well as having a more critical attitude to normality—took the possible need for exorcism more seriously: the imagined ascent back up to heaven required us to strip off the characters we have accumulated here, including the "normal" one. The therapists who disapproved of Allison's exorcism of the more hostile and angry multiples in his charge may not have thought him simply deluded (after all, it is not uncommon for therapists to play along with their clients' belief-sets and stage dramatic scenes in the hope of effecting a "cure").

---

65 *Ennead* III.4 [15].3, 18–24.
66 See Prince, *Dissociation of a Personality*, which became the template for many subsequent investigations and would-be-helpful therapies.
67 Ross, *Dissociative Identity Disorder*, 226f.

The problem may have been rather that they didn't suppose that *any* element of the patient's soul should be so roughly removed.[68] But surgery, however brutal, may occasionally be needed. There are some selves, or would-be selves, that must be acknowledged only to be dismissed, just as there are some possible lifestyles and opinions that we shouldn't even discuss,[69] some voices that we shouldn't lend any strength to; whether exorcism "works" as well as Origen and others have supposed is another matter.

The other crux, of course, is indeed that there may be disagreement about the *origin* of alters, especially those that Allison identifies as "Imaginary Companions." The persona that is first presented to the world, and the therapist, is itself most likely *imaginary*: someone or something devised to deal with the outer world, usually by an abject conformity. Is it possible that the companions are *invoked*—as people around the world suppose that gods, demons and the departed dead may be invoked? Or are they "only imagined"? Is there any clear distinction between these options?

What is it, after all, to "imagine" something? Our predecessors would have found our belief in our own personal *creativity* odd. The sculptor locates the statue in the marble, and rubs or chips away at the stone till it emerges.[70] The composer *hears* the music that he then writes down.[71] Only what is really there already can truly and vividly be imagined, perhaps at first in a dream. When Homer invokes his Muse,[72] the Muse responds. How different

---

68 Beahrs, Unity and Multiplicity, 129, 141–65.
69 "It is not necessary to examine every problem and every thesis but only one about which doubt might be felt by the kind of person who requires to be argued with and does not need castigation or lack perception. For those who feel doubt whether or not the gods ought to be honoured and parents loved, need castigation, while those who doubt whether snow is white or not, lack perception": Aristotle, Topics 1.105a4–8 1.11.
70 As the Kwakiutl suppose (according to Harré, Personal Being, 88), and also our own predecessors: Ps-Dionysius Mystical Theology, ch. 2 (1025ab), in Complete Works, 138.
71 The notion that Mozart (especially) "dreamed his music" and that such musical composition takes place in a relaxed state of free association is widely canvassed. It sounds plausible, though it may also be adopted as a way of diminishing Mozart's achievements: see Karhausen, Bleeding of Mozart, 187–89.
72 "Of Peleus' son, Achilles, sing, O Muse, the vengeance, deep and deadly; whence to Greece unnumbered ills arose; which many a soul of mighty warriors to the viewless shades untimely sent": Homer Iliad 1.1–4, trans. Edward, Earl

is that from the way we dream, on the cusp of waking? Even today we may find it helpful to allow dream figures to act out their dramas in the hypnogogic state of consciousness between sleep and waking, or listen to the songs they sing, waking only in time to take some note of what they did.

> In meditation and the hypnogogic state the individual can watch symbols form. By looking at feelings, associations, and the situation being autosymbolized [sic], it is possible to penetrate the symbol. These states instruct in the matter of symbolism. One gradually feels that the symbol is the means by which something higher and more interior speaks to the conscious self. It is an intelligent guidance system. Since it is in a higher language than we are accustomed to, the searcher needs to enter into this inner realm to understand its language.[73]

Whether, so many centuries later, we can always manage to read the symbols, may be doubtful, but we may at least be moved by them, even without formal understanding: we are, after all, still human. And maybe the "intelligent guidance system" is still here. The image we create for ourselves (we think) of some superior angel is perhaps that angel's presence to us. Can we hope to be wholly taken up into that angel, as we may also fear to be "taken down" into some less friendly "demon"? What would it be like?

> Often I have woken up out of the body to my self and have entered into myself, going out from all other things; I have seen a beauty wonderfully great and felt assurance that then most of all I belonged to the better part; I have actually lived the best life and come to identity with the divine; and set firm in it I have come to that supreme actuality, setting myself above all else in the realm of Intellect. Then after that rest in the divine, when I have come down from Intellect to discursive reasoning, I am puzzled how I ever came down, and how my soul has come to be in the body when it is what it has shown itself to be by itself, even when it is in the body.[74]

---

of Derby [1864]: www.gutenberg.org/files/6150/6150-h/6150-h.htm.
73 Van Dusen, *The Presence of Other Worlds*, 35.
74 *Ennead* IV.8 [6].1, 1–12.

The world as we ordinarily experience it is ruled by unvoiced assumptions, foolish hopes and fears, stereotypical judgments about this and that. Identifying the demons which are at work in us may be the first slight step towards discovering what we might really be without them—or with the help of a superior god or *daimon*. We need Athena, as it were, to tug us round.[75] "Our normal waking consciousness, rational consciousness as we call it, is but one special type of consciousness, whilst all about it, parted from it by the filmiest of screens, there lie potential forms of consciousness entirely different."[76] Turning around, or waking up to the "*real* world," may not be merely a return to common sense, as though it were *obvious* that Morton Prince had more sense than Sally. Like Markandeya in the Hindu story, we may fall out of the sleeping Vishnu's mouth into "the immense silence of the night of Brahma" to discover truth![77] But unlike Plotinus (and maybe Markandeya) we immediately forget: "it is as if people who slept through their life thought the things in their dreams were reliable and obvious, but, if someone woke them up, disbelieved in what they saw with their eyes open and went to sleep again."[78]

PRINCIPLES AND PERSONS

The gods, demons, angels of our own and our ancestors' imagination may really be all around us still. "The angels keep their ancient places"[79] despite our unbelief. But what are those places, and what sort of "being" do such spectres have? Our modern commonsensical assumption—not very well supported even by our own modern science—is, roughly, Aristotelian. Discrete and countable "substances" (*ousiai*) are the primary existents, each of which are the bearers of what exists in other "categories": properties like colour or weight or location can only be predicated of those primary existents. More seemingly amorphous

---

75 *Ennead* VI.5 [23].7, 9f.; cf. Porphyry, *Life*, 23.
76 James, *Varieties of Religious Experience*, 388.
77 Zimmer, *Myths and Symbols*, 38–39.
78 *Ennead* V.5 [32].11.
79 Francis Thompson, "The Kingdom of God" [c. 1885], in *Works*, 2:226: "The angels keep their ancient places; / Turn but a stone and start a wing! / 'Tis ye, 'tis your estrangèd faces, / That miss the many-splendoured thing."

stuffs, like water or fog or fire, turn out to be mere aggregates of smaller discrete bits which alone determine the behaviour of the stuffs. Many such discrete existents may display or suffer similar qualities or events but those shared properties don't themselves have any "independent" being: there is no single "headache" that everyone trapped in a stuffy room may share, even though they all do "have a headache" (that is to say, their heads ache, or they, as it were, "headache"). All attempts to formalize or rationalize these commonsensical observations, though, end in some confusion: the primary existents themselves can't really exist without their "properties," and their own continued being seems to come down to some apparent property's continued manifestation, without which they will vanish. Meanwhile scientific theory continues to grope to identify those smallest "bits" which maybe compose all larger things: the bits, the supposed unbreakable atoms, turn out themselves first to be composites and then to be merely, as it were, a range of possibilities for continued action or observation. If all such identified "particles" turn out be weirdly "identical" (so that it is even almost rational to suggest that there is only one such particle, looping back and forth in time[80]) why may we not consider a non-Aristotelian, sort of Platonic, ontology instead? What are manifest in our experience are Qualities, with identities that allow them to be present in many times

---

80 "[John] Wheeler relayed to [Richard] Feynman that he had figured out why all the electrons ever detected have identical charges, masses, and other properties. There is only one electron in the universe, he explained. All the electrons we see are simply the same one racing forward and backward in time — ricocheting through perpetuity like a racquetball in a court. That is why every electron appears the same": Halpern, *Quantum Labyrinth*, 76. This hypothesis does not of itself explain why that singular electron *retains* its properties forever. Better suppose that all the appearances are of a singular *timeless* somewhat. So Boethius, *Consolation* 5.6 (*Tractates*, 423) distinguishes Eternity from what simply lasts "forever": "Eternity is the whole, simultaneous and perfect possession of boundless life, which becomes clearer by comparison with temporal things. For whatever lives in time proceeds in the present from the past into the future, and there is nothing established in time which can embrace the whole space of its life equally, but tomorrow surely it does not yet grasp, while yesterday it has already lost. And in this day to day life you live no more than in that moving and transitory moment. Therefore whatever endures the condition of time, although, as Aristotle thought concerning the world, it neither began ever to be nor ceases to be, and although its life is drawn out with the infinity of time, yet it is not yet such that it may rightly be believed to be eternal."

and places, and to merge or separate themselves very much like the ancient gods. Our error in considering those ancient—and not so ancient—stories is to suppose that gods and demons and angels were ever supposed to be discrete and countable entities of the sort we imagine ourselves to be (mistakenly). Aristotle's God identically *is theoria*, and not a singular being who happens to "theorize."[81] It does not follow (it is a common error) that such a god, demon or angel is merely an aspect of our own individual soul: it is rather a presence that can occupy, inspire or else contaminate us—and our own souls are similarly incorporeal. Our chief error—to which I shall return—is to suppose that existence is always local.

In his treatise on the doctrine that dreams are sent from God, Philo of Alexandria insisted that it was important to know oneself before presuming to talk about the cosmos: "Now this disposition the Hebrews call Terah [who was Abram's father], and the Greeks Socrates; for they say also that the latter grew old in the most accurate study by which he could hope to know himself, never once directing his philosophical speculations to the subjects beyond himself. But he was really a man; but Terah is the principle itself which is proposed to every one."[82] The story of Abram's family is allegorized to represent successive stages in the proper exploration of ourselves and the world.

> The information that Terah left the land of Chaldaea and migrated to Haran, taking with him his son Abraham and his kindred, is given us not with the object that we may learn as from a writer of history, that certain people became emigrants, leaving the land of their ancestors, and making a foreign land their home and country, but that a lesson well suited to man and of great service to human life may not be neglected.[83]

Terah deserts the astrological confines of Chaldaea, to live amongst immediate Sense Experience, "here and now." Abram (as he was first called) leaves Haran too behind to be instructed in the truth.

---

81 Aristotle, *Metaphysics* 12.1072b13–28; see *Nicomachean Ethics* 10.1177b28–34.
82 Philo, *On Dreams* 10.58, in *Collected Works*, 5:327.
83 Philo, *On Dreams* 10.52, in *Collected Works*, 5:323.

For Isaac is a figure of knowledge gained by nature, knowledge which listens to and learns from no other teacher but itself, while Abraham is a figure of knowledge gained by instruction; and Isaac is a dweller on his native soil, while Abraham is an emigrant and a stranger in the land. For, abandoning the foreign alien tongue of Chaldaea, the tongue of sky-prating astrology, he betook him to the language that befits a living creature endowed with reason, even the worship of the First Cause of all things.[84]

Jacob, in his turn, relied on exercises and practisings,[85] so completing (for Philo) the threefold structure of education. What Abram/Abraham did by instruction and Isaac by nature, Jacob was to learn by painful practice. MacCulloch offers an interesting gloss on Jacob—specifically on the story of his wrestling with God, or an angel:

Around Abraham's rackety grandson Jacob are woven several engaging tales of outrageous cheating and deceit, and they culminate in an all-night wrestling match with a mysterious stranger who overcomes Jacob and is able to give him another new name, Israel, meaning "He who strives with God." Out of that fight in the darkness, with one who revealed the power of God and was God, began the generations of the Children of Israel. Few peoples united by a religion have proclaimed by their very name that they struggle against the one whom they worship. The relationship of God with Israel is intense, personal, conflicted. Those who follow Israel and the religions which spring from his wrestling match that night are being told that even through their harshest and most wretched experiences of fighting with those they love most deeply, they are being given some glimpse of how they relate to God.[86]

So what does it mean that Socrates was a man but Terah is a principle, a *logos* (specifically, *ho logos ho peri tou gnonai tina heauton prokeimenos hoia dendron euernestaton*: "a way of thinking set before us

---

84 Philo, *On Dreams* 26.160–61, in *Collected Works*, 5:381.
85 Philo, *On Dreams* 27.168, in *Collected Works*, 5:385.
86 MacCulloch, *History of Christianity*, 50, citing Genesis 32.24–32. See also Abraham's argument with God about the proposed fate of Sodom: Genesis 18.17–33.

as a tree of great luxuriance")?[87] It might as easily be suggested, after all, that Socrates was also taken to be a "principle": at once an ideal example of unrelenting and incorruptible enquiry and an actual enlivening spirit. Indeed, it is likely that more philosophers invoked that spirit than Hebrews regularly invoked Terah (unless an identical spirit may be found within the Kabbalah). It is the God of Abraham, Isaac, and Jacob that is remembered by the servants of that God, and Terah is but a name. But the question remains: when does a remembered example, or a rule of thought, or the practice of self-reflection, become something more like a "person," an agency at least as independent as the selves we imagine ourselves to be? Does it have a history of its own? Can we ever converse with it?

A similar question arises in considering Hesiod's cosmogeny:

> First of all Chaos came into being, then broad-breasted Earth, the ever-safe foundation of all the deathless ones, who live on the peaks of snowy Olympos, and shadowy Tartaros in a hiding place of the earth with its wide ways, and Eros, who is the most beautiful of all the deathless gods, who relaxes the limbs and overwhelms the mind and wise counsel in the breasts of all the gods and men. From Chaos came Darkness and black Night, and from Night came Brightness and Day, whom Night conceived and bore by uniting in love with Darkness. Earth bore starry Sky first, like to her in size, so that he covered her all around, everywhere, so that there might always be a secure seat for the blessed gods. And Earth gave birth to the blessed Mountains, the pleasant halls of the gods, the nymphs who live in the wooded hills. She bore the barren waters, raging with its swell, Sea, without making delightful love.[88]

These firstborn out of Chaos seem (to us) mostly to be "mere abstractions" or—at best—mere geographical features: Darkness and Night, Brightness and Day, mountains and barren waters.

> And again the goddess murky Night, though she lay with none, bare Blame and painful Woe, and the Hesperides

---

87 Philo, *On Dreams* 26.150, in *Collected Works*, 5:381.
88 Hesiod, *Poems*, 36–37 [*Theogony* 116–38].

who guard the rich, golden apples and the trees bearing fruit beyond glorious Ocean. Also she bore the Destinies and ruthless avenging Fates, Clotho and Lachesis and Atropos, who give men at their birth both evil and good to have, and they pursue the transgressions of men and of gods: and these goddesses never cease from their dread anger until they punish the sinner with a sore penalty. Also deadly Night bore Nemesis (Indignation) to afflict mortal men, and after her, Deceit and Friendship and hateful Age and hard-hearted Strife. But abhorred Strife bore painful Toil and Forgetfulness and Famine and tearful Sorrows, Fightings also, Battles, Murders, Manslaughters, Quarrels, Lying Words, Disputes, Lawlessness and Ruin, all of one nature, and Oath who most troubles men upon earth when anyone wilfully swears a false oath.[89]

These are already edging towards a more animated and personal existence: nymphs live in the wooded hills and Earth may or may not "make delightful love" before she can give birth. The next generation more obviously consists of named "persons": "uniting with Sky, Earth bore deep-swirling Ocean, and Koios, Kreios, Hyperion, Iapetos, Theia, Rhea, Themis, Mnemosynê, golden-crowned Phoibê, and beloved Tethys. After them was born crooked-counselled Kronos, the youngest and most terrible of these children, who hated his powerful father."[90] In the Egyptian story Shu and Tefnut, the Moist and Dry, acquire personalities enough to feel desire and jealousy and even affection almost from the start. In Hesiod's the process is more delayed — and even those powers which are also personalities are closely identified with their functions.[91] Mortals like us — and even the younger gods — have lives outside their functions, precisely because we — and even those younger gods — are puppets, subject to the influence of many different moods and modes of being:

---

89 Hesiod, *Theogony* 212-31.
90 Hesiod, *Poems*, 37 [*Theogony*, 116-38].
91 See Proclus, *Elements*, 105 [Proposition 119]: "neither [the gods'] goodness nor their unity is a quality superadded upon other qualities; they are pure goodness, as they are pure unity" (*ou gar allo hekastos, eita agathon, alla monon agathon, hosper oude allo, eita hen, alla monon hen*); ibid., 107 [Proposition 120]: "every god is an excellence."

Powers and Personalities

Let us conceive of it in the following way. Let us suppose that each of us living creatures is a puppet of the gods, whether contrived as some kind of toy or for some serious purpose; for as to that we know nothing, but we do know that these inner affections of ours, like sinews or cords, drag us along and, being opposed to one another, pull against each other in opposing actions.[92]

Plato himself would deny that any real gods could be similarly divided in their souls,[93] but the ancient stories disagree: even Zeus may be drawn aside from his real purposes by love or lust, when Hera craftily borrows Aphrodite's girdle to seduce him.[94]

> Her broider'd cestus, wrought with ev'ry charm
> To win the heart; there Love, there young Desire,
> There fond Discourse, and there Persuasion dwelt,
> Which oft enthralls the mind of wisest men.[95]

In that last story Zeus, once awake, angrily rebukes his wife, reminding her of a past quarrel and its aftermath:

> Hast thou forgotten how in former times
> I hung thee from on high, and to thy feet
> Attach'd two pond'rous anvils, and thy hands
> With golden fetters bound, which none might break?
> There didst thou hang amid the clouds of Heav'n;
> Through all Olympus' breadth the Gods were wroth;
> Yet dar'd not one approach to set thee free.
> If any so had ventur'd, him had I
> Hurl'd from Heav'n's threshold till to earth he fell,
> With little left of life.[96]

As I observed before, Stoic philosophers, and others, sought to turn these *persons* back into principles and stuffs:

> The scholiast of A wrote: "It is a question why Zeus mistreats Hera so disgracefully on account of the mortal Heracles." He then proceeds to give an allegorical interpretation

---

92 Plato, Laws 1.644d7–654a3.
93 Plato, Phaedrus 246ab: "We will liken the soul to the composite nature of a pair of winged horses and a charioteer. The horses and charioteers of the gods are all good and of good descent, but those of other races are mixed."
94 Homer, Iliad 14.154–352.
95 Homer, Iliad 14.240–43, trans. Edward, Earl of Derby.
96 Homer, Iliad 15.20–29.

of the kind reputedly begun by Theagenes of Rhegium and continued by the Stoics: Zeus is the aether, or fiery upper air, Hera the middle air, the two anvils are earth and water, and the chain brings moisture down from the air and binds the changing of the elements together. Thus the whole symbolizes the stability of the universe. Porphyry gives much the same explanation but interprets the chain as the heavenly fire; and he connects the passage, rightly, with *Iliad* 1.590, where Hephaestus is thrown out of Heaven for having tried to rescue Hera from Zeus.[97]

It is likely enough that some sort of *hieros gamos*, sacred marriage of Earth and Sky, lies behind Homer's satire (if so it was), and also that there was a metaphysical meaning (or at least a metaphysical interpretation) for Hera's punishment, as well as Zeus's threat to the whole body of the Olympians in an earlier passage.

> Ye all shall know
> In strength how greatly I surpass you all.
> Make trial if ye will, that all may know.
> A golden cord let down from Heav'n, and all,
> Both Gods and Goddesses, your strength, apply:
> Yet would ye fail to drag from Heav'n to earth,
> Strive as ye may, your mighty master, Jove;
> But if I choose to make my pow'r be known,
> The earth itself, and ocean, I could raise,
> And binding round Olympus' ridge the cord,
> Leave them suspended so in middle air:
> So far supreme my pow'r o'er Gods and men.[98]

As Plotinus records, matter is bound everywhere by golden chains.[99] And the One holds a golden veil or barrier before itself, which is to say the whole intelligible world.[100] Zeus, in this account, stands for the primary controlling power: no lesser principle can overpower him, since he is himself the power that they must use: *dunamis panton*, the power of all things.[101]

---

97 Whitman, "Hera's Anvils," 37.
98 *Iliad* 8.19-26, trans. Edward, Earl of Derby.
99 *Ennead* I.8 [51].15.
100 *Ennead* I.6 [1].9.
101 *Ennead* III.8 [30].10; see also Aristotle, *De Motu Animalium* 699b35–700a3, citing this same passage; see Segev, *Aristotle on Religion*, 127–28. Might the phrase be an echo of a prayer of the dead to Ra, addressing him as "the mighty one

A similar metaphysical interpretation makes better sense of the "silly story" of Hephaestus's trapping of Ares and Aphrodite than the astronomical possibility I mentioned earlier.[102] Ares and Aphrodite (Strife and Love) are trapped within the glittering chains, "fine as spiders' webs," cast by the Maker: that is, the world contains those twin principles so as to provide a spectacle for divine onlookers. Hermes, on Apollo's ribald suggestion, offers to enter in those bonds himself, and Poseidon persuades the injured husband to relent, himself standing bail for Ares. On one level, maybe, the story is simply what it seems: "We see a husband restoring both the integrity of his *oikos* and his own honour by a public act of shaming. Yet at the same time the banter of Apollo and Hermes reminds us that this is not human society; the consequences of actions are not as serious."[103] But in fact (in fancy) neither Ares nor Aphrodite are ashamed, nor even a little discouraged.[104] As a warning to potential adulterers it lacks force! Proclus, though acknowledging the scandalous nature of the superficial story (as also the story of Hera's seduction of Zeus), nonetheless insists that "[Homer] is clearly in a state of inspiration, and that he composed these myths through being possessed by the Muses."[105]

> The union of Ares and Aphrodite creates "harmony and order for the opposites"; that of Hephaestus and Aphrodite creates in this world beauty and radiance "to make the world the most beautiful of all visible things." The hypercosmic nuptial embrace and the encosmic adultery are, in fact, simultaneous and eternal, but the mythoplasts have distorted the account according to the familiar pattern. If the cuckolded husband observes the encosmic goings-on from his hypercosmic perch and binds the couple together, the truth behind the screen is that this world

of victories, who art the power of [all] Powers" (Romer, *Egyptian Book of the Dead*, 76)?
102 *Odyssey* 8.266-369.
103 Brown, "Ares, Aphrodite and the Laughter of the Gods," 291.
104 *Odyssey* 8.361-6: "The two, when they were freed from that bond so strong, sprang up straightway. And Ares departed to Thrace, but she, the laughter-loving Aphrodite, went to Cyprus, to Paphos, where is her demesne and fragrant altar. There the Graces bathed her and anointed her with immortal oil, such as gleams upon the gods that are forever. And they clothed her in lovely raiment, a wonder to behold."
105 Proclus, *Commentary on Republic*, 1.193, in Lamberton, *Homer the Theologian*, 190.

has need both of the power of separation (Ares) and of that of combination (Aphrodite), and if he subsequently breaks the chains (at the urging of Poseidon, whose pre-eminent role it is to preside over the cycle of coming to be and passing away), it is because a static union of the two would bring the process to a standstill—Hephaestus's act simultaneously destroys the physical universe and (since eternal destruction and eternal coming to be are the life of that universe) creates it anew.[106]

To this analysis we could add that it is Hermes who, at Apollo's prompting, offers to enter the bonds of visible creation to help *break* Love's ties with Strife. What Empedocles himself meant by speaking of himself as one "putting [his] trust in the insanities of strife"[107] is contested: Plotinus himself suggested that such trust was what had condemned Empedocles (and us) to mortal life.[108] But this is not altogether a "Bad Thing":

> There must not be just one alone—for then all things would have been hidden, shapeless within that one, and not a single real being would have existed if that one had stayed still in itself, nor would there have been the multiplicity of these real beings which are generated from the One, if the things after them had not taken their way out which have received the rank of souls.[109]

Our escape—or else our passage to a better life—is either by the dissolution of all bonds, or—perhaps—by the new creation when it is Hermes—which is Understanding—rather than Ares who joins himself with Aphrodite.

---

106 Lamberton, *Homer the Theologian*, 228, citing Proclus, *Commentary on Republic* 1.141.17-21.
107 Empedocles 31B115DK, 13, in Waterfield, *First Philosophers*, 154.
108 *Ennead* IV.8 [6].1; Kingsley has argued that it is rather the reverse: he must now rely on "Strife"—which is what permits the existence of distinct individuals—so as to resist the lethal blandishments of "Love," intent on merging all existence into one: Kingsley, *Reality*, 430-45.
109 *Ennead* IV.8 [6].6, 1-6. So also Descola, *Beyond Nature and Culture*, 203: "In Plotinus, for example, the generative world soul that, through its emanations, creates the chain of being has one essential property, that of creating otherness; for if the universe is at peace with itself, even if its parts are often in conflict, it is because this conforms with reason, and the unity of reason stems from the contraries that it encompasses. Reason makes things different from one another, in fact as different as possible."

Lamberton himself plainly dislikes this exegesis. "The whole emotional texture of the Homeric passage is lost," he complains, "the rage and bitter frustration of Hephaestus, the comic impatience of Ares to jump into the trap, and the laughter of the gods."[110] Obviously, he is correct: the story is there to be enjoyed at the supposedly "superficial" level, whatever its metaphysical, astronomical, or sardonically moralistic meaning. But it is hardly fair to blame Proclus for seeking to make these stories more worthy of respect, any more than to blame Philo, Origen or Augustine for dealing in similar ways with the dramatic but disturbing stories in Genesis and the other books of the Bible. Either the writers were lying about the gods, or those gods don't deserve respect, or else the stories are to be understood as conveying a more complex message.

And yet there is perhaps still something worth acknowledging in even the "superficial" story. To revert to biblical myths:

> The sequence of mythic traditions found in Genesis *Rabba* 5. 2-4 marks a certain transformation of the relationship of God to the pooling of the waters mentioned in Scripture [Genesis 1.9: "let the waters under heaven be gathered into one place, so that dry land may appear"]; for while the divine command in Genesis is uttered in impersonal and staid terms (as befits the impersonal nature of the elements in this imperious creation myth), the rabbinic revision introduces personal and dramatic elements.[111]

Making a "personal" story of what might otherwise be merely an abstract, even a mechanical, account of things is not necessarily an error. It is too easy for us — and even perhaps for Proclus — to interpret the gods of myth as nothing more than powers or principles or even fundamental "stuffs." But it is true for many more than merely the ancient Egyptians that they "lived in a universe composed not of things, but of beings."[112] Most moderns assume, without much argument, that the universe is composed of "things": that is, mere objects, having only "objective" properties of a sort that (perhaps) exist before, outside, and after anyone's

---

110 Lamberton, *Homer the Theologian*, 229.
111 Fishbane, *Biblical Myth*, 118.
112 Allen, *Genesis in Egypt*, 8.

experience. We accept, without much argument, that there were many billion years before there was sentient life, and that there are many billion worlds beyond our reach or sight. That merely "material" universe is without any "subjective" being, and the emergence of such "subjects" as ourselves is an unpredictable and inexplicable event: inexplicable because we have laid it down that merely material things have no subjective quality, and that there is therefore no essential link between—for example—a particular frequency of electromagnetic radiation and particular colours as experienced by multiple sorts of animal. The so-called "hard problem of consciousness" is indeed an artefact, an effect of that initial decision that the world is really made only of "objects." Our predecessors were wiser—or at least more innocent: they had not imagined the merely material into being, and therefore took it for granted that the world was composed of cooperating and conversing *subjects*. Whatever life we encounter (human or crow or oaktree) is also encountering us. "Whatever possesses a soul is a subject, and whatever has a soul is capable of having a point of view."[113] This sudden confrontation—the moment when we recognize Another and, perforce, admit that Other into our own experience—is at the root of Martin Buber's account of the I/Thou relationship, which he did not confine to human relations.

> The tree is no impression, no play of my imagination, no aspect of a mood; it confronts me bodily and has to deal with me as I must deal with it—only differently. One should not try to dilute the meaning of the relation: relation is reciprocity. Does the tree then have consciousness, similar to our own? I have no experience of that. But thinking that you have brought this off in your own case, must you again divide the indivisible? What I encounter is neither the soul of a tree nor a dryad, but the tree itself.[114]

The tree itself, as also the sense of a particular place or time or principle, is something at once outside our own sense of self and something that intrudes itself on us as a real centre of experience.

---

113 De Castro, "Cosmological Deixis and Amerindian Perspectivism," 476, cited in Descola, *Beyond Nature and Culture*, 139.
114 Buber, *I and Thou*, 58–59.

Powers and Personalities

And once it is acknowledged as that, it is free to be itself. It is free, strangely, to be a "person."

> A person is a mystery, never totally circumscribed by a definition, that is, as an essence or a "what." A person is not a "what" but a "who," and "who" you are, just as Who God is, is ultimately indefinable, undetermined, and of infinite depth. To say "what" something is, is to circumscribe that something in terms of essence or essential definition; to say "who" is to speak, not of some "thing" which can be defined in terms of its essence, but of some "one," an ultimately uncircumscribable and indefinable "who."[115]

So, after all, the superficial story of strange happenings amongst the immortals may really be closer to reality than any merely mechanical or abstract story.

> Which came first, nature-allegories about personalized thunder in the mountains, splitting rocks and trees; or stories about an irascible, not *very* clever, red-beard farmer, of a strength beyond common measure, a person (in all but mere stature) very like the Northern farmers, the bœndr by whom Thórr was chiefly beloved? To a picture of such a man Thórr may be held to have "dwindled," or from it the god may be held to have been enlarged. But I doubt whether either view is right—not by itself, not if you insist that one of these things must precede the other. It is more reasonable to suppose that the farmer popped up in the very moment when Thunder got a voice and face; that there was a distant growl of thunder in the hills every time a story-teller heard a farmer in a rage.[116]

The Rabbis were wise to make the *personal* element of the Genesis story clear. We may need to face up to our fears, and realize that "religion" is not seeking "explanations" but acknowledging the mystery of being. We do still live in a world of beings, not of things.

> Possibly the most pathetic of all the delusions of the modern students of primitive belief is the notion they have about the thing they call anthropomorphism. They believe that primitive men attributed phenomena to a god

---

115 Rossi, "Presence, Participation, Performance," 79.
116 Tolkien, *Monsters and the Critics*, 124.

in human form in order to explain them, because his mind in its sullen limitation could not reach any further than his own clownish existence. The thunder was called the voice of a man, the lightning the eyes of a man, because by this explanation they were made more reasonable and comfortable. The final cure for all this kind of philosophy is to walk down a lane at night. Anyone who does so will discover very quickly that men pictured something semi-human at the back of all things, not because such a thought was natural, but because it was supernatural; not because it made things more comprehensible, but because it made them a hundred times more incomprehensible and mysterious. For a man walking down a lane at night can see the conspicuous fact that as long as nature keeps to her own course, she has no power with us at all. As long as a tree is a tree, it is a top-heavy monster with a hundred arms, a thousand tongues, and only one leg. But so long as a tree is a tree, it does not frighten us at all. It begins to be something alien, something strange, only when it looks like ourselves. When a tree really looks like a man, our knees knock under us. And when the whole universe looks like a man we fall on our faces.[117]

But *pace* Chesterton, the point is not that trees or hills or the whole universe look "like men," unless "men" here means "beings." So also William Blake:

> Each grain of sand,
> Every stone on the land,
> Each rock and each hill,
> Each fountain and rill,
> Each herb and each tree,
> Mountain, hill, earth, and sea,
> Cloud, meteor, and star,
> Are men seen afar.[118]

---

117 Chesterton, *Heretics*, 63. A common suggestion nowadays is that we are programmed to see patterns, and especially faces, in the undergrowth, as our ancestors needed to notice possible threats: better that "a bush should seem a bear" than that we miss the real live bears. So Apollonius remarked (Philostratus, *Life of Apollonius*, 1:183 [2.22.2]): "the things passing through the sky are shapeless and haphazard as far as god is concerned, but we, because imitation is in our nature, rearrange and create them." But better still to acknowledge that both bush and bear are *real*: it is that latter revelation that is at issue here.
118 Blake, Letter to Butts (2 October 1800), in *Complete Writings*, 804-5.

~5~
Families and Dysfunctional Divinities

"I do not think it a sign of modesty to be on bad terms with any of the gods. It is more modest to speak well of every god."[1]

WAR IN HEAVEN

But there is still more to be said about the lurid superficialities of myth. "The more paradoxical and prodigious the riddle is," so the Emperor Julian and many others have insisted, "the more it seems to warn us not to believe simply the bare words but rather to study diligently the hidden truth."[2]

> Why need I enumerate the outrageous stories of the Greeks about the gods which are obviously shameful even if they are to be interpreted allegorically? At any rate, in one place Chrysippus of Soli, who is considered to have adorned the Stoic school of philosophers by his many intelligent treatises, expounds the meaning of a picture at Samos, in which Hera is portrayed as performing unmentionable obscenities with Zeus. This honourable philosopher says in his treatises that matter receives the generative principles of God, and contains them in itself for the ordering of the universe. For in the picture at Samos matter is Hera and God is Zeus.[3]

Unfortunately, if there is a hidden meaning to the myths it is often one that would have been conveyed through personal contact, from priest or sage to acolyte or disciple: we have now lost the line, and must *imagine* our way to understanding. But perhaps there must be limits to our hermeneutical charity? Such

---
1 Philostratus, *Life of Apollonius*, 2:101 [6.3.5].
2 Julian, *Speeches*, 2:105 [Oratio 7].
3 Origen, *Contra Celsum*, 223 [4.48].

stories as we have about the Egyptian gods (if "gods" is what they were) are often even more chaotic and unprincipled than the Greek! If they are "allegorical" the allegory is deeply buried beneath the soap-operatic drama. Seth kills and dismembers his brother Osiris; Osiris's wife and sister, Isis, collects all the parts except Osiris's penis and reconstructs the body, with an artificial penis, so as to enable her conception of Horus; Horus, once grown, demands the kingship back from his wicked uncle, and the council of "gods" debates the issue fruitlessly for eighty years; during one staged contest, Isis wounds first Horus (accidentally) and then Seth, who pleads that he is her brother and persuades her to release him; Horus, angered by this betrayal, cuts off Isis's head (but of course, since she is a "goddess," she survives); Seth attempts to sodomise his nephew, who (with Isis's encouragement) surreptitiously intrudes his own semen (via lettuce) into Seth (so that at the council it is Seth who is shown to have been—humiliatingly—buggered); the dispute continues till at last Osiris, lord of the dead, the harvest, and most tellingly the vengeful demons of the Underworld, insists that his son Horus is to be king of Egypt (and Seth may reside in the solar boat, to fight off the snake Apophis—which is the Nothing before all things—until the end of time,[4] or possibly, by another account, be utterly destroyed, without any part left to bury).[5]

> The struggle between Osiris and Seth has been variously interpreted as the tension between the fertile, controlled Egypt (Osiris) and her chaotic deserts (Seth); as the contrast between the Nile inundation (Osiris) and the storm (Seth); as the struggle between two brothers for their father's crown at the start of the dynastic age; or as a reflection of the ancient (and unproven) tradition

---

[4] "Thus, it is precisely Seth, the rebel, the foreigner, the thunderer, and the murderer of Osiris, who has been chosen to defeat Apopis [sic] and thereby ward off ultimate chaos and cosmic catastrophe": Schweizer, *Sungod's Journey through the Netherworld*, 141.
[5] See Tyldesley, *Myths and Legends*, 103-9 and 133-55, drawing chiefly on Plutarch's *Isis and Osiris* for the earlier part of the story, and a papyrus dating from Ramesses V [reigned 1149-45 BC], "The Contendings of Horus and Seth" for the later.

of slaying old and infirm kings during the *heb-sed*, the jubilee celebration held after thirty years of rule.[6]

Maybe so, but it is difficult to imagine what agricultural, meteorological, astronomical, or even political advice is contained in the story of the "Contendings" (except that wicked uncles should not be allowed to usurp the throne forever, and that senatorial rule, as it were, is ineffective). As Tyldesley acknowledges, "the struggle for the throne is not a straightforward contest fought fair and square. Each bout is won by trickery and cheating, and the all-divine cast [including the supposed "Universal Lord"] is weak, indecisive and, occasionally, ridiculous."[7] The stories read far more — as I have already hinted — like modern soap operas that have "jumped the shark" in search of ratings.[8] Conversely, such soap operas, in a future forgetful age, may be read as myths, and their characters seen as "gods," abiding personalities which shape the imagination of their spectators: the 1990s sitcom, *Friends*, might be a moral and allegorical text, and its characters (Chandler, Joey, Monica, Phoebe, Rachel, Ross) the object of half-serious, half-satirical devotion. Critics of their behaviour will (quite properly) be reminded that representation is not the same as recommendation (and also that times change). Devotees of the show do not have to imitate their heroes: they may rather expect to learn from their mistakes.

Might not the same be said of the oldest stories? Kronos emasculated Ouranos, and was dealt the same injury in his turn, by Zeus. Gaia — having first incited both Kronos and Zeus to their deeds — creates monsters and giants in fury to try to bring down the Olympians. Other Olympians gang up on Zeus, and he is only rescued — despite his claims to be stronger far than all of them together — by the help of Thetis and many-handed Briareus. Or so Achilles reminds his mother, Thetis:

---

6 Tyldesley, *Myths and Legends*, 120.
7 Tyldesley, 142.
8 "Jon Hein and his University of Michigan roommate Sean Connolly coined the phrase in 1985 in response to Season Five, Episode 3, 'Hollywood: Part 3,' of the sitcom *Happy Days* [September 1977]": https://en.wikipedia.org/wiki/Jumping_the_shark (accessed October 14, 2022). It seems that the sitcom survived the event. As did the Egyptian stories.

HOW THE WORLDS BECAME

> For I remember, in my father's house,
> I oft have heard thee boast, how thou, alone
> Of all th' Immortals, Saturn's cloud-girt son
> Didst shield from foul disgrace, when all the rest,
> Juno, and Neptune, and Minerva join'd,
> With chains to bind him; then, O Goddess, thou
> Didst set him free, invoking to his aid
> Him of the hundred arms, whom Briareus
> Th' immortal Gods, and men Ægeon call.
> He, mightier than his father, took his seat
> By Saturn's side, in pride of conscious strength:
> Fear seiz'd on all the Gods, nor did they dare
> To bind their King.[9]

On the other hand, as I observed on an earlier page, Zeus is reckoned the Lord of All.[10]

The allegorical interpretations advanced by the Stoics or hinted at by Plotinus may be apposite, but the superficial story still seems to deserve Plato's contempt. Is this how gods behave?

To which question the answer seems to be "yes." Across mythologies and mythic histories it seems that divine or heroic persons are everlastingly at odds: as jealous and quarrelsome as any clearly human families. In one Mesopotamian story the goddess Inanna[11] descends to the Underworld, losing all her jewellery, clothes, and at last her very flesh, to seek to unseat Ereshkigal from her throne. She is at last restored to life by finding someone else to die for her — and selects her husband Dumuzi for the role because he hasn't mourned her well enough.[12] Dumuzi's faithful sister eventually retrieves him, and he and Inanna alternate their stay in the Underworld. Jacobsen offers an agricultural reading:

> Thus, at its simplest, we would see the death of Inanna
> in the emptying of the storehouse, her revival and the
> resultant death of Dumuzi in the replenishing of the

---

9 Homer, *Iliad* 1.396–406, trans. Edward, Earl of Derby.
10 Homer, *Iliad* 8.19–26; 15.16–21.
11 Characterised as "the numen of the storehouse, as rain goddess, as goddess of war, as goddess of the morning and evening star, and as goddess of harlots," and also "lady of the myriad offices," by Jacobsen, *Treasures*, 141; see also Jacobsen, *Treasures*, 23–74, for a more detailed account of stories about Inanna's marriage, and Dumuzi's various deaths.
12 Jacobsen, *Treasures*, 55–61.

storehouse with fresh meat when the flocks return from the desert and its withering pasturage in late spring and early summer. The last part of the tale, Geshtinanna's search for her brother, seems to be a myth belonging to Dumuzi under his aspect of power in the grain and the beer; this was originally a separate myth concerned with explaining the difference in timing of the grain crop and the grape crop, of beer and wine.[13]

Did the Mesopotamian audience "believe" that the brewing of grain and grape repeated a timeless story of love and loyalty, estrangement and ambition? Or were the stories only meant to convey the proper agricultural techniques to a suitably alert and educated audience? The former possibility seems more realistic: who could seriously learn agricultural technique from the story? More likely they might learn or reinforce *moral* lessons. Just possibly the story provided a "sacramental" meaning: farmers and brewers could conceive themselves to be embodying eternal relationships, or repeating a foundational event, in which the immortals acted out a story with meanings more than we can see. For us, at least, the story is simply an odd adventure, and the immortal beings it describes seem even odder. But that is because we have come to assume that the Very Beginning was well-ordered (and so vastly improbable by current standards),[14] whereas our

---

13 Jacobsen, *Treasures*, 63.
14 Mersini-Houghton, *Before the Big Bang*, 67–68: "Cosmic inflation offers the whole cosmic origin story in one irresistible package. But it does so at the cost of one assumption: a finely tuned start of the universe at high energies on an exquisitely smooth tiny patch of space. And this is a huge assumption, because everything else we know about the workings of the universe tells us that the odds of our universe starting the way it did, in a tailor-made initial state of exceptional order with an entropy state of nearly zero, are ominously small! [Roger] Penrose had made a splash in the 1970s by pointing out this embarrassing fact, and it led to some even more embarrassing implications. Since starting a universe with this state is more improbable than any other possibility, then even what might be conceived of as outrageously impossible will have a higher chance of existing than our universe does. Consider this spooky example as a dramatic statement of the unlikeliness of our existence: The spontaneous formation of a brain in empty space stands a much greater chance (statistically) of occurring than the creation of our universe through cosmic inflation!" Mersini-Houghton's own research provides a partial answer to the puzzle (on which more hereafter), by invoking the notion of a "multiverse": the initial singularity expands in all possible ways, and those which can sustain an inflation produce sufficient space, time, and stuff to allow galaxies,

predecessors seem almost all to have assumed that it was Chaos: the Nothing that we can only imagine as the undivided Sea.

There are many suggestive remarks even in the Hebrew records referring to the Lord's defeat of "the dragon in the deep."

> You it was who smashed Sea (Yam) with Your might,
> Who battered the heads of (the) (tanninim) monsters
>   in the waters;
> You it was who crushed the heads of Leviathan,
> Who left them for food for the denizens of the desert;
> You it was who cut springs and torrents,
> You made the rivers run dry;
> Yours is the day, and also the night;
> You established the moon and sun;
> You fixed the boundaries of the earth;
> Summer and winter—You made them.[15]

The imagined back story seems to echo the story of Marduk's dealings with Tiamat, as recounted in Mesopotamian myth, and perhaps to hint at a need for random procreation to be controlled at the human level as well as the cosmological!

> Rav Yehuda said in the name of Rab: All that the Holy One, blessed be He, created in His world He created male and female. Even Leviathan the slant serpent and Leviathan the twisting serpent He created male and female; and had they mated with one other they would have destroyed the whole world. (So) what did the Holy One, blessed be He, do? He castrated the male and killed the female, preserving her in salt for the righteous in the world to come, as it is said, "And He will slay the dragon in the sea" (Isaiah 27.1) ... (And the reason He killed her was because) fish are dissolute. The general theme of the profusion of the primordial waters is now condensed around two sea creatures. Nevertheless, here again we have a myth in which a threat to the world due to sexual profligacy is aborted—this time by castration and killing.... One may even suspect that the prototype for such primordial proliferation goes back to ancient

---

stars, and planets to emerge. "Our universe's chance of existence is high simply due to evolutionary selection, determined by the quantum dynamics of gravity and matter": Mersini-Houghton, ibid., 151.
15 Psalm 74.13-17; see also Isaiah 51.9-11.

Families and Dysfunctional Divinities

Mesopotamian mythology, where it is precisely the mating of the primordial sea-gods Apsu and Tiamat, and later Laḥmu and Laḥamu, that produced a proliferation of gods and a noisy commotion—all of which resulted in the great battle between Marduk and the sea monster Tiamat, and Tiamat's death.[16]

As I observed in an earlier chapter, even modern cosmologists can hardly conceive mere Nothing as anything but Chaos (in the later sense): a chaos that is always apt to subvert domestic or celestial peace, but which is also needed for the continued life of the cosmos. The Gap itself—the space between and within all bodies—turns out to determine much of our world's history: the distances between galaxies is increasing because "Space" itself is expanding. And our present world, it has been proposed, is weirdly unstable: at any moment the present "false vacuum" (the Higgs field) which determines the mass of particles may be transformed into a more stable "true vacuum" and eliminate us all.[17] The dragon in the deeps, it seems, is never wholly conquered.

In the Babylonian story (and also in the Greek) that dangerous Chaos, whether manifest in the Earth or in the Sea, is perceived as female, to be mastered, eventually, by male gods.

> She who fashions all things,
> Added matchless weapons, bore monster-serpents,
> Sharp of tooth, unsparing of fang.
> [With venom] for blood she has filled their bodies.
> Roaring dragons she has clothed with terror,
> Has crowned them with haloes, making them like gods,
> So that he who beholds them shall perish abjectly.[18]

Once defeated, Tiamat, the first mother of all gods and monsters, is made into the world:

> [Marduk] first split Tiamat in two and made heaven of one half, providing for bolts and guards so that her waters could not escape. Traversing the newly made heaven looking for a building plot, he came upon the spot where

---

16 Fishbane, *Biblical Myth*, 115–16, citing *Enuma Elish* I.1–10; IV.20–120, in Lambert, *Babylonian Creation Myths*, 51, 87.
17 See Mack, *End of Everything*, 142–43.
18 *Enuma Elish* 2.132–9, 4.70–80, in Pritchard, *Ancient Near Eastern Texts*, 64, 67.

he directly confronted Ea's dwelling, Apsu, below. Here, after first carefully measuring the shape of Apsu, he built an exact duplicate of it, his own great estate, Esharra. The text tells us that the name means "the sky." Marduk next made constellations, organized the calendar, fixed the polestar, and instructed the moon and the sun.[19]

But the original matrix is not universally female: in the Norse stories of the beginning (recorded many centuries later), told to Gylfi by three kings (the High; the Equally High; the Third), it is the giant Ymir—born in the Gap between the Fire and the Ice, and father of the (supposedly evil) Frost Giants, perpetual enemies of the gods—that is killed and dismembered by the sons of Borr:

> Harr [the High] answered: "The sons of Borr slew Ymir the giant; lo, where he fell there gushed forth so much blood out of his wounds that with it they drowned all the race of the Rime-Giants, save that one, whom giants call Bergelmir, escaped with his household; he went upon his ship, and his wife with him, and they were safe there." The sons of Borr then took "Ymir and bore him into the middle of the Yawning Void, and made of him the earth; of his blood the sea and the waters; the land was made of his flesh, and the crags of his bones; gravel and stones they fashioned from his teeth and his grinders and from those bones that were broken." And Jafnharr [the Equally High] said: "Of the blood, which ran and welled forth freely out of his wounds, they made the sea, when they had formed and made firm the earth together, and laid the sea in a ring round about her; and it may well seem a hard thing to most men to cross over it." Then said Thridi [the Third]: "They took his skull also, and made of it the heaven, and set it up over the earth with four corners; and under each corner they set a dwarf: the names of these are East, West, North, and South. Then they took the glowing embers and sparks that burst forth and had been cast out of Muspellheim, and set them in the midst of the Yawning Void, in the heaven, both above and below, to illumine heaven and earth. They assigned places to all fires: to some in heaven;

---

19 Jacobsen, *Treasures*, 179, summarizing *Enuma Elish* 4.135–5.22; see Pritchard, *Ancient Near Eastern Texts*, 67–68; see Schweizer, *Sungod's Journey through the Netherworld*, 167–68.

some wandered free under the heavens; nevertheless, to these also they gave a place, and shaped them courses. It is said in old songs, that from these the days were reckoned, and the tale of years told, as is said in *Voluspa*: 'The sun knew not where she had housing; The moon knew not what might he had; The stars knew not where stood their places. Thus was it ere the earth was fashioned.'"[20]

Our world is constructed from the ruins of an older world — as many modern cosmologists hope may really be true: that our "Big Bang" was an emergent bubble from an older and wider world, or else a "white hole" that reversed the "black hole" in which that older world had perished. The temptation to believe in an eternally oscillating reality, forever interrupted by the "conflagration" which eliminates all distinctions, is as powerful now as ever. The fire and ice — or perhaps either the fire or the ice — will overwhelm us — but we may hope that a new world will emerge again. "In that time the earth shall emerge out of the sea, and shall then be green and fair; then shall the fruits of it be brought forth unsown,"[21] and the Golden Age return, at least for a little while.

The partial and temporary victory over Chaos does not eliminate all quarrels, either among the immortal gods of Greece or the long-lived gods of Egypt and the North. In the Hebrew stories God Himself stands above all such quarrels more unambiguously than Zeus: in the beginning it was He who alone made heaven and earth by His mere word. The gods of the nations are said to be His subordinates, even if those other nations are permitted to harass and conquer the "chosen people." Even before those nations began, dispersed from the failed and fabled Tower of Babel,[22] we managed to quarrel and kill each other, and the stories of those killings and betrayals constitute the acknowledged history of the Hebrews and us all, from Cain's killing of his brother onwards. The message in all the traditions, whether couched as stories about gods or merely about our human ancestors, seems to be that we do not, or cannot, avoid such quarrels, and that we shall all suffer the effects.

---

20 Sturluson, *Prose Edda*, 19–20 ("Beguiling of Gylfi," ch. 7).
21 Sturluson, *Prose Edda*, 83 ("Beguiling of Gylfi," ch. 53).
22 Genesis 11.1–9.

> In that time [which is all times] brothers shall slay each other for greed's sake, and none shall spare father or son in manslaughter and in incest; so it says in *Voluspa*: Brothers shall strive and slaughter each other; Own sisters' children shall sin together; ill days among men, many a whoredom: An axe-age, a sword-age, shields shall be cloven; A wind-age, a wolf-age, ere the world totters.[23]

Sudden disasters, "acts of God," will overthrow established empires — and those empires will thereby be proved wanting, as a warning to later humanity:

> Now this was the sin of your sister Sodom: She and her daughters were arrogant, overfed and unconcerned; they did not help the poor and needy. They were haughty and did detestable things before me. Therefore I did away with them as you have seen. Samaria did not commit half the sins you did. You have done more detestable things than they, and have made your sisters seem righteous by all these things you have done. Bear your disgrace, for you have furnished some justification for your sisters. Because your sins were more vile than theirs, they appear more righteous than you. So then, be ashamed and bear your disgrace, for you have made your sisters appear righteous.[24]

"Believing in God" or at least the God of Abraham, whatever else it is, is a commitment to the possibility and eventual success of Justice. Believers bind themselves to a cause, and nourish their commitment by reciting and acting out the stories that give weight and sense to it — which is not simply to the present order of society, but to an hypothesized ideal: to do justice and love mercy. Marx was right at least in this: "Religion is the sigh of the oppressed creature, the heart of a heartless world, and the soul of soulless conditions. It is the opium of the people."[25] The point of religion, or religion of the mainstream Abrahamic sort,

---

23 Sturluson, *Prose Edda*, 77–78 ("Beguiling of Gylfi," ch. 51).
24 Ezekiel 16.49–52; see also Isaiah 3.9; Jeremiah 23.14. The repeated attempt to blame Sodom's fall on her citizens' supposed toleration of "sodomy" is inane. The charge is that Sodom and Samaria had neglected and oppressed the poor, threatened guests with forced buggery or gang rape, and idolatrously preferred demons to the God of Justice.
25 Marx, "Critique of Hegel's Philosophy of Right: Introduction," 57.

is not, *pace* Marx's own inference, to reconcile us to iniquity, but to remind us of an alternative. A belief in God's Omnipotence does not necessarily require that we believe that everything that now happens is His Will, but that His Will shall prevail, His Kingdom come. "Magna est veritas, et praevalebit." Believing in the Divine Trinity is believing in the possibility and hope of love, the community of the holy ones.

> May not Christians... be allowed to believe the divinity of our Saviour, or that in Him God and man make one Person, and be verily persuaded thereof, so far as for such faith or belief to become a real principle of life and conduct? inasmuch as, by virtue of such persuasion, they submit to His government, believe His doctrine, and practise His precepts, although they form no abstract idea of the union between the divine and human nature; nor may be able to clear up the notion of *person* to the contentment of a minute philosopher.[26]

This interpretation of doctrine seems easier in supposedly "primitive" religions. Raising sceptical doubts about the actors who don ceremonial masks to impersonate or represent the many gods of popular Hindu religion, or Voodoo, or the Australian Dreamtime, looks much like the crasser forms of Christian missionary endeavour. It would be like telling Star Trek enthusiasts that there is no Federation, or that Vulcans and Earth-humans could not possibly interbreed. It is more easily assumed that even Star Trek enthusiasts know that very well, and that even "primitive polytheists" are aware that they are *acting*.

And why not? The very thing that makes us human (maybe) is our imaginative capacity, our talent and our desire for imaginative fictions that can gather up our manifold experience, offer engaging characters and plots for ourselves to take on board, and unite into a single story people who might otherwise be enemies. Unlike other animals — at least as we conceive them — we each live within at least two worlds: the world of ordinary sensibilia, and the world of imagination. Sometimes that imagined world so permeates the sensible that we see no difference. Sometimes

---

26 Berkeley, *Alciphron* (Euphranor speaks): *Works* 3:298; see my "Berkeley's Philosophy of Religion."

we can convince ourselves that the imagined world is *more* real than the sensible. The epic of an expanding universe, dark matter, black holes, and supernovas sprinkling the elements of life around the galaxies impresses us as "real," even though we mostly pay no attention at all to it. We may be the more easily persuaded that traditional religion teaches truth precisely because the gods it imagines are obviously present with us, in ordinary life as well as ceremonial. No one can seriously doubt the reality of Aphrodite, or Ares, or Apollo, whether they are gods or demons or only allegorical fictions. And as Apollonius is said to have remarked, "I do not think it a sign of modesty to be on bad terms with any of the gods, as Hippolytus was with Aphrodite. It is more modest to speak well of every god."[27]

Poets and fantasists nowadays don't invent new gods, but they do invent characters and superheroes, which then become common stock for individual and collective fantasy. We know very well that Sherlock Holmes, James Bond and Wonder Woman "don't exist," any more than Santa Claus or Terry Pratchett's Death. But we also know that these characters are influential, and can be invoked to structure our personal motives. It is pointless, naïve, absurdly literal-minded, to complain about an author's obvious inconsistencies or creative attitude to history — unless the critic is cooperating in creating the imagined world,[28] or unless she has her own commitments to a different theme than the author's. In either case the point would not be to insist that the created world is at odds with "reason," or is not "realistic," but at most that the unchallenged inconsistency disturbs our aesthetic trance. Artists, authors, and the founders of religions are expanding our imaginative experience, sometimes roughly. Whether we are inspired to join them in their endeavour, or to denounce them in whatever terms we wish, is not a matter for *reason* to decide, but imagination and desire.

---

27 Philostratus, *Life of Apollonius*, 2:101 [6.3.5], referring to Theseus's son Hippolytus, said to have foolishly insulted Aphrodite (see Euripides, *Hippolytus*).
28 Consider the "Great Game" invented by Ronald Knox in 1912, and played by other Sherlockians since: for example, was Dr. Watson wounded in leg or shoulder, and was he "John" or "James"? Or better suppose that he was "John Hamish," and "James" a wifely joke: see Sayers, *Unpopular Opinions*, 148-51.

GENESIS

So the stories may be read as moral warnings more easily than as metaphysical cyphers. Do they perhaps have a more positive moral too? Some at least of the stories emphasise our common ancestry, and this is intended to have some eirenic effect.

> Thus, for example, in 1625, the philosopher Nathanael Carpenter in his *Geography* maintained that Moses' motivation, in writing his genealogical lists, was so that all people would understand themselves to be descended from the same original "then which there is no greater meanes to conciliate and ioyne mens affections for mutuall amitie and conversation" (*Geography Delineated Forth in Two Books* [Oxford, 1625], 2:207). Similarly, in 1656, the year of La Peyrère's *Men before Adam*, John White remarked in his commentary on Genesis that the reason for God's having created only one couple was to unite all men in love to one another so that "we cannot shut up our bowels of compassion from any man, of what Nation or Kindred soever he be" (*A Commentary upon the Three First Chapters of Genesis* [London, 1656], 1:111). Some forty years later, Richard Kidder, Bishop of Bath and Wells, suggested that the origin of all people was from one man to ensure that claims of racial superiority could not arise, that "men might not boast and vaunt of their extraction and original... and that they might think themselves under an obligation to love and assist each other as proceeding from the same original and common parent" (*A Commentary on the Five Books of Moses* [London, 1694], 1:6).[29]

This was also the chief reason for the widespread medieval belief that there were no habitable lands on the other side of the world: the earth, undoubtedly, was a globe, but the other side, being inaccessible because of the trackless ocean and the impassable heats of the equator, could not—they supposed—have been colonized by our human ancestors. We had better suppose, like Palamas, that there was only landless ocean there, rather than run the risk of encountering or imagining "people" unrelated to

---

29 Almond, "Adam, Pre-Adamites, and Extra-Terrestrial Beings in Early Modern Europe," 168–69.

ourselves.³⁰ Augustine had the same problem.³¹ The discovery that tropic heats and the wastes of water are not after all impassable, and that we have human cousins of the same stock on the other side of the world, has resolved that issue—though nowadays we wonder and worry instead about the possibility of encountering "people" of a sort on *other* worlds.

The obvious retort is that family feeling does not, in practice, seem to count for much. It may be true that people often do recognize strangers as "human" despite their difference, and feel some slight affection for the human form itself. Certainly, they should.

> Mutual attraction between [humans] is also something natural. Consequently, the mere fact that someone is [human] makes it incumbent on another [human] not to regard him as alien.³²

Unfortunately, this dictum has often been used to make the further claim, that "everything else was created for the sake of [humans] and gods, but these for the sake of community and society; consequently [humans] can make beasts serve their own ends without contravening rights."³³ This (Stoic) opinion has had a long life. According to the *Catechism of the Catholic Church*:

> Of all visible creatures only man [*homo*] is "able to know and love his creator." He is "the only creature on earth that God has willed for its own sake," and he alone is called to share, by knowledge and love, in God's own life. It was for this end that he was created, and this is the fundamental reason for his dignity. Being in the image of God the human individual possesses the dignity of a person, who is not just something, but someone. He is capable of self-knowledge, of self-possession and of freely

---

30 Palamas, *The 150 Chapters*, 9–14.
31 Augustine, *City of God*, 664 [16.9].
32 Cicero, *On Ends* 3.62–8 (Cato speaks, on behalf of Stoic philosophers), in Long and Sedley, *Hellenistic Philosophers*, 1:348 [57F]. Long and Sedley misleadingly translate "homo" as "man" rather than "human."
33 Long and Sedley, *Hellenistic Philosophers*, 1:349, citing Chrysippus. The claim can be given some slight force by the suggestion that only humans and gods have any concept of the world as a whole: other creatures—or so we suppose—are aware only of their own little worlds (see my "Going Beyond Our Worlds").

giving himself and entering into communion with other persons. And he is called by grace to a covenant with his Creator, to offer him a response of faith and love that no other creature can give in his stead.[34]

The *Catechism* goes on to insist, on the word of John Chrysostom, that man is "more precious in the eyes of God than all other creatures! For him the heavens and the earth, the sea and all the rest of creation exist."[35] The same assumption is routinely made in seemingly secular circles nowadays, without even the faint excuses provided by Stoic philosophy or (faulty) biblical exegesis. Apollonius drew a different moral from our supposed priority: "everything Earth produces is for humanity's sake, and those who are willing to live at peace with animals have need of nothing. They can gather or reap, as the seasons dictate, from the nourishing earth. But some people, as if deaf to the earth, sharpen knives against animals for the sake of clothing and food."[36]

The humanistic assumptions involved are, I think, unwarranted. But it is worth looking again at the Creation narratives of *Genesis* with these thoughts in mind. Their significance as *foundational myths* is perhaps more important than their apparent cosmological or historical meaning.

> The opening statement [of the Book of Genesis] that in the beginning God created the world...was not meant as a speculation about the origin of the natural order in past history at all, but rather as a poem about the world which *could* be created by God-in-man if man lived up to his full human stature; nature appears in the story as the No-thing out of which the world is to be made, the chance realm which is fundamentally "without form and void," although it throws up, purely *by* chance, patterns which can be starting-points for creating a world.[37]

---

34 CCC 356–57, www.vatican.va/archive/ENG0015/_INDEX.HTM.
35 John Chrysostom, *In Gen. sermo* 2, 1, in *Patrologia Graeca* 54:587D–588A. So also Apollonius: "mankind has a sort of kinship with God, and hence he is the only animal who knows the gods, and speculates about his own nature and in what way he partakes of divinity": Philostratus, *Life of Apollonius*, 2:347 [8.7.20]. Neither Chrysostom nor Apollonius seem to have worried about the roots of this conviction.
36 Philostratus, *Life of Apollonius*, 2:339 [8.7.13].
37 Wren-Lewis, "What I Believe," 236.

The priestly author of the first chapter of Genesis was seeking to put the world in imaginative order, to describe—and so create for his readers—a sense of the cosmos around us not as an arena of oppressive powers but as an available, orderly home. Even the Mesopotamian stories can be read to similar effect:

> World origins, it holds, are essentially accidental: gods were born out of a mingling of the primeval waters and they engendered other gods. The active nature of the gods led to conflict with the older powers who stood for inertia, repose, and, in subtle ways, for the dead hand of a powerful old cultural tradition. World ordering is essentially the outcome of youthful leadership: conscious, creative intelligence in a born ruler, Marduk. He created the present universe, overcame old fears and hatreds by magnanimously granting amnesty to the gods he captured in battle, provided the gods with leisure (based on the slave labor of man), and assigned them offices in his administration. Thus was the world established as a state, a well-run paternalistic monarchy with permanent king, capital, parliament, and royal palace in Babylon. As a view of world order this is in many ways impressive. It sees the universe as grounded in divine power and divine will: even those wills traditionally felt as older, more authoritative, or hostile, are unified under the leadership of a single ruler who governs through consultation, persuasion, and conviction. It is religiously of great profundity, leading in its picture of Marduk toward the aspects of awe and majesty. Moreover, it is intellectually admirable in providing a unifying concept of existence: political order pervades both nature and society. Finally, it is humanly satisfying: ultimate power is not estranged from mankind, but resides in gods in human form who act understandably. The universe is now moral and meaningful and expression of a creative intelligence with valid purpose: order and peace and prosperity.[38]

In those older Mesopotamian stories humankind was created, from the blood of Tiamat's general Kingu, to do the jobs that

---

38 Jacobsen, *Treasures*, 191.

the lesser gods found tedious.³⁹ In the Egyptian we were made from Atum's tears. Times changed in Mesopotamia and Egypt, allowing more hope to humans, and creating a civilized order. In the Hebrew story we are made to be God's viceroys and representatives in an open world: the *political* effect especially is different.

Hanegraaff offers a similar reading of the story in the Hermetic text *Poimandres*, while still supposing that the Genesis story is a simple creation myth.

> As for *Corpus Hermeticum* I, I would see it as a prime example of the phenomenon ... of a text getting misframed as something different from what it really was. Reassured by apparent similarities with the Genesis account and probably adapting it further to fit Christian tastes, scribes and scholars miscategorized as a creation myth what was in fact the account of a visionary revelation.⁴⁰

The cosmological sense of the stories should not be ignored: that the world of our experience is brought into being simply by God's Word is a deliberate change from earlier and cruder myths. It is an answer to the cosmological query from which I began this study: why is there anything at all? But the world it describes is still the world *as it is for us*: the world of our possible experience and action. And it seems that there is a subtext in later poems and prophecies which involves a primordial battle with the Sea and its monsters. The world is laid out for us to love and embellish, allowing each level of being its due, but this is not entirely without its risks.

> Our analysis of biblical myth and mythmaking has focused on this *agon* model, because it allows us to see how the common ancient Near Eastern *topos* of divine combat with the sea was realized in Israelite sources. Careful analysis shows that, at the level of imagery and terminology, there is no disjunction between the pagan and monotheistic texts, and in fact many of the

---

39 See *Enuma Elish* 6.1–10, in Pritchard, *Ancient Near Eastern Texts*, 68: "Blood I [Marduk] will mass and cause bones to be. I will establish a savage, 'man' shall be his name. Verily, savage-man I will create. He shall be charged with the service of the gods that they might be at ease!" See Jacobsen, *Treasures*, 117–18, 180–81.
40 Hanegraaff, *Hermetic Spirituality*, 139, speaking of *Poimandres* (Copenhaver, *Hermetica*, 1–7).

nominalizations of the sea (Yam, Leviathan, Nahash) and its attributes (*bariaḥ* and *ʾqalaṭon*) comport with common Canaanite prototypes. At the same time, there is no indication in the biblical materials that the sea is a fully distinct divine personality with its own biography, as we can know it from Canaanite texts, or that the theomachy is a recurrent seasonal phenomenon. Rather, in a distinctive manner, the biblical versions link the prototypical conflict at the beginning of the world order (*Urzeit*) with its recurrence within the sacred history of Israel during the exodus from Egypt, and its anticipated recurrence in new forms thereafter, up to and including the final defeat of the sea in the future (*Endzeit*).[41]

"In that day YHWH will punish, with His cruel, great, (and) mighty sword, Leviathan the slant serpent (*naḥash bariaḥ*), Leviathan the twisting serpent (*naḥash ʾqalaṭon*); He will slay the dragon (*tanin*) in the sea."[42] Creation is not yet complete.

So the story of our descent from the first human couple (and our descent from the remnant left alive from Noah's Flood) was to be believed on moral more than historical grounds (like the suggestion that the other side of the world is largely ocean): it asserted our common humanity (and also acknowledged our constant failure to live up to that humanity). So also the Hebrew Creation story established, for better or worse, our human pre-eminence. We are not, it seems, merely side-effects of a chaotic cosmos, an afterthought, but called to complete creation. The power that brought Adam and Eve safely out of the Garden, Noah's family from the Flood, and Israel out of Egypt, will also save Jerusalem from herself.

The other biblical creation story, solely of Adam and Eve, has a further moral, to outline the roots of our constant failure to live out the vision. The story is about us all, not simply a fable about the putative parents of all humankind—a fable which is now difficult to believe, in the face of palaeontological and genetic evidence. It

---

41 Fishbane, *Biblical Myth*, 63–64; see ibid., 41: "All these cross-references and shared depictions suggest that ancient Israel drew upon a bundle of mythic traditions that circulated throughout the Syro-Palestinian region, and used them in order to depict battles against sea dragons—albeit for its own purposes and in its own ways."
42 Isaiah 27.1.

Families and Dysfunctional Divinities

may be, of course, that the fable was never truly intended to be about the very first human beings: notoriously, Adam's and Eve's sons needed wives from somewhere. Perhaps we are dealing not with the failures of the very first humans, but of the very first prophets, drawn out, like later prophets, from the common mass of the people (or at least the first recorded prophets). But taking the fable on its word, what was the mistake our first parents were thought to have made, and why should it matter to us?

"In the middle of the garden, [the Lord God] set the tree of life and the tree of the knowledge of good and evil,"[43] and told Adam not to eat from the second tree. That is, the Lord God set before them the same choice as in a book about later events: "the choice of life and good, or death and evil."[44] "The knowledge of good and evil," in brief, is itself death and evil: the habit of discriminating and dismissing any part of the creation. The serpent, it is said, suggested that by eating from the tree of knowledge we would be "like gods"[45]—but not, it turned out, like the gods we were meant to be.[46] What did the choice amount to? Adam had already named each living creature[47] before he was divided into male and female: that is, he already knew their names and natures. So if Adam already knew the names and natures of all living creatures, what did "the knowledge of good and evil" add? We begin to experience some things, some creatures, as "good" and some as "evil," whereas the Lord God "hates nothing that He has made."[48] We learnt discrimination, and so condemnation. The antidote conceived, for example, in the words of Jesus, is that we should not "judge,"[49] nor seek to disentangle "good" and "evil" influences,[50] but behave "like God," so "that you may be the children of your Father who is in heaven: for he makes his sun

---

43 Genesis 2.9.
44 Deuteronomy 30.15.
45 Genesis 3.5.
46 That serpent, we must presume, had itself eaten the fruit, and was coiled about the tree, like the dragon Lagon who guarded the apples of the Hesperides: "an immortal dragon with a hundred heads, offspring of Typhon and Echidna, which spoke with many and diverse sorts of voices": see Apollodorus, *Library*, 2.5.11.
47 Genesis 2.19–20.
48 Wisdom of Solomon 1.24.
49 Matthew 7.1–3.
50 Matthew 13.24–30.

to rise on the evil and on the good, and sends rain on the just and on the unjust."[51]

The effect of this mistake in our relations with the nonhuman as well as the human is that we think creatures "good" if they serve our purposes, and enemies or vermin if they don't. Before we began to discriminate, we could acknowledge that all things created were, in their way, beautiful—and this thought does still surface in both pagan and Abrahamic literature. As Aristotle said, there is something wonderful and beautiful in even the smallest, commonest, and apparently "base" of living creatures.[52] If we are ever to be "holy" we must love even our enemies, even "vermin," and so realize that they are not vermin. According to Muslim tradition, "One day Jesus was walking with his followers, and they passed by the carcass of a dog. The followers said, 'How this dog stinks!' But Jesus said, 'How white are its teeth.'"[53] "To the pure all things are pure."[54]

Another way of allegorizing the story of Adam and Eve and the Snake—one rather more in accord with other late antique philosophy—was expounded by Augustine: the original wisdom of the androgynous Adam was first divided into two, representing an old distinction between Wisdom (*sapientia*) and Knowledge (*scientia*), which were meant to work together.[55] Such allegorizing was familiar, practised—as we have seen—by pagan and Jewish philosophers as well as Christian:

> Are the stories related by your inspired Hesiod in the form of a myth about the woman [Pandora] to be interpreted allegorically when they say that she was given to men by Zeus as an evil, as the price of the fire, whereas you think that there is no deeper and hidden meaning

---

51 Matthew 5.45; cf. *Ennead* IV.4 [28].42, 1517: "the wicked draw water from the streams and that which gives does not know itself to what it gives, but only gives."
52 Aristotle, *De Partibus Animalium* 1.645a15f.
53 Meyer, *Unknown Sayings*, 140, after al-Ghazali, *Revival of the Religious Sciences* 3.108.
54 Titus 1.15.
55 Augustine, *On the Trinity*, 102 [12.25]: "to wisdom belongs the intellectual cognition of eternal things, but to knowledge the reasonable cognition of temporal things." In Greek the distinction is between *Sophia* and *Phronesis* (which are virtues), or else *Nous* and *Dianoia* (which are distinct faculties or even distinct elements).

at all in the story that the woman was taken and made by God from the rib of the man who fell asleep after a trance? But it is not treating the matter fairly to refuse to laugh at the former as being a legend, and to admire the philosophical truths contained in it, and yet to sneer at the biblical stories and think that they are worthless, your judgment being based upon the literal meaning alone.... Are the Greeks alone allowed to find philosophical truths in a hidden form, and the Egyptians too, and all barbarians whose pride is in mysteries and in the truth which they contain?[56]

On Augustine's account the story is about the relationship between different modes of thought: our *knowing* part, sadly, was (and is) tempted to rely entirely on what is experienced through the senses we share with beasts, and so to corrupt the original vision. From that failure stems our own reliance on material things and sensual appetite: jealousy and possessiveness, fratricide and war.

> Whenever that carnal or animal sense, therefore, forces upon the intention of the mind, which uses the living force of reason in temporal and corporeal things for the purpose of carrying out its functions, some inducement to enjoy itself, that is, to enjoy itself just as in some private and personal good and not as in a public and common good, which is an unchangeable good, then the serpent, as it were, addresses the woman. But to consent to this inducement is to eat of the forbidden tree.[57]

This Augustinian reading, unfortunately, plays neatly into the humanistic arrogance I have identified before, and also the masculine tendency to think women, at best, merely "helpmates." Augustine himself acknowledges that women "are with us co-heirs

---

56 Origen, *Contra Celsum*, 213 [4.38].
57 Augustine, *On the Trinity*, 95 [12.12]. Plotinus similarly blames our "fall" into merely material existence on *tolma*: we lose our grip on intelligible reality when we're bored with being together and each seek to have all things *our* own way (*Ennead* V.1 [10].1). Or as George MacDonald put it: "the one principle of Hell is 'I am my own. I am my own king and my own subject. I am the centre from which go out my thoughts; I am the object and end of my thoughts; back upon *me* as the alpha and omega of life, my thoughts return'" (MacDonald, "Kingship," in *Unspoken Sermons*, 158); see also www.online-literature.com/george-macdonald/unspoken-sermons/30/ (accessed January 19, 2023).

of grace,"[58] and that "the image of God does not remain except in that part of the mind of man [humanity] in which it clings to the contemplation and consideration of the eternal reasons, which, as is evident, not only men but also women possess."[59] But the damage remains.

SUB-CREATION

"The god was never a symbol or hieroglyph representing the sun. The sun was a hieroglyph representing the god. Primitive man... went out with his head full of gods and heroes, because that is the chief use of having a head."[60]

Human beings tell stories. Whether any other earthly creatures do, we cannot tell, but it is very easy to pretend that this is a special excellence of our humanity, another imagined proof that we have access to worlds beyond our own. Many of our stories are hardly more than gossip, and perhaps a necessary device for maintaining group cohesion. Dunbar has argued indeed that we need to gossip because even small human tribes have too many members for the older primate system of mutual grooming to keep us all together.[61] When we need to unify still larger groups, of people we haven't met, we can share at least the common stories of gods and heroes, or exemplary regions and households. Our conversation can be about Odysseus or Moses, monarchs, or sportsmen, or singers, or celebrities, or about imaginary characters in soap operas or long-running dramas. Not all such characters are admired: they are merely worth remembering, talking about or mocking. Sometimes they have been created of set purpose by the rulers of our day, as openly propagandistic icons. Sometimes they have only emerged into popular esteem from the works of particular artists: Sherlock Holmes or James Bond or Superman or Miss Marple. All such characters outlive their makers, and take on manifold descriptions—as did the heroes of Greek myth in multiple Attic tragedies.

---

58 Augustine, *On the Trinity* 91 [12.12], citing Galatians 3.26-8: "in Christ, there is neither Jew nor Greek, there is neither slave nor freeman, there is neither male nor female." Augustine still, unfortunately, reveals in his language ("women are with *us* co-heirs of grace") that he thinks he is writing exclusively for *men*.
59 Augustine, *On the Trinity*, 92 [12.12].
60 Chesterton, "The Priest of Spring," in *Miscellany of Men*, 53-54.
61 Dunbar, *Grooming, Gossip, and the Evolution of Language*.

Families and Dysfunctional Divinities

The stories, and their constant characters, can be projected onto the local landscape. Even now we like to visit places with particular, personal, tribal, or national associations, and quarrel a little (or a lot) over the precise stories we hope to remember there: are we to think of a local benefactor with affection, or of a known slavetrader with contempt? Is Ayodhya to be remembered as Rama's birthplace or the ancient Babri Masjid mosque?[62] Is Uluru the same as Ayers Rock? Are Londonderry and Doire Colmcille [aka Derry] the same place?

> The answer is first that no proper name of place or person names any place or person *as such*; it names *in the first instance only for* those who are members of some particular linguistic and cultural community, by identifying places and persons in terms of the scheme of identification shared by, and perhaps partly constitutive of, that community. The relation of a proper name to its bearer cannot be elucidated without reference to such identifying functions. And secondly that "Dore Colmcille" names— embodies a communal intention of naming—a place with a continuous identity ever since it became in fact St. Columba's oak grove in 546, and that "Londonderry" names a settlement made only in the seventeenth century, and presupposes the legitimacy of that settlement and of the use of the English language to name it.[63]

In any case we cannot easily escape the memories.

In times past we also projected the stories on the heavens, so that the sun's passage spoke to us of past and future Pharaohs, or the Pleiades of gossipy stories about young men and maidens. We wrote the stories on the heavens, and maybe longer ago than is now easily imagined. Whether the stars are really gods matters less, on this account, than that we see the gods in them.

> Let us assume for the moment...that nothing actually exists corresponding to the "gods" of mythology: no personalities, only astronomical or meteorological objects. Then these natural objects can only be arrayed with a personal significance and glory by a gift, the gift of a

---

62 See Gandhi, *Sita's Kitchen*, for an attempted theoretical reconciliation of that dispute, which climaxed, in 1992, in the destruction of the mosque.
63 MacIntyre, "Relativism, Power and Philosophy," 7.

person, of a man. Personality can only be derived from a person. The gods may derive their colour and beauty from the high splendours of nature, but it was Man who obtained these for them, abstracted them from sun and moon and cloud; their personality they get direct from him; the shadow or flicker of divinity that is upon them they receive through him from the invisible world, the Supernatural.[64]

And this, so Tolkien proposed, is as it should be:

> Though all the crannies of the world we filled with Elves and Goblins, though we dared to build Gods and their houses out of dark and light, and sowed the seed of dragons, 'twas our right (used or misused). The right has not decayed. We make still by the law in which we're made.[65]

He even suggested that our inventions might eventually be endorsed:

> So great is the bounty with which he [Christian Man] has been treated that he may now, perhaps, fairly dare to guess that in Fantasy he may actually assist in the effoliation and multiple enrichment of creation. All tales may come true; and yet, at the last, redeemed, they may be as like and as unlike the forms that we give them as Man, finally redeemed, will be like and unlike the fallen that we know.[66]

Our fictions, properly developed, will then have wills and purposes of their own. Perhaps they do already.

One response may be to denounce all this as idolatry, and to hope—like Sprat—that these fancies can all be forgotten. It is an old dispute. In late antiquity some thinkers at least were ready to insist that art objects *could* be given life, or else the life recognized in them.

> A particularly difficult moment occurs when Hermes remarks that humans imitate the supreme Creator by making terrestrial gods. Evidently Asclepius's face betrays incredulity or even stupefaction about that statement, for

---

64 Tolkien, "On Fairy Stories," in *Monsters and the Critics*, 123.
65 Tolkien, "Mythopoeia," in *Tree and Leaf*, 87; see also Tolkien, "On Fairy Stories," in *Monsters and the Critics*, 143–45.
66 Tolkien, "On Fairy Stories," in *Monsters and the Critics*, 156–57.

Families and Dysfunctional Divinities

Hermes interrupts his discourse to address him directly: "Does that cause you to wonder, or do you too have doubts, like so many?" Asclepius readily admits to being confused and at a loss about what to say, but declares himself willing to be convinced. Clearly his puzzlement remains, for a similar prickly moment occurs not much further on, when an evidently still incredulous Asclepius blurts out "You aren't talking about statues, are you?," to which Hermes responds with evident irritation: "It is you who are talking about statues! Look at your incredulity...You are talking about beings endowed with *nous* and spirit [*pneuma*] and call them 'statues'..."[67]

Asclepius is startled by the claim, but might have been eased into a readier acceptance by noting, along with Nilus Scholasticus some centuries later (born c. AD 400), that *all* statues are somehow infused with life:

"All Satyrs are fond of jeering," Nilus playfully asks a statue, "but tell me, thou too, why, looking at everyone, dost thou pour forth this laughter?" And the statue replies "I laugh because I marvel how, being put together out of all kinds of stones, I suddenly became a Satyr."[68]

The same author, speaking of a Christian icon: "How daring it is to give form to the incorporeal! But yet an image [of the archangel Michael] beckons us to spiritual recollection of heavenly beings."[69] So also Agathias (AD 536–582):

Greatly daring was the wax that formed the image of the invisible Prince of the Angels, incorporeal in the essence of his form. But yet it is not without grace; for a man looking at the image directs his mind to a higher contemplation. No longer has he a confused veneration, but imprinting the image in himself he fears him as if he were present. The eyes stir up the depths of the spirit, and Art can convey by colours the prayers of the soul.[70]

---

67 Hanegraaff, *Hermetic Spirituality*, 65, citing *Asclepius* 23–24 according to the Coptic version recovered from Nag Hammadi (NH VI8, 69); cf. Copenhaver, *Hermetica*, 81 (this latter version, from the Latin text, sounds rather less irritated).
68 Paton, *Greek Anthology*, 5:307 [16.247].
69 Paton, *Greek Anthology*, 1:31 [1.33].
70 Paton, *Greek Anthology*, 1:34, quoted by Mathew, *Byzantine Aesthetics*, 78.

Other thinkers insisted instead that all such idols, even Christian icons, be demolished: the only secure or lasting centre for our loyalty and national attention must be the One Creator. And this too is an old idea:

> Numa [753-672 BC] ascribed the greater part of his oracular teachings to the Muses, and he taught the Romans to pay especial honours to one Muse in particular, whom he called Tacita, that is, the silent, or speechless one; thereby perhaps handing on and honouring the Pythagorean precept of silence (*ekhemuthia*). Furthermore, his ordinances concerning images are altogether in harmony with the doctrines of Pythagoras. For that philosopher maintained that the first principle of being was beyond sense or feeling, was invisible and uncreated, and discernible only by the mind. And in like manner Numa forbade the Romans to revere an image of God which had the form of man or beast. Nor was there among them in this earlier time any painted or graven likeness of Deity, but while for the first hundred and seventy years they were continually building temples and establishing sacred shrines, they made no statues in bodily form for them, convinced that it was impious to liken higher things to lower, and that it was impossible to apprehend Deity except by the intellect (*noesis*).[71]

Even Byzantine Christians who defended icons against the iconoclasts conceded that there might be problems—especially with statues:

> In reference to icons, we should be confident that every work made in the name of God is good and holy. But stay away from idols and statues. For these as well as their makers are evil and portentous. An icon of a holy prophet is one thing, a statue or a small figure of Cronos, Aphrodite, the Sun or the Moon is another.[72]

"Good" Hebrew kings like Hezekiah tore down "idolatrous" images, in obedience to the command of their jealous God.[73]

---

71 Plutarch, *Numa* 8.6-8, cited by Buxton, *Forms*, 184. Note that Pythagoras himself [570-495 BC] could not be Numa's source: "Silence," as an inspiration, preceded him.
72 John of Damascus, *Orationes de imaginibus tres* 3.73, quoted by Papaioannou, *Michael Psellus*, 180.
73 2 Kings 18.3-8.

"Bad" kings, like Ahab, took it that it was his royal right to slander, rob and murder.[74] The only accepted "images" of God were the ordinary living human beings that Egyptian texts had also considered part of "the sacred herd of God."[75] We had better prefer the *real* living beings.

> Are not the more lifelike statues the more beautiful ones, even if others are better proportioned? And is not an uglier living man more beautiful than the beautiful man in a statue?[76]

But are we sure that Hermes was incorrect, along with "Egyptian wise men," to suppose that pictures or even statues might be infused with "real life" of their own? Certainly Isaiah (c. 760–c. 690 BC) mocked those who cut down a tree and shape it for different aims: "some of it he takes and warms himself; some he kindles and bakes bread on it; and some he makes into a god and prostrates himself, shaping it into an idol and bowing down before it."[77] Herodotus reports a different moral, telling of Amasis, who made himself king of Egypt.[78] Finding that the Egyptians despised him for his common birth, he had a footbath (in which the courtiers had vomited and pissed, as well as washing their feet) made into a golden statue, to which they paid great reverence. Pointing this out to them, he insisted that he too should now be reverenced: what mattered was the function, not the stuff. And some Egyptians, at least, would be ready to admit that Amasis himself could be present through the statue. Is that enough?

> The Hermes who speaks in the *Logos Teleios* [aka *Asclepius*] may be sincere in his praise of statue animation, but his pious convictions are clearly old-fashioned and quite naïve. He still believes that statues can come alive and the true gods inhabit them as long as the sacred practice of daily sacrifice continues; but in fact he is being duped by ruthless priests of Neilos's ilk. He does not realize that the entire machinery of temple worship no longer serves

---

74 I Kings 21.1–29.
75 Hornung, *Conceptions of God*, 138.
76 *Ennead* VI.7 [38].22, 30–32.
77 Isaiah 44.15–16; see also Wisdom of Solomon 13.11–14.10; 15.7–13.
78 Herodotus, *Histories* 2.172.

divinity but has fallen under the control of the enemy—
those very same "wicked angels" that (in his own words)
are teaching "unnatural things" to human beings and try to
poison their souls through the passions of the body. That
statues come alive is an illusion produced by technical arti-
fice, as Zosimos [of Panopolis] knows all too well. However,
the daily sacrificial practice of statue animation does have
the effect of attracting daimons, because such entities are
nourished and replenished by the incense and smoke. In
other words, although the statues are empty of any divine
power, the temples are in fact full of sinister daimons![79]

It does not seem necessary to suppose that the statues "literally" moved: they "came alive" in imagination as the outward form of those internal statues that Plotinus urged us to polish. But it is indeed also possible that they were sometimes mechanical artefacts:

Aristotle reported that Democritus described statues that
were made to move by pouring quicksilver, analogous to
the human *psychê*, into them. If such a thing existed, it
may have been moved by magnets. And, although after
Plato's era, Pliny the Elder describes a statue of iron,
another "marvel," suspended in space by magnets at the
Temple of Arsinoe in 3rd century BC Alexandria.[80]

Whether these automata *deceived* the faithful may be moot: they would rather have been considered marvels, even if (or precisely because) human engineers had made use of the mysterious power of magnets. The real issue is whether there was anything *more* than their own imagination. Were the mechanisms *only* something that was made by men? Or were the worshippers truly encountering Another?

Isaiah's challenge emphasised the distinction between the symbols we make for ourselves and for our comfort, and the realities amongst which we live. Those who think that they can "make up" the images, rules, and standards by which they judge themselves and others cannot be confident that they themselves will hold to them in the face of threats or bribes. Why should they?

---

79 Hanegraaff, *Hermetic Spirituality*, 96, describing the attitude of Zosimos of Panopolis (fl. c. AD 300).
80 Moore, "Plato's Puppets," 42, citing Aristotle, *De Anima* 406b15-22; Pliny, *Natural History* 34.148.

The subjectivist in morals, when his moral feelings are at war with the facts about him, is always free to seek harmony by toning down the sensitiveness of the feelings. Being mere data, neither good nor evil in themselves, he may pervert them or lull them to sleep by any means at his command. Truckling, compromise, time-serving, capitulations of conscience, are conventionally opprobrious names for what, if successfully carried out, would be on his principles by far the easiest and most praiseworthy mode of bringing about that harmony between inner and outer relations which is all that he means by good. The absolute moralist, on the other hand, when his interests clash with the world, is not free to gain harmony by sacrificing the ideal interests.[81]

So even if "religion," and its associated stories, ceremonies, invocations, and ideal figures, is a human construction, a way of making a house a home or a chance-met aggregate of persons into a true community, it is probably a more stable construct if people *suppose* that it reflects or embodies reality, the way things truly are, and that it is not dependent for its power on anything we have made ourselves. Maāt, according to the Egyptian story, is both the common task for gods and humankind, "to build a living order that allows space for creative breath,"[82] and the order established "at the very beginning." It is better, that is, that the God or gods of the cult turn out to be the world's creators, that "God" (that is, the object or felt presence) turns out also to be "God" (that is, the first creator, without whom there is only "Nothing"). The only statues worth our reverence are those whose life and beauty have been discovered or invoked, and not merely invented. Conversely, the natural order of all things comes to be imagined as somehow validating or supporting more or less "humane" values. The connection may be hard to make. In the old cultic Credo of the Hebrews, so von Rad proposed, "there was nothing about Creation": what came first was the saving history, and it took time and effort to make a connection between that

---

81 James, "Rationality, Activity and Faith," 82.
82 Hornung, *Conceptions of God*, 216. Euthyphro and Socrates agreed: our task was to join the gods in making many and beautiful things (Plato, *Euthyphro* 13d—a passage often ignored because Socrates demands further detail).

and the wider, cosmic story.[83] That connection—the claim that the one focus of our own loyalty is really and truly the Creator and Lord of all (for how else can we be confident of its eventual triumph?)—does raise further problems, which I shall address later. Is the cosmos really and truly ever on "our" side? Is it not evident that it is sometimes very much against us, and that God or the gods have gone?

Disasters are a problem for theodicy, it is true, but not for all religion. On the contrary, the very fact or fancy that "the gods have gone" is a religious revelation. Famously, Hermes Trismegistus warns his disciple of the end of Egypt:

> The land that was the seat of reverence will be widowed by the powers and left destitute of their presence.... In their weariness the people of that time will find the world nothing to wonder at or to worship. This all—a good thing that never had nor has nor will have its better—will be endangered. People will find it oppressive and scorn it. They will not cherish this entire world.... Nothing holy, nothing reverent nor worthy of heaven or heavenly beings will be heard or believed in the mind. How mournful when the gods withdraw from mankind. Only the baleful angels remain to mingle with humans, seizing the wretches and driving them to every outrageous crime.[84]

There may have been some contemporary relevance to the apparent prophecy:

> While the empire descended into chaos [during the third-century AD], the infrastructure of Egyptian religion fell apart. Such developments were obviously traumatic for Egyptians who still tried to hold on to their ancestral traditions. As for the "new laws" and "prohibitions" that are mentioned twice in the Asclepius fragment, they most probably have to do with an imperial decree issued in 199 CE by the Roman prefect of Egypt Q. Aemilius Saturninus. It imposed capital punishment on anybody found guilty of practicing divination, consulting oracles, engaging in public processions of cult images, or claiming

---

83 Von Rad, *Old Testament Theology*, 136-37.
84 *Asclepius* chs. 24-25, in Copenhaver *Hermetica*, 81-82.

Families and Dysfunctional Divinities

higher knowledge based on "written documents supposedly granted in the presence of a deity." The decree was publicly displayed in every Egyptian city or village and must have been deeply intimidating to practitioners of traditional Egyptian religion, temple priests in particular. It is true that this attempt to put an end to Egyptian "superstition" seems not to have been very successful; but whatever its effectiveness, such an imperial decree meant that from the beginning of the third century onwards, not just ritual worship of temple images but even divinely inspired discourses such as we find in the *Asclepius* were officially illegal and punishable by death.[85]

So the prophecy of Egypt's doom, and the world's, was more an observation than a prediction. There may even be a dim memory of an earlier catastrophe, recorded in Tutankhamun's day:

> The temples of the gods and goddesses were desolated from Elephantine as far as the marshes of the Delta, their holy places were about to disintegrate, having become rubbish heaps, overgrown with thistles. Their sanctuaries were as if they had never been, their houses were trodden roads. The land was in grave disease [*znj-mnt*]. The gods have forsaken this land.[86]

When such events are seen and described as God's withdrawal, for whatever divine purpose, the disaster itself has a religious, *binding*, significance. Even if God or the gods were solely our creation their very absence is a reason to remember them, and to pray for their return—as Holmes from the Reichenbach Falls, or King Arthur back from Avalon.

MIGHT-HAVE-BEENS THAT MAYBE ARE

But the wish to have our fictions realized, or the past return, is problematic. If Tolkien's Middle Earth were real, so would be orcs, Shelob, Sauron and other still worse creatures. Maybe—from

---

85 Hanegraaff, *Hermetic Spirituality*, 75. Note that this attack on Egyptian spirituality long preceded any merely "Christian" demolition of the ancient order.
86 Assmann, *Moses the Egyptian*, 27, quoting Tutankhamun's "Restoration Stela" (Wolfgang Helck, *Urkunden IV: Urkunden der 18. Dynastie*, vol. 22 [Berlin: Akademie Verlag, 1958], 2025ff.). Assmann adds that "the trauma resulting from the events of the Amarna period reflected both the experience of religious otherness and intolerance and the suffering caused by a terrible epidemic."

the Creator's perspective—that is fine: creativity need have no limits, and every sort of creature—including psychopathic villains—is to be cherished merely for what it is. God hates nothing that He has made, and every creature, however small and base, has something of the divine in it. Those familiar, hopeful judgements, from Hebraic and Hellenic thinkers, may help us in our daily doings even as we seek to oppose, or cure, or even kill the villains. Kipling pictures how "Evarra—Man—maker of gods in lands beyond the sea" devises one god after another, proclaiming each time that this alone is how gods must be made, and at last comes before the One True God:

> Yet at the last he came to Paradise,
> And found his own four Gods, and that he wrote;
> And marvelled, being very near to God,
> What oaf on earth had made his toil God's law,
> Till God said mocking: "Mock not. These be thine."
> Then cried Evarra: "I have sinned!"—"Not so.
> If thou hadst written otherwise, thy Gods
> Had rested in the mountain and the mine,
> And I were poorer by four wondrous Gods,
> And thy more wondrous law, Evarra. Thine,
> Servant of shouting crowds and lowing kine."[87]

Kipling's Evarra then casts out his gods as being patently unworthy, but Kipling's God does not! So also Stapledon's imagined Star Maker, who devises many strange worlds, apparently in sequence.[88] He even imagines a world in which mortals are arbitrarily condemned either to timeless bliss or never-ending agony. He also imagines what has come to be called the "Multiverse":

> In one inconceivably complex cosmos, whenever a creature was faced with several possible courses of action, it took them all, thereby creating many distinct temporal dimensions and distinct histories of the cosmos. Since in every evolutionary sequence of the cosmos there were very many creatures, and each was constantly faced with many possible courses, and the combinations of all their courses

---

87 Kipling, "Evarra and his Gods" (1890), in *Complete Verse*, 338-40.
88 Stapledon followed Plotinus in suggesting that "myths" embody timeless relationships in narrative, sequential, form: see *Ennead* III.5 [50].9, 24-29.

were innumerable, an infinity of distinct universes exfoliated from every moment of every temporal sequence in this cosmos.[89]

And maybe that is our very own reality. All possibilities are realized—including worlds with radically different "laws," some of which may be more hospitable than ours.[90] This story, the Multiverse Hypothesis,[91] may seem (to some) to vindicate "Free Will," but is actually rigidly deterministic. Stoic philosophers reckoned that only what was real was possible. Epicureans suggested instead that everything possible was, somewhere or other, real. The two theses are logically though not semantically equivalent.[92] I may not at this moment know which time-line I am myself embedded in, but that line, like every other line, is fixed. Even if someone otherwise "just like me," even one "identically" me, is due to endure or enjoy some radically other life-line, *my* future here is as concrete as my past. If everything possible really happens, I can never *choose* one course of action rather than another because I can never *eliminate* any possibility. And even if I seem to myself to have resisted some temptation or succeeded in some task, I must now admit that at the same time I—or someone "identically" me—did not.

Conversely, the fact that *not* all possibilities are realized is what makes action possible and history open, though we often forget this truism:

> As history is taught, nearly everybody assumes that in all important past conflicts, it was the right side that won. Everybody assumes it; and nobody knows that he assumes it. The man has simply never seriously entertained the other notion. Say to him that we should now all of us be better off if Charles Edward and the Jacobites had captured London instead of falling back from

---

89 Stapledon, *Star Maker*, 118.
90 See Ćirković, *Astrobiological Landscape*, 86–108; Mersini-Houghton, *Beyond the Big Bang*, 161–62.
91 See, e.g., Deutsch, *Fabric of Reality*, for the empirical basis for the hypothesis; and Rubenstein, *Worlds without End*, for a sympathetic study of its literary uses.
92 Compare the logical equivalence of "All crows are black" and "All non-black things are non-crows" (or, "No non-black things are crows"). So (by strict logic) red pillar boxes tend to confirm the thesis that all crows are black.

Derby, and he will laugh. He will think it is what he calls a "paradox."[93]

Alternate histories—the things that *didn't* happen—are untestable, except in fantasy creations:[94] the best we can manage is to devise psychologically or physically *plausible* ones, without even any clear sense of the distinct identities of those imagined worlds. Is the world where the Jacobites captured London the very same world as the one where Peter III of Russia did *not* marry the would-have-been Catherine the Great, or the one where the Qianlong Emperor of China died untimely (all imagined events occurring or not in 1745)? If all possibilities are realized there are also multiple answers to those same questions.

Indeed, the problem is still worse. Many possible futures open from this moment—and also many possible pasts converge on it.

> That is why Carneades [the Academic Sceptic, d. 129 BC] used to say that not even Apollo could foretell the future, apart from things whose causes were embodied in nature in such a way as to render their coming necessary. For by inspecting what could even the god himself tell that Marcellus who was three times consul would die at sea? This is something that was true from eternity but did not have causes working to bring it about. Thus he held that Apollo did not even know those *past* facts of which no signs survived as traces. How much less could he know the future?[95]

Commonsensically, we can merely agree that we don't now know exactly what will happen, nor exactly what has happened: the present evidence is compatible, as far as we can tell, with

---

93 Chesterton, *The Thing*, 131–32. That "we" would be better off is doubtful: why should we imagine that we would have been born at all? But maybe the people who would be here instead would be happier than we are (or, clearly, the reverse).
94 That there are indeed or have been *some* other real alternates is a better supported theory: see Mersini-Houghton, *Beyond the Big Bang*, 171–73, on the successful prediction of "scars" from the early entanglement of our cosmos with others. What is happening in them remains beyond our grasp.
95 Cicero, *On Fate*, 30–32, in Long and Sedley, *Hellenistic Philosophers*, 1:464–65 [70G]. The assumption that all truths are "true from eternity" is not, as Aristotle knew, a reason to think them "necessary" (see Aristotle, *On Interpretation*, 19a22–30: "all things must be or not be, or must come or not come into being, at this or that time in the future. But we cannot determinately say which alternative must come to pass").

many pasts as well as many futures, though there is only one "real world." But if all those possibilities are *real*, we cannot now be troubled by any seeming contradictions in the record: our records here-and-now are of many converging pasts.

> [Hawking and Herzog] claim that the Universe had no unique beginning. Instead, they argue, it began in just about every way imaginable (and maybe some that aren't). Out of this profusion of beginnings, the vast majority withered away without leaving any real imprint on the Universe we know today. Only a tiny fraction of them *blended* [my emphasis] to make the current cosmos, Hawking and Hertog claim.... We should picture the Universe in the first instants of the Big Bang as a superposition of all these possibilities, they say; like a projection of billions of movies played on top of one another. This might sound odd, but it is precisely the view adopted by quantum theory. Think of a particle of light reaching our eye from a lamp. Common sense suggests that it simply travels in a straight line from the bulb to the eye. But to make correct predictions about the particle's behaviour, quantum mechanics must consider all other possible paths too, including ones in which, say, the photon bounces around the walls thousands of times before reaching us. This summation of all paths, proposed in the 1960s by physicist Richard Feynman and others, is the only way to explain some of the bizarre properties of quantum particles, such as their apparent ability to be in two places at once. The key point is that not all paths contribute equally to the photon's behaviour: the straight-line trajectory dominates over the indirect ones. Hertog argues that the same must be true of the path through time that took the Universe into its current state. We must regard it as a sum over all possible histories.[96]

Sometimes the differences are too great to be made compatible, and the world divides. If our past is indeterminate in detail, our present time-line has indeed absorbed many minor variations, and also split away from larger variations. We may seem to ourselves

---

96 Ball, "Hawking rewrites History," after Hawking and Hertog, "Populating the Landscape."

to remember events that turn out not to have secured a fixed being, or to have made no other distinguishable difference in our continuing story. We may also entirely forget them. And if this is true we can no longer dismiss obvious inconsistencies in the records, nor hope to identify a single consistent past: false memories, faulty references, or even the so-called "Mandela Effect,"[97] are merely signs that we here-now have many origin stories, and as many distinct origins. Whether we could retain any notion of rational inquiry in such a world seems doubtful.

And yet the real possibility that some possible worlds and histories are real remains attractive, and psychologically significant. Our cosmos, and this world here, might really have been very different. We might, all of us, have done differently in the past. We have many possibilities to realize that in fact we won't. We can wish that we could really see and understand those other possible lines, whether they depend on cosmological accident, geological or historical difference, or the choices of individual creatures. We may wish that we could "go back" and pick a different line, whether or not that eliminates *this* line or leaves it really unchanged while we enjoy (or endure) the other choice.[98] Realistically we may suspect that if we were really given the chance to relive and re-engineer our lives, we might do worse, or even choose "again" to do exactly what we did, even while half-remembering that we really shouldn't: that is, after

---

97 See www.healthline.com/health/mental-health/mandela-effect for a brief outline of the problem, drawing its title from the widespread belief that Nelson Mandela died in prison, rather than surviving to be the President of South Africa and dying only in 2013.
98 SF writers, oddly, tend to suggest that attempts to change the time-line end either in disaster or in a return to the line we already know: see, e.g., Brunner, *Times without Number*. Card's *Pastwatch* is one of very few that envisage a succession of improvements, engineered by time-travelling interventions: Columbus, in our own line, was apparently persuaded to sail west rather than crusade against the Muslim east, in order to prevent the conquest of Europe by the Mesoamerican Tlaxcalan Empire (which waged war, like the Aztecs, chiefly to win human sacrifices for its dreadful gods). The genocidal outcome of the European conquest of the Americas is in turn to be negated by converting him and his men to a more humane ideal (and infecting everyone with antibodies against the Eurasian diseases that—in our history—devastated the Americas). In Card's imagining our own line will thereby be simply cancelled: we here-now will never really have been, and the interventionists marooned in Mesoamerica will have come into the world from nowhere.

all, exactly what we felt and did this time![99] But imagining the worlds that *might* have happened, whether because the Big Bang took a different course, or different phyla evolved from the Cambrian Era,[100] or the Jacobites took London, may still fulfil a little of Tolkien's ambition, and not need to be entirely cast out from Paradise.

---

99 See Ouspensky, *Strange Life of Ivan Osokin*. Other authors have felt a little more optimistic about their chances: see, e.g., North, *First Fifteen Lives of Harry August*.
100 See Gould, *Wonderful Life*, and my "Does the Burgess Shale Have Moral Implications?"

↩6↪
Ritual and Belief

"Poetry and Hums aren't things which you get, they're things which get *you*. And all you can do is to go where they can find you."[1]

FAITH WITHOUT BELIEF

The stories we tell and the images we identify or make all help to bind us together, both as the individual persons we hope to be, and in the communities that support us. They answer especially the "anagogical" question, *quo tendas?*[2] Without such shared stories we have less to talk about, and fewer ideas about what to do or to avoid. But is it necessary for us exactly to *believe* the stories, or think that the images are of presently existent beings? Do Pyrrhonian Sceptics need to *believe* in the truth of the everyday assumptions by which they live? Sanity, as Chesterton observed, lies in accepting what we cannot prove[3]—but does it require us to accept that what we accept is *true*?

> Attending to what is apparent, we live in accordance with everyday observances, without holding opinions—for we are not able to be utterly inactive. These everyday observances seem to be fourfold, and to consist in guidance by nature, necessitation by feelings, handing down of laws and customs, and teaching of kinds of expertise. By nature's guidance we are naturally capable of perceiving and thinking. By the necessitation of feelings, hunger conducts us to food and thirst to drink. By the handing down of customs and laws, we accept, from an everyday point of view, that piety is good and impiety bad. By

---

1 Milne, *House at Pooh Corner*, 146.
2 As Plotinus argued in *Ennead* VI.9 [9], the *unity* of any being is granted by its *goal*, a point I have tried to explicate in my *Commentary on* VI.9.
3 Chesterton, 'Philosophy for the Schoolroom,' in *Daily News*, June 22, 1907; reprinted in Maycock, *The Man Who Was Orthodox*, 92f.

teaching of kinds of expertise we are not inactive in those which we accept.⁴

Such sceptics follow "the customary observances," but without any need to consider them either "correct" or "incorrect." Even rationalists of Descartes' school, who hope to believe all and only what is certainly correct, must always in practice fall back on popular assumptions. "It is custom and example that persuade us, rather than any certain knowledge."⁵ Other possibilities *could* be true: maybe this is a virtual reality; maybe we are controlled by aliens; maybe there is a worldwide military-industrial complex financed by the Rothschilds. It would be hard to *prove* otherwise. Most of us are content to ignore these exotic possibilities. We also ignore even the stories that we think are *certainly* true: that the world is very big, very old, and very strange, and that each of us is mortal. If Pyrrhonians follow nature, feeling, custom, and the rules of art, what is it they *aren't* doing? The very word, *peithesthai*, which we translate as "to believe," can signify this compliance. What else is believing than complying? If I cheerfully drink something, don't I *show* I believe it drinkable? But a nonrational animal, or a Pyrrhonian, doesn't need to believe that it's *true* that it is drinkable, that it will do her good, that anything which contradicts that claim is false, and that anyone who acts or imagines otherwise is wrong.⁶ Nor do they need to consider all the implications of those imagined truths, or their larger context. Such observations as they make are contextual—and so immune to the arguments of Academic Sceptics (for example: that if I really knew even that this is a computer, I would also *know* that there are no pixies or mischievous aliens deliberately deceiving me on this point: not *knowing* the latter I do not *know* the former).⁷ Further, whereas rationalists believe that "the truth

---

4 Sextus Empiricus, *Outlines of Scepticism*, 9 (1.23–4). See my "Living the Pyrrhonian Way."
5 Descartes, *Discourse on Method* (1637), in *Philosophical Writings*, 1:119.
6 Pyrrho, according to Diogenes Laertius, *Lives*, 9.68, pointed to a pig's indifference to the threat of ship-wreck as a good example of serenity in action, and an explanation of his own failure to panic.
7 See Lehrer, "Why Not Scepticism?" Strangely, it is apparently widely supposed that to rebut Pyrrho it is enough to say that knowledge claims are contextual, without the global implications on which Lehrer's argument relies. But

is one, without a flaw,"[8] Pyrrhonians don't insist: they don't need to synthesise their various hypotheses because they aren't considered *truths*. And this too is not unusual, even amongst scientists: "in this respect physicists are like ordinary people. If they can't resolve a contradiction, and the contradiction is not pressing, they just disregard it and give their attention to those aspects of the theory (or theories) that are pleasantly consistent."[9]

Descartes' first maxim, before he satisfied himself (but not many philosophers since) that there were some literally unquestionable dogmas, was "to obey the laws and customs of my country, holding constantly to the religion in which by God's grace I had been instructed from my childhood, and governing myself in all other matters according to the most moderate and least extreme opinions—the opinions commonly accepted in practice by the most sensible of those with whom I should have to live."[10] The fantasy writer H. P. Lovecraft, intellectually convinced—*contra* Descartes—that the wider cosmos had no human meaning, and that even our own conceptions of what was right or good had no solid foundation, adopted a similar stance:

> Amidst this variability [that is, the relative and changing nature of "the good"] there is only one anchor of fixity which we can seize upon as the working pseudo-standard of "values" which we need in order to feel settled and contented—and that anchor is tradition, the potent emotional legacy bequeathed to us by the massed experience of our ancestors, individual or national, biological or cultural. Tradition means nothing cosmically, but it means everything locally and pragmatically because we have nothing else to shield us from a devastating sense of "lostness" in endless time and space.[11]

Or as John Buchan supposed a savage might speak to a missionary for the wider world:

---

this response simply agrees with Pyrrho!
8 Boethius, *Consolation of Philosophy* 5.3 (Tractates, 403), as translated by Waddell, *Medieval Latin Lyrics*, 59.
9 Malin, *Nature Loves to Hide*, 90.
10 Descartes, *Discourse on Method*, in *Philosophical Writings*, 123.
11 Lovecraft, *Selected Letters* 2.356-57, quoted by Joshi, *Subtler Magick* (Kindle location 836).

Ritual and Belief

> Wherefore my brittle gods I make
> Of friendly clay and kindly stone,—
> Wrought with my hands, to serve or break,
> From crown to toe my work, my own.
> My eyes can see, my nose can smell,
> My fingers touch their painted face,
> They weave their little homely spell
> To warm me from the cold of Space.
> My gods are wrought of common stuff
> For human joys and mortal tears;
> Weakly, perchance, yet staunch enough
> To build a barrier 'gainst my fears,
> Where, lowly but secure, I wait
> And hear without the strange winds blow.—
> I cannot worship what I hate,
> Or serve a god I dare not know.[12]

But must not this appeal merely to tradition weaken our morale, quite as much as—by William James's account—any merely subjective story of the rules we follow? It takes a strong *belief* to step knowingly off a cliff, even with a rope, and even if there is a visible ledge a few feet down. It also takes a strong belief to defy or disobey tyrants. If the tyrant *could* be in the right, Pyrrhonians may find it easier not to disturb the status quo. Like other Hellenistic schools, their original aim is *ataraxia*, serenity or equanimity: where others hope to achieve that state by securing a conclusion, the Pyrrhonian achieves it by surrendering that hope, and will thereafter follow custom and impulse where they lead. And maybe that is after all enough even for rebellion. Sextus suggests that obedience to custom, unhampered by beliefs about how bad it is to suffer, will help us defy tyrants, or at least ignore them,[13] without succumbing to hatred or conceit.

> The profession of the Pyrrhonists is to waver, doubt and inquire, to be assured of nothing.... Now this foundation of their judgement, straight and inflexible, receiving

---

12 John Buchan, "Stocks and Stones," in *The Moon Endureth*, 160–62. Buchan appended the poem to a distinctly Lovecraftian story, "Space," about what lurks around us in some normally invisible direction. He may, of course, have been entirely wrong about the likely feelings of "savages" (so-called), as well as about the cosmic horrors.
13 See Naess, *Scepticism*, 65, after Sextus Empiricus, *Against the Ethicists*, 160–67.

> all objects without application or consent, leads them to their *ataraxia;* which is a condition of life that is peaceful, composed, exempt from the agitations which we receive from the impression of the opinion and knowledge that we think we have of things. From this arises fear, avarice, envy, immoderate desires, ambition, pride, superstition, the love of novelty, rebellion, disobedience, obstinacy, and the majority of bodily ills. In this way, to be sure, they exempt themselves from jealousy for their discipline, for they debate in a very mild manner. They do not fear rebuttal in their arguments.[14]

An attack on their arguments and assumptions is not an attack on *them,* nor are they easily bribed or threatened (which is the usual fate of "natural slaves," including most of us).

Some critics have argued that this sort of life, while *possible,* is personally destructive. Impulsive people, responding to every movement of the psychic weather, are what Aristotle supposed the "further barbarians" to be (and the deranged).[15] They can't be counted on to keep their promises, nor sustain a project longer than it takes the wind to change. Or do Pyrrhonians hold themselves to familiar custom, at the expense of impulse, "heathens" rather than "savages?" How are they to balance these demands?

On the one hand, it seems that Pyrrhonians must be identified, in practice, with their impulses or their tribal customs, with no reason to resist or to reform them. On the other, they must be detached from exactly those impulses and customs, even while they act them out. Whereas ordinary agents choose one thing over another (raspberries over strawberries; peace over war) as being *better* than the other, Pyrrhonians make no such claim. Confronted by the questionnaires and opinion polls endemic in our age and region, the Pyrrhonian is happy to count as a "Don't Know," and so is immune—in a way—to demagogues (but may of course "go along" with what the demagogues require).

But must this detachment not be constantly subverted? Some things *matter* to us in ways that are difficult to forget. These may not be the things most often mentioned. Bodily pain gets our

---

14 Montaigne, *Apology,* 64–65.
15 Aristotle, *Nicomachean Ethics* 7.1149a10.

attention, but we can moderate its effects by conceiving that this is only a rather unpleasant dream, from which one may soon awaken. At least it is not *certain* that pain is an evil (even if it feels that way).[16] On other occasions these dreamy thoughts can be disciplined by a swift reminder of the recalcitrance of things![17] There is a thought and feeling familiar to depressives, that there isn't any point getting up, or going out, or bothering to eat: *argument* is unlikely to dislodge depression, but Pyrrhonism sometimes may, by suggesting that this all-pervasive mood is not one's self, nor certainly veridical, or even allowing the possibility of a divine inspiration. "If someone is able to turn around, either by himself or having the good luck to have his hair pulled by Athena herself, he will see God and himself and the All."[18]

That latter escape from depression and unbelief may indeed be our only real hope:

> My disease [so Al-Ghazali says of his own acute depression] grew worse and lasted almost two months, during which I fell prey to skepticism (*safaa*), though neither in theory nor in outward expression. At last, God the Almighty cured me of that disease, and I recovered my health and mental equilibrium. The self-evident principles of reason again seemed acceptable; I trusted them and in them felt safe and certain. I reached this point not by well-ordered or methodical argument, but by means of a light God the Almighty cast into my breast, which light is the key to most knowledge.[19]

In this age and region, we are encouraged to believe that only

---

16 According to T. E. Lawrence, as portrayed in David Lynch's film *Lawrence of Arabia* (1962), "the trick [about enduring pain] is not minding that it hurts."
17 See O'Flaherty, *Dreams, Illusions*, 301: "When life—*samsara*—becomes too full of suffering, or even too full of happiness, we tell ourselves, 'This must be a dream,' hoping in this way to transform the all-too-real into what we define as unreality. By contrast, we sometimes find ourselves caught up in a dream that we cannot get enough of, a dream so wonderful that, when we wake, we cry to dream again. Then we pull this moment closer to us, telling ourselves, 'This is real life; I am awake,' hoping in this way to turn the dream into what we define as reality."
18 *Ennead* VI.5 [23].7, 11–13. See Homer, *Iliad* I.197f., where Athena (the goddess of good sense) recalls Achilles from a murderous rage, as she might also recall us from a suicidal depression.
19 Al-Ghazali (1058–1111), *Deliverance from Error and Mystical Union with the Almighty* (1106/7), 67.

"material facts" are known or knowable. But are there not moral truths which we are far less likely to abandon than even the best supported materialistic theories? Even the Neo-Darwinian theory of evolution might conceivably be mistaken, but most of us cannot suppose that there might "really" be nothing wrong with torturing children, even though — at some risk to the purity of our imaginations — we can envisage the state of mind and character required to believe this. There are possible worlds where terrestrial life was planted, cultivated, and weeded by envoys of the Galactic Empire, but there are no really possible worlds where the rape and murder of children is correct. Can Pyrrhonians reply? When Pyrrho, it is said, grew enraged on his sister's behalf, it was not in obedience to an abstract doctrine (that one should defend one's female relatives), but following natural impulse, in immediate recognition of someone dear to him.[20] Similarly, Kuzminski suggests that "in the absence of rationalizing, soothing, or distracting dogmatic beliefs about what [was] going on [in a Roman arena], there would be revulsion and disgust" at the spectacle.[21] Because the Pyrrhonian is not persuaded that "reason" is a superior faculty she is less likely to feel superior, and so more likely to be kind. Montaigne's *Apology* is at once a defence of Pyrrhonism and of sympathy for the nonhuman! Maybe doctrines are what subvert the immediate and honest response to iniquity? Faith does not, or need not, depend on a reasoned belief that such and such a proposition is really, truly true: it is rather a determination to go on living by a particular vision,[22] including (sometimes) a determination to make our theories consistent, however hard that may seem. "One must not then suppose that the gods and the 'exceedingly blessed spectators' in the higher world contemplate propositions (*axiomata*), but all the Forms we speak about are beautiful images in that world, of the kind which someone imagined to exist in the soul of the wise man, images not painted but real."[23]

---

20 Kuzminski, *Pyrrhonism*, 23, commenting on Diogenes Laertius, *Lives* 9.66.
21 Kuzminski, 106.
22 As Puddleglum determines, in Lewis's *Silver Chair*, 190, to live as like a Narnian as he can, even if there is no Narnia.
23 *Ennead* V.8 [31].5f., citing Plato, *Symposium* 215b; see also IV.3 [27].18, 6–8: "in the crafts reasoning (*logismos*) occurs when the craftsmen are in perplexity, but when there is no difficulty, the craft dominates and does its work."

SOUNDS AND MUSIC

But isn't this naïve? "Believe Christ and His Apostles that there is a class of men whose whole delight is in destroying."[24] There are real and deadly alternatives to the sort of sympathy that is disgusted by the Roman spectacles—why else would there ever be such spectacles? Whatever the metaphysical reality may be, our daily experience is of antagonistic spirits, and our constant need is for some way of ordering the horde. Maybe we need to invoke Zeus, or maybe, like Blake, we hope instead to be "just and true to our own Imaginations, those worlds of eternity in which we shall live for ever in Jesus our Lord."[25]

That conclusion may of course be helped by careful argument, and most especially by arguments *against* whatever other view of things there may be. The starting point for obviously "philosophical" argument will often—and maybe always—be a puzzle. According to Heracleitos, "the lord whose oracle is in Delphi [that is, Apollo] neither speaks nor suppresses, but indicates."[26] As Iamblichus also declared, Apollo (together with the eldest of the Muses, Calliope) is the inspiration of philosophers not because he speaks "rationally" and "clearly," but because he poses riddles: he is "a god of impossible enigmas,"[27] and perhaps of insoluble antinomies. Dialectic deals with ambiguity and homonymy, "and the ferreting out of any double meaning." It is conducted in disputatious dialogue—which is why Hermes carries, so Iamblichus says, a staff with two snakes looking toward each other, poised to test themselves against each other![28] But even disputation itself, though valuable, is not of the essence: the eristical mode, though attractive especially (perhaps) to the young, is not dialectic.

---

24 Blake, Milton, Preface, in Complete Writings, 480.
25 Blake, ibid.; see also Blake, "Descriptive Catalogue," Complete Writings, 571: "The gods of Priam ... are visions of the eternal attributes, or divine names, which, when erected into gods, become destructive of humanity.... When separated from man or humanity, who is Jesus the Saviour, the vine of eternity, they are thieves and rebels, they are destroyers."
26 Heracleitos 22B93DK, in Waterfield, First Philosophers, 40.
27 Kingsley, Story Waiting to Pierce You, 43.
28 Iamblichus, Letters, 14–15: "Letter to Dexippus, on Dialectic"; see also ibid., 39: "these are the purifications of the intellect through refutations, juxtaposing opposite opinions for those engaged in disputation and testing them against each other." See also Dillon, "Letters of Iamblichus," 59–60.

"When he thinks that he is reasoning he is really disputing, just because he cannot define and divide, and so know that of which he is speaking; and he will pursue a merely verbal opposition in the spirit of contention and not of fair discussion."[29] The proper goal of philosophical dispute is not winning arguments (nor silencing opponents), but rather "the purification of the intellect through refutation."[30] And perhaps our awakening is an effect of intellectual despair — the moment when we acknowledge that we cannot any longer cope.[31] "He who has thoroughly comprehended himself, thoroughly despairs of himself... And the man who has despaired of himself is beginning to know Him that is."[32]

And if this is so perhaps we should reexamine Plotinus's scorn for those who rely on "magic chants" to invoke or control demons.[33] Such chants may not influence the gods and *daimones* of the Neo-Platonic cosmos, considered as real beings of an older, stronger and wiser sort than us. But perhaps they influence their human audience, and the singers themselves, even if their chants are deliberately couched so as not to resemble any familiar words.

"In Egypt the priests, when singing hymns in praise of the gods, employ the seven vowels, which they utter in due succession; and the sound of these letters is so euphonious that men listen to them in place of flute and lyre."[34] Janowitz notes that those seven vowels are sometimes aligned with the planets,[35]

---

29 Plato, *Republic* 5.454a; see also Plato, *Meno* 75cd: "if he were a philosopher of the eristic and antagonistic sort, I should say to him: You have my answer, and if I am wrong, your business is to take up the argument and refute me. But if we were friends, and were talking as you and I are now, I should reply in a milder strain and more in the dialectician's vein; that is to say, I should not only speak the truth, but I should make use of premises which the person interrogated would be willing to admit."
30 Iamblichus, *Letters*, 15 (Stobaeus, *Anthologia* 2.2.5).
31 See Zimmer, *King and the Corpse*, 202–38.
32 Philo, *On Dreams* 10.60, in *Collected Works*, 5:327–29.
33 *Ennead* II.9 [33].14, 1–12.
34 Demetrius, *De Elocutione*, trans. Roberts; cf. *Asclepius* 38 on honouring earthly gods (or idols) "with hymns, praises and sweet sounds in tune with heaven's harmony" (Copenhaver, *Hermetic*, 90), cited by Fowden, *Egyptian Hermes*, 118; see Cox Miller, "In Praise of Nonsense," 482–86.
35 Janowitz, *Icons of Power*, 49; see also ibid., 59–60. Plutarch mentions a Chaldean trope, that "there are seven vowels in the alphabet and seven stars that have an independent and unconstrained motion; that E is the second in order of the vowels from the beginning, and the sun the second planet after the moon, and that practically all the Greeks identify Apollo with the Sun" ("The

though there seems to be no single, universally agreed, association between particular vowels and particular planetary gods. To us, this sounds like gibberish—and perhaps it sounded like gibberish even to the singers, while still having an effect.

> The first thing to note is the succession of the seven vowels of the Greek alphabet: this string "a e ē i o u ō"—appears in many places elsewhere in the *Papyri Graecae Magicae* as well, and was often understood as a divine name that could be turned into a formula. The vowels appear to represent divine powers that reside in the seven planetary spheres, and as the number of vowels is successively expanded, we get $1 + 2 + 3 + 4 + 5 + 6 + 7 = 28$ powers. Each vowel is followed by the same number of omegas (ω) plus one. Since the ceremony is initiated from down below, the intended sequence must be as follows: Moon (α), Mercury (ε), Venus (η), the Sun (ι), Mars (o), Jupiter (υ), and Saturn (ω). As the number of these vowels expands progressively, the total number of powers that are being invoked at each step expands as well ($1-3-6-10-15-21-28$; or even $3-8-15-24-35-48-63$ if one includes the omegas); hence each line of vocalizations takes considerably more time than the previous one; and furthermore, we may readily assume that the powers themselves were believed to get more potent the closer they were to the hypercosmic domain. Therefore, we are watching an exponential build-up of numinous power, culminating in the long series of fifteen omegas sealed by the word *zōzazōth*.[36]

Should we find this surprising? Even unbelieving, would-be secular, auditors are moved by musical sounds, without any expectation that the sounds make any rational sense: sometimes, indeed, we had rather not know what words are joined to the music. And very often we prefer mere sounds, whether made by the human voice, or wolves, or whales, or else by musical instruments, which do not even sound like words. "Sounds can 'do things' because they are icons of divinity, audible and accessible bits of the inaudible

---

E at Delphi" 386b, in *Moralia*, 5:207).
36 Hanegraaff, *Hermetic Spirituality*, 291, after Nag Hammadi Codex VI6.56, 10-22 ("The Ogdoad Reveals the Ennead").

and inaccessible divine world."[37] They may have their effect even without being euphonious: their point is to correct the damage we have already done our souls, and this may require us to be bent back, as woodworkers do with crooked wood.[38]

> In the sacred rites, it is by ugly spectacles and sounds that we are delivered from the damage that results from practicing those ugly things ["ambition, distraction, uglification, and derision," maybe].[39] These rites are therefore practiced in view of healing our soul, to moderate the evils that have become attached to it because of the fact of generation, to liberate it and relieve it from its chains.[40]

Music has an advantage over other forms of art — or so Aristotle supposed. "Visual works of art are not representations of character but rather the forms and colours produced are mere indications of character."[41] Music actually evokes the appropriate feelings and characters.

> Rhythms and melodies contain representations of anger and mildness, and also of courage and temperance and all their opposites and the other moral qualities, that most closely correspond to the true natures of these qualities (and this is clear from the facts of what occurs — when we listen to such representations we change in our soul).[42]

For this very reason care must be taken, so Plato also insisted,[43] over the choice of musical modes. But perhaps neither Plato nor

---

37 Janowitz, *Icons of Power*, 61.
38 Aristotle, *Nicomachean Ethics* 2.1109b5-7.
39 The four branches of arithmetic, according to Carroll's Mock Turtle: *Alice in Wonderland*, 97.
40 Hanegraaff, *Hermetic Spirituality*, 112, quoting Iamblichus, *Response to Porphyry* [*De Mysteriis*] I, 11. See also Mahé & Meyer, "Discourse on the Eighth and the Ninth," 418: "O grace! After this, I thank you by singing a hymn to you. You gave me life when you made me wise. I praise you. I invoke your name hidden in me, A ŌEE ŌĒĒĒ ŌŌŌIII ŌŌŌŌOOOO ŌŌŌŌŌUUUUU ŌŌŌŌŌŌŌŌŌŌ ŌŌŌŌŌŌŌŌŌŌ. You exist with spirit. I sing to you with godliness."
41 Aristotle, *Politics* 8.1340a32-3.
42 Aristotle, *Politics* 8.1340a19-21; see also Butcher, *Aristotle's Theory of Poetry and Fine Arts*, 128-32.
43 Plato, *Republic*, 96-97 [3.398c-400c]: he prefers the Dorian and Phrygian modes. The Dorian, he said, "properly captures the tones and variations of pitch of a brave man's voice during battle or any other enterprise he'd rather not be involved in." The Phrygian "captures his voice when he's engaged in peaceful enterprises."

Aristotle would have been ready to take the further, Hermetic, step: might not music—or properly articulated sounds—do more than represent and encourage familiar feelings and moral characters? "Someone in grief wishes his grief to be allayed by the pipe, someone happy to become more cheerful still, someone in love to become more passionate, someone devoted to religion (*philothutes*) to become more inspired (*entheoteros*) and enchanted (*humnodes*)."[44] May we not hope to call down gods, or else—equivalently—raise us up to the divine?

> [M]ore admirable than all other wonders is the fact that man has been able to discover the divine nature and make it manifest. As our ancestors were very much confused as to what the gods were all about (for they were unbelieving and inattentive to worship and divine reverence), they invented a procedure for manifesting the gods. They empowered their invention by adding a virtue drawn from the nature of the world, thus bringing both natures together and mixing them. As they could not make souls, they evoked the souls of daimons or angels, drawing them into these images through sacred and divine mystery rites, so that these idols could have the power to produce good and evil.[45]

Even if "the divine" means only that state of feeling that we sometimes encounter, and project upon the wider world, it may be our chief source of joy. "Man [*anthropos*] is a shadow's dream [*skias onar*]," said Pindar, "but when (a) god [*theos*] sheds a brightness then shining light is on earth, and life is as sweet as honey."[46]

Oswald Spengler was not entirely wrong to suggest that we ourselves, inheritors of the "Faustian" experiment, may find more of the divine in music than in the visual arts.

---

44 The flute player Canus (then "the most skilful player in the world") explaining the effects of his art: Philostratus, *Life of Apollonius*, 2:37-39 [5.3].
45 Hanegraaff, *Hermetic Spirituality*, 68-69, citing *Asclepius* 37, in Copenhaver *Hermetica*, 90. Cf. Purves, *Holy Smoke*, 19: "Sculpture, like music, has a peculiar power to start communicating at the place where logic and experience have to stop. Great statues, like music, speak to small children with a directness not to be underestimated."
46 Pindar, *Pythian* 8.95-7.

The plurality of separate bodies which represents Cosmos for the Classical soul, requires a similar pantheon—hence the antique polytheism. The single world-volume, be it conceived as cavern or as space, demands the single god of Magian or Western Christianity. Athene or Apollo might be represented by a statue, but it is and has long been evident to our feeling that the Deity of the Reformation and the Counter-Reformation can only be "manifested" in the storm of an organ fugue or the solemn progress of cantata and mass.[47]

Whereas Dio Chrysostom thought that Pheidias had fixed the image of Olympian Zeus,[48] the God of Christian devotion is better experienced—for Spengler at least—in Bach or Handel. But our predecessors—even our Classical predecessors—were not after all deaf to music.

> Pythagoras advised people that when they arose at dawn, before setting off on any activity, they should apply themselves to music ["the Muse"] and to soothing melody, so that the confusion of their souls resulting from arousal out of sleep should first be transformed into a pure and settled condition and an orderly gentleness, and so make their souls well-attuned and concordant for the actions of the day. It also seems to me that the fact that the gods are invoked with music and melody of some sort—with hymns and *auloi*, for instance, or with Egyptian *trigonoi*—shows that we desire them to listen to our prayers with kindly gentleness.[49]

---

47 Spengler, *Decline of the West*, 1:247; see also Spengler, *Decline*, 1:412: "about 1700 painting has to yield to instrumental music—the only art that in the end is capable of clearly expressing what we feel about God. Consider, in contrast with this, the gods of Homer. Zeus emphatically does not possess full powers over the world, but is simply 'primus inter pares,' a body amongst bodies, as the Apollinian world-feeling requires." See Mendel, "Spengler's Quarrel with the Methods of Music History."
48 Dio Chrysostom, "Man's First Conception of God," in *Discourses* 2:59 (12.53). I shall address the further implications of that claim below.
49 Ptolemy, *Harmonics* 3.100, in Barker, *Harmonic and Acoustic Theory*, 379. *Auloi* are double pipes; *trigonoi* are triangular harps. Spengler was perhaps right at least in this: Classical musicians, and philosophers, were mainly entranced by singular notes, and did not conceive of "harmony," the simultaneous sounding of different notes and instruments, in the sense that we now mean. Whether Egyptian music was the same, I do not know.

SILENCE AND SELF-CONTRADICTION

The stories we tell about ourselves, societies and the world are not always consistent. Indeed, the very dream of an absolute consistency, of "truth without a flaw," is itself a story, an unrealized hope. Rationalistic moralists may urge us to act only on those principles that we can suppose to be universally acknowledged and acted on, and so to treat other creatures, or at least other people, as we can suppose *all* to be treated without contradiction. The only real rights that anyone can have are those which can be endorsed and applied for everyone. The only duties, correspondingly, are those that everyone can and must perform. It follows, of course, that moral rights and duties cannot be changed by changing times and locations. It may be true, for example, that homosexual acts were *criminal* in Rome, but not in Persia, as Sextus says.[50] But it can't be true that right and wrong (as distinct from "lawful" and "unlawful") depend on national boundaries. Nor can the evil of oppression be mitigated or excused by simply declaring the victim unworthy of any care. Similarly, in discovering how the world "really works" we must make our theories consistent both with observation and with other well-supported theories: the General Theory of Relativity and Quantum Mechanics cannot both be "true," though each is as well-supported as the other. In practice, both moralists and scientists are content to ignore the contradictions, and to follow custom as good Pyrrhonian sceptics. Fully consistent moralists (if any such exist) are reckoned overzealous. Scientists who worry too much about the "real truth" are advised instead to "shut up and calculate."[51] This latter diktat seems to have arisen chiefly from wartime necessities (as understood at the time), but had further lasting effects within the physics community: "Anything that smacked of 'interpretation,' or worse, 'philosophy,' began to carry a taint for many scientists who had come through the wartime projects. Conceptual scrutiny of foundations struck many as a luxury."[52]

---

50 Sextus, *Outlines*, 38 (1.152).
51 A diktat attributed to David Mermin as a summary of the Copenhagen interpretation of quantum theory. He did not himself endorse the rule: see Kaiser, "History: Shut up and calculate!"
52 Kaiser, "History," 155.

The rationalizing, "philosophical," drive is not entirely extinct in either ethics or metaphysics, nor would I welcome such an extinction, however distant the realization of the dream. But it is worth considering whether the drive may itself be mistaken. Ancient mythographers, at any rate, seem content to multiply divisions and distinctions without seeking fully to rationalize the stories. And, as I have implied, this is also how we moderns still behave in practice.

On past occasions I have argued that both the content of commonsensical reasoning and the methods and axioms that we identify with "reason," or "scientific reason," are themselves accepted "on faith," though we may call it "intuition" or "intellect."[53] I have also suggested that this faith is at least more "reasonable," or consistent, when couched in theistic terms. So far from theism's being at odds with "science," science, both historically and logically, gives some support to theism: at least the apparent success of science is better explained, and more expectable, on a theistic account than on a naturalistic. The words that David Hume invented for Philo have a wider impact than is usually acknowledged: "what peculiar privilege has this little agitation of the brain which we call 'thought' that we must thus make it the model of the whole universe?"[54] What indeed? Why should we suppose that the patterns we discern are ones that the whole universe obeys? We recognize that we have the sensory organs and modalities we do because these were the ones that helped our ancestors survive and procreate, and that other creatures, for equivalent reasons, sense and treat things differently. Our senses have a very limited range, bounded by our own biology.[55] Why should our intellec-

---

53 The next few paragraphs are drawn partly from my essay, "Folly to the Greeks." In summary: First Principles cannot, by definition, be proved from any more fundamental principles. Worse still, we are always being confronted by apparent contradictions, even in the "best supported" theories, and by repeated failures even in the best contrived experiments. Continued (and costly) investigations depend on our determination to carry on seeking 'truth without a flaw.'
54 Hume, *Dialogues concerning Natural Religion* (1779), part 2, in Gaskin, *Dialogues*, 50.
55 A quotation from one of H. P. Lovecraft's early, and otherwise inferior, tales, "From Beyond" [1920], in Joshi, *Dream*, 23-29: "What do we know... of the world and the universe about us? Our means of receiving impressions are absurdly few, and our notions of surrounding objects infinitely narrow. We see things

tual gifts be any better fitted to an understanding of worlds and ages far away? "Darwin's theory makes the testable prediction that whenever we use technology to glimpse reality beyond the human scale, our evolved intuition should break down."[56] What has been called the unreasonable effectiveness of mathematics[57] is a sort of confirmation that we have the root of the matter in us, that our intellect is a spark of the universal reason, an image of the God on whom everything depends.[58] Or else, of course, we should rather abandon that conviction, and with it any confidence that mathematics is more than a sometimes-useful fiction. The "success" of science can only be pragmatic, parochial, transient, and we have no reason to extrapolate the patterns that *we* happen to see here-now to a vastly wider world. Nor can we reasonably suppose both that there are no universal binding obligations (that is, that there is no God) and also that there is a universal binding obligation to pursue "the truth." If atheistical naturalists are correct we cannot reasonably expect to discover truths beyond, at best, the parochial, nor do we have any obligation to try. The geneticist Steven Jones commented a few years ago that some young Muslims had left his lectures when he began to talk about neo-Darwinian evolution, and suggested that this was an example of the way "religious" people refuse to listen to reason.[59] On the contrary, they were simply obeying his own (and other

---

only as we are constructed to see them, and can gain no idea of their absolute nature. With five feeble senses we pretend to comprehend the boundlessly complex cosmos, yet other beings with a wider, stronger, or different range of senses might not only see very differently the things we see, but might see and study whole worlds of matter, energy, and life which lie close at hand yet can never be detected with the senses we have."

56 Tegmark, *Our Mathematical Universe*, 5. Strangely, Tegmark still trusts our mathematical intuitions.

57 Wigner, "The Unreasonable Effectiveness of Mathematics in the Natural Sciences."

58 So also Benedict XVI (2009): "the objective structure of the universe and the intellectual structure of the human being coincide; the subjective reason and the objectified reason in nature are identical. In the end it is 'one' reason that links both and invites us to look to a unique creative Intelligence": www.vatican.va/holy_father/benedict_xvi/messages/pont-messages/2009/documents/hf_ben-xvi_mes_20091126_fisichella-telescopio_en.html (accessed November 25, 2022).

59 Steven Jones, "Islam, Charles Darwin and the denial of science," *Daily Telegraph*, December 3, 2011: www.telegraph.co.uk/news/science/8931518/Islam-Charles-Darwin-and-the-denial-of-science.html (accessed December 13, 2022).

evolutionary theorists') suggestion: that we are likely to believe only what will be socially and reproductively useful (and that is therefore all we should do or can be expected to do). The young Muslims perhaps calculated accordingly that it would do them no good to let themselves be infected by a socially disadvantageous meme. Most creatures, as Plotinus pointed out, manage quite well without "reasoning,"[60] and so do most people. Conversely, if we can and should pursue and prefer the "real truth," then a form of theism is, essentially, correct: we really *should* listen to reason.

I do not wish to withdraw these claims. My belief is that we *can* and should rely on "reason," even though we should also acknowledge that it is often obscured by ignorance, stupidity, self-conceit, wishful thinking, malice, and all other sorts of sin. The principal dogmas of mainstream Abrahamic theism provide a proper context for that cautious confidence. There is a single source for all things; this source is expressed in the Logos, and the Logos is, at least, *available* to us. This does not constitute a "proof" of those dogmas—I doubt if there are ever any final or conclusive or universally persuasive proofs of anything—but atheistical naturalists are at least condemned to a more incoherent doctrine than are theists, as they must believe simultaneously that creatures like us are very unlikely to be equipped to understand the cosmos (or even have reason to want to), and that they themselves know enough to know that theism is mistaken.

Though the principles of abstract reason (never to accept a contradiction; never to believe without "sufficient" evidence; always to discount one's own position, feelings and inchoate intuitions, while at the same time assuming that the world outside our experience is just like the world within, and so on) aren't helpful as absolute rules, we may continue commonsensically to think that we can tell the "rational" from the "irrational," the ignorant, or insane. We cannot, practically speaking, live like "rationalists" of the stricter sort, but we may often find it wise to suspend judgement upon many things, or at least not leap too quickly to conclusions. This pragmatic, commonsensical approach to "reasoning" is compatible even with those "animistic" habits of

---

60 *Ennead* I.4 [46].2.31–43.

Ritual and Belief

mind that modern atheists despise: imagining ourselves into the life of stars, clouds, trees, engines, or elementary particles may make it easier to live with them, and even easier to predict what they will do. But we may still feel that "right reason" requires a commitment to a universal truth, and to disown error. That ascetic demand, to purge ourselves of error even when that error is very useful, has a theological origin.

But such a purgation is not entirely obligatory—nor even entirely helpful. According to Emile Durkheim, most devotees of any particular cult "feel that the real function of religion is not to make us think, to enrich our knowledge, nor to add to the conceptions which we owe to science others of another origin and another character, but rather, it is to make us act, to aid us to live." He did also acknowledge that religion "is not merely a system of practices—but also a system of ideas whose object is to explain the world."[61] He might have added that, conversely, "science," considered as a social practice, is not merely a system of ideas but—as above—an apparatus for helping us deal with immediate problems, and to live! But the primary purpose of "religion," in its broadest sense, may indeed be rather to inspire than to explain.

> The believer who has communicated with his god is not merely a man who sees new truths of which the unbeliever is ignorant; he is a man who is stronger. He feels within him more force, either to endure the trials of existence, or to conquer them. It is as though he were raised above the miseries of the world, because he is raised above his condition as a mere man; he believes that he is saved from evil, under whatever form he may conceive this evil. The first article in every creed is the belief in salvation by faith.

To cultivate and maintain that faith we need the cult:

> Whoever has really practised a religion knows very well that it is the cult which gives rise to these impressions of joy, of interior peace, of serenity, of enthusiasm which are, for the believer, an experimental proof of his beliefs.

---

61 Durkheim, *Elementary Forms of the Religious Life*, 428.

> The cult is not simply a system of signs by which the faith is outwardly translated; it is a collection of the means by which this is created and recreated periodically. Whether it consists in material acts or mental operations, it is always this which is efficacious.[62]

Faith is not credulity. It is the repeated invocation of a sustaining spirit through cultic practices, a spirit no less efficacious for being, perhaps, imaginary. The cultic practices themselves may have a natural origin: we don't need a religious education to find it natural to rouse, for example, a spirit of righteous anger by stomping up and down and shouting. Nor do we need romantic comedies to learn how to encourage ourselves and others to season our lusts with humour. But common practices and artistry play a role in channelling our spirits into particular forms, and may also offer doctrines to "believe in," doctrines that may last longer than the first emotions. The doctrines flow from the rituals, and the rituals from the emotions, but doctrines then influence rituals, and rituals the emotions. And much the same is true for the fervent practice of "scientific reason": the experimentalist needs a devout and sturdy *faith* in the procedures, and the whole community of helpful—and critical—scientists.[63] Faith—and also awe:

> Those who entered on the path of Hermes were taught first of all to open their hearts so as to look at the world not with the gaze of narrow selfish desires but with the eyes of wonder and admiration. This is Hermes' message when he goes out into the street to tell the people to wake up: he tells them to "look up with the eyes of the heart" because the true light of divinity can be seen "only with your *nous* and your heart."[64]

The merely practical uses of "science" are not the only reason to devote one's life to science, and even the wish to "understand" the world is of less importance than the initial admiration. On the one hand, this is familiar.

---

62 Durkheim, 416–17.
63 Consider the psychological effects of a discovery that some alien civilization has been systematically distorting the results of our experiments: Liu, *Three-Body Problem*.
64 Hanegraaff, *Hermetic Spirituality*, 200, citing CH 7.1-2 (see Copenhaver, *Hermetica*, 24).

Ritual and Belief

To be a follower of Hermes did not mean sitting in some kind of school, memorizing the teacher's statements about God and the cosmos. It meant practicing a way of spiritual transformation to find true knowledge, peace of mind, ultimate salvation, and perfect enlightenment.[65]

And that "true knowledge" itself did not consist in a system, or even a string, of propositions which could be easily taught in school. Even when a scientific or mathematical investigation does lead to a definite proposition, there is more to the discovery than verbal agreement. Most of us can recall a few scientific or mathematical formulae, but we do not demonstrate our understanding merely by repeating the words, nor even by translating them into our mother tongue. We begin to understand them when we can *see* them, and the little flutter of delight that accompanies such dawning comprehension is a hint of the spirit that more dedicated lovers feel: "these experiences must occur whenever there is contact with any sort of beautiful thing, wonder and a shock of delight and longing and passion and a happy excitement (*ptoesin meth'edones*)."[66] But sometimes there is no adequate proposition to discover or repeat.

> As for what Diotima is trying to tell Socrates [in Plato's *Symposium*], one point is absolutely essential to our concerns: she makes clear to him that neither she nor anybody else will ever be able to "tell him the truth" about ultimate reality, because it is not the kind of thing that can be told. The best she can do is tell him about it.[67]

---

65 Hanegraaff, *Hermetic Spirituality*, 122.
66 *Ennead* I.6 [1].4, McKenna's translation.
67 Hanegraaff, *Hermetic Spirituality*, 189, after Plato, *Symposium* 201-12; see Plato, *Seventh Letter* 341c-341d: "Thus much at least, I can say about all writers, past or future, who say they know the things to which I devote myself, whether by hearing the teaching of me or of others, or by their own discoveries—that according to my view it is not possible for them to have any real skill in the matter. There neither is nor ever will be a treatise of mine on the subject. For it does not admit of exposition like other branches of knowledge; but after much converse about the matter itself and a life lived together, suddenly a light, as it were, is kindled in one soul by a flame that leaps to it from another, and thereafter sustains itself." The authenticity of this "seventh letter" is disputed: see Burnyeat and Frede, *Pseudo-Platonic Seventh Letter*. Denyer, "The Seventh Letter," 291, endorses their hostile conclusion, disparagingly saying that "[the letter's] author intends not so much to philosophize as to give the impression of someone philosophizing." The doctrine it declares, however, is one that later Platonic tradition accepts—and thereby rebukes most of us!

So can we say anything sensible *about* that longed-for condition, or the reality it discovers? According to William James, "the keynote of [the 'other' forms of consciousness] is invariably a reconciliation. It is as if the opposites of the world, whose contradictoriness and conflict make all our difficulties and troubles, were melted into unity."[68] The route that we must follow to that vision is itself one that we can talk about once we have traversed it, but the travel itself need not be—perhaps must not be—accompanied by verbal monologues.

> The soul runs over all truths, and all the same shuns the truths we know if someone tries to express them in words and discursive thought; for discursive thought, in order to express anything in words, has to consider one thing after another: this is the method of description; but how can one describe the absolutely simple [the One]? But it is enough if the intellect comes into contact with it; but when it has done so, while the contact lasts, it is absolutely impossible, nor has it time, to speak; but it is afterwards that it is able to reason about it.[69]

In other words, we can talk about the truth, but seeing the truth is positively inimical to speech. "In proportion as the confidence is clearer, the contemplation is quieter... [and] what it utters, it utters because of its deficiency, with a view to examining it, trying to learn thoroughly what it possesses."[70] Nor is speech the only or the best route upwards to the truth.

> Nor do I think that we should suppose that they use speech in the intelligible world, and altogether, even if they have bodies in heaven, there would be none of that talk there which they engage in here because of needs or over doubtful and disputed points; but as they do everything they do in order and according to nature they would not give orders or advice and would know by intuition (*sunesis*) what passes from one to another. For here below, too, we can know many things by the look in people's eyes when they are silent; but there all

---

68 James, *Varieties of Religious Experience*, 388.
69 *Ennead* V.3 [49].17.
70 *Ennead* III.8 [30].6, 14 and 27–29.

their body is clear and pure and each is like an eye, and nothing is hidden or feigned, but before one speaks to another that other has seen and understood.[71]

Speech may actually disguise our meaning — so "let [one who wishes to understand] abandon the verbal signification and grasp the meaning of what is being said":[72] a plea that any author must occasionally murmur, though with a less metaphysical purpose! Only a few authors resort to deliberate nonsense of a strangely evocative sort — employing, like Tom Bombadil, "an ancient language whose words were mainly those of wonder and delight."[73]

Is this indeed a "state of consciousness" that has any relevance for the ancient myths? Consider again the emergence of Atum from "nothing." That Nothing, the original Chaos or Gap, is difficult or impossible to conceive or describe: as Edwards said, any attempt to do so results in conceiving *something*, even if that is only darkness, or sludge, or a sea of "virtual particles" that roll between being and non-being.[74] There are no divisions there, no boundaries or distinct identities.[75] The Nothing which is called Nun quickly becomes Apophis, the eternal serpent who will one day consume the world. But if we seriously attempt to think of the emergence of distinct entities, or even of their eventual end, it is clear that we cannot suppose that Nothing is itself a Thing. We cannot conceive it at all — but that does not necessarily mean that we must abandon any thought of it, or that we cannot, in some way, encounter it. The incomprehensible X before, behind

---

71 *Ennead* IV.3 [27].18; see also V.8 [31].4, and II.3 [52].7. The phrase is also used by Kadowaki, *Zen and the Bible*, 33: working on Zen koans has the object of extending enlightenment from the mind's eye through the whole body, so that "the whole body is an eye." Kadowacki (ibid., 13, 49) also emphasises the body language that precedes "oral speech."
72 *Ennead* VI.4 [22].2; see also IV.8 [6].9.
73 Tolkien, *Lord of the Rings*, 1:158.
74 Cf. Plato, *Republic* 5.477a6–478e5.
75 Some Stoic philosophers preferred to think of this condition as "the life of Zeus, when the world is dissolved and the gods have been blended together into one, when nature comes to a stop for a while" (Seneca, *Letters* 9.16, in Long and Sedley, *Hellenistic Philosophers*, 277 [46A]). Others, perhaps more consistently, thought there was no need for any such condition — as "God" was already all there is: we are mistaken in seeing any really distinct identities. See, further, Long and Sedley, *Hellenistic Philosophers*, 274–79. As usual, it is impossible to conceive of Nothing.

and after Atum seems indistinguishable from the goal of "mystical" endeavour. Plotinus may speak of this Nothing as "Matter," and reckons it as difficult, as impossible, to conceptualize as the One itself. None of us ever encounters Matter directly, but only the golden chains that bind it,[76] just as Being serves as a golden screen or advance guard between us and the Good Itself.[77] Only what lies between Nothing and the One can be appreciated or spoken of "intellectually." "Before" Soul, "before" experience, there is neither time nor space nor any distinct quality: whatever existed then, or exists beyond the reach of Soul, is not to be described as anything like what is experienced. Being Nothing, it looks like nothing![78] How then, as Hume enquires, "do you mystics, who maintain the absolute incomprehensibility of God, differ from sceptics or atheists who assert that the first cause of everything is unknown and unintelligible?"[79] The appropriate response to either would seem to be silence, but there may be different sorts of silence.

The most obvious context for wordless experience is the mystical appreciation of the One.

> It is there that one lets all study go; up to a point one has been led along and settled firmly in beauty and as far as this one thinks that in which one is, but is carried out of it by a kind of swell and sees suddenly, not seeing how, but the vision fills his eyes with light and does not make him see something else by it, but the light itself is what he sees.[80]

The transcendent cause of everything is not itself a thing.

> It is therefore truly ineffable: for whatever you say about it you will always be speaking of a "something." But "beyond all things and beyond the supreme majesty of

---

76   *Enneads* I.8 [51].15.
77   *Ennead* I.6 [1].9.
78   As Lem says (though still managing somehow to believe in the real existence of a material world that is not, and cannot be, experienced), 'one can say that an ocean exists when there is no one there, but one cannot ask what it looks like then. If it looks a certain way, it means that there is someone looking at it": Lem, *Summa Technologiae*, 215.
79   Hume, *Dialogues*, 4, in Gaskin, *Dialogues*, 60-61.
80   *Enneads* VI.7 [38].36.

Ritual and Belief

Intellect" is the only one of all the ways of speaking of it which is true; it is not its name, but says that it is not one of all things and "has no name," because we can say nothing of it: we can only try, as far as possible, to make signs to ourselves about it.[81]

What we cannot talk about we cannot reason about either, nor do we discover it by any familiar form of *reasoning*. Notoriously, this makes it difficult to understand what Plotinus meant.

> The perplexity arises especially because our awareness of the One is not by way of reasoned knowledge (*episteme*) or of intellectual perception (*noesis*) as with other intelligible things, but by way of a presence superior to knowledge. The soul experiences its falling away from being one and is not altogether one when it has reasoned knowledge of anything; for reasoned knowledge is a rational process (*logos*), and a rational process is many. The soul therefore goes past the One and falls into number and multiplicity. One must therefore run up above knowledge and in no way depart from being one, but one must depart from knowledge and things known, and from every other, even beautiful, object of vision.... Therefore, Plato says, "it cannot be spoken or written," but we speak and write impelling towards it and wakening from reasonings to the vision of it, as if showing the way to one who wants to have a view of something.[82]

Even the One itself can neither speak nor know Itself.

> If [the intellect] directed its gaze to a single object without parts, it would be without thought or word (*elogethe*): for what would it have to say about or to understand? For if the absolutely partless had to speak itself, it must, first of all, say what it is not; so that in this way too it would be many in order to be one. Then when it says "I am this," if it means something other than itself by "this," it will be telling a lie; but if it is speaking of some incidental property of itself, it will be saying that it is many or saying "am am" or "I I."[83]

Is this wholly beyond our power to recognize? The mystery

---

81 *Enneads* V.3 [49].13.
82 *Enneads* VI.9 [9].4, citing Plato, *Letter* 7.241c5.
83 *Enneads* V.3 [49].10; see also VI.7 [38].35.

is ubiquitous, but we can understand a little more about it by considering again the *personal* encounter. After all, even our own intimacies are often beyond our grasp!

> Man knows that there are in the soul tints more bewildering, more numberless, and more nameless than the colours of an autumn forest.... Yet he seriously believes that these things can every one of them, in all their tones and semi-tones, in all their blends and unions, be accurately represented by an arbitrary system of grunts and squeals. He believes that an ordinary civilized stockbroker can really produce out of his own inside noises which denote all the mysteries of memory and all the agonies of desire.[84]

Silence does indeed seem better, in the face of mystery![85]

When Frodo asks Bombadil who he is, Bombadil replies "Tell me, who are you, alone, yourself and nameless?"[86] No one is to be summed up simply as a particular sort of creature, even an accidentally unique one.

> In every sphere, in every relational act, through everything that becomes present to us, we gaze toward the train of the eternal You; in each we perceive a breath of it, in every you we address the eternal You, in every sphere according to its manner. All spheres are included in it, while it is included in none. Through all of them shines the one presence.[87]

The usual assumption, for those who thus emphasise the mystery of personal being, is that it is only in *human beings*, people, that the mystery is encountered. "We characterize God's mode of being as *personal*, primarily because it corresponds to the experience we have of human personal existence: existence with self-consciousness, with rational relatedness, with ecstatic (active) otherness and freedom from any predetermination."[88] That is not entirely my own experience, though I accept Yannaras's

---

84 Chesterton, G. F. *Watts*, 88.
85 So Apollonius, speaking of Pythagoras: "he made riddling a precept when he invented speech as the teacher of silence": Philostratus, *Life of Apollonius*, 2:131 [6.11.13].
86 Tolkien, *Lord of the Rings*, 1:142.
87 Buber, *I and Thou*, 150.
88 Yannaras, *On the Absence and Unknowability of God*, 85.

characterization of God's activity as one of "personal relationship and loving communion." Anything at all may suddenly be *there* for us, may wake us up, whether an octopus suddenly looking back at us or a tree suddenly more than a merely leafy plant. "Each grain of sand, every stone on the land, each rock and each hill, each fountain and rill, each herb and each tree, Mountain, hill, earth, and sea, Cloud, meteor, and star, Are men seen afar"[89]—not because Blake imagined them to be our conspecifics, nor even that they were "like" us, but because each such thing is more than its own form.

The Darkness from which all things come is, as it were, a "dazzling darkness."[90]

But there may still be a problem. Lovecraft, in his attempts to transcend the merely human and domestic scene, populated his mythological landscape with the literally "indescribable," and unfamiliar feelings compounded of terror, dread, curiosity, and (imagined) objects beyond ordinary taxonomies (vegetable, animal, mineral) and geometries. He was even, at times, attempting the same task as Plotinus in his attempt to describe what lies before or behind all form!

> We in our travail do not know what we ought to say, and are speaking of what cannot be spoken, and give it a name because we want to indicate it to ourselves as best we can. But perhaps this name "One" contains [only] a denial of multiplicity. This is why the Pythagoreans symbolically indicated it to each other by the name of Apollo, in negation of the multiple [that is, A—*Pollon*: Not Many].[91]

Lovecraft called that ultimately indescribable Somewhat Azathoth instead, disclaiming any association with beauty, intelligence or meaning. To that I shall return.

---

89 Blake, Letter to Thomas Butts (2 October 1800), in *Complete Writings*, 804-5. Raine (*Blake and the New Age*, 116-18) identifies Swedenborg as the source of Blake's conception.
90 Vaughan, *Silex Scintillans*, 300.
91 *Ennead* V.5 [32].6, 23-29. Apollo—remember—was not, as so many commentators suppose, a god of *clarity* and *order*, but of impossible enigmas and brutal force: the Christians who chose to speak instead of "Apollyon," the Destroyer, had some reason on their side—though the same might also be said of YHWH.

~7~
Monotheisms

> "No one can serve two masters; for either he will hate the one and love the other, or else he will be loyal to the one and despise the other. You cannot serve God and Mammon."[1]

MODERN DEROGATIONS OF MONOTHEISM

It has been fashionable of late to suggest that "monotheism" is essentially intolerant and exclusivist: if we are to have no other "gods" but the one "true" god, the devotees of other faiths must be entirely wrong. The same intolerance may be displayed by those who insist that there is one true way to knowledge, and that all other faiths are dangerous superstitions. Polytheists—who recognize that there are many different sources of comfort and inspiration, and many different ways of interpreting and learning from experience—may be broadly tolerant of dissensions, though there will always be some limit to their tolerance (as there are also likely limits for Pyrrhonian doubt). Even polytheists may attempt to construct some framework for those varied gods and goals, some single order, and even tidy their variety by identifying seemingly discrete divinities.

> The polytheistic religions overcame the primitive ethnocentrism of tribal religions by distinguishing several deities by name, shape, and function. The names are, of course, different in different cultures, because the languages are different. The shapes of the gods and the forms of worship may also differ significantly. But the functions are strikingly similar, especially in the case of cosmic deities; and most deities had a cosmic function. The sun god of one religion is easily equated to the sun god of another religion, and so forth. Because of their functional equivalence, deities of different religions can be equated.

---

[1] Matthew 6.24.

Monotheisms

In Mesopotamia, the practice of translating divine names goes back to the third millennium BC... In the second millennium, this practice was extended to many different languages and civilizations of the Near East. The cultures, languages, and customs may have been as different as ever: the religions always had a common ground. Thus they functioned as a means of intercultural translatability. The gods were international because they were cosmic. The different peoples worshipped different gods, but nobody contested the reality of foreign gods and the legitimacy of foreign forms of worship.[2]

Some of these identifications may seem strange: none more so, perhaps, than the equation of YHWH and Dionysos,[3] or the suggestion that Hera and Aphrodite are the same, as both being or representing the Soul of Zeus.[4] The political and metaphysical effects of these proposed identities are notable. The stories change as they are rationalized into almost-consistency.

In considering where the ascendancy of the ruler metaphor has led, we note that the whole view of existence appears to have changed. The earlier world in which things happened more or less by themselves and the gods were "intransitive" powers has yielded to a planned, purposeful universe actively administered and ruled by

---

2 Assmann, *Moses the Egyptian*, 3; see also ibid., 45: "The meaning of a deity is his or her specific character as it is unfolded in myths, hymns, rites, and so on. This character makes a deity comparable to other deities with similar traits. The similarity of gods makes their names mutually translatable. But in historical reality, this correlation has to be reversed. The practice of translating the names of the gods created a concept of similarity and produced the idea or conviction that gods are international."
3 Plutarch, *Quaestiones Convivales* 4.6.1–2. See Amzallag, "Was Yahweh Worshiped in the Aegean?" But is the equation so doubtful? Dionysos subverted order almost as much as YHWH: both are consummate Outsiders!
4 *Ennead* III.5 [50].8, 19–24. Plotinus here adopts the suggestion that female deities represent the souls accompanying the distinct intellects who are represented as male deities. Blake seems to borrow the notion: each creative energy has a female emanation, and the division of these constitutes our fall. "Man divided from his Emanation is a dark Spectre, His Emanation is an ever-weeping melancholy Shadow" (Blake, *Jerusalem*, ch. 3, plate 54, in *Complete Writings*, 684). See Billigheimer, "Conflict and Conquest," for a sympathetic account of Blake's account of Fall and Redemption, via the relations of Intellect and Soul, or Male and Female. Women, of course, have reason to be irritated by the assumption that they are properly only the helpmates of their lords and masters, but the metaphors involved are not wholly misogynistic.

gods who have broadened their concerns far beyond what we call nature: to society as upholders of the legal and moral order, and to politics, deciding about victory and defeat. They have come to control and shape history.[5]

Mediterranean religion, perhaps especially Roman religion, was mostly syncretic and inclusive. Even such rites as struck most ordinary Romans as indecent might still have their respect: the rites of Cybele, for example, which sometimes included ecstatic self-castration, were nonetheless parts of Roman official religion, as linking them to their purported Trojan ancestors.[6] Conversely, child sacrifice was an evil mostly because it was practised by the Carthaginians! Minucius Felix (died c. AD 250) records the judgment that this (limited) tolerance was the real secret of the Romans' imperial success:

> Thus it is that their power and authority has embraced the circuit of the whole world, and has advanced the bounds of empire beyond the paths of the sun, and the confines of ocean; while they practise in the field god-fearing valour, make strong their city with awe of sacred rites, with chaste virgins, with many a priestly dignity and title; besieged and imprisoned within the limits of the Capitol, they still reverenced the gods, whom others might have spurned as [enraged], and through the ranks of Gauls amazed at their undaunted superstition [the audacity of their superstition] passed on armed not with weapons but with godly reverence and fear; in captured fortresses, even in the first flush of victory, they reverence the conquered deities; everywhere they entertain the gods and adopt them as their own; while they raise altars even to the unknown deities, and to the spirits of the dead. Thus is it that they adopt the sacred rites of all nations, and withal have earned dominion.[7]

It was not only the Hebrews who resented this assimilation, and subordination, of their own gods, rituals, and stories,[8] but

---

5 Jacobsen, *Treasures*, 90.
6 Beard, "The Roman and the Foreign."
7 Minucius Felix, *Octavius*, 329 [6.2–3].
8 See Caseau, "Sacred Landscapes," 21: the citizens of Gholaia in Libya, as soon as the Roman legionnaires had withdrawn in 270, "carefully desecrated the religious spaces within the Roman camp and destroyed the cult statues."

Monotheisms

the *principle* was perhaps the only one available to the empire. And it can be admitted that there are metaphysical as well as political advantages to such a structured polytheism, as Armstrong noted:

> Even if we retain any sense of a divine presence in the world, we have to admit that it manifests itself in innumerably various, apparently clashing, often inscrutably odd and terrifying ways. Divine unity, not divine plurality, requires an effort of reflection and faith to attain it; and when attained, it does not necessarily exclude plurality.[9]

It follows that despite any strength there may be in monotheistic theory our lives here-now are subject to a plurality of laws and purposes, none of which is clearly dominant forever. It seems folly to follow *one* goal, cultivate *one* habit of mind and practice, or expect *one* universal law to explain just everything. Even those who are most firmly and rationally "monotheistic" should recognize that any proffered image of the God will only be an idol. "The divine word at the beginning forbids that the Divine be likened to any of the things known by men, since every concept which comes from some comprehensible image by an approximate understanding and by guessing at the divine nature constitutes an idol of God and does not proclaim God."[10] Even the most rational of scientists should acknowledge that even the best current theory is not a *final* theory, nor likely to cover *all* cases. Even those who look forward to establishing a single Global Authority must recognize that there will always — or at least as long as our descendants are still human — be very many nations, sects, professions, and personal entanglements that each serve a separate vision.[11]

And yet the notion of a *single* authority, a *single* source of being, retains its own power. Blake, who also acknowledge the compresence of many "gods," was adamant that they were only "thieves and rebels" if they were "separated from man or humanity, who is Jesus the Saviour."[12] And those who worshipped the various

---

9 Armstrong, "Some Advantages of Polytheism," 184.
10 Gregory of Nyssa, *Life of Moses*, 81 (2.166).
11 A point elaborated in my "Sphere with Many Faces," and also "Global Religions."
12 Blake, "Descriptive Catalogue" (1809), no. 3 (Chaucer and the pilgrims), in *Complete Works*, 571.

Olympians also expected them all to be obedient to Zeus: "Zeus, the mighty lord, holding the reins of a winged chariot, leads the way in heaven, ordering all and taking care of all; and there follows him the array of gods and demigods, marshalled in eleven bands."[13] If there are still many gods, there may be a divine hierarchy which is more or less stable, and also always at risk. Amon-Ra may lose his position when once Isis compels him to reveal his real name. Kronos has long been overthrown—and Zeus himself may have reason to fear some future son.

> A more radical way of consolidating powers was to unify them by identifying their several divine bearers as but aspects of one and the same deity. This was not new; in all periods the line between the epithets and names of a deity had been fluid, and the decision in a given case as to whether one or more gods were involved must already have been a difficult one for the ancients. What is new in the first millennium, though, is a remarkable readiness to bring such uncertainty about separateness or identicalness, to bear upon major, well defined, clearly distinct deities. As an example, a text that baldly states: "Ninurta is Marduk of the hoe, Nergal is Marduk of the attack, Zababa is Marduk of the hand-to-hand fight, Enlil is Marduk of lordship and counsel, Nabium is Marduk of accounting, Sin is Marduk, the illuminator of the night, Shamash is Marduk of justice, Adad is Marduk of rains." As will be seen even from this excerpt a remarkable number of major gods are here simply identified with aspects of Marduk, that is to say, with functions of his that correspond to their own characteristic natures, functions, and powers.[14]

Cosmologically, many different stuffs and energies turn out to be, or are presumed to be, aspects of some single stuff or energy, even if we cannot yet provide a single theory to accommodate, for example, both the general theory of relativity and quantum mechanics, and even if the number of different sorts of particle or wave-form seems to increase with every investigation!

---

13 Plato, *Phaedrus* 247a (trans. Benjamin Jowett).
14 Jacobsen, *Treasures*, 234–35, citing Cuneiform Texts from Babylonian Tablets in the British Museum, XXIV pl. 50, no. 47406 obv. 3-10.

Politically, we hope for or fear some universal agreement between disparate tribes and legal systems, or else (more practically) work out particular accommodations when a special agreement is needed, without supposing that the same accommodation will be acceptable elsewhere. Psychologically, we accept that we have many different interests and delights, but profess still to believe that we are each single individuals, from birth or conception to brain death, and each accountable for all that we have done. The appearance of any radical disunity is considered madness or hypocrisy, unless (perhaps) we are persuaded that our unity is only an aspiration, and our identity is easily deconstructed. By this last account, we need to be disabused, disillusioned, and enlightened by the Buddhist insight: that there is no self. In the *Questions of King Milinda* (which is Menander, ruling in the second century BC in northwest India) the Buddhist philosopher Nagasena explains to Menander that no complex entity is anything but a collection of parts: better still, such words as seem to name that complex entity are only convenient designations for what has no substantial being. "Nagasena" itself is "but a way of counting, term, appellation, convenient designation, mere name for the hair of the head, hair of the body... brain of the head, form, sensation, perception, the predispositions and consciousness. But in the absolute sense there is no ego to be found."[15]

But perhaps there is after all.

> For every man, whatever the Culture to which he belongs, the elements of the soul are the deities of an inner mythology. What Zeus was for the outer Olympus, Nous was for the inner world that every Greek was entirely conscious of possessing—the throned lord of the other soul-elements.... The Classical soul, therefore, with its parts and its properties, imagines itself as an Olympus of little gods, and to keep these at peace and in harmony with one another is the ideal of the Greek life-ethic of *sophrosune* and *ataraxia*.[16]

---

15 Radhakrishnan and Moore, *Sourcebook*, 281–84. Rhys-Davies, *Milinda Panha*, 16–17 offers a milder version of the claim, acknowledging that Nagasena, like other things, is a real complex of many parts.
16 Spengler, *Decline of the West*, 1:411–12.

The further question is whether this unifying somewhat is transcendent or immanent (or of course both).

> There is either one first principle or many. If there is one, we have what we are looking for; if there are many, they are either ordered or disordered. Now if they are disordered, their products are more so, and the world is not a world but a chaos; besides, that which is contrary to nature belongs to that which is non-existent. If on the other hand they are ordered, they were ordered either by themselves or by some outside cause. But if they were ordered by themselves they have something in common that unites them, and that is the first principle.[17]

AKHENATEN AND AFTER

The first explicitly monotheistic and exclusive cult of which we have any current knowledge was Akhenaten's: in Hornung's summary, "there is no god but Aten, and Akhenaten is his prophet," as "the Aten's nature is not revealed in mythical images, but is accessible only through intellectual effort and insight—and hence is not revealed to everyone, but only to Akhenaten and those whom he teaches."[18] Akhenaten (in the late 14th century BC) replaced the multifarious gods by one singular image, one worshipful cause of life and light and being, dismissing all the others as inglorious fictions.

Whatever the metaphysical significance of Akhenaten's cult, its political effects seem to have been unwelcome. The Egyptians of his time had conceived of themselves as members of a town or city rather than as members of a nation, let alone as members of a single universal God-ordained collective.

> The city was where they belonged and where they wanted to be buried. Belonging to a city primarily meant belonging to a deity as the master of that city. This sense of belonging to a god or goddess was created and confirmed by participating in the feasts. The abolition of the feasts [by Akhenaten] must have deprived the individual Egyptians of their sense of identity and, what is more,

---

17 Aristotle, Ross Fragments 88 [fr. 17].
18 Hornung, Conceptions of God, 248.

Monotheisms

their hopes of immortality. For following the deities in their earthly feasts was held to be the first and most necessary step toward otherworldly beatitude.[19]

Whether this was a genuinely "religious" revolution, or merely a political power-grab, is moot. His attempt did not succeed — though later priests and would-be theologians seemingly accepted the need for unity in the heavens, though of the syncretic rather than the strongly imperial sort.

> "All gods are three," we read in an Egyptian text, which then states that these three gods are just aspects of One God: "All gods are three: Amun, Re, and Ptah, whom none equals. He who hides his name as Amun, he appears to the face as Re, his body is Ptah." All gods are three, and these three are encompassed and transcended by a god who is referred to only as "He," whose name is Amun, whose cosmic manifestation is Re, and whose body, or cult image, is Ptah. Even the name of "Amun," the "Hidden One," is just an epithet screening the true and hidden name of this god, of whom another hymn states: "People fall down immediately for fear if his name is uttered knowingly or unknowingly. There is no god able to call him by it." This text was written in the thirteenth century, when the monotheistic revolution by Akhenaten had already been overturned and the traditional religion with its plethora of temples and deities was reinstituted. Despite this external restitution, however, Akhenaten's revolution had left a deep impression on Egyptian thought and had led to a veritable explosion of explicit theological discourse, which now concentrated more than ever on the topic of the oneness of God. The traditional paradigm of creation and sovereignty is now complemented by the new paradigm of hiddenness and manifestation.[20]

This unity represents an "inclusive" rather than Akhenaten's "exclusive" monotheism.[21]

---

19 Assmann, *Moses the Egyptian*, 26.
20 Assmann, *Akhenaten to Moses*, 13-14; see Allen, *Genesis in Egypt*, 62; Hornung, *Conceptions of God*, 219.
21 See Assmann, *Of God and Gods*, 53.

> The author of the Memphite treatise has skilfully incorporated all the widely known and accepted great traditions into his own system; instead of attempting to replace these old traditions with something new, he has appropriated their weight of authority for the benefit of Ptah.[22]

Other divine names and stories are conceived as manifestations of an underlying unity, in tune with earlier accounts of many gods as each themselves multifaceted, "lords of faces":[23] a notion that is echoed, at least in Plotinus's evocation of the Divine as a sphere "all faces, shining with living faces."[24]

> The attempt to eliminate the many was rejected, in its place the view was propounded that the many are manifestations of the one. The success of the new theology is illustrated by its longevity, still being encountered in the texts of the Graeco-Roman temples of Egypt and in late magical texts.[25]

In more than merely *magical* texts: the inclusive form is explicit, for example, in the speech the "Middle Platonist" Apuleius ascribed to Isis in his picaresque novel, *The Golden Ass*.

> I, mother of the universe, mistress of all the elements, first born of the ages, highest of the gods, queen of the shades, first of those who dwell in heaven, representing in one shape all gods and goddesses. My will controls the shining heights of heaven, the health-giving sea-winds, and the mournful silences of hell; the entire world worships my single godhead in a thousand shapes, with diverse rites, and under many names. The Phrygians, first born of mankind, call me the Pessinuntian Mother of the gods; the native Athenians the Cecropian Minerva; the island-dwelling Cypriots Paphian Venus; the archer Cretans Dictynnan Diana; the triple-tongued Sicilians Stygian Proserpine; the ancient Eleusinians Actaean Ceres; some call me Juno, some Bellona, others Hecate, others Rhamnusia; but both races of Ethiopians,

---

22 Ockinga, "The Memphite Theology," 101.
23 Hornung, *Conceptions of God*, 126.
24 *Ennead* VI.7 [38].15, 25.
25 Ockinga, "The Memphite Theology," 111–12.

those on whom the rising and those on whom the setting sun shines, and the Egyptians who excel in ancient learning, honour me with the worship which is truly mine and call me by my true name: Queen Isis.[26]

The gods, however they are named, are universal:

> God is not senseless nor inanimate nor subject to human control. As a result of this we have come to regard as gods those who make use of these things and present them to us and provide us with things everlasting and constant. Nor do we think of the gods as different gods among different peoples, nor as barbarian gods and Greek gods, nor as southern and northern gods; but, just as the sun and the moon and the heavens and the earth and the sea are common to all, but are called by different names by different peoples, so for that one rationality which keeps all these things in order and the one Providence which watches over them and the ancillary powers that are set over all, there have arisen among different peoples, in accordance with their customs, different honours and appellations. Thus men make use of consecrated symbols, some employing symbols that are obscure, but others those that are clearer, in guiding the intelligence toward things divine, though not without a certain hazard. For some go completely astray and become engulfed in superstition; and others, while they fly from superstition as from a quagmire, on the other hand unwittingly fall, as it were, over a precipice into atheism.[27]

As Assmann observes, "the deity whose theology was most strongly informed by this universalist concept was Isis—not in her traditional Egyptian form, but in the form she assumed in Greco-Egyptian syncretism."[28]

Many centuries later the Norse All Father claimed a similar preeminence.

---

26 Apuleius, *Golden Ass*, 197–98 [11.5]. Hornung, *Conceptions of God*, 86: "in the Graeco-Roman period the goddess Isis was still simply the 'one of many names,' as was appropriate to the richness and diversity of her nature." See also Hanegraaff, *Hermetic Spirituality*, 264–65.
27 Plutarch, "Isis and Osiris" 67, in *Moralia*, 5:156–57.
28 Assmann, *Moses the Egyptian*, 47. See ibid., 48–50 for similar contemporary declarations that Isis was to be worshipped under many names.

Most of his names have been given him by reason of this chance: there being so many branches of tongues in the world, all peoples believed that it was needful for them to turn his name into their own tongue, by which they might the better invoke him and entreat him on their own.[29]

The very notion of a "true name" lay behind an earlier story—of how Isis managed to depose Ra by learning the real name behind his manifestations as "Khepry in the morning, Re at midday, Atum in the evening."[30] Names—that is, "true names"—embody real natures: the things as they are understood in the original language, or in the "mind of God." The Name, as much as the statue, is the god's active presence.

> Creation, according to the Shabaka Stone [inscribed 8th century BC, and the principal evidence for "the Memphite Theology"], was both a spiritual or intellectual creation as well as a physical one. It was through the divine heart (thought) and tongue (speech/word) of Ptah as the great causer of something to take shape in the form of the physical agent of creation Atum, through which everything came forth. Importantly, creation was first and foremost an intellectual activity and only then a physical one. The intellectual principles of creative thought and commanding speech were realized in Ptah and could be said to be embodied in him. He is that which "causes every conclusion to emerge" (line 56). Just as important though, at several points earlier in the text, as well as within the Memphite Theology, Ptah is identified as Ta-tenen, the primeval mound that Atum sat upon arising from the waters of Nun as he

---

29 Sturluson, Prose Edda, 34 ("Beguiling of Gylfi," ch. 20).
30 Hornung, Conceptions of God, 88; see Pritchard, Ancient Near Eastern Texts, 12-14. Cf. Schweizer, Sungod's Journey through the Netherworld, 46: 'Re as the daytime sky, Atum as the western horizon, Khepri as the eastern horizon, and Osiris as the embodiment of the netherworldly, nocturnal sun. Re is the active ruler of the sky and the daytime world; Osiris is the passive, albeit beloved, god of the realm of the dead; Atum is the aged god who descends into the depths, worn and weary from his day's labors; and Khepri is the newborn solar child who is greeted with jubilation at daybreak. All of these are aspects of one and the same truth, of the unique Great Soul whose totality can best be described as a fourfold process of transformation.'

created the gods (see lines 2, 3, 13c, 58, 61, and 64). So, while Ptah is the intellectual and creative principle that "in-forms" and precedes all matter, he is also "a physical principle that is the font of all matter, conceptualized in his identification with Ta-tenen," and in his imparting of life to Atum who, standing on Ta-tenen, carried out physical creation. Thus, in keeping with the notion that the things of the universe are for the Egyptians beings with distinct wills and personalities, it is through both spiritual and physical principles and actions—personified in and derived from Ptah—that the world becomes a reality. It did not take scholars long to recognize that in the ideas of the Memphite Theology there was an approach similar to the Greek notion of *logos*.[31]

In this notion, that is, the cosmos begins in a genuine creation, precisely because the creator God holds His purpose and Form already, "before" it is realized in the material world, "before" He is, as it were, incarnate. The *Logos*—to give it the later title—exists "before" the world is made, contains the forms of all that is to be, and is incarnate in that world to make it. Augustine reasonably replied to those pagans who disputed the possibility, or the decency, of a divine incarnation: "You (sc. Porphyry) who say that all body must be avoided, kill the universe! You are saying that I should escape from my flesh: let your Jupiter [taking Jupiter here to be the World Soul] escape from heaven and earth!"[32]

That *Logos* also outlasts the world and all its creatures: "You will roll them up like a robe; like a garment they will be changed. But you remain the same, and your years will never end."[33] In the meantime that *Logos* is active in all existing things, though its nature is not exhausted by those things. And the power that makes and sustains all things has its own ideas about what should be (and often isn't):

> I did four good deeds within the portal of the horizon.
> I made the four winds so that every man might breath in his surroundings.

---

31 Bodine, "Shabaka Stone," 18–19; see Allen, *Genesis in Egypt*, 44–47.
32 Augustine, *Sermon* 241.7, in O'Daly, *Augustine's Philosophy of Mind*, 67.
33 Hebrews 1.12.

That is one of the deeds.
I made the great flood so that poor and rich might have power.
That is one of the deeds.
I made every man like his fellow.
I did not ordain that they do wrong.; their hearts disobeyed what I had said.
That is one of the deeds.
I caused that their hearts should not forget the west, so that offerings be presented to the gods of the nomes.
That is one of the deeds.34

THE HEBREW STORY

The other exclusive monotheism that—maybe—issued from Egypt was the Hebraic. Some have found some congruence, or even an historical connection, between Akhenaten's revolution and the Mosaic,35 but there are also considerable differences. Akhenaten was attempting to centralize authority, and replace the pluriform images by a much thinner, rationalistic, account of the divine, symbolized solely in the sun's visible disc. Mosaic Law was also political, but the community being created did not, at least at first, lend authority to any human monarch, nor did it rest on abstract reasoning, and explicitly rejected *any* picture of the divine, including the Sun, Moon and Stars. The God that Moses perhaps proclaimed (the God of Abraham, Isaac, and Jacob) was recognized in the command to come away from Ur and Haran, and "to let His people go." It is that memory, of liberation from slavery, from a divinized monarch, and from the Babylonian tyranny of the stars, that was to be maintained throughout Hebrew history—even when the people of Israel were so rash as to require a king to make themselves more respectable in the eyes of their neighbours.36 Their constant error, according to the Hebrew Scriptures,

---

34 *Coffin Texts* VII, 462dff., cited by Hornung, *Conceptions of God*, 198–99. From the Old Kingdom until the end Egypt was divided into roughly 42 districts (22 in Upper and 20 in Lower Egypt around the Delta): "nomes."
35 The best evidence of a connection, by whatever unknown route, is the verbal and structural correspondence between the *Hymn to Aten* (Pritchard, *Ancient Near Eastern Texts*, 369–71) and Psalm 104. See Levenson, *Creation and the Persistence of Evil*, 60–64.
36 1 Samuel 8.4–22.

was to be seduced by the gods of other nations, and to join their temple rituals. Those same scriptures recorded, or invented, the ruthless suppression of such alien ways. Phinehas, son of Eleazer, for example, killed an Israelite and a Midianite woman in their bed, "pinning them together," and so — it was said — turned the Lord's wrath away from Israel, and so ended a plague in which twenty-four thousand had already died.[37] In later life Phinehas encouraged the general assault on the tribe of Benjamin for the atrocious rape and murder of the Levite's concubine.[38] Any sign of mercy to the other tribes, and their ways, was mercilessly rebuked and punished. On the other hand, the very same chapters that decree such grievous penalties for fraternizing insist that "when an alien settles among you, you shall not oppress him. He shall be treated as a native born among you, and you shall love him as a man like yourself, because you were aliens in Egypt."[39] Moses's wife was herself a Midianite, and David, Israel's favourite king, was the greatgrandson of a Moabite.[40]

One obvious, familiar, response is to treat the stories as allegorical — very much as we now read the Psalmist's pleas to cast his enemies into the pit,[41] or his gloating fantasy of dashing Babylon's children against the rocks.[42] What must be driven out is sin, and there is a penalty for failure. But "it is all very well to say that the Canaanites that we should root out are vice and sinfulness, but we still have texts that speak rather clearly of slaughtering human beings."[43]

---

37 Numbers 25.6–18. Later Rabbis did not doubt that Phinehas was in the right, but they were disturbed that "due process" had not been followed, and were cautious in the morals they drew from the story. Philo preferred to allegorize it entirely, seeing Phinehas as that Reason which refuses the wiles of Pleasure: see Feldman, "The Portrayal of Phinehas by Philo, Pseudo-Philo, and Josephus." Ps-Philo even identified Phinehas with the prophet Elijah, and suggests that he will live on till the Last Day.
38 Judges 20.28; see Judges 19.16–30 for the story of the murder.
39 Leviticus 19.33–4.
40 Ruth 4.13–22; see also Matthew 1.6.
41 Psalm 55.23.
42 Psalm 137.9 — the verse is now usually omitted when the psalm is read in church. Perhaps it shouldn't be: it is an abrupt and terrible end to one of the most moving of the psalms of exile: "By the rivers of Babylon we sat down and wept when we remembered Zion." We need to remember what our hearts desire.
43 Collins, "Zeal of Phinehas," 19.

> They did not destroy the peoples round about,
> As the Lord had commanded them to do,
> But they mingled with the nations,
> Learning their ways;
> They worshipped their idols
> And were ensnared by them.
> Their sons and their daughters
> They sacrificed to foreign demons;
> They shed innocent blood,
> The blood of sons and daughters
> Offered to the gods of Canaan,
> And the land was polluted with blood.
> Thus they defiled themselves by their conduct
> And they followed their lusts and broke faith with God.[44]

It may also be that the stories don't record the *actual* incursion into Palestine, but are rather "ideological fictions," warnings, centuries later, to such Israelites as were tempted by the alien gods. Phinehas's (imagined?) example helped to fire up Mattathias, father of Judas Maccabaeus, to the murder of an Israelite traitor in the days when Antiochus Epiphanes was seeking to demolish Israel, and so led on to the Maccabaean revolt.[45]

But before we finally disown those earlier passages—composed many centuries after the events—as demonstrating a merely xenophobic, pathologically doctrinaire attitude, it is as well to set them in context. The Israelites were not alone in practicing (or imagining) the total eradication of alien populations, their "dedication" to the god of their devotion.

> A famous parallel is provided by the Moabite Stone, erected by the ninth-century king Mesha: "And Chemosh said to me, 'Go, take Nebo from Israel'. So I went by night and fought against it from the break of dawn until noon, taking it and slaying all, seven thousand men, boys, women, girls, and maid-servants, for I had devoted them to destruction for (the god) Ashtar-Chemosh."[46]

---

[44] Psalm 106.34–39. See also Ecclesiasticus 45.23, which names Phinehas as "third in renown" after Moses and Aaron.
[45] I Maccabees 2.23–28.
[46] Collins, "Zeal of Phinehas," 5. See also Stern, *The Biblical Herem*; Pritchard

So also, when Odysseus returned at last to Ithaca, he killed the suitors infesting his home, and also executed supposedly disloyal slaves and slavegirls, with — apparently — his gods' approval.[47] A few centuries later the Athenians were only a little less destructive when they slaughtered all the *adult* males of Melos and enslaved the rest, without bothering to claim more than their own power to do so as a sufficient excuse.[48] And the record of later, supposedly "enlightened" persons is not very much better.

At least the biblical story offers a slightly better reason for this fierce intolerance: that the Canaanites (allegedly) killed children,[49] and by implication also served their gods or demons by promiscuous sex. The plague that was killing thousands, it is reasonable to suppose, was sexually transmitted.[50] The rules that Israel accepted were required if the people were to live. Seduction, under the circumstances, was an act of war, and a desperate population chose the only way they could see to survive. That we now have other ways, perhaps, is because they *did* survive, somehow maintaining the sense to see that ethnic origin was not the issue, and that there was a path to justice.

This very impulse, to survive as a national unity, demanded that the god of their worship be more than simply a tribal patron. The land of Canaan, it was supposed, was His to give His people, and to cleanse from squatters. And the only way that this could seem possibly true was for the Lord also to be the Creator and thereby the Owner of all lands and peoples. He must therefore stand *outside* the natural order, as its sole origin and master.[51] At the same time, that Lord was introduced from the beginning, exactly, as the Liberator from all oppressive masters — including the lesser "gods" and their human or demonic servants.

"Moabite Stone," *Ancient Near Eastern Texts*, 209–10.
47 *Odyssey* 22.456–74.
48 Thucydides, *History of the Peloponnesian War* 5.116.
49 See also Deuteronomy 12.31, 18.10; Micah 6.7; Jeremiah 19.4–5.
50 My thanks to Martha Sherwood of Oregon for pointing out the possibility that these strict sexual rules were required to counter endemic venereal disease.
51 Jacobsen (*Treasures*, 6) suggests that the Burning Bush (Exodus 3.2-6) indicates a transcendent god, whereas Mesopotamians would have taken the god to be immanent in the bush.

Unfortunately, this leads at once to some version of "the problem of evil": if the God of the cult (who requires justice and mercy) is also the Grand Creator, how is it that the natural world, the world apart from human contrivance, is so obviously unjust and merciless? Our own failures to do justice and love mercy and walk humbly with our God may reflect badly only upon us: the Creator's failure reflects badly upon Him! Answers to the puzzle have abounded, sometimes blaming "natural evil" on the work of rebellious spirits allowed — like us — their way, sometimes urging that such evils are proper punishments for "sin," and sometimes suggesting that what we think evil may, in the end, be necessary steps towards some greater good, or at least be of little significance in the light of a glorious future. The most obvious answer has always been that the God of religion is *not* after all the Creator, but rather the power that seeks to remake and mend the mess: the Nothing from which, in the earlier story, Everything emerged, is increasingly considered to be "Something," as intimated in earlier chapters. "Chaos" comes to mean something other than the mere "Gap" or "Yawn" that its Greek etymology indicates: it is rather an abiding Evil that must be ordered and transformed into a new beauty, and that always struggles against that re-creation.[52] "Thou rulest the surging sea, calming the turmoil of its waves. Thou didst crush the monster Rahab with a mortal blow and scatter thy enemies with thy strong arm."[53]

This may be truer to our own personal experience — though that very experience then suggests that we cannot be entirely confident (to say the least) that the "Good God" (so to call it) will triumph over the "Bad," that Maāt will be the conclusion as it already is the beginning. And yet we need to believe exactly that if there is to be any chance that He will. The story about Rahab and other such Chaotic monsters may indeed lurk in the Bible's background, but a more radical claim emerges that even the monsters are God's pets rather than His enemies.

> How many are Your works, O LORD!
> In wisdom You have made them all;

---

52 See Levenson, *Creation and the Persistence of Evil.*
53 Psalm 89.8-10.

the earth is full of Your creatures.
Here is the sea, vast and wide,
teeming with creatures beyond number,
living things both great and small.
There the ships pass,
and Leviathan, which You formed to frolic there.[54]

It is not an easy story to remember.

Ceremonies and sacred places are the place where Heaven meets Earth—that is, the hope of a bright eternity is given temporary form here-now. Our hope is that the future kingdom is always already realized, despite the seeming evil of our present day. "The blessed dead and the gods are rejuvenated in death and regenerate themselves at the wellsprings of their existence":[55] that renewal is possible, and maybe even certain, because there is an escape from the cycles of this world, a "flight to the Alone."[56] And perhaps we should be relieved, rather than perturbed, that the Creator delays His judgement.

> A significant step toward a solution ["why bad things happen to good men"] was only made later, in the middle of the first millennium, by the religious genius of Israel: the treatment of the problem in the *Book of Job*. Here, in God's speech, the imbalance is redressed. The personal, egocentric view of the sufferer—however righteous—is rejected. The self-importance which demands that the universe adjust to his needs, his righteousness, is cast aside, and the full stature of God as the majestic creator and ruler of the universe is reinstated. The distance between the cosmic and the personal, between God in his infinite greatness and mere individual man, is so great and so decisive that an individual has no rights, not even to justice: "Then Job answered the Lord and said, 'I know that thou canst do everything, and that no thought can be withholden from thee. Who is he that hideth counsel without knowledge? Therefore have I uttered that I understood not; things too wonderful

---

54 Psalm 104, 24–26.
55 Hornung, *Conceptions of God*, 160: though the term (axw) here translated as "blessed dead" may mean little more than "ghosts."
56 See *Ennead* VI.9 [9].11, 51.

for me, which I knew not. Hear, I beseech thee, and I will speak. I will demand of thee, and declare thou unto me. I have heard of thee by hearing of the ear: but now mine eyes seeth thee. Wherefore I abhor myself, and repent in dust and ashes."[57]

There is perhaps another robust answer:

> A manifold life exists in the All and makes all things, and in its living embroiders a rich variety and does not rest from ceaselessly making beautiful and shapely living toys. And when men, mortal as they are, direct their weapons against each other, fighting in orderly ranks, doing what they do in sport in their war-dances, their battles show that all human concerns are children's games, and tell us that deaths are nothing terrible, and that those who die in wars and battles anticipate only a little the death which comes in old age—they go away and come back quicker. But if their property is taken away while they are still alive, they may recognize that it was not theirs before either, and that its possession is a mockery to the robbers themselves when others take it away from them.[58]

The war of each against all is, perhaps, only a dream from which we shall and should awaken.

---

57 Jacobsen, *Treasures*, 163, citing Job 42.1-6.
58 *Ennead* III.2 [47].15, 31-43; see also Boethius, *Consolation* 2.2 (*Tractates*, 181-83): "I may say quite firmly that if those things the loss of which you complain of were really yours, you would never have lost them."

~8~
How to Escape

> Simultaneously with the construction of the Heaven He contrived the production of days and nights and months and years, which existed not before the Heaven came into being. And these are all portions of Time; even as "Was" and "Shall be" are generated forms of Time, although we apply them wrongly, without noticing, to Eternal Being. For we say that it "is" or "was" or "will be," whereas, in truth of speech, "is" alone is the appropriate term.[1]

TIME AND THE TRANSIENT

Being constrained by days, months, years, we are ourselves transient beings, forever losing what we almost begin to be, and intermittently aware that there was and will be a world outside all our experience. Plato, and the Greeks in general, might suppose that there were wholly immortal beings—gods and perhaps our own discarnate souls—but this was not a universal judgment. "Thoth, the scribe and archivist of the gods and reckoner of time who 'reckons years, months, days, hours, and moments' assigns a fixed lifespan not only to people but also to the gods."[2] How might we lay hold on that Great World, which was and is and will be—or rather, eternally "is"? How, in language drawn from Buddhist thought, might we escape, or put an end to, *dukkha*?

Early tradition offers, initially, three images of something at least a little less transient than our usual lives: the astronomical, the historical, and the mathematical. Each of these can be accepted within a broadly "naturalistic" framework acceptable to would-be modern thinkers. Each can also suggest a more radical conclusion: that we may be something more than lately evolved primates on a minor rocky planet, and more even than merely mortal slaves of almost immortal powers.

---
1 Plato, *Timaeus* 37e.
2 Hornung, *Conceptions of God*, 155.

The first, implicit in my earlier astronomical or astrological accounts, is to feed on the abiding spectacle of the heavens' rotation. Up aloft the stars need not remember where they've been, nor yet be anxious about what is still to come: their travels are conceived as circular. The point is not simply to look toward their example to get some sense of what our real lives should be like, or are like, but to internalize their neverending motion. As Plato suggested, we "must correct the orbits in the head which were corrupted at our birth."[3] Plotinus added that our real selves were already thus "in orbit," and that it was only our lower selves that needed the reminder to "imitate the soul of the universe and of the stars."[4] The motion that Plotinus has in mind, obviously, isn't spatial: "one must use 'centre' analogically."[5] "Circular motion" is—in principle—unending, and never nearer or further from its goal. It is therefore more "perfect" than "linear motion," since its end and its beginning are the same: it has nowhere *else* to get to, but is not simply static. So also Ps-Dionysius, who suggests that the "circular" motion of the soul is that by which "it separates itself from external things and concentrates its spiritual powers."[6]

Nowadays, of course, we understand that the heavens' apparent rotation is an effect rather of the Earth's rotation, but that need not change the *spiritual* effect: in place of the merely *apparent* rotation we can now imagine the real circuits, of the Earth and other planets around the Sun, of the Sun around the Galaxy, of this and other galaxies' movements towards and away from each other. Modern citydwellers are also shielded from the sight of uncountably many stars, but can be compensated by the yet more detailed view of the heavens through the Hubble and James Webb telescopes: there are more visible galaxies than we once supposed there were stars, and galaxy and galactic cluster house stars past all human imaginings. The world is always wider, and yet more populous—and even if (as it currently appears) all galaxies are doomed to go on flying apart, and the whole cosmos dissipate

---

3 Plato, *Timaeus* 90d.
4 *Ennead* II.9 [33].18, 32.
5 *Ennead* II.2 [14].2, 10.
6 Maximus, *Writings*, 219n58, after Ps-Dionysius, *Divine Names* 705ab, in *Complete Works*, 78.

and disintegrate in time, we can conceive it true that there will be, that there already are, still other "cosmic bubbles." The story simultaneously reminds us of our own small, transitory being and exalts us through the imagining of that story.

> Astronomy is peculiarly adapted to remedy a little and narrow spirit.... There is something in the immensity [of astronomical distances] that shocks and overwhelms the imagination; it is too big for the grasp of a human intellect: estates, provinces and kingdoms vanish in its presence.[7]

For those who choose to be intimidated by the immensity of things, Arthur Ransome's riposte (via his young character, Dick Callum) is—possibly—germane:

> Those little stars that seemed to speckle a not too dreadfully distant blue ceiling were farther away than he could make himself think, try as he might. Those little stars must be enormous. The whole earth must be a tiny pebble in comparison. A spinning pebble, and he, on it, the astronomer, looking at flaming gigantic worlds so far away they seemed no more than sparkling grains of dust. He felt for a moment less than nothing, and then, suddenly, size did not seem to matter. Distant and huge the stars might be, but he, standing here with chattering teeth on the dark hillside, could see them and name them and even foretell what next they were going to do.... He felt an odd wish to shout at them in triumph, but remembered in time that this would not be scientific.[8]

"Triumph" is clearly a slightly silly response—but the term perhaps better refers to a sense, exactly, of exaltation: the astronomer is lifted away from ordinary sense experience and can, briefly, identify with the wider world, and even find other lives "out there."

---

7 Berkeley, "Guardian Essay on Minute Philosophers," in Works 7:207–8. Strictly, on Berkeleian principles, such distances are only virtual, but they may still have a salutary effect!
8 Ransome, Winter Holiday, 34. The philosopher Frank Ramsey said something similar, though he was actually, it appears, of the opinion that astronomy was only concerned with certain visual impressions of human, and maybe also animal, experience (Ramsey "Epilogue," 249)! Which is an entirely different sentiment.

But this astronomical escape in imagination from here-and-now is not the only route. The second to be considered is more literally "historical," which does not seem to have much excited Classical sentiments in quite the way that now affects us heirs of a "Western" sensibility. Classical humanity, as Spengler proposed, held the singular human form as its chief image (and for that very reason most of the philosophers we now remember were not entirely "Classical," but rather—in Spengler's terms—were "Magian"[9]), and had little interest in historical times past or yet to come. Anything beyond an easy journey or a living memory vanished into myth or fable. Even those "fathers of history," Herodotus and Thucydides, relegated times only a few generations earlier to the realm of myth and folklore. Only recent history was worth examining.

> After the destruction of Athens by the Persians, all the older art-works were thrown on the dust heap (whence we are now extracting them), and we do not hear that anyone in Hellas ever troubled himself about the ruins of Mycenae or Phaistos for the purpose of ascertaining historical facts. Men read Homer but never thought of excavating the hill of Troy as Schliemann did; for what they wanted was myth, not history.[10]

Even not-quite-Classical thinkers and artists were less concerned about their merely *historical* origins than we: the story, for example, that Plato professed to have learned from Critias—and he from family tradition of Solon's visit to Egypt—all about the prehistorical conflict of Atlantis and primeval Athens, was obviously

---

9   The Mediterranean basin was never exclusively occupied by merely "Classical" humans. Egyptian culture and civilization was a fascinating presence in the south, precisely because it was, by Classical standards, weird. Babylonian water-works, especially, were an inspiration to early Classical sages such as Thales. Phoenician merchants, and their colony city Carthage, were powerful in trade, and in later years, in war. Hebrews were acknowledged to be a "nation of philosophers" in their supposed commitment to a single, universal deity who required both moral and ceremonial purity. It is likely that Asoka's Buddhist missionaries infected at least some Mediterranean schools, persuading Epicureans indeed that there was no single abiding self, but only (and sufficiently) a fluid swarm of atoms. And some of the greatest of supposedly Classical philosophers were persuaded that they were not, after all, singular human bodies, but transmigrating souls of the same kind as the immortal gods. "I am a child of earth and starry heaven, but my race [*genos*] is of heaven alone," according to the Orphic Tablets. See further my "New Histories of the World."
10 Spengler, *Decline*, 1:14.

fiction.[11] But what the Egyptian priests were said to have said is perhaps a more plausible story: the Egyptians could look back on many hundred years of Egyptian life, and plausibly suggest that their neighbours' history had been set back by various disasters. The world is even older, and the sun's passage through the heavens:

> Millions of years have gone over the world; I cannot tell the number of those through which thou hast passed. Thy heart hath decreed a day of happiness in thy name of Traveller. Thou dost pass over and dost travel through untold spaces [requiring] millions and hundreds of thousands of years [to pass over]; thou passest through them in peace, and thou steerest thy way across the watery abyss to the place which thou lovest; this thou doest in one little moment of time, and then thou dost sink down and dost make an end of the hours.[12]

Maybe humankind has indeed been around "forever," as Aristotle and the Preacher speculated,[13] and those ages had been forgotten—except in Egypt. Or rather, any gaps in that long history were camouflaged: Akhenaten attempted a serious break, and in response the memory of that episode was erased, and so also the intervention of a non-Egyptian dynasty, the Hyksos. Successive Pharaohs constructed time capsules—pyramids in the earlier days, and lavish tombs thereafter—to carry their name forward, and so license their dynastic heirs.

> Kings who carved their name throughout their land were...taking practical steps to ensure that they would indeed live for ever. Conversely, kings who attempted to erase the names of their predecessors from the official records were pushing those earlier pharaohs a step nearer to permanent obliteration.[14]

---

11 Plato, Timaeus 24e et seq.; see Gill, "Plato's Atlantis Story and the Birth of Fiction."
12 Romer, Book of the Dead, 14: "Hymn to Ra when He Ariseth" (trans. Wallis-Budge).
13 Ecclesiastes 1.10: "Is there anything of which one can say, 'Look this is new'? No, it has already existed, long ago before our time. The men of old are not remembered, and those who follow will not be remembered, by those who follow them."
14 Tyldesley, Myths and Legends, 170. Cf. Spengler, Decline of the West, 1:14–15: "The Egyptian soul, conspicuously historical in its texture and impelled with

Perhaps this is to be understood merely as a "genealogical" identity, perhaps the only way in which such creatures as ourselves could hope to bypass death — by remembering our ancestors and caring about our descendants.[15] Pythagoreans too had a larger sense of history, grounded in their identification with past lives — and may have borrowed the idea from Egypt.

> It seems to me also that the discourse (*logos*) of the Pythagoreans, which prepares souls to recollect their former lives as well, imitates this historical study of the Egyptians. For just as in the case of one man — or one soul rather — duty requires that he grasp his different lives, so too in the case of one race it requires that they grasp their different cycles. So as among the former the recollection of their previous existences is perfective of their souls, so too among the latter the historical study of earlier cycles contributes very greatly to their perfection in wisdom.[16]

It is an option that we here-now may find more useful than the astronomical, particularly if we no longer believe the heavens to be anything but indifferent, and even if we do not accept a firmly Pythagorean or Platonic conception of our possible earlier lives. Better, perhaps, to identify ourselves with tradition, with some long lineage, with the human past, remembered or invented. Lovecraft, for example, wrote to August Derleth that "time, space, and natural law hold for me suggestions of intolerable bondage, and I can form no picture of emotional satisfaction which does not involve their defeat — especially the defeat of time, so that one may merge oneself with the whole historic stream and be

---

primitive passion towards the infinite, perceived past and future as its whole world, and the present (which is identical with waking consciousness) appeared to him simply as the narrow common frontier of two immeasurable stretches. The Egyptian Culture is an embodiment of care — which is the spiritual counterpoise of distance — care for the future expressed in the choice of granite or basalt as the craftsman's materials, in the chiselled archives, in the elaborate administrative system, in the net of irrigation works, and, necessarily bound up therewith, care for the past. The Egyptian mummy is a symbol of the first importance. The body of the dead man was made everlasting, just as his personality, his 'Ka,' was immortalized through the portrait-statuettes."

15 The only sort of immortality that earthly beings could hope for, according to Aristotle in his more naturalistic mood: Aristotle, *De Anima* 2.415a22–b7. See also Philostratus, *Life of Apollonius*, 1:167 [2.14.4]: "So for all creatures children are their life."

16 Proclus, *Commentary on Timaeus*, 219 [I.124, 5–13].

How to Escape

wholly emancipated from the transient and the ephemeral."[17] That stream may encompass more than human historical records: we can now look back at billions of years of evolutionary change, and trace our ancestry back through all those ages. Once upon a time "we" were small agile furry creatures scuttling around the feet of gigantic dinosaurs. Earlier still, "we" clambered adventurously out of the sea to explore the marshy shores. And in some imagined future "we" will take many new shapes, all still (perhaps) somehow "human" (or maybe "hominin").

Both astronomical and historical (or genealogical) escapes may merely allow us an *imaginative* grasp of time and distance larger than our own brief lives, without any hint that we might ourselves have any real presence "there." Lovecraft and his readers could imagine themselves into the Great Race of his fantasy (which migrates through times and worlds to collate all available information), and thereby contemplate—in thought—the manifold other lives and places of the cosmos. One character, displaced from here-and-now to allow one of the "Great Race" to sample twentieth-century life (as Olaf Stapledon's Neptunian, from many million years in the future, also samples it), is permitted conversations with manifold other minds similarly entrapped in the very long ago (and mostly borrowed from other "weird fictions" by Lovecraft's fellow authors).

> There was a mind from the planet we know as Venus, which would live incalculable epochs to come, and one from an outer moon of Jupiter six million years in the past. Of earthly minds there were some from the winged, starheaded, half-vegetable race of palaeogean Antarctica; one from the reptile people of fabled Valusia; three from the furry pre-human Hyperborean worshippers of Tsathoggua; one from the wholly abominable Tcho-Tchos; two from the arachnid denizens of earth's last age; five from the hardy coleopterous species immediately following mankind, to which the Great Race was some day to transfer its keenest minds en masse in the face of horrible peril; and several from different branches of humanity. I talked with the mind of Yiang-Li, a philosopher from the

---

17 Lovecraft, Letter to August Derleth, November 21, 1930, in Schultz and Joshi, *Essential Solitude*, vol. 1.

cruel empire of Tsan-Chan, which is to come in 5,000 AD; with that of a general of the greatheaded brown people who held South Africa in 50,000 BC; with that of a twelfth-century Florentine monk named Bartolomeo Corsi; with that of a king of Lomar who had ruled that terrible polar land one hundred thousand years before the squat, yellow Inutos came from the west to engulf it. I talked with the mind of Nug-Soth, a magician of the dark conquerors of 16,000 AD with that of a Roman named Titus Sempronius Blaesus, who had been a quaestor in Sulla's time; with that of Khephnes, an Egyptian of the 14th Dynasty, who told me the hideous secret of Nyarlathotep, with that of a priest of Atlantis's middle kingdom; with that of a Suffolk gentleman of Cromwell's day, James Woodville; with that of a court astronomer of pre-Inca Peru; with that of the Australian physicist Nevil Kingston-Brown, who will die in 2,518 AD; with that of an archimage of vanished Yhe in the Pacific; with that of Theodotides, a Greco-Bactrian official of 200 BC; with that of an aged Frenchman of Louis XIII's time named Pierre-Louis Montagny; with that of Crom-Ya, a Cimmerian chieftain of 15,000 BC; and with so many others that my brain cannot hold the shocking secrets and dizzying marvels I learned from them.[18]

So also Colin Wilson imagines the archaeological narrator of one of his Lovecraftian fantasies identifying with Nineveh and the enduring earth (though with much less invented detail), to the point of feeling disdain for his own transitory existence:

> Just inside the farmyard there was a large pool of grey water, rather muddy. As I was taking the clothes from the line, my mind still in Nineveh, I happened to notice this pool, and forgot for a moment where I was or what I was doing there. As I looked at it, the puddle lost all familiarity and became as alien as a sea on Mars. I stood staring at it, and the first drops of rain fell from the sky, and wrinkled its surface. At that moment I experienced a sensation of happiness and insight such as I had never known before. Nineveh and all history suddenly became as real and as alien as that pool. History became

---

18 "The Shadow out of Time," in *The Dreams in the Witch House and Other Weird Stories*, 334–96. That none of these other lives are female is all too familiar a neglect.

such a *reality* that I felt a kind of contempt for my own existence, standing there with my arms full of clothes.[19]

But both routes of escape—the astronomical and the historical—may also begin to suggest the other, stranger, and more "Magian" thought: that we really may have been present, as the selves we truly are, in those earlier times and galaxies far away. So in Lovecraft's "Dream Quest of Unknown Kadath" the central character, Randolph Carter, passes "amidst [both through and around] backgrounds of other planets and systems and galaxies and cosmic continua; spores of eternal life drifting from world to world, universe to universe, yet all equally himself... His self had been annihilated and yet he—if indeed there could, in view of that utter nullity of individual existence, be such a thing as he—was equally aware of being in some inconceivable way a legion of selves."[20] My life here-now and my immediate sense of self may be overwhelmed in identifying instead with Soul: not "my soul" merely, but the Soul that animates all things.

Both routes may aim to realize the ancient notion of a philosopher, in Plato's description, as a "spectator of all time and all existence."[21] It is an ambition that Stapledon also dramatized in his imagined future histories, especially *Star Maker* (1937), whose narrator—like Carter—drifts from one world to another, back and forth in time, accumulating other selves, part friends, part alter egos. Whether Stapledon had read any of Lovecraft's work is uncertain—there seem to be no traces in the Stapledon Archive at Liverpool University[22]—Lovecraft, on the other hand, had read *Last and First Men* (1930) with enthusiasm.[23] Stapledon openly professed an idealistic, Platonic philosophy, while Lovecraft's own conviction that the cosmos had no meaning—not even an "inhuman" meaning—rested on a merely materialistic,

---

19 Wilson, *Mind Parasites*, 18. Wilson may perhaps have drawn this case not merely from his own experience, but from the writings of Arnold Toynbee, who recounted similar episodes in his own growth as a fully engaged historian: Wilson, *Religion and the Rebel*, 125–26, quoting Toynbee, *Study of History*, 10:130, 139.
20 Joshi, *Dreams*, 155–251.
21 Plato, *Republic* 6.486a; see also *Ennead* III.2 [47].15, 44f.
22 Personal communication from Andy Sawyer, one time curator of the University's science fiction library.
23 Letters to Fritz Leiber (18 November 1936), in Lovecraft, *Selected Letters* V, 357, 375.

post-Darwinian thought. But his stories, despite his philosophy, permit his adventurers to escape their bodies so as to experience both the terrestrial past and the sidereal present.

That Magian outlook is also strongly connected with the third way of escape from here-and-now, which is also sometimes entangled with the astronomical: namely, the mathematical. It is a way, perhaps, that is even less accommodated to our usual mental powers and sensibilities than the astronomical or historical. It is said (probably falsely) that Plato had this dictum inscribed over the entrance to his Academy: "Let no one ignorant of geometry enter here."[24] Strictly, Plato distinguished arithmetic and geometry.[25] Geometry especially should be studied, he is said to have said, to help guide the Greeks away from the ways of war:

> A party of Delians... requested Plato, as a geometer, to solve a problem set them by the god in a strange oracle. The oracle was to this effect: the present troubles of the Delians and the rest of the Greeks would be at an end when they had doubled the altar at Delos.... Plato, recalling the Egyptian, replied that the god was rallying the Greeks for their neglect of education, deriding, as it were, our ignorance and bidding us engage in no perfunctory study of geometry; for no ordinary or near-sighted intelligence, but one well versed in the subject, was required to find two mean proportionals, that being the only way in which a body cubical in shape can be doubled with a similar increment in all dimensions. This would be done for them by Eudoxus of Cnidus or Helicon of Cyzicus; they were not, however, to suppose that it was this the god desired, but rather that he was ordering the entire Greek nation to give up war and its miseries and cultivate the Muses, and by calming their passions through the practice of discussion and study of mathematics, so to live with one another that their intercourse should be not injurious, but profitable.[26]

---

24 See Fowler, *The Mathematics of Plato's Academy*, 200–201.
25 Plato, *Republic* 7.527c; Aristotle followed him in insisting that arithmetical proofs had no place in geometry, nor vice versa: *Posterior Analytics* 1.75a39–75b22; *Posterior Analytics/Topica*, 61–63. Significantly, we would now think them both mistaken.
26 Plutarch, "On the Sign of Socrates," 579bcd, in *Moralia* 7:397–99; see also "The E at Delphi," 386d, in *Moralia*, 5:211. The problem cannot be solved simply

MAKE MATHS, NOT WAR

But for Platonists the study was not merely a relaxation of passions, nor even merely a way of managing the affairs of this world. Both numbers and geometrical figures had a real existence beyond their phenomenal and physical representations. We must, he argued, carry the "memory" of these realities with us — not because we were geometers in some earlier human life,[27] but because we knew and know them *directly* in our discarnate existence, as it were "in the nether realms," prior to our immersion in the here-and-now. Almost equivalently, Aristotle held that our knowledge at least of the very first principles was by direct intuition, not simply from experience or deduction. Nous, that primary intuition, came "from outside,"[28] rather than being built up from sense-experience or simply accepted by biological necessity. The baffling success of mathematical analysis, founded on first principles, was an indication — fervently accepted by later scientists, philosophers, and theologians — that our minds were attuned to the One Mind.[29] Mathematical truths are eternal — and so must be the minds that incorporate them.[30] That God is always doing

---

with straight edge and compass, as it requires the construction of an (irrational) cube root.

27 As the priests whom Socrates invokes might seem to suggest: "Seeing then that the soul is immortal and has been born many times, and has beheld all things both in this world and in the nether realms, she has acquired knowledge of all and everything; so that it is no wonder that she should be able to recollect all that she knew before about virtue and other things" (Plato, *Meno* 81c). Socrates goes on to lead a seemingly uneducated slave to understand how to double the size of a square (*Meno* 82–86), and suggests that this is because he already knew the truth from direct discarnate experience.

28 Aristotle, *Generation of Animals* 2.736b27–28; it is likely that Aristotle would identify this as *nous poietikos*, the active *nous*, mentioned in De Anima 3.430a14–17. Commentators vary: either this is simply a way of noting that we have things to learn from others (as modernists prefer), or else it is to be taken fairly "literally," and Aristotle here acknowledges an immortal, unearthly, element in our consciousness — an element which should be what we take most seriously (see *Nicomachean Ethics* 10.1177b31–1178a4). Later Platonic and neo-Pythagorean philosophers mostly accepted the latter reading.

29 As above: see Wigner, "The Unreasonable Effectiveness of Mathematics in the Natural Sciences."

30 "If the intelligible objects are eternal, and knowledge is the same as its object, knowledge should also be eternal. Such mind enters into humans for their brief lives" (Polansky, *Aristotle's De Anima*, 466, cited by Connell, "Nous Enters from Outside," 120). On Connell's own account, the story is to be taken not quite literally: "When, through a long and arduous process, human beings

geometry is, so Plutarch says, a genuinely Platonic thought, even if it is not stated in the surviving Platonic texts.[31] Other Platonists and Pythagoreans made much of triangles, squares, pentagons or hexagons in plane geometry, and the so-called "Platonic solids" in solid geometry (tetrahedra, cubes, octahedra, dodecahedra, icosahedra). Astronomy in turn could be viewed as the study of *motion* in three dimensions, and music itself as a final form of applied mathematics.[32] In all these studies we can be acquainted with something that outlasts the years: both the objects of our study, and the self that studies them.

We are, accordingly, "gods," but have forgotten ourselves, tiger-cubs raised among goats, according to Sri Ramakrishna,[33] or feral children. Astronomy, history, arithmetic may give us simple reminders, but the final realization must come through a conscious effort, and the help of senior gods.

> [The Hymn of the Pearl] tells us the edifying story of a prince who is sent by his royal parents to search for the pearl in a foreign land. It lies buried under the Egyptian Sea, which is guarded by a fearsome dragon. The son sets off, but soon he forgets his mission and his royal (divine) origin, losing himself entirely in Egypt's lust for worldly pleasures. Only when an eagle brings him a letter from his homeland does he suddenly remember his noble ancestry and his original task: "Rise up and awake out of sleep, and hearken unto the words of the letter; and remember that you are a son of kings; lo, you have come under the yoke of bondage. Remember the pearl for which you were sent into Egypt. Remember your garment spangled with gold. Your name is named in the book of life." Heeding the message, he breaks free of his worldly bonds and dives down into the depths of the Egyptian Sea, where he soon finds the pearl. After taming the

---

are able to grasp eternal truths and contemplate them, the part of themselves that achieves this becomes one with these objects of knowledge. Thus, a person, when she is thinking of these truths, becomes like God, pure thought"—but this does not guarantee her a post-mortem life, only a diversion from pressing material engagements. My own suspicion is that Aristotle wavered.
31 Plutarch, "Table Talk," *Moralia* 8.718c, vol. 9, p. 127. The remark is slightly misleading: God obviously has no need to *do* geometry, in the manner of Euclid.
32 Plato, *Republic* 7.524d–535a on the potential philosopher-kings' curriculum.
33 See Zimmer, *Philosophies of India*, 5–8.

dragon that guards the treasure, he seizes the pearl and departs for his homeland in the East (sunrise!). Along the way, he recovers his shining gold garment, and soon after his return, he dedicates his most precious treasure to God on high.[34]

Till then we live among shadows.

> Allowing one's life to be dominated by the destructive passions that worked through the body meant falling under the sway of death. Because this condition of "living in darkness" was an almost inevitable side effect of embodiment, as we have seen, such a severely diminished way of living (a kind of dim or shadowy half-life) was the default human condition from which Hermetic practitioners were trying to heal themselves and others. That most people "keep wandering in darkness, deluded by the senses and subject to death" therefore does not refer to their physical mortality but to their failure to live life as it should be lived.[35]

FAIRYLAND

Is it wrong, or weak, or unrespectable to wish to escape from here-and-now, even if only in thought? Is it wrong, or weak, or unrespectable to tell imaginative fictions, "Fairy Tales" (as some have called them), to help us?

> I have claimed that Escape is one of the main functions of fairy-stories, and since I do not disapprove of them, it is plain that I do not accept the tone of scorn or pity with which "Escape" is now so often used. Why should a man be scorned if, finding himself in prison, he tries to get out and go home? Or if he cannot do so, he thinks and talks about other topics than jailers and prison-walls?[36]

The point is all the stronger when we consider that our usual preoccupations, and the sorts of story which more "naturalistic" readers prefer, are themselves diversions from a truer and more honest account of things.

---

34 Schweizer, *Sungod's Journey through the Netherworld*, 127–28, citing "The Acts of Thomas," 109–13, in Elliott, *Apocryphal New Testament*, 489.
35 Hanegraaff, *Hermetic Spirituality*, 274.
36 Tolkien, "On Fairy Stories" [1947], in *Tree and Leaf*, 60.

> If we were all on board ship and there was trouble among the stewards, I can just conceive their chief spokesmen looking with disfavour on anyone who stole away from the fierce debates in the saloon or pantry to take a breather on deck. For up there, he would taste the salt, he would see the vastness of the weather, he would remember that the ship had a whither and a whence. He would remember things like fogs, storms, and what had seemed in the hot, lighted rooms down below to be merely the scene for a political crisis would appear once more as a thin eggshell moving rapidly through an immense darkness over an element in which men cannot live.[37]

Lovecraft—though his nihilistic views were themselves the effect of contemporary materialistic philosophies and preoccupations—at least had a clearer insight into the sort of cosmos those philosophies dictated, and a better memory for the monsters that once dominated our imaginations:

> All my tales are based on the fundamental premise that common human laws and interests and emotions have no validity or significance in the vast cosmos-at-large. To me there is nothing but puerility in a tale in which the human form—and the local human passions and conditions and standards—are depicted as native to other worlds or other universes. To achieve the essence of real externality, whether of time or space or dimension, one must forget that such things as organic life, good and evil, love and hate, and all such local attributes of a negligible and temporary race called mankind, have any existence at all. Only the human scenes and characters must have human qualities. These must be handled with unsparing realism, (not catch-penny romanticism) but when we cross the line to the boundless and hideous unknown—the shadow-haunted Outside—we must remember to leave our humanity—and terrestrialism—at the threshold.[38]

---

37 Lewis, *Of Other Worlds*, 59–60.
38 Letter to Farnsworth Wright, July 5, 1927, borrowed from www.hplovecraft.com/writings/quotes.aspx (accessed December 15, 2022); see Schultz and Joshi, *Essential Solitude*, vol. 1.

How to Escape

Why should we worry if the Outside is "shadow-haunted" or "hideous"? And isn't Fairyland imagined to be fun? Obviously, not entirely.

Consider two related sorts of myth: the first, about the dead; the second, the travels of Gilgamesh or Odysseus, "beyond the fields we know."[39] Actually, the two kinds are barely distinguishable — and that is itself a clue. In the Field of Reeds, those who have survived Maāt's judgment (when their hearts have been weighed against a feather to determine their innocence of all wrongdoing) and the many other perils on the way, may live as comfortably as any prosperous peasant, aided (perhaps) by magical *ushabti* to do the harder work. The dead and their helpful servants exist in living imagination, more happily than Homer's dead. According to the prayers and charms collated in the Egyptian *Book of the Dead* — a work constructed or reconstructed from fragments found in pyramids or coffins[40] — the dead must both proclaim their innocence, and identify with assorted divine powers to escape the monsters that besiege them on their journey through "the twelve hours of night."[41] "It is a journey from death and burial to the darkest caverns and to the eternal stars, and on the way the dead enter fiery pits, confront snakes and flesh-eaters; they meet ferrymen and gods and kings."[42] Will they move on from there, either reincarnated back to our own living world or elevated to the heavens? "The Field of Reeds was, of course, only a part of the afterlife existence. As the *akh* spirit journeyed forever onwards, the bird-headed *ba* spirit either haunted the land of the living or travelled across the sky with Re, before returning to the tomb at night."[43]

---

39 The familiar phrase is drawn from Dunsany, *King of Elfland's Daughter*, one of the most significant of twentieth-century fantasies.
40 Strictly, "the Book of the Dead is a scholarly illusion conjured from the randomly surviving relics of a distant past. No 'genuine' ancient version of it has ever been discovered and, considering that it was compiled from a wide variety of sources, nor is such a find remotely likely": Romer, *Book of the Dead* (Kindle location 530).
41 Described in the *Amduat* (composed c. 1500 BC), in Darnell and Darnell, *Ancient Egyptian Netherworld Books*, 127–248; see Schweizer, *Sungod's Journey through the Netherworld* for a sympathetic, psychological reading of the journey.
42 Romer, *Book of the Dead* (Kindle location 552).
43 Tyldesley, *Myths and Legends*, 167.

I shall explore the different souls attested in Egyptian thought in a little more detail in the next chapter. My present focus is on the Otherworld, including the land of the dead. The traveller there encounters monsters and other strange beings, who may or may not be helpful. So also Gilgamesh must deal with the gods' caprices: fighting and being reconciled with the wild man Enkidu, insulting the goddess Ishtar, defeating an ogre and the Bull of Heaven, and at last—depressed by Enkidu's death—travelling in quest of an end to age and death. He too encounters gods and monsters—scorpion people, stone people, and the ferryman over the river of death, on the way to interview Utnapishtim and his wife, the great survivors of the Mesopotamian flood and now uniquely immortal. Gilgamesh fails in his quest, losing even the secret of a renewed youth to an opportunistic serpent, and must return to an everyday existence.[44] That last story, of the snake who steals the secret, "has been convincingly traced to Melanesian and Annam folklore by Julian Morgenstern... At what time these Far Eastern folktale motifs spread to Mesopotamia is not easy to determine."[45] Or more probably, it is another relic of an ancient, global culture—not that the stories are passed down, and across, without any alteration. Tracing their descent is even trickier than tracing phylogenetic evolution, which is very like the transmission and constant reinvention of attractive stories.

> It is fascinating to reflect that stories that are so compelling and well-crafted as these were not plotted by the creative genius of any individual author, but developed over the course of generations through a process of cumulative descent with modification—rather like those "organs of extreme perfection and complication" that so inspired Darwin.[46]

What "the original story" might have been is probably beyond our grasp. But the Otherworld journey most familiar still to most readers of this book is likely to be the Odyssey. Despite occasional efforts to track Odysseus's journey around the Mediterranean—an enterprise almost as pointless as to seek out Atlantis—it is far

---

44 See Helle, *Gilgamesh*.
45 Jacobsen, *Treasures*, 214, citing Morgenstern "On Gilgamesh."
46 Tehrani, "Descent with Imagination," 286.

How to Escape

more likely that he travelled beyond the borders of everyday, and only returned by courtesy of the Phaeacians.

> It must not be thought that interpretations of this kind are forced, and nothing more than the conjectures of ingenious men; but when we consider the great wisdom of antiquity, and how much Homer excelled in intellectual prudence, and in an accurate knowledge of every virtue, it must not be denied that he has obscurely indicated the images of things of a more divine nature in the fiction of a fable.[47]

According to Odysseus's own account of his travels, as told to the court of Alcinous in Phaeacia, he gradually lost all his crew at one mysterious island or another. After his pirate raid on the Cycones, a tempest drove the surviving ships away, first to the land of the Lotus-Eaters, and then the island where the Cyclopes each managed their own flocks and household. He tricked the voracious Polyphemus into a drunken stupor, and blinded his one eye, but foolishly allowed Polyphemus, son of Poseidon, to know his real name (Odysseus rather than Oudeis, No-One) — and so earned the god Poseidon's hostility.[48] In the next island he encountered the god of the winds, and his twelve incestuous children.[49] His crew, convinced that Aeolus had given Odysseus treasure, foolishly released the winds that might have carried them home, and Aeolus refused any further help. After another land of cannibals (the Laestrygonians), they reached Circe's Island, and — only with Olympian assistance — escaped from being all turned into animals.[50] Circe directed them to visit the borders of Hades, principally to get Teiresias's advice, but also managing encounters with other heroes and relatives.[51] They must also brave the Sirens (with Odysseus tied to the mast and his crews' ears stopped against the Sirens' enchantments), the monstrous Scylla and Charybdis (twice), and finally the Isle of Helios — where Odysseus's crew ignore a vehement prohibition and slaughter the

---

47 Porphyry, *On the Cave of the Nymphs*, ch. 18, in Taylor, *Select Works*, 199–200; see Edwards, "Porphyry's 'Cave of the Nymphs' and the Gnostic Controversy."
48 *Odyssey* 9.82–115.
49 *Odyssey* 10.1–75.
50 *Odyssey* 10.134–546.
51 *Odyssey* 11.1–640.

Sun-god's cattle. Odysseus is at last the sole survivor, and kept on Calypso's Island till the Olympians once again require his release.

The lands that he encountered each seem to represent deviations from familiar human behaviour—the most extreme being offered by Circe and Calypso: if Circe has her way, Odysseus will be an "animal"; if Calypso holds his affections, he will be made a god. The Cyclops as well as the Laestrygonians and the Sirens think of humans as mere meat—better meat indeed than the sheep the Cyclops cares for. The Sun-god, contrariwise, forbids that any should kill his cattle. The most obvious moral of the visit to the Dead is that it is better to enjoy domestic peace in life than to seek for a passing glory—but not to surrender to the laziness of the Lotus-Eaters, nor yet the inbred court of Aeolus. The route back into the everyday requires Odysseus to pass between contrasting dangers, at last with the help of the Phaeacians.

The Phaeacians may seem at first to be just like any other Hellenic nation—but there are clues to their odder status. "On either side of the [palace] door there stood gold and silver dogs, which Hephaestus had fashioned with cunning skill to guard the palace of great-hearted Alcinous; immortal were they and ageless all their days."[52] And the climate is as serene as the Land of Reeds!

> Therein grow trees, tall and luxuriant, pears and pomegranates and apple-trees with their bright fruit, and sweet figs, and luxuriant olives. Of these the fruit perishes not nor fails in winter or in summer, but lasts throughout the year; and ever does the west wind, as it blows, quicken to life some fruits, and ripen others; pear upon pear waxes ripe, apple upon apple, cluster upon cluster, and fig upon fig.[53]

The Phaeacians kindly ferry Odysseus back to his own land, and leave him sleeping there. But their involvement enrages Poseidon enough to turn the returning ship to stone, and so block Scheria's harbour against any further exchanges with what is Here and Now.[54] Fairyland is cut off from Here forever (or until the gods should change their minds again).

---

52 *Odyssey* 7.91–94.
53 *Odyssey* 7.114–20.
54 *Odyssey* 12.160–65.

How to Escape

Odysseus wakes, back in Ithaca, in the Cave of the Nymphs, by the harbour of Phorcys, the old man of the sea:

> There is in the land of Ithaca a certain harbor of Phorcys, the old man of the sea, and at its mouth two projecting headlands sheer to seaward, but sloping down on the side toward the harbor. These keep back the great waves raised by heavy winds without, but within the benched ships lie unmoored when they have reached the point of anchorage. At the head of the harbor is a long-leafed olive tree, and near it a pleasant, shadowy cave sacred to the nymphs that are called Naiads. Therein are mixing bowls and jars of stone, and there too the bees store honey. And in the cave are long looms of stone, at which the nymphs weave webs of purple dye, a wonder to behold; and therein are also ever-flowing springs. Two doors there are to the cave, one toward the North Wind, by which men go down, but that toward the South Wind is sacred, nor do men enter thereby; it is the way of the immortals.[55]

For Porphyry, this cave represents the cosmos, and is an echo or original version of Plato's imagined Cave: full of distracting beauties and an ambiguous refuge.[56] From here Odysseus must take up his usual duties—for a while, at least. Once he has cleared his court and country of the ambitious suitors and the servants they have suborned, he must—by Teiresias's account—take another voyage, far away from the sea, and the passions of earthly life.

> When thou hast slain the wooers in thy halls, whether by guile or openly with the sharp sword, then do thou go forth, taking a shapely oar, until thou comest to men that know naught of the sea and eat not of food mingled with salt, aye, and they know naught of ships with purple cheeks, or of shapely oars that are as wings unto ships. And I will tell thee a sign right manifest, which will not escape thee. When another wayfarer, on meeting thee, shall say that thou hast a winnowing-fan on thy stout

---

55 *Odyssey* 13.93–114; see also ibid., 13.348–50. Cf. Larson, *Greek Nymphs*, 229: "One of the apocryphal stories of Plato's life is that his parents brought him to a cave on Mount Hymettos to be blessed by Pan, the nymphs, and Apollo Nomios; upon returning from the sacrifice, Periktione found her child's mouth filled with honey by the bees, the agents of the nymphs."
56 See Edwards, "Porphyry's 'Cave of the Nymphs' and the Gnostic Controversy."

> shoulder, then do thou fix in the earth thy shapely oar and make goodly offerings to lord Poseidon—a ram, and a bull, and a boar that mates with sows—and depart for thy home and offer sacred hecatombs to the immortal gods who hold broad heaven, to each one in due order. And death shall come to thee thyself far from the sea, a death so gentle, that shall lay thee low when thou art overcome with sleek old age, and thy people shall dwell in prosperity around thee. In this have I told thee sooth.[57]

For Porphyry this is a story about the escape from this "blood-drinking life, from its sickening whirlpools, in the midst of its billows and sudden surges," that the Delphic oracle assured him that his master Plotinus had achieved.[58] Other, later, stories of Odysseus's end carried rather different morals: perhaps he was inadvertently killed by his own son (by Circe), Telegonus—a further example of the fraught relationships of Hellenic father and son![59] Or perhaps, by Dante's account, he chose to travel still further afield, and only saw Mount Purgatory from a distance before the sea swallowed him and his crew, and consigned him to the Hell of Fraudsters.

> Neither the sweetness of a son, nor compassion for my old father, nor the love owed to Penelope, which should have made her glad, could conquer within me the ardor that I had to gain experience of the world and of human vices and worth; but I put out on the deep, open sea alone, with one ship and with that little company by which I had not been deserted.[60]

---

57 *Odyssey* 11.119-36.
58 The oracle offered to Amelius after Plotinus's death, as recorded by Porphyry, *Life* 22.31-3; see Lamberton, *Homer the Theologian*, 133.
59 Apollodorus, "Epitome," 7.36-7, in *Library*, 3:303-5: "When Telegonus learned from Circe that he was a son of Ulysses, he sailed in search of him. And having come to the island of Ithaca, he drove away some of the cattle, and when Ulysses defended them, Telegonus wounded him with the spear he had in his hands, which was barbed with the spine of a stingray, and Ulysses died of the wound. But when Telegonus recognized him, he bitterly lamented, and conveyed the corpse and Penelope to Circe, and there he married Penelope. And Circe sent them both away to the Islands of the Blest." The story was variously told in lost works by Eugammon of Cyrene (author of *Telegonus*) and Sophocles.
60 Dante, *Inferno*, 421 [Canto 26.94-102]. Dante drew his account of Odysseus's character from Roman poets rather than from Greek, but there was some ambiguity even among Greek authors: Odysseus's intelligence was perhaps better

How to Escape

Dante's account of Odysseus (named Ulysses after Virgil's example) is of an intelligence warped for deceitful ends, joined with an urge to transcend the everyday:

> "O brothers," I said, "who through a hundred thousand perils have reached the west, to this so brief vigil of our senses that remains, do not deny the experience, following the sun, of the world without people. Consider your sowing: you were not made to live like brutes, but to follow virtue and knowledge."[61]

This is not Homer's Odysseus, who very much prefers his son, his wife, his father, and the land of Ithaca and its nymphs[62] either to the life of brutes,[63] or the life of gods. But it is an image that clearly resonates with many more recent authors—an early example, it seems, of a standard SF hero, always wishing to "go beyond." Our ancestors were, perhaps with reason, rather more cautious about such wishes. Fairyland may be closer than we think, but it is always behind a barrier which we would be wise to respect.

Even (or especially) Tolkien had doubts about the effect of going too far outside our "comfort zone," quite apart from the obvious dangers of going "where the Mewlips feed" or where "horny Fastitocalon, an island good to land upon," can drown unwary sailors.[64] The nameless narrator of one poem has been

---

considered *deinotes* than *phronesis* (see Aristotle, *Nicomachean Ethics* 6.1144a23–29). He was, as his patron goddess says, a compulsive liar (*Odyssey* 13.294–6).
61 Dante, *Inferno*, 422 [Canto 26.112–20].
62 Larson, *Greek Nymphs*, 25–26: "The Ithakan nymphs are never presented as active players in the narrative the way Athena is. We see places associated with them, and we hear characters praying to them, but they do not show themselves. Odysseus is now back in the 'real' world as opposed to the fantastic world of his travels, and the only overt supernatural element in the Ithakan narrative is Athena herself. On the other hand, the unseen presence of the nymphs is constantly suggested. By a sort of divine metonymy, they are the island itself, and they represent all that Odysseus is struggling to regain, homecoming in every sense of the word—not merely a physical homecoming and reclaiming of the land but recognition of his true identity."
63 Plutarch, in his *Gryllos*, imagines that one of Odysseus's crew at least greatly prefers a pig's life, as being calmer and more rational than the usual human. Few commentators can quite imagine that Plutarch was being serious—but the arguments that Gryllos offers are confirmed in other of Plutarch's works (see Buxton, *Forms of Astonishment*, 138–40).
64 Middle Earth, it seemingly needs to be said, is as dangerous and sometimes horrifying in its detailed history as any dystopian fantasy. The Fellowship is mostly walking through a ruined landscape, beset by invincible horrors whose

lost in fairy, in the wider world, and—rejected by that realm for his conceit—finds a way back home. Except that there is no home for him, any more than for poor Frodo.

> Houses were shuttered, wind round them muttered,
> Roads were empty. I sat by a door,
> And where drizzling rain poured down a drain
> I cast away all that I bore:
> In my clutching hand some grains of sand,
> And a sea-shell silent and dead.
> Never will my ear that bell hear,
> Never my feet that shore tread
> Never again, as in sad lane,
> In blind alley and in long street
> Ragged I walk. To myself I talk;
> For still they speak not, men that I meet.⁶⁵

Better, sometimes, to have stayed "home."

Fairyland is of its nature "once upon a time," and the fairies have always gone. "Once upon a time," the gods walked freely among us. Once upon a time, they went away—though when exactly they departed may be difficult to decide. Our talk of them is a lament, an attempt to recreate in memory an imagined glory.

> The literature of lament [in Mesopotamia] was directed to powers lost, difficult or impossible to regain: the dead young god of fertility in the netherworld, the destroyed temple, the dead king or ordinary human. In the lament the vividness of recall and longing was an actual magical reconstitution, an attempt to draw back the lost god or temple by recreating in the mind the lost happy presence.⁶⁶

Did they leave when we began farming, or when we began to work with iron, or when we neglected the ceremonial seasons?

---

principal is only defeated—this time round—by "chance" (if chance it be). Not even the Shire is "cosy"! And the best that even the greatest of the Elves can manage is "through ages of the world [to fight] the long defeat": *Lord of the Rings*, 1:372. And again: "Far, far below the deepest delvings of the Dwarves, the world is gnawed by nameless things. Even Sauron knows them not. They are older than he. Now I have walked there, but I will bring no report to darken the light of day": Tolkien, *Lord of the Rings*, 2:150.

65 Tolkien, *The Adventures of Tom Bombadil*, "The Sea Bell," 19-21.
66 Jacobsen, *Treasures*, 15.

How to Escape

> Farewell, rewards and fairies,
> Good housewives now may say,
> For now foul sluts in dairies
> Do fare as well as they.
> And though they sweep their hearths no less
> Than maids were wont to do,
> Yet who of late for cleanness
> Finds sixpence in her shoe?[67]

And the dead too are known as the Departed.

IN THE BEGINNING

Once upon a time nonhuman animals could all talk—or else we humans could listen. Once upon a time there was no definite boundary between the many sorts of being.

> We must remember, above all, that if there is a virtually universal Amerindian notion, it is that of an original state of undifferentiation between humans and animals, described in mythology. Myths are filled with beings whose form, name and behaviour inextricably mix human and animal attributes in a common context of intercommunicability, identical to that which defines the present-day intra-human world. The differentiation between "culture" and "nature," which Levi-Strauss showed to be the central theme of Amerindian mythology, is not a process of differentiating the human from the animal, as in our own evolutionist mythology. The original common condition of both humans and animals is not animality but rather humanity. The great mythical separation reveals not so much culture distinguishing itself from nature but rather nature distancing itself from culture: the myths tell how animals lost the qualities inherited or retained by humans. Humans are those who continue as they have always been: animals are ex-humans, not humans ex-animals.[68]

This is more than an Amerindian notion. Once upon a time, we were all "human"—that is, we were all members of a single family.

---

67 Richard Corbet [1582–1635], "Farewell, Rewards and Fairies" [1612], in Eliot, *English Poetry*, 324; cf. Sprat, *History of the Royal Society*, 340.
68 De Castro, "Cosmological Deixis," 471-72.

In those days there was nothing odd in imagining hybrid forms, or thinking that the gods could take on many shapes. How then did we come to suppose that "being human" was something very special? Why were hybrid forms offensive? How did we leave "fairyland" and the talking beasts behind?

> There are ancient limitations from which fairy-stories offer a sort of escape, and old ambitions and desires (touching the very roots of fantasy) to which they offer a kind of satisfaction and consolation. Some are pardonable weaknesses or curiosities: such as the desire to visit, free as a fish, the deep sea; or the longing for the noiseless, gracious, economical flight of a bird, that longing which the aeroplane cheats, except in rare moments, seen high and by wind and distance noiseless, turning in the sun: that is, precisely when imagined and not used. There are profounder wishes: such as the desire to converse with other living things. On this desire, as ancient as the Fall, is largely founded the talking of beasts and creatures in fairy-tales, and especially the magical understanding of their proper speech. This is the root, and not the "confusion" attributed to the minds of men of the unrecorded past, an alleged "absence of the sense of separation of ourselves from beasts." A vivid sense of that separation is very ancient; but also a sense that it was a severance: a strange fate and a guilt lies on us. Other creatures are like other realms with which Man has broken off relations, and sees now only from the outside at a distance, being at war with them, or on the terms of an uneasy armistice. There are a few men who are privileged to travel abroad a little; others must be content with travellers' tales. Even about frogs.[69]

The message of Attic comedy is similar to the dream of fairy:

> Actors appear in the very transparent guise of dogs and cheese-graters, hoopoes and barbarian gods. Choruses of clouds, birds, or frogs sing and dance and join in the action. Part of comedy's delight is therefore, as Plato noticed, the vicarious liberation it provides from our ordinary roles in life that nature and society join to enforce, firmly distinguishing female from male, human from

---

69 Tolkien, "On Fairy Stories," in *Monsters and the Critics*, 151–52.

beast, animate from inanimate nature. For a brief time, the barriers are broken down.[70]

Even today our children's stories — and many more adult fantasies — are full of talking beasts. And maybe these fables serve the truth rather better than more immediately plausible stories: as Apollonius is said to have remarked, Aesop "was more devoted to truth than the poets. They give their own stories a forced appearance of plausibility, while he, by promising a story that everyone knows to be untrue, tells the truth precisely in not undertaking to tell the truth"![71]

But on the other hand, our children's stories are, after all, realistic, or at least rest on realistic reasons. Once upon a time — and not all that long ago — our own human ancestors were of one species with the ancestors of all modern apes, of all mammals, of all vertebrates — and indeed of every living thing on Earth. Once upon a time there were many different hominin species, subtly or largely different from our own human norm. There were, in biological reality, creatures whom we could fairly characterize as elves or dwarves or hobbits, exactly as our folk stories intimate. Once upon a time our ancestors had good reason also to try and understand the moods and motives of many other sorts of creature, both like and unlike themselves. In brief, our present conviction that "we human beings" are of a radically other kind than other living things is incompatible with our own preferred theories of evolutionary change, and the smug conceit with which too many commentators address "anthropomorphic fantasies" as suitable only for "children" has no clear intellectual basis.

But might it have a sort of *moral* basis? Many people find fault with the very idea of merging "animal" and "human" characters. Even the combination of cow egg and human DNA, for the purposes of stem-cell research, is allowed only on condition that the zygote is never even an embryo, let alone a neonate. And even quite hardheaded scientists express some disapproval even of such hybrid forms as we can already create, like geeps (goat-sheep

---

70 Buxton, *Forms*, 72, citing Reckford, *Aristophanes' Old-and-New Comedy*, 99.
71 Philostratus, *Life of Apollonius*, 2:25 [5.14.3]. He adds, "it is also a charming trait to make dumb animals nicer and deserving respect from humans" (ibid., 2:27 [5.14.3]).

hybrids), not only because their creation may involve physical and mental pains in the failed as well as the successful artefacts. Some opposition to Darwinian theory (indeed to almost any evolutionary theory) has always arisen from disapproval of the suggestion that we are "animals," and especially that we have no stable essence.

> The sub-conscious popular instinct against Darwinism was... that when once one begins to think of man as a shifting and alterable thing, it is always easy for the strong and crafty to twist him into new shapes for all kinds of unnatural purposes. The popular instinct sees in such developments the possibility of backs bowed and hunch-backed for their burden, or limbs twisted for their task. It has a very well-grounded guess that whatever is done swiftly and systematically will mostly be done by a successful class and almost solely in their interests. It has therefore a vision of unhuman hybrids and half-human experiments much in the style of Mr. Wells's Island of Dr Moreau... The rich man may come to be breeding a tribe of dwarfs to be his jockeys, and a tribe of giants to be his hall-porters.[72]

In other words we may *deliberately* breed different human species: that is, the powerful may breed them (and maybe maintain a small class of scholars or innovative engineers to do the actual work). Maybe this need not be overt oppression: after all, it would pay the powerful to ensure that each of their new specimens *preferred* the life they lead, and it is doubtful that any of these could *sue* for having been made the way they are. Nor need they suppose that the new kinds are "inferior": on the contrary, a "good dwarf" would be valued as much as a good horse, however strange she looked by mainstream standards. But there still seems something wrong.

Ethical humanism depends on the intuition that humanity is both a moral norm and a constitutive reality. Every one of our conspecifics stands in for all: to kill one human is to kill anyone.[73]

---

72 Chesterton, *What's Wrong with the World*, 259.
73 As stated in the *Koran* 5.32: "whosoever killeth a human being for other than manslaughter or corruption in the earth, it shall be as if he had killed all humankind, and whoso saveth the life of one, it shall be as if he had saved the life of all humankind." The concession in this verse apparently has to do with capital punishment for particularly outrageous crimes against the community.

Even animal liberationists are more affected by a human corpse than by a cat's (or a wasp's), and not just because it's bigger. However ridiculous it may be, on almost any moral theory, to suggest that a hybrid of ape and human would have or should have fewer rights than us, such a phantom does, somehow, excite quite different attitudes. On the one hand, she has a claim to be human; on the other, it is but an ape, and even people who care for apes don't usually see them as "divine." Humanism, in order to safeguard the interests of other *human* tribes, requires us to turn from the nonhuman.

It is not difficult to see why, on the other hand, many animals *have* struck us as divine, and why rulers have often sought to seize their mystique for themselves, choosing lion or eagle or horse or wild boar as their emblems. We recognize their beauty and their power — and much of the outrage felt at factory farming, and bad zoos, has more to do with the sense that the creatures should not be thus diminished than with the mere judgement (true as it often is) that they are, as individuals, miserable or in pain.

> If the most noted of the philosophers, observing the riddle of the Divine in inanimate and incorporeal objects, have not thought it proper to treat any thing with carelessness or disrespect, even more do I think that, in all likelihood, we should welcome those peculiar properties existent in natures which possess the power of perception and have a soul and feeling and character.[74]

Chimps, perhaps, are too undignified to get much worship, but gorillas inspire awe. These emotions, of course, don't necessarily result in our treating individual animals fairly: being an incarnate god was always a mixed blessing, even in Ancient Egypt. The individual is only an *instance* or an echo of that god, and can, with proper ritual, be killed. Even while alive it is likely to be coerced into behaving as a proper emblem rather than as its own recalcitrant self (that is why kings have so often kept royal menageries, uncaring that the "symbolic beasts" are, as individuals, wretched). And it is all too often the case that romantics turn from praising the beauty of animals to gobbling their factory-farmed flesh.

---

74 Plutarch, "Isis and Osiris" 76, in *Moralia*, 5:180.

The "first conception of God" as Dio Chrysostom represented it amounts to the elevation of human mind and judgement over the "brute beasts" of passion and disorder — an elevation that has often been employed also to defend imperial control of recalcitrant *human* populations. *Parcere subiectis et debellare superbos*: to spare the conquered and beat down the proud.[75] This image of divinity clearly had an influence on later Christian centuries: by contemplating God's glory, as represented in art, we could be reconciled to our own troubles, we could be seduced by splendour, and could expect our enemies to be defeated. The difference is that Christ Pantokrator was still, indelibly and doctrinally, the Crucified: the cross his "disgraceful symbol" because it marked him as a criminal condemned by imperial power to a naked, humiliating, *excruciating* (exactly) death. "It isn't *nomos*, but one who was nailed to the cross by *nomos* who is the imperator! This is incredible, and compared to this all the little revolutionaries are *nothing*."[76]

We have not fully internalized that message, nor understood that the victims of our human pride are all around us. Early Christians were derided for worshipping, as it was said, a man with an ass's head. Perhaps we should have taken the charge more seriously, and not simply returned the insult (as did Tertullian).[77] It is worth noting in passing that the Vatican ruled (in 1987) that a notorious graffito found in Rome (of the crucified Christ with donkey's ears and a schoolboy pointing a finger at him) was not, as is usually assumed, a juvenile insult, but a genuine mark of devotion![78] But they probably didn't draw my moral!

It is of course problematic. If animals are seen as worshipful we may hope to embody something of their characters, and thereby

---

75 Virgil, *Aeneid* 6.853.
76 Taubes, *The Political Theology of Paul*, 24, cited by Baker, "Now We Have Been Delivered from the Law," 376.
77 Tertullian, *To the Nations*, Bk. 1, ch. 11: "Suppose that our God, then, be an asinine person, will you at all events deny that you possess the same characteristics with ourselves in that matter? (Not their heads only, but) entire asses, are, to be sure, objects of adoration to you, along with their tutelar Epona; and all herds, and cattle, and beasts you consecrate, and their stables into the bargain! This, perhaps, is your grievance against us, that, when surrounded by cattle-worshippers of every kind we are simply devoted to asses!"
78 At least according to the *Chicago Tribune* (December 29, 1987): www.chicagotribune.com/news/ct-xpm-1987-12-29-8704060660-story.html.

lose a little of our own humanity—or so the suspicion runs. We may reasonably not much care for rulers who self-identify as lions or eagles, however gloriously they posture. We may reasonably be worried by anyone who seeks to copy what he thinks is "animal behaviour" (by which he will usually intend "amoral" or "uninhibited" or "natural" behaviour).

So perhaps we should still take warning against both imitation and miscegenation from the older stories. Modern genetic engineers now often propose that a genome is more like a loose-leaf folder than a clearly edited volume, and that we may happily transfer genetic material from one kind to another. As Freeman Dyson has proposed: "We are moving rapidly into the post-Darwinian era, when species will no longer exist, and the evolution of life will again be communal."[79] Genes will be shared around as easily amongst us as they are amongst bacteria (for which *species*-distinctions have always been moot). Dyson, it seems to me, is a great deal too optimistic in his description of the early years:

> In the post-Darwinian era, biotechnology will be domesticated. There will be do-it-yourself kits for gardeners, who will use gene transfer to breed new varieties of roses and orchids. Also, biotech games for children, played with real eggs and seeds rather than with images on a screen. Genetic engineering, once it gets into the hands of the general public, will give us an explosion of biodiversity. Designing genomes will be a new art form, as creative as painting or sculpture. Few of the new creations will be masterpieces, but all will bring joy to their creators and diversity to our fauna and flora.

Even ordinary dog-breeders have managed to create varieties of dog with innate deformities. What "the general public" will do if licensed to perform such vivisections I cannot quite imagine, nor endure. Will we be able to resist the fashion? How long will there be "a general (unmodified?) public" in the sense that Dyson imagines? Maybe there should even be some support for the panic reaction of one of Lovecraft's characters, faced by what he imagines is an improper mixture of kinds? "Hippopotami should

---

79 Dyson, "The Darwinian Interlude." Dyson takes his cue from Woese, "A New Biology for a New Century."

not have human hands and carry torches... men should not have the heads of crocodiles," his fictional Houdini exclaims in a story ghostwritten for Harry Houdini himself.[80] Lovecraft's point was, exactly, that they might, that our particular sort of life is not a cosmic norm, and that species boundaries are in the end no more than long-lasting *social* ones. Maybe we should still be cautious: the ethic of universal humanism, founded on the feeling or conviction that all *human beings* are kin, is still not sturdy enough to stop us "othering" even our closest neighbours. That we are *all* of one blood, whatever our outward apparel, and that we *all* contain some portion of the divine, may be a conviction far beyond us all.

And yet it is a conviction that some of our ancestors managed. Folkstories are full of clever and kindly beasts, who should not be taken to be merely metaphors. Once upon a time we understood them better.

Is this happy confusion of forms one root of Egyptian images, of gods with animal heads, or gods embodied in actual animals (cats, or the bull of Apis)? Those images, of course, were probably not intended to be realistic portraits: they were ideograms, not pictograms, to indicate the properties or functions of the god. But Egypt's neighbours were not entirely wrong to think that the Egyptians did respect, or even "worship," the animal forms of gods. Even such sympathetic commentators as the first century Platonist, Plutarch of Chaeronea, thought that portraying the gods as animals must lead "the weak and innocent into 'superstition' (*deisidaimonia*), and the cynical and bold into 'atheistic and bestial reasoning' (*atheos kai theriodes logismos*)."[81] Even the author of the Wisdom of Solomon, who insisted that God hates nothing that He has made, mocked the Egyptians for their worship of "vermin."[82] Only in the Human, we are to suppose, can anything worth worshipping be found—and the notion retains its power even for those who claim to have no god. So Apollonius disputed with the Egyptian or Ethiopian "Naked Ones" (with whom he was clearly on bad terms):

---

80 Lovecraft, "Under the Pyramids" [1924], in *Thing on the Doorstep*, 74.
81 See Gilhus, *Animals, Gods and Humans*, 98, after Plutarch "Isis and Osiris" 71, in *Moralia*, 5:166–67.
82 Wisdom of Solomon 11.24; 11.15–20.

"Doubtless if you envisage the shape of Zeus, you must see him together with the heaven, the seasons, and the planets, as Pheidias ventured to do in his day. If you are planning to portray Athena, you must think of armies, intelligence, the arts, and how she sprang from Zeus himself. But if you create a hawk, an owl, a wolf, or a dog, and bring it into your holy places instead of Hermes, Athena, or Apollo, people will think animals and birds worth envying for their images, but the gods will fall far short of their own glory." "You appear," said Thespesion [speaking for the Naked Ones], "to be examining our practices without due scrutiny. If there is one respect in which the Egyptians are wise, it is that they are not presumptuous about the forms taken by the gods. They make these forms symbolic and suggestive, since in that way they seem more venerable."[83]

On this at least, I side with the Egyptians! Some, like Apollonius, have supposed that it was "the Greeks" who saved us from such supposed superstitions:

> The great superiority of the Hellenes over the Orientals and the Egyptians lies in the fact that they conceived their gods in a form which was beautiful, human, and unaffected by the disfigurements of old age; and it was Homer who first taught them this lesson.[84]

Homer (as well as Hesiod) in fact allowed his gods to take on many nonhuman shapes, which classical scholars often prefer to suppose mere similes, as though Athena (for example) merely flew as quickly as a bird, rather than as a bird. But the Human Form Divine did indeed come to predominate Hellenic thought and artistry.

> In times past, because we had no clear knowledge, we formed each his different idea, and each person, according to his capacity and nature, conceived a likeness for every divine manifestation and fashioned such likenesses in his dreams; and if we do perchance collect any small and insignificant likenesses made by the earlier artists, we

---

83 Philostratus, *Life of Apollonius*, 2:157 [6.19.3].
84 Buxton, *Forms*, 32, paraphrasing (sceptically) Wilamowitz-Moellendorff, *Der Glaube der Hellenen* [1931–32], 1:144.

do not trust them very much nor pay them very much attention. But [Pheidias] by the power of [his] art first conquered and united Hellas and then all others by means of this wondrous presentment, showing forth so marvellous and dazzling a conception, that none of those who have beheld it could any longer easily form a different one.[85]

The philosopher Xenophanes, not noticing that older artists had not in fact been so unimaginative, observed that "if cows and horses or lions had hands, or could draw with their hands and make things as men can, horses would have drawn horse-like gods, cows cow-like gods,"[86] with the implication that all such images were biased. And Numa, supposedly, forbade the Romans, as Moses forbade the Hebrews, to revere an image of God which had the form of either man or beast.[87] Even the storytellers were not so sure that the gods were only human, or even like any usual creature: Semele's request to see her lover "in his true form" proved disastrous.[88] Zeus is not something so easily encountered.

> So will you say "God is invisible"? Don't speak like that. Who is more visible than he is? He has made everything so that you might see him through all that is. That is God's goodness, therein lies his excellence: to make himself apparent through all that is. For nothing is invisible, not even among the incorporeals. *Nous* shows itself in the act of *noēsis*, God in the act of creating.[89]

---

85 Dio Chrysostom, "Man's First Conception of God," in *Discourses* 2:59 [12.53]. See also *Ennead* V.8 [31].1; Cicero, *Orator* 11.8-9, on the form that Zeus *would* take if he were incarnate.
86 Xenophanes 21B15DK, in Waterfield *First Philosophers*, 27.
87 Plutarch, *Numa* 8.6-8; cf. Exodus 20.4-5; 20.22-24.
88 See Buxton, *Forms*, 50, 148-50, 158-59.
89 *Corpus Hermeticum* 11.22, in Hanegraaff, *Hermetic Spirituality*, 219 (see Copenhaver, *Hermetica*, 42).

∞9∞
Other Identities

> Here below we can know many things by the look in people's eyes when they are silent; but There all their body is clear and pure and each is like an eye, and nothing is hidden or feigned, but before one speaks to another that other has seen and understood.[1]

SURVIVING LIFE[2]

According to Plotinus's exegesis of Homer, Heracles's image or shadow is in Hades, but he himself is among the gods.[3] Most commentators suggest that some copyist, desperate to reconcile entirely conflicting traditions, had added the line about "Heracles himself," distinct from the shade of Heracles. In the earlier text or oral recitation, it is supposed, Heracles was no more than another hero, whose "afterlife" was no real life at all. At death, *The Iliad* repeatedly declares, our force (*menos*), will (*thumos*), guts (*phrenes*) and breath (*psyche*) itself all leave the bodily remains behind, but not so as to constitute a real surviving entity. All that can be found in the Unseen, in Hades, are memories and images of the departed, perhaps to be given momentary life by the blood of sacrifice, but best walled off from the life of the survivors.[4] If there is any conscious experience there at all it is a life of regretful memory—a notion that in later years amounts to eternal damnation, whether or not particular punishments are imagined.[5] A quite different notion of our "soul" (still *psyche*) permitted the idea that we *are* souls, able to wander away even during this mortal life, and destined for real life hereafter. In

---

1 Ennead IV.3 [27].18, 19–24.
2 This section partly repeats, and corrects, my "Souls, Stars and Shadows," originally composed for a Prometheus conference at Chingford in 2015, and for a conference at Bath Spa University in 2016.
3 Ennead I.1 [53].12; see also IV.3 [27].32; after *Odyssey* 11.601–2.
4 See Heath, "Blood for the Dead."
5 See Hillman, *Dream and the Underworld*, 56.

Homeric or pre-Homeric times, such "life souls" may be reserved for the special few, who are being raised to life immortal, even to godhead (like Heracles himself,[6] or Dionysos), or granted a special escape from death, an everlasting home in Elysion, as Zeus's son-in-law (a fate prophesied for Menelaus). In *The Odyssey* even the great hero Achilles was left in Hades, though an alternative tradition suggested that his mother took him away instead to the "White Island."[7] That Island may be Elysion — or it may be merely an island in the Black Sea, his putative burial place. A different editor might have added a gloss to Achilles' gloomy conversation with Odysseus to accommodate the stories.

But these differing accounts need not have had different sources, as though one tradition or poetic lineage firmly supposed that even heroes only survived as shadows, and another insisted rather that they were raised immortal. The likelier story is that we have always held apparently conflicting views about the present whereabouts of those we can no longer touch or hold. The dead still exist at least "in our mind's eye," in dreams or sudden reminiscences: do they also exist in graveyards, or in the imagined West, or the Underworld, or Heaven, independent of our memory? Do they grow and change there, or remain forever what they were, or simply fade to be forgotten? By Homer's account, shadow-Heracles goes on hunting, Rhadamanthus judges, and Achilles, of course, complains. We may hope that "real heroes" manage rather better! But there need have been no rationalizing copyist to distinguish shadow-Heracles and Heracles-the-god: gods and heroes (that is, persons well remembered whether for good or evil) differ from the rest of us — but there may be and may always have been the same uncertainty, the same ambivalence, even about the non-heroic dead. A body (buried or burnt or mummified) may be an aide-memoire, and reason for leaving flowers in graveyards; so also may be the name and reputation of the dead, or an occasional

---

6 "Mighty Heracles, the valiant son of neat-ankled Alcmena, when he had finished his grievous toils, made Hebe the child of great Zeus and goldshod Hera his shy wife in snowy Olympus. Happy he! For he has finished his great work and lives amongst the undying gods, untroubled and unaging all his days": Hesiod, *Theogony*, 951–56.
7 See Burgess, *Death and Afterlife of Achilles*, 78–110; Edwards, "Achilles in the Underworld."

phantom-glimpse, or some more stable icon, or—perhaps—a real immortal identity beyond our imagination.

Even if these ambiguities are familiar ones, and need no special explanation, they may also provide the seeds of more developed theories. On the one hand the dead—if they are not merely buried or burned bodies—are shadows, *eidola*, dream-images of the real bodily beings that had real effects in the world, and real choices. On the other, perhaps they can be counted—or some of them can be counted—alongside really immortal—or at least long-lasting—beings, tangible divinities. The ancient Egyptian story suggested that "one aspect of the god's nature, his *ba*, is in heaven; another one, his body, rests in the realm of the dead."[8] Even the human dead may have at least three modes of "survival": the *ka* is given form through the body's mummification, the array of funeral goods, and seems to persist simply as an echo of the once-living being; the *ba*, represented as a bird with a human head, can hope to join the Sun in his progress across the heavens, maybe as a star, probably in the constellation Orion (the sidereal home of Osiris).[9] A third, the *akh*, transcends all usual possibilities. There may, in short, be a systematic theory of the Afterlife, developed in Egypt, and persisting (perhaps) in Homer, and (more certainly) in Plotinus.

But there is another possibility to be faced and considered first: perhaps we should give up the fixed belief that we are ourselves discrete and determinate beings: why not suppose—as consistent materialists must suspect is true—that there is only *stuff* in motion, that the boundaries between this and that, or even now and then, are as fictitious as the boundaries between nation-states.

> Democritus occasionally does away with sensible phenomena, saying that none of them really and truly presents itself to the senses, but is only thought to do so, while the only truth in existing things is the existence of atoms and void. He says: "Sweet exists by convention, and so does bitter, warm, cold, and colour; in reality there are atoms and void."[10]

---

[8] Morenz, *Egyptian Religion*, 151, after the Leiden Hymns (13th century BC).
[9] Griffith, 'Sailing to Elysium: Menelaus' Afterlife,' 215, after Pyramid Text utterances (24th century BC).
[10] Democritus 68B9, in Waterfield *First Philosophers*, 176.

Still more obviously, the names we give to particular aggregates are solely "by convention." "'Nagasena' is but a way of counting,"[11] and Chuang Tzu was right not to fear extinction:

> A good craftsman, casting metal, would not be too pleased with metal that jumped up and said "I must be made into a sword like Mo Yeh." Now given that I have been bold enough to take on human shape already, if I then said, "I must be a human! I must be a human!" the Maker of All would eye me somewhat askance.... Peacefully we die, calmly we awake.[12]

On another occasion Chuang Tzu enquired why he should be expected to grieve because the stuff that had been moulded into his wife now had a different shape.[13] What real substance do individual forms have, whether the real stuff is an homogenous continuum or a cloud of atomic bits? The thought was explicit in a Sicilian thinker: "no mortal thing has a beginning, nor does it end in death and obliteration; there is only a mixing and then a separating of what was mixed."[14]

But interestingly the very thinkers who most emphasised the transformative possibilities of living nature were also known to believe in distinct and immortal souls, of another sort than the souls which were the life of distinct, individual bodies. Material stuff cannot provide unities, but—at best—only *continuities*, and so real unitary beings must get their being elsewhere.[15] Long ago we were gods, and some of us—Empedocles said—remember this. In realizing our imprisonment, he presented himself to Acragas in Sicily as "an immortal god, mortal no more."[16] Hesiod's gods are condemned to lie frozen by the Styx when they break their oath, and Zuntz's aphorism is almost correct: "the banished god described by Hesiod is—Man."[17] Almost correct, but not exactly: for the point Empedocles is making is that the banished god

---

11 Radhakrishnan and Moore, *Sourcebook*, 281–84.
12 *Book of Chuang Tzu*, 54.
13 *Book of Chuang Tzu*, 150–51.
14 Empedocles 31B8DK, in Waterfield, *First Philosophers*, 145.
15 Plotinus concludes that soul itself cannot provide that unity, being intrinsically diverse: unity comes only from the One, as "final cause." See *Ennead* VI.9 [9].1–3, on which I have attempted a brief account in my *Commentary* on VI.9.
16 Empedocles 31B112DK, in Waterfield *First Philosophers*, 140.
17 Hesiod, *Theogony* 775–806; Zuntz, *Persephone*, 267.

isn't *essentially* human, even if it may be born among humans "as prophets, singers of hymns, healers and leaders"[18]—and among beasts as lions, or laurels amongst trees.[19]

The banished god that finds itself embodied here is not necessarily tied down to its body, even while that body lives. Hermotimus of Clazomenae, for example, set his soul roaming round the world while his body lay seemingly lifeless (till his treacherous wife, bored with his long silence, had the body burnt).[20] He was, it was said, an earlier incarnation of the soul that also animated Pythagoras, and himself claimed to have had the same soul as a hero of the Trojan War, Euphorbus.[21] An even odder character, Aristeas of Proconnesus (an island *polis* in the Propontis, between the Mediterranean and the Black Sea), in the seventh century BC, is said to have vanished from his home after seeming to fall dead, and reappeared seven years later to deliver a poem, the *Arimaspea*, about his travels, "possessed by Apollo," in the North. More oddly still, he reappeared—or someone claiming to be him appeared—240 years later, in southern Italy, saying he had been with Apollo, as a raven.[22]

Some later Platonists, like Iamblichus, were wary of the notion that our human soul could ever be incarnate as an "animal" (for reasons all too familiar), but it seems clear that others—from Plato to Plotinus—were content that we might be embodied as ants or bees or eagles, depending on the form of life we had chosen.[23] Plato, in his "myth of Er," suggested that we all have *chosen* the lives we had to live, and must make the best of it: "Orpheus chose the life of a swan,...Thamyras chose a nightingale's life, while a swan and other songbirds opted for change and chose to live as human beings.... The same kind of thorough exchange and shuffling of roles occurred in the case of animals too, as they became men or other animals—wild ones if they'd been immoral (*adika*), tame ones otherwise."[24] That being born

---

18 Empedocles 31B146DK, in Waterfield, *First Philosophers*, 141.
19 Empedocles 31B127DK. Waterfield, for some reason, omits this fragment.
20 Pliny, *Natural History* 7.174.
21 Diogenes Laertius, *Lives* 8.4.
22 See Culianu, *Psychanodia* I, 37.
23 See Stamatellos, "Plotinus on Transmigration."
24 Plato, *Republic* 10.617d–620d (a passage that I foolishly ignored in my earlier publication!).

"tame" is always a reward or an improvement is perhaps naïve. Perhaps, Plotinus added, we might all hope for a better part next time—as actors hope for a more significant role once they have shown their talents.[25] The story would be easier to comprehend or accept if all of us—not simply the favoured few like Hermotimus or Empedocles—could *remember* being "a boy and a girl, a shrub and a bird and the fish that leaps from the sea."[26] Memory is not the criterion of identity here: on the contrary, the stories about past events that come into my mind here-now are only *memories* if it was I that was their subject or their agent. Conversely, there are many true stories about "my own" past actions that I do not now recall. But at least, if I were to *seem* to remember being (say) Hermotimus I would have some slight reason to consider it might be true. But the story about our life hereafter actually emphasises that hardly anyone will remember—and that this is as it should be: Euphorbus, Hermotimus, and Pythagoras are different lives, with different duties. Each life we live has its own time and reason, even if those lives do, somehow, share "a soul."

So what criterion of identity for souls is relevant? Plotinus reckoned that we could simply *recognize* our friends hereafter, as Pythagoras recognized his friend, in the sound of a beaten dog.[27] "For here below, too, we can know many things by the look in people's eyes when they are silent; but There all their body is clear and pure and each is like an eye, and nothing is hidden or feigned, but before one speaks to another that other has seen and understood."[28] "There," that is, we apparently have recognizable, and naked, bodies—or at least we have *some* public presence, even if that presence is not so easily locatable, nor yet as divisible, as our present corporeal being. Are these "bodies" merely the shadowy

---

25 *Ennead* III.2 [47]. 17, 45–53.
26 Empedocles DK31B117, in Waterfield, *First Philosophers*, 154. Ian Stevenson, a prolific scholar, spent time and energy recording and assessing apparent memories of earlier lives: see Stevenson, *Twenty Cases Suggestive of Reincarnation*; cf. Kelly, *Science, the Self, and Survival after Death*. Whether or not those memories were veridical, they do serve to show the empirical basis for the widespread doctrine.
27 According to Xenophanes of Colophon DK21B7: see Diogenes Laertius, *Lives* 8.36. For a less literal interpretation of the story, see my essay "Can Animals Be Our Friends?"
28 *Ennead* IV.3 [27].18, 19–24.

images that Homer led us to expect, even though we can expect to be more like Teiresias (who kept most of his wits) than the common Homeric mass? But images of what? Precisely because these souls—or better, perhaps, these *daimones* or *spirits*—are not identical with any one of their earthly lives—we cannot expect to recognize (say) Socrates merely from the look of things: his spirit is not snub-nosed, even symbolically. But if there were no individualized public presences we might have to expect that there is just *one* spirit for all of us, wholly indistinguishable and therefore wholly identical. That indeed seems, sometimes, to be the implication of the philosophers' account: "mind is the god in us—whether it was Hermotimus or Anaxagoras who said so—and mortal life contains a portion of some god."[29] And maybe this is common knowledge: "all men are naturally and spontaneously moved to speak of the god who is in each one of us *one and the same*."[30]

Just occasionally, Plotinus remarked, we may glimpse that possibility, when the world we see grows dreamlike. "Often I have woken up out of the body to myself, and have entered into myself, going out from all other things; I have seen a beauty wonderfully great and felt assurance that then most of all I belonged to the better part."[31] But what wakens is not just *Plotinus*, a particular third-century Egyptian. Remember that caterpillars, in one ancient and respectable account, are not *turned into* butterflies, but only lay the eggs (the chrysalids) from which the butterflies will hatch![32] And *"psyche"* means both soul and butterfly. Our present selves are grubs in the great tree of nature.[33] Or maybe we are leaves.

The immortal soul or spirit, then, is effectively a *daimon*, with an unearthly body that somehow still reveals an abiding character and form of life, and which is in turn a twig of Soul-as-Such. There is a difference between "the absolute Socrates" and the Socrates that lived in Athens.[34] In the stories that Plato several

---

29 Aristotle, *Protrepticus*, in Ross, *Select Fragments*, 42 [fr.10c]; see Betegh, *The Derveni Papyrus*, 284. Indeed, Aristotle sometimes goes further: "*everything* has by nature something divine," not only things "with mind": *Nicomachean Ethics*, 7.1153b32.
30 *Ennead* VI.5 [23].1 (my emphasis).
31 *Ennead* IV.8 [6].1.
32 Aristotle, *De Historia Animalium* 5.551a3.
33 *Ennead* IV.3 [27].4, 26–30. The notion is given an explicit SF shape in Eric Frank Russell, *Sentinels from Space*.
34 *Ennead* V.7 [18].1, 3–8.

times appends to his dialogues these spirits will be sorted out in Hades: most may have to endure purgatorial torments, a few will pass on—for a while—to the Elysian Fields.[35] Almost all will be returned to natural existence, in whatever form best suits them. A very few will be discarded forever, or else break free forever from the wheel. In later developments of the story—echoing the Egyptian myth—our spirits must ascend, as I have described before, through seven planetary spheres, shedding the qualities or vices we acquired in our earlier descent, and so return at last to heaven as stars[36]—which are themselves indivisible points. Free so to pass through space we must have a sort of local presence, an *okhema*, a vehicle or "astral body"—though Plotinus flatly denied that we had any need of this to manage our return.[37]

As stars, so Plotinus also insisted, we have no need of memory: everything of importance will then be immediately present and we shall have no more need than the true Heracles to recall our earthly lives. This will be our longed-for return:

> Even before this coming to be we were there, men [that is, *anthropoi*] who were different, and some of us even gods, pure souls and intellect united with the whole of reality; we were parts of the intelligible, not marked off or cut off but belonging to the whole; and we are not cut off even now.[38]

How different is this hope from the Stoic suggestion that the wise at least, by identifying with or attaching to their idea of the cosmos, are effectively immortal as the single Mind all really rational beings share? That would seem to be at odds with Plotinus's declaration that we shall recognize our—plural—friends, as well as with Socrates' hope of conversing with past heroes if he survives his execution.[39] According to Porphyry, the oracle at Delphi declared that Plotinus, freed "from the wave of this blood-drinking life" and from "the tomb (*sema*) that held [his]

---

35 Plato, *Phaedo* 107a–115a; *Republic* 10.614–21; *Gorgias* 523a–525a.
36 Proclus, *Elements of Theology*, 307n2, on Proposition 209; see Rist, *Plotinus: The Road to Reality*, 190–91; see also *Enneads* IV.3 [27].15; II.3 [52].9, 7ff.
37 *Ennead* I.6 [1].8, 16–28; see Finamore, *Iamblichus and the Theory of the Vehicle of the Soul*.
38 *Ennead* VI.4 [22].14, 18ff.
39 Plato, *Apology* 40c5–41c7.

Other Identities

daimonic soul," had joined "the dance of immortal love," alongside Minos, Rhadamanthus, Aeacus, Plato and Pythagoras.[40] Such confusions, as I pointed out before, are commonplace, and do not signify that Socrates (or Plato or Plotinus or the Oracle) is being "ironic." Whatever the world we wake to at our deaths may be, they are confident at any rate that we shall wake,[41] and waking realize that we are none of us what we once thought we were. Our earthly deaths will be an initiation into a sacred reality[42]—but what that is like, God knows.

Following the Egyptian clue, we have at least three "souls"—first, the mere shadow or image of a sometime mortal life (*ka*), and second a spirit who may join the gods in glory (*ba*). A third soul, the *akh*, originally reserved for Pharaohs, is elevated even higher. The Egyptian story may suggest that there are even more such "soulish" elements (including *sahu* or "spiritual body," which seems to function like the later *okhema*; *shut* or shadow, and *ren* or name and reputation).[43] The third significant soul may be reflected in Plotinus's own occasional distinction between the usual *daimon* and a god: "*some* of us even gods," but perhaps not all, or not yet all. In our ascent to heaven, we may come to the star "which is in harmony with the character and power which lived and worked in [us] and each will have a god of this kind as its guardian spirit, either the star itself or the god set above this power."[44] Whether the *daimon* or the god is to be thought our own "higher self," or else a distinct and higher soul, is a question without clear answer. There is perhaps a faint echo of these elements in Paul's distinction between flesh, soul, and spirit,[45] and his hopes to be raised a "spiritual body."[46]

In any case, we may hope that we are all, like Heracles, to be freed from memory of past follies and misadventures. An interesting analogy (at least) has recently surfaced in psychological study: a woman who has no "first-person, episodic" memory of her own life, though she may know many facts about it:

---

40 Porphyry, *Life of Plotinus* 22: 34, 45, 53–57.
41 *Ennead* IV.8 [6].1.
42 Plutarch fr. 165 (Stobaeus 4.52.49), cited by Segal, *Life after Death*, 217.
43 See also Romer, *Book of the Dead* (Kindle location 1272), where Wallis-Budge enumerates nine distinct material and "spiritual" elements.
44 *Ennead* III.4 [15].6, 27ff.; see also VI.5 [23].12, 32–34.
45 Paul [?], 1 Thessalonians 5.23.
46 Paul, 1 Corinthians 15.42–4.

McKinnon is the first person ever identified with a condition called severely deficient autobiographical memory. She knows plenty of facts about her life, but she lacks the ability to mentally relive any of it, the way you or I might meander back in our minds and evoke a particular afternoon.[47]

Just so most of us can acknowledge that we were born at such and such a time and place, had an unremembered infancy, and have since done many things we don't ourselves recall.[48] Losing *all* our episodic memory would not necessarily render us incapable. We might think it an improvement! "Memories that would be searing to anyone else leave little impression on [McKinnon].... She doesn't know what it's like to linger in a memory, to long for the past, to dwell in it." And maybe we can get some comfort even in this earthly life from the story told of Proclus: in his last illness "though he forgot almost all human things as the paralysis advanced... he completed the hymns [he had asked to be chanted] and the greater part of the Orphic verses... read out in his presence."[49] Those suffering from dementia and losing their "personal" memories, even their autobiographical memories, may still be able to sing.[50] Our predecessors would have inferred that this is what was worth remembering.

> An aged man is but a paltry thing,
> A tattered coat upon a stick, unless
> Soul clap its hands and sing, and louder sing
> For every tatter in its mortal dress.
> Nor is there singing school but studying
> Monuments of its own magnificence;
> And therefore I have sailed the seas and come
> To the holy city of Byzantium.[51]

---

47 Erika Hayasaki, "In a Perpetual Present," *Wired Magazine*, April 2016: www.wired.com/2016/04/susie-mckinnon-autobiographical-memory-sdam/ (accessed December 21, 2022).
48 Cf. Chesterton, *Autobiography*, 1: "my birth is an incident which I accept, like some poor ignorant peasant, only because it has been handed down to me by oral tradition."
49 Marinus, "Life of Proclus," in Edwards, *Neoplatonic Saints*, 89.
50 As McKinnon also can. See also Sacks, *Anthropologist on Mars*, and *Musicophilia*, 371–86.
51 Yeats, "Sailing to Byzantium" [1927], in *Collected Poems*, 163.

DREAMING THE WORLD ALIVE

Fairyland is also the Dreamworld—but are we entirely sure what the Waking World might be? "What proof could you give if anyone should ask us, now, at the present moment, whether we are asleep and our thoughts are a dream, or whether we are awake and talking to each other in a waking condition?"[52]

Myles Burnyeat argued that "Greek philosophy does not know the problem of proving in a general way the existence of an external world."[53] Perhaps so, but his argument depends on a confusion between a belief that *something* is the case, and a belief that we are immediately acquainted with that thing. Even if we are dreaming, even if there is only Me dreaming, there would be a fact of the matter distinct from my imagining it. It does not follow that there must be a *material* fact, or that all my common-sense beliefs are definitely true, *pace* Chesterton! Travelling to Fairyland may lead to some suspicion that our ordinary lives are the real dream—so Frodo returning at last (and only for a little while) to the familiar Shire declares that it is like falling asleep again.[54]

Even Chesterton, despite his laudable insistence on the unprovable dogmas of our common sense, acknowledged a wilder possibility—as I remarked before. Of the ending of *Midsummer Night's Dream*, he said:

> One touch is added which makes the play colossal. Theseus and his train retire with a crashing finale, full of humour and wisdom and things set right, and silence falls on the house. Then there comes a faint sound of little feet, and for a moment, as it were, the elves look into the house, asking which is the reality. "Suppose we are the realities and they the shadows." If that ending were acted properly any modern man would feel shaken to his marrow if he had to walk home from the theatre through a country lane.[55]

---

52 Plato, *Theaetetus* 157c–158e, cited by O'Flaherty, *Dreams, Illusions*, 39. The often-unnoticed irony of this remark is that it occurs within a work of fiction: "Socrates" and "Theaetetus," even if they had "real-world counterparts," are dream figures.
53 Burnyeat, "Idealism and Greek Philosophy," 19.
54 Tolkien, *Lord of the Rings*, 3:276.
55 *Good Words*, vol. 45 (September–October 1904), 621–26; see www.gkc.org.uk/gkc/books/midsummer_nights_dream.html (accessed September 19, 2022).

HOW THE WORLDS BECAME

Titania had, after all, affirmed that claim:

> The spring, the summer,
> The childing autumn, angry winter, change
> Their wonted liveries, and the mazed world,
> By their increase, now knows not which is which:
> And this same progeny of evils comes
> From our debate, from our dissension;
> *We are their parents and original.*[56]

Intrigue and confusion in the Other World engenders like confusion here-and-now.

Exactly what that Other—and maybe Original—World may be is something that we here-now cannot say.

> What do we know... of the world and the universe about us? Our means of receiving impressions are absurdly few, and our notions of surrounding objects infinitely narrow. We see things only as we are constructed to see them, and can gain no idea of their absolute nature. With five feeble senses we pretend to comprehend the boundlessly complex cosmos, yet other beings with a wider, stronger, or different range of senses might not only see very differently the things we see, but might see and study whole worlds of matter, energy, and life which lie close at hand yet can never be detected with the senses we have.[57]

Our ignorance is, strangely, both acknowledged and ignored by most modern, "naturalistic," thinkers, who repeatedly conclude that we cannot, on current evolutionary theory, expect to be able to discern distant and humanly irrelevant truths, but continue to insist that we do after all "know" (for example) that all real things are material, and that "there is no God." On the contrary, as I have observed before, if we can and should pursue and prefer the Truth, then some form of theism is, essentially, correct: we really *should* listen to reason. But what does Reason tell us?

"To know that one is dreaming is to be no longer perfectly asleep. But for news of the fully waking world you must go to

---

56 *Midsummer Night's Dream*, Act 2, Scene 1 (my italics).
57 Lovecraft, "From Beyond" [1920], in Joshi, *Dream*, 23-29.

my betters."[58] Our ancestors, and our own most faithful scribes, made stories to remind us that our usual world could only be a small part of the Real, and that its borders were neither fixed nor firm. We are living in a small part of the world, so Plato caused his Socrates to say, like ants or frogs about a pond or puddle:

> Now we do not perceive that we live in the hollows, but think we live on the upper surface of the earth, just as if someone who lives in the depth of the ocean should think he lived on the surface of the sea, and, seeing the sun and the stars through the water, should think the sea was the sky, and should, by reason of sluggishness or feebleness, never have reached the surface of the sea, and should never have seen, by rising and lifting his head out of the sea into our upper world, and should never have heard from anyone who had seen, how much purer and fairer it is than the world he lived in. I believe this is just the case with us; for we dwell in a hollow of the earth and think we dwell on its upper surface; and the air we call the heaven, and think that is the heaven in which the stars move.[59]

We may now dispute some of the details of Plato's fantasy, but cannot wholly forget the truth. We live within a fiction only partly of our own making, and sometimes glimpse reminders of the wider and older world. There were powers at work in the world before us, whose motives we can only guess.

When Frodo asks, "Can't a hobbit walk from the Water to the River [in our own Shire] in peace?" Gildor, the High Elf, replies: "It is not your own Shire. Others dwelt here before hobbits were; and others will dwell here again when hobbits are no more. The wide world is all about you: you can fence yourselves in, but you cannot for ever fence it out."[60] One of the strangest and most robust of our modern delusions is that it is "realistic" to forget the future, and to suppose that nothing really changes, or has changed.[61] "It is as if people who slept through their life

---

58 Lewis, *Four Loves*, 160; cf. Rappe, *Reading Neoplatonism*, 62: "Once [the dreamer] realizes the fact about his own creations [that he himself projects the *phantasmata* seen in the dream], he is no longer subject to them."
59 Plato, *Phaedo* 109cd.
60 Tolkien, *Lord of the Rings*, 1:93.
61 Cf. Wells, *World Set Free*, 18: "The sober Englishman at the close of the

thought the things in their dreams were reliable and obvious, but, if someone woke them up, disbelieved in what they saw with their eyes open and went to sleep again":[62] for that very reason it is clear that genre fiction, science fiction, or fantasy (including most "historical fiction"), is really more realistic, at a deep level, than the so-called "realistic novel"!

The theme — that we might be dreaming — has recently been given an even more striking descant. We are now familiar with the making of "virtual worlds," fictions that we can experience in highly persuasive detail, so as wholly to suspend any disbelief. We can reasonably suspect that the art form will improve, until there will be no way of telling, from within, that we are not "really" engaged in the adventures we imagine. From which it follows, as Bostrom has observed, that there would be good reason to suspect that we are now within exactly such a virtual adventure, perhaps devised by experts only a few generations later than the time we now suppose ourselves to live in.[63] But there is an even more distant and confusing possibility: maybe the experts who have made our virtual world are of an entirely other order, from an age unimaginably distant from our own. The denizens of that far future world, for whom this era, in the Big Bang's afterglow, is a very distant moment, may attempt a reconstruction, or several reconstructions, or complete inventions.[64]

And if they do, how would we tell whether *this* is the reconstruction, or the "original version" (if there ever was one)? The problem has a further aspect. On the alarmingly plausible argument initiated by Brandon Carter, it is far more likely that we are *not* after all surprisingly early humans, but members of the

---

nineteenth century could sit at his breakfast-table, decide between tea from Ceylon or coffee from Brazil, devour an egg from France with some Danish ham, or eat a New Zealand chop, wind up breakfast with a West Indian banana, glance at the latest telegrams from all the world, scrutinise the prices current of his geographically distributed investments in South Africa, Japan, and Egypt, and tell the two children he had begotten (in place of his father's eight) that he thought the world changed very little. They must play cricket, keep their hair cut, go to the old school he had gone to, shirk the lessons he had shirked, learn scraps of Horace and Virgil and Homer for the confusion of cads, and all would be well with them." See further my "Eradicating the Obvious."

62 *Ennead* V.5 [32].11, 19–23.
63 Bostrom, "Are You Living in a Computer Simulation?"
64 See Tipler, *Physics of Immortality*.

largest—and probably almost the last—generation of humankind.⁶⁵ If there ever is a Final Population at "the end of time" we are enormously more likely to be in it, than in any of the tiny populations of the early days. And if that Final Population ever exists, it will have access to all the power and information it needs to generate indefinitely many reconstructed Early Day Adventures. It may even have had access to the many alternate worlds spawned from the quantum singularity we might as well call Atum. So on both counts this—the world that we now seem to ourselves to live in—is by far more likely to be a reconstructed version than the supposed original, and we have every hope of "waking up" one day to realize our continued presence in the unimaginable end-days, or the more hospitable Other Cosmos.

> Once I, Chuang Tzu, dreamed I was a butterfly and was happy as a butterfly. I was conscious that I was quite pleased with myself, but I did not know that I was Tzu. Suddenly I awoke, and there was I, visibly Tzu. I do not know whether it was Tzu dreaming that he was a butterfly or the butterfly dreaming that he was Tzu.⁶⁶

We may also suspect that the Real World is not, after all, much like our "virtual" world, nor even one that can be imagined as the fulfilment of obvious trends here-now. Perhaps in the end-days our waking selves are something a lot more like a butterfly than like a hominin. Perhaps some of our peers in the end-days are playing here as butterflies. And maybe what they are playing in, this world, is not even a reconstruction, but a pure fantasy, with sufficient clues internally to allow us the half-joking understanding that the real world is something else than this. "We... have dreamt the world. We have dreamt it as firm, mysterious, visible, ubiquitous in space and durable in time; but in its architecture we have allowed tenuous and eternal crevices of unreason which tell us it is false."⁶⁷

And perhaps we could "wake up" to grasp what cannot now be "seen."

---

65 See Leslie, *End of the World*, for a sympathetic summary of the many possible ways for the world to end.
66 *Book of Chuang Tzu*, 20.
67 Borges, "Avatars of the Tortoise."

> Those who choose to remain ignorant of what is immortal see only that which is mortal. Their own bodies are subject to death and decay, like all composites made from the elements of dark nature; and the five senses with which they are endowed can perceive nothing but other composite bodies, all mortal too. If this is your entire reality, so the message goes, it means that you are wandering in darkness—you are literally living your life "in death" because everything you hold to be real is only finite and mortal.[68]

Waking Up is indeed an important metaphor if we are ever to understand the life of faith.[69] Respectable philosophers in the past have agreed that this life, this world, is a dream and a delirium from which we should gladly wake.[70] So also Philo: "The dreamer finds on rising up that all the movements and exertions of the foolish man are dreams void of reality. Yea Mind itself turned out to be a dream."[71] This world here-now is not the Real World. So Chesterton was perhaps not quite correct: it is not after all a *sure* mark of sanity to think we are awake already. He may still have been right to suggest that we should take the dream seriously. "Whether it's reality or a dream, doing what's right is what matters. If it's reality, then for the sake of reality; if it's a dream, then for the purpose of winning friends for when we awaken."[72] And perhaps it is easier to "do what's right" if we remember that material gains are fairy gold, that vanish on our waking. Better to lay up treasures for ourselves "in Heaven," in the real waking world, if we can do it[73]—though the Selves that really exist "there" are not what we now conceive ourselves to be. It is at least bad manners to neglect the seeming duties of this seeming world: after all, the story is that we have *chosen* to embark on it, with others.

---

68 Hanegraaff, *Hermetic Spirituality*, 178, expounding *Poimandres* (Copenhaver, *Hermetica*, 1–7 [CH.I]).
69 I began examining it in "Waking-up: A Neglected Model for the After-life," and have addressed the issue periodically since then. See especially *Understanding Faith*, 158–71.
70 Marcus Aurelius, *Meditations* 2.17.1.
71 Philo, *Allegorical Interpretations*, 3.81, in *Collected Works*, 1:487.
72 Calderón de la Barca, *Life's a Dream*, 137 (Sigismund speaks).
73 Matthew 6.19–21.

~10~
Talking of the End

Freyr shall contend with Surtr, and a hard encounter shall there be between them before Freyr falls: it is to be his death that he lacks that good sword of his, which he gave to Skirnir. Then shall the dog Garmr be loosed, which is bound before Gnipa's Cave: he is the greatest monster; he shall do battle with Tyr, and each become the other's slayer. Thor shall put to death the Midgard Serpent, and shall stride away nine paces from that spot; then shall he fall dead to the earth, because of the venom which the snake has blown at him. The Wolf shall swallow Odin; that shall be his ending. But straight thereafter shall Vidarr stride forth and set one foot upon the lower jaw of the Wolf: on that foot he has the shoe, materials for which have been gathering throughout all time. With one hand he shall seize the Wolf's upper jaw and tear his gullet asunder; and that is the death of the Wolf. Loki shall have battle with Heimdallr, and each be the slayer of the other. Then straightway shall Surtr cast fire over the earth and burn all the world.[1]

MIGHT THE MONSTERS WIN?

Lovecraft and Tolkien both, as well as other writers of their day, made it their business to remind us that the world is wider than we had imagined, and that we do not own it. It is not "our Shire": others dwelt here before us, and will again when hobbits—or *Homo sapiens*—are no more. The world does not acknowledge the borders that we draw, nor do the heavens mourn the death of princes. This is not simply an atheistical insight: on the contrary, it is one born in *theological* enquiry. Precisely because we do not, and cannot, know God's purposes, we must not project our own on what is "really there." It is easy still to suppose that

---

[1] Sturluson, *Prose Edda*, 79–80 ("Beguiling of Gylfi," 81).

though the outer world has its own rules and rulers we may at least be masters of our own souls: surely we must at least know our own purposes! Unfortunately, as many of our oldest stories show, this isn't true.

There is perhaps another and more worrying theme to consider yet again. Fairyland is full of monsters—and so may be the wider world outside. "When we cross the line to the boundless and hideous unknown—the shadow-haunted Outside," as Lovecraft said, "we must remember to leave our humanity—and terrestrialism—at the threshold."[2] Have we any good reason to suppose that the Real World is humane? Our ancestors were not convinced that it was so: witness the Mesopotamian gods who made us to be servants, and chose to destroy us when we were making too much noise. Witness also the likely end of the better sort of god in Norse mythology.

> Make it your hope
> To be counted worthy on that day to stand beside them;
> For the end of man is to partake of their defeat and die
> His second, final death in good company. The stupid, strong,
> Unteachable monsters are certain to be victorious at last,
> And every man of decent blood is on the losing side....
> Know your betters and crouch, dogs;
> You that have Vichy water in your veins and worship the event
> Your goddess History (whom your fathers called the strumpet Fortune).[3]

In his *Letters to Malcolm*, Lewis wrote:

> You know my history. You know why my withers are quite unwrung by the fear that I was bribed—that I was lured into Christianity by the hope of everlasting life. I believed in God before I believed in Heaven. And even now, even

---

2 Letter to Farnsworth Wright, July 5, 1927, borrowed from www.hplovecraft.com/writings/quotes.aspx (accessed December 15, 2022).
3 Lewis, "Cliché Come Out of Its Cage," in *Poems*, 3-4; see also Tolkien, *Monsters and the Critics*, 25-26: "It is the strength of the northern mythological imagination that it faced this problem, put the monsters in the centre, gave them victory but no honour, and found a potent but terrible solution in naked will and courage."

Talking of the End

if—let's make an impossible supposition—His voice, unmistakably His, said to me, "They have misled you. I can do nothing of that sort for you. My long struggle with the blind forces is nearly over. I die, children. The story is ending"—would that be a moment for changing sides? Would not you and I take the Viking way: "The Giants and Trolls win. Let us die on the right side, with Father Odin"?[4]

It is common now to claim that our opponents are "on the wrong side of history," as though it were obvious that "history" is on *our* side, and that as time passes we shall make fewer mistakes. "The arc of the universe is long, but it bends toward justice."[5] It does not follow that all new things are just, even if we can persuade ourselves that "justice" will in the end prevail, and that all error and injustice will in the end be past. But why should we think it obvious that history is, in this sense, "progressive," let alone that any self-styled "progressive person" is correct? Why should we so easily expect that "evolution" always improves the breed, merely because some heritable traits are somewhat more successful, in some particular circumstances, than their available rivals? It seems clear that this is a fantasy, even if it is an encouraging and fairly helpful one. Natural Selection does not select "the best," and evolution is not essentially "progressive." Better (perhaps) ignore this, and believe that life will certainly improve for all than that we shall die unmourned and obsolete. "There shall be no want, no oppression, no fear of man, no fear of God, but only love. 'There is a good time coming,' so we all believe when we are young and full of life and healthy hope."[6]

---

4 Lewis, "Letter 22," in *Letters to Malcolm*, 99. See also Lewis, *That Hideous Strength*, 418: "If the universe was a cheat, was that a good reason for joining its side? Supposing the Straight was utterly powerless, always and everywhere certain to be mocked, tortured, and finally killed by the Crooked, what then? Why not go down with the ship?"
5 A remark made famous by Martin Luther King in 1958, which seems to have originated in a sermon by Theodore Parker in 1853: see https://quoteinvestigator.com/2012/11/15/arc-of-universe/, citing Parker, *Ten Sermons*, 84–85, who went on to say "Jefferson trembled [*Notes on the State of Virginia* (1788), query 18: p. 173] when he thought of slavery and remembered that God is just. Ere long all America will tremble."
6 Parker, *Ten Sermons*, 84.

But perhaps we are mistaken.

> Vanity of vanities, says the Preacher, vanity of vanities! All is vanity. What does man gain by all the toil at which he toils under the sun? A generation goes, and a generation comes, but the earth remains forever. The sun rises, and the sun goes down, and hastens to the place where it rises. The wind blows to the south and goes around to the north; around and around goes the wind, and on its circuits the wind returns. All streams run to the sea, but the sea is not full; to the place where the streams flow, there they flow again. All things are full of weariness; a man cannot utter it; the eye is not satisfied with seeing, nor the ear filled with hearing. What has been is what will be, and what has been done is what will be done, and there is nothing new under the sun. Is there a thing of which it is said, "See, this is new"? It has been already in the ages before us. There is no remembrance of former things, nor will there be any remembrance of later things yet to be among those who come after.[7]

Utopian fictions falter when the author seeks to imagine how we would likely live in seemingly prosperous and well-ordered ages, or how we would evade whatever external event might easily disrupt our contentment: plague, volcanic eruption, nearby supernova, alien invasion, or some strange decay of space and time themselves. Some authors put their trust in superheroes, equipped by magic or mathematics to defeat all ogres. Others, perhaps more credibly and certainly more humanely, propose that we shall prevail by ordinary, domestic, virtues, combined with cheerful resistance to all would-be tyrants (and a lot of cunning). The Human—on either image—will prevail (some say). But how shall these things be? Parker was explicitly and vehemently theistic:

> [God's] justice, our morality working with that, shall one day create a unity amongst all men more fair than the face of nature, and add a wondrous beauty, wondrous happiness, to this great family of men. Will you fear lest a wrong should prove immortal? So far as anything is false, or wrong, it is weak; so far as true and right,

---

[7] Ecclesiastes 1.2-11.

is omnipotently strong. Never fear that a just thought shall fail to be a thing; the power of God, the wisdom of God, and the justice of God are on its side, and it cannot fail,—no more than God himself can perish. Wrong is the accident of human development. Right is of the substance of humanity, justice the goal we are to reach.[8]

In the perceived absence of such a God, the humanistic faith seems weak. We may partly believe that human beings are often, or even essentially, both kind and clever, but it is also sadly clear that they are also often cowardly and cruel—and that the powers, whatever they may be, that seem to rule the world care even less for mortal creatures than we do ourselves. "To Mercy, Pity, Peace and Love all pray in their distress,... for Mercy has a human heart, Pity a human face, and Love, the human form divine, and Peace, the human dress,"[9] but it is uncomfortably also obvious that "Cruelty has a Human Heart, and Jealousy a Human Face."[10] "The shadow-haunted Outside" is as likely to be full of monsters as our own past and present.

What lies behind and before the cosmos for Lovecraft is much more like the darkness "that the gods hate" (in Plotinus's words):[11] "that nuclear chaos beyond angled space which the Necronomicon had mercifully cloaked under the name of Azathoth,"[12] who deserves no worship.

> Out in the mindless void the daemon bore me,
> Past the bright clusters of dimensioned space,
> Till neither time nor matter stretched before me,
> But only Chaos, without form or place.
> Here the vast Lord of All in darkness muttered
> Things he had dreamed but could not understand,
> While near him shapeless bat-things flopped and fluttered
> In idiot vortices that ray-streams fanned.

---

8 Parker, Ten Sermons, 99–100.
9 Blake, "The Divine Image" [1789], in Complete Writings, 117.
10 Blake, "A Divine Image" [1794], in Complete Writings, 221.
11 Plotinus, Ennead V.1 [10].2, 24–27.
12 "The Whisperer in Darkness" [1930], in Call of Cthulhu, 200–67. Whether Lovecraft had come across the Hermetic "zōzazōth," the culmination of a magical sequence of vowels invoking deities, I do not know: see Nag Hammadi Codex VI.56, 10–22 ("The Ogdoad Reveals the Ennead"). If so, he gave it an entirely un-Hermetic meaning.

They danced insanely to the high, thin whining
Of a cracked flute clutched in a monstrous paw,
Whence flow the aimless waves whose chance combining
Gives each frail cosmos its eternal law.
"I am His Messenger," the daemon said,
As in contempt he struck his Master's head.[13]

"If there is a meaning," so Stapledon's Last Men say in their final hours, "it is no human meaning,"[14] and so might as well be no real meaning. As Robert Anton Wilson remarks:

> Lovecraft and Stapledon succeeded more thoroughly than anyone else in creating truly "inhuman" perspectives, artistically sustained and emotionally convincing. That HPL makes the "inhuman" or the "cosmic" a frightening and depressing thing to encounter, while Stapledon makes it a source of mystic awe and artfully combined tragedy-and-triumph, registers merely that they had different temperaments.[15]

Stapledon and Lovecraft agreed that it is part of our duty as ordinarily human beings to acknowledge that there is more to the worlds than us, and somehow to find, despite the world's indifference, a way of living humanely. Our friends, our family, our native soil, our histories don't matter to the wider world or its more powerful residents: they may still matter to us, and those who allow themselves to be infected by indifference, indiscipline, cruelty, and cultish stupidity are still to be resisted when we can—or even if, in the end, we can't.

But the story does have its comic aspects. Witness Bertrand Russell's grandiloquence:

> Blind to good and evil, reckless of destruction, omnipotent matter rolls on its relentless way; for Man, condemned to-day to lose his dearest, to-morrow himself to pass through the gate of darkness, it remains only to cherish, ere yet the blow falls, the lofty thoughts that ennoble his little day; disdaining the coward terrors of

---

13 *Fungi from Yuggoth*, no. 22: "Azathoth."
14 Stapledon, *Last and First Men*, 605.
15 Wilson, "My Debt to H. P. Lovecraft": http://rawilsonfans.org/my-debt-to-h-p-lovecraft/, accessed January 6, 2023.

the slave of Fate, to worship at the shrine that his own hands have built; undismayed by the empire of chance, to preserve a mind free from the wanton tyranny that rules his outward life; proudly defiant of the irresistible forces that tolerate, for a moment, his knowledge and his condemnation, to sustain alone, a weary but unyielding Atlas, the world that his own ideals have fashioned despite the trampling march of unconscious power.[16]

To which Logan Pearsall Smith's retort ("By Jove, that is a stunt!") is probably the best immediate response,[17] and John Wren-Lewis's is not far behind:

> Real science knows nothing of Omnipotent Matter, for it is a continual process of changing both our concepts and our experience of matter. The only constant factor in real science—the science of the experimental method—is Potent Man, man who constantly strives to use matter to express the creativity of his own inner life. Omnipotent Matter is as much a paranoid fantasy as the traditional concept of Omnipotent God, and serves the same neurotic purpose of providing grounds for not taking the inner life of human beings really seriously in its own right. Where traditional religion insists upon the subordination of man's inner life to the supposed Divine Plan behind the scenes, materialism overrides the inner life by dismissing it in the name of a "tough-minded" assertion of man's utter insignificance in face of the inflexible laws of an indifferent universe.[18]

But maybe Wren-Lewis had less reason for his confidence than he supposed.

MALICE OR INDIFFERENCE?

It is probably already clear that I am turning a little away from the ancient stories. Modern writers, especially of Science Fiction and fantasy, are trying to live up to Chesterton's appeal, for imaginative use of our latest information. Some have managed to create whole worlds for others to elaborate or at least enjoy.

---

16 Russell, "The Free Man's Worship" (1903), in *Mysticism and Logic*, 46–57.
17 Smith, *All Trivia*, 81. Smith was Russell's brother-in-law at the time.
18 Wren-Lewis, *What Shall We Tell the Children?*, 70.

Amongst many others worth attention, I shall make principal use of Stapledon, Lovecraft, Tolkien.

Stapledon managed, throughout his life, to believe in the value of sane intelligence, even if it was always under threat from both internal and external evils. The final vindication of such intelligence, however, could only be metaphysical: maybe there was indeed a Star Maker existing beyond our time and space, in whom all good things would be (were) eternal, and all disappointments remedied.

> At length... the Star Maker created his ultimate and most subtle cosmos, for which all others were but tentative preparations. Of this final creature I can say only that it embraced within its own organic texture the essences of all its predecessors; and far more besides. It was like the last movement of a symphony, which may embrace, by the significance of its themes, the essence of the earlier movements; and far more besides.[19]

But even then, so he imagined, there would be (there were) intolerable costs: "as I strove to hear more inwardly into that music of concrete spirits in countless worlds, I caught echoes not merely of joys unspeakable, but of griefs inconsolable."

> Yet obscurely I saw that the ultimate cosmos was nevertheless lovely, and perfectly formed; and that every frustration and agony within it, however cruel to the sufferer, issued finally, without any miscarriage, in the enhanced lucidity of the cosmical spirit itself. In this sense at least no individual tragedy was vain. But this was nothing. And now, as through tears of compassion and hot protest, I seemed to see the spirit of the ultimate and perfected cosmos face her maker. In her, it seemed, compassion and indignation were subdued by praise. And the Star Maker, that dark power and lucid intelligence, found in the concrete loveliness of his creature the fulfilment of desire. And in the mutual joy of the Star Maker and the ultimate cosmos was conceived, most strangely, the absolute spirit itself, in which all times are present and all being is comprised; for the spirit which was the

---

19 Stapledon, *Star Maker*, 321–25.

issue of this union confronted my reeling intelligence as being at once the ground and the issue of all temporal and finite things.[20]

This was not something that Stapledon's narrator could comfortably endure, despite his efforts to believe that he should:

> It was with anguish and horror, and yet with acquiescence, even with praise, that I felt or seemed to feel something of the eternal spirit's temper as it apprehended in one intuitive and timeless vision all our lives. Here was no pity, no proffer of salvation, no kindly aid. Or here were all pity and all love, but mastered by a frosty ecstasy. Our broken lives, our loves, our follies, our betrayals, our forlorn and gallant defences, were one and all calmly anatomized, assessed, and placed. True, they were one and all lived through with complete understanding, with insight and full sympathy, even with passion. But sympathy was not ultimate in the temper of the eternal spirit; contemplation was. Love was not absolute; contemplation was. And though there was love, there was also hate comprised within the spirit's temper, for there was cruel delight in the contemplation of every horror, and glee in the downfall of the virtuous. All passions, it seemed, were comprised within the spirit's temper; but mastered, icily gripped within the cold, clear, crystal ecstasy of contemplation.

Our ancestors would perhaps have found it easier to acknowledge that the powers which rule the world were unlikely to be humane. It was, perhaps, possible to respect or even to worship beings that to us seem devils, just as we admire tigers and tyrannosaurs. Later in life, Stapledon himself found it yet harder to

---

20 Stapledon *Star Maker*, 325. Cf. Tolkien, *Silmarillion*, 5: "Then Ilúvatar spoke, and he said: 'Mighty are the Ainur, and mightiest among them is Melkor, but that he may know, and all the Ainur, that I am Ilúvatar, those things that ye have sung, I will show them forth, that ye may see what ye have done. And thou, Melkor, shalt see that no theme may be played that hath not its uttermost source in me, nor can any alter the music in my despite. For he that attempteth this shall prove but mine instrument in the devising of things more wonderful, which he himself hath not imagined.'" Melkor had attempted to "interweave matters of his own imagining that were not in accord with the theme of Ilúvatar; for he sought therein to increase the power and glory of the part assigned to himself." As Plotinus agreed, the cause of the fall, our fall, is *tolma*.

endorse that sort of joy: "Were the masters of Buchenwald my ministers?," asks Stapledon's imagined Creator God with heavy irony in Stapledon's last work.[21]

Apparently, they might be—but it does not directly follow that these "gods" or godlike attitudes are to be copied by us. The proper moral may always be that we *aren't* gods, and that trying to behave "like gods (or devils)" of this sort is to infringe their prerogatives. We may need to acknowledge their power, and our own ultimate weakness. We may even have to abandon the Norse delusion that we might somehow fight on the side of the more lovable sort of god: such wars will only end in ruin, even if we could safely identify which gods are really more lovable. "Nothing" will one day swallow up the world: that is, the world and all its purposes will in the end be nothing.

What the ancient stories intended in their predictions of final and absolute catastrophe we cannot now be certain. Some story tellers hoped, as some modern cosmologists still hope, that the worlds will begin again, and that our immediate, transient world is only one of infinitely many, some of which may be better (and some worse). Others expected only "that calm Sunday that goes on and on/ when even lovers find their peace at last, /and Earth is but a star, that once had shone."[22] In the absence of final proof we carry on imagining. The spread of humankind across the sidereal universe has often been an SF dream, to culminate in a world where, after all, there is nothing that is not symbolical, nothing that is truly alien. Nature may be neutral *now*, but will not be forever. The stars themselves—the fantasy suggests—will one day serve our species or its descendant kinds, and be as familiar as contemporary traffic lights. It will then be literally true that the lights in the firmament of heaven exist "for signs, and for seasons, and for days and years."[23] Looking outward at the heavens we shall see, as our medieval predecessors thought they saw, the animated stars look back at us, with whatever twist of mischief or compassion. Nowhere will there be anything wholly *other*, wholly alien. Alternatively, if it chances that the wider world

---

21 Stapledon, *Opening of the Eyes*, 8.
22 James Elroy Flecker, "The Golden Journey to Samarkand" (1913).
23 Genesis 1.14.

is already populous, maybe we shall be able to join in that larger conversation. One day we shall realize, perhaps, that the signs we see of "natural events" (exploding stars, colliding galaxies) are vast engineering projects—or appalling acts of war.[24] What that imagined conversation might be like will also vary. Some writers conceive it to be merely human and probably rather boring after all, even though it is conducted between creatures of an entirely different ancestry and nature.

But a few writers, even in the act of describing the conversation between those angels in the skies, begin to suspect that their ways are not ours. Perhaps they are mechanical intelligences, forever hostile to the prolific and irrational life of animals like us. Perhaps they are star-spanning hives, with just as much intelligence as they need to seek out and incorporate their prey, and without any merely *human* interest in close companionship, or art, or religion, or even science. Perhaps we shall discover that both human religiosity and human curiosity are only byproducts of our biology (most usually, of our long childhoods and our deference to alpha males and females), one that other rational intelligences do not begin to comprehend. Perhaps indeed those intelligences are indistinguishable in what they do from merely physical happenings: if the stars are ruled by utterly alien Powers it is as much as to say that they are not *ruled* at all: and the only wills in question are our own. When Stapledon's peace-loving and peace-making Tibetan mystics (in one of the alternate futures envisaged in his *Darkness and the Light*) finally discover the "truth" it is as if they woke to a frozen landscape trampled by indifferent giants. Whether those giants are deaf because they are witless or because they are callous hardly matters; even their ill-will—if they are malevolent—is immune to prayer, and so as natural and fixed a fact as any.

As the Cambridge Platonist Ralph Cudworth remarked in a sermon before the House of Commons in 1647: "Surely this will make us either secretly to think, that there is no God at all in the World, if he must needs be such, or else to wish heartily, there were none."[25]

---

24 Ćirković, *Astrobiological Landscape*, 214, after Lem, "The New Cosmology."
25 Patrides, *Cambridge Platonists*, 107.

In brief, Science Fiction seems well suited to the needs and fantasies of an irreligious age, easily persuaded that there are no *transcendent* purposes, and that the only meanings that we could comprehend will be the ones created by our own descendants or by creatures enough like us to share our lives. In their absence the merely *natural* world is empty of significance, even if it is at last controlled by some single alien purpose that can never be our own. And in World's End all purposes are made null.

That vision is used in Blish's *Black Easter*—and it is there, explicitly, a weapon in the hands of a black magician, who instructs a demon as follows:

> Thou shalt straightaway go unto him, not making thyself known unto him, but revealing, as it were to come from his own intellectual soul, a vision and understanding of that great and ultimate Nothingness, which lurks behind those signs he calls matter and energy, as thou wilt see it in his private forebodings, and that thou remainest with him and deepen his despair without remittal, until such time as he shall despise his soul for its endeavors, and destroy the life of his body.[26]

That black magician, in Blish's fable, is willing to sell his soul for "knowledge"—and loses, in the story's end, the knowledge he has accumulated, and also his own soul. All purposes in the end prove empty. It is perhaps in order to avoid this deep depression—which older thinkers called "accidie"—that some of us prefer to stifle thought, by giving allegiance to whatever exciting cult may come our way.[27] Excitement at least enthuses us a while!

APOCALYPSE AND THE END OF DAYS

Most Science Fiction is founded on a naturalistic hypothesis: that is, whatever happens and whatever exists is assumed to be part of a single "closed" system—and this is not very different

---

26 Blish, *Black Easter*, 87.
27 Sayers, *Unpopular Opinions*, 11: "In the list of the Seven Deadly Sins which the Church officially recognises there is the sin which is sometimes called Sloth, and sometimes Accidie. The one name is obscure to us; the other is a little misleading. It does not mean lack of hustle: it means the slow sapping of all the faculties by indifference, and by the sensation that life is pointless and meaningless, and not-worth-while."

from "the original Bronze Age Myth" that I described before! Intrusions "from outside" are impossible, since there can never be a true "outside," as the hardheaded captain of Heinlein's generation ship insists, in the face of evidence that there is a world outside that ship.[28] If there is another world, another life beyond the life we know, this can only be a separate region of the manifold, and its inhabitants as subject to the "laws of nature" as ourselves. Those imagined "laws," strictly speaking, are only descriptive, and not constructive (as Wittgenstein remarked),[29] but they do perhaps depend on more powerful intuitions: that nothing comes out of Nothing, and that all real truths are universal truths. If such-and-such happens here-now, then it also happens everywhere (even if we have to redescribe what happens here to secure the universal story). And energy can neither be created nor destroyed: the sums always add up.

It is a plausible story, but it is, in the end, just a story, which cannot be finally *proved*. Maybe there is, after all, a truly Other world whose energies (being infinite) are never depleted, and which can intrude on all our ordered lives. Science, as the study of what generally happens here-and-now, or what can be expected to happen in a consistently ordered cosmos, can neither expect nor wholly disbelieve stories about such intrusions.

> Science is the study of the admitted laws of existence; it cannot prove a universal negative about whether those laws could ever be suspended by something admittedly above them. It is as if we were to say that a lawyer was so deeply learned in the American Constitution that he knew there could never be a revolution in America. Or it is as if a man were to say he was so close a student of the text of *Hamlet* that he was authorised to deny that an actor had dropped the skull and bolted when the theatre caught fire. The constitution follows a certain course, so long as it is there to follow it; the play follows a certain course, so long as it is being played; the visible order of nature follows a certain course if there is nothing

---

28 Heinlein, "Common Sense" (1941), in *Orphans of the Sky*, 189: "The most obvious fact of nature is the reality of the Ship itself, solid, immutable, complete. Any so-called fact which appears to disprove that is bound to be an illusion."
29 Wittgenstein, *Tractatus*, 85 (6.371).

behind it to stop it. But that fact throws no sort of light on whether there is anything behind it to stop it. That is a question of philosophy or metaphysics and not of material science.[30]

For traditional theists, nature is an *open* system, and God's miraculous intrusions can't be ordered or evaded. Nor is that God merely another element within a wider system: She/He/It and They is rather the Place of all.

Even Plotinus, who was firmly convinced that there could be no better image of the Divine than this world here, with all its seeming inconveniences, suspected that there were after all better things yet unseen.

> The god therefore who is bound [that is, Kronos] so that he abides the same, and has conceded the government of this universe to his son [that is, Zeus] — for it would not have been in character for him to abandon his rule in the intelligible world and go seeking a later one because he had had enough of the beauties there — lets this world go and establishes his father [Ouranos] in himself, extending as far as him on the upper side; and on the other side he has established what begins with his son in the place after himself, so that he comes to be between the two, by the otherness of his severance from what is above, and by the bond which keeps him from what comes after him on the lower side; he is between a better father and a worse son.[31]

And on the other hand, Zeus (that is, Soul) is only the one of Kronos's children who lives outside his Father (*Nous*, or Spirit), for a good purpose (so that there should be "a beautiful image of beauty and reality") but is still bound to be surpassed by those offspring that have stayed "within," the worlds that have not (yet) had temporal or phenomenal reflections.[32]

---

30 Chesterton, *The Thing*, 137.
31 *Ennead* V.8 [31].13, 1–11.
32 *Ennead* V.8 [31].12–13. See also Copenhaver, *Hermetica*, 20 (5.9): "He is himself the things that are and those that are not. Those that are he has made visible; those that are not he holds within him.... There is nothing that he is not, for he also is all that is, and this is why he has all names, because they are of one father, and this is why he has no name, because he is father of them all."

Talking of the End

The walls of the world may yet be broken down. On the Christian account, especially, they already have been, though it may take centuries for the news to spread, and the effects of past apostasy to be reversed. Babylon's walls are breached.³³ Nor is it only a *Christian* hope.

> Ye are wise men and know the mighty gods
> are called immortal, over us: their lives
> Sufficient are to them; in youth or eld
> As first they broke to being, so they are.
> They drive man's generations as a wind
> Tosses in wave on wave to shoreward: time
> Dwells not amid their might, for centuries
> Pass at their feasts in one cup-lifting. Yet
> There is a darkness beyond all the gods,
> Where once in many ages that which Is
> In Its eternal sleep whose dreams we are
> Heaves suddenly and shudders half-awake.
> Then, as an earthquake rends the seas and shores
> Making all strange, so the All-being moves,
> And all the visible and invisible worlds
> In that sole motion ruin and are re-born
> Into fresh lands, new nations, other gods.³⁴

So what might that new world, "what rough beast, slouching toward Bethlehem to be born,"³⁵ be like? What will happen when Brahma stirs from sleep? Is the object only to restart the game? After the worst has happened, so the Norse supposed, a new world will appear, and maybe begin in peace.

> In that time the earth shall emerge out of the sea, and shall then be green and fair; then shall the fruits of it be brought forth unsown. Vidarr and Vali shall be living, inasmuch as neither sea nor the fire of Surtr shall have

---

33 Cf. Herodotus, *Histories* 1.191: "Owing to the vast size of the place, the inhabitants of the central parts (as the residents at Babylon declare) long after the outer portions of the town were taken, knew nothing of what had chanced, but as they were engaged in a festival, continued dancing and revelling until they learnt the capture but too certainly."
34 Williams, *Chapel of the Thorn*, 103–4. Williams here imagines a pagan priest's response to changing times; his immediate source is more likely Hindu than Celtic or Hermetic.
35 After Yeats, "Second Coming" [1921], in *Collected Poems*, 158.

harmed them; and they shall dwell at Ida-Plain, where Asgard was before. And then the sons of Thor, Modi and Magni, shall come there, and they shall have Mjolnir there. After that Baldr shall come thither, and Hodr, from Hel; then all shall sit down together and hold speech with one another, and call to mind their secret wisdom, and speak of those happenings which have been before: of the Midgard Serpent and of Fenris-Wolf. Then they shall find in the grass those golden chess-pieces which the Aesir had.[36]

Will that truly be a new world, or only the old repeated? And shall we be remembered in it?

One hope or fancy is that our descendants or successors will think our time was special enough to remember (as above): the century in which artificial or virtual realities wholly displaced "natural" reality as the context of human life, or that in which genetic engineering began to be applied even to the human genome, and we budded into multiple varieties that signalled the end. Or else the century of the Sixth Extinction. Maybe the changes that are coming upon us will indeed mark a radical alteration in the way humankind experiences itself. Maybe, though much less plausibly, they will mark an alteration in solar history, or Galactic. It may instead turn out that our successors feel no special interest in these days, but rather—as we do ourselves—will run the generations and the centuries together, more or less equating the discovery of fire and the development of nuclear power, the migration out of Africa and the solar Diaspora. Imagining that our particular history will be remembered, except as remotest, vaguest legends, is most probably conceit. As the spirit of his ancestor warned Scipio Africanus:

> How long do you think they will remember us or even desire to remember us? Let us even grant that future generations will desire to remember us. Think about the deluges and conflagrations which descend on the earth at set intervals. These disasters make it impossible for our glory to last for any length of time, let alone for eternity.[37]

---

36 Snorri, *Prose Edda*, 83 ("Beguiling of Gylfi," ch. 52).
37 "Dream of Scipio," Cicero, *De Re Publica* Bk. 6. See also Boethius, *Consolation* 2.7 (*Tractates*, 219): "if you really consider the infinite space of eternity, have you any reason to rejoice in the long life of your own name? For, one moment

Talking of the End

The very fact that we can disown our past, of course, makes it more likely that our successors will do just the same — and disown us! "Empires break; industrial conditions change; the suburbs will not last forever."[38] And why, after all, should we imagine that we can always *see* the seeds that will one day blossom? There have been very many *plausible* futures: the Caliphate, for example, just a few centuries ago could confidently have expected soon to conquer, when it could be bothered, the last few grubby barbarians of Northern Europe. Nor did those barbarians necessarily think otherwise. Chesterton again:

> What was the meaning of all that whisper of fear that ran round the West under the shadow of Islam, and fills every old romance with incongruous images of Saracen knights swaggering in Norway or the Hebrides?... The answer is that hundreds of people probably believed in their hearts that Islam would conquer Christendom; that Averroes was more rational than Anselm; that the Saracen culture was really, as it was superficially, a superior culture.[39]

Things might always have gone quite differently, both from the way they did, and from the way that was expected. One of William Gibson's minor stories has his narrator periodically plunged into the world imagined by pulp-writers of the 1930s: "it had all the sinister fruitiness of Hitler Youth propaganda."[40] We can be glad that most of our *actual* futures grew from seeds and characters that had no special prophetic aura. Looking backward we imagine that our present was always bound to come, but we can be fairly sure, in reason, that it wasn't. So also our own future: why should we expect to know its origin? And if we don't, then — paradoxically — it will be the least plausible, least obvious, futures that are far more likely! As the Euripidean tag

---

compared with ten thousand years, since each is a determinate length of time, is a certain proportion, even if a very small fraction; but even that length of years, or any multiple of it, cannot be compared at all with the infinite length of time."
38 Chesterton, *Ball and the Cross*, 99.
39 Chesterton, *Everlasting Man*, 294. King John of England is said to have offered, in 1212, to convert himself and all his people, to become the Caliph al-Nāṣir's vassal: see Shoval, *King John's Delegation to the Almohad Court*.
40 Gibson, "Gernsback Continuum."

has it: "the things that men expect to happen do not happen. The unexpected, God makes possible." Even those fantasists that make most effort to imagine an unlikely future, of course, are usually trapped by their own assumptions and psychology. "I can make the future as narrow as myself," so Chesterton observed: "the past is obliged to be as broad and turbulent as humanity."[41]

It is one thing to extrapolate a future, whether from commonly acknowledged trends in the present or from hidden possibilities—hidden, that is, from everyone but the author. It is another to conceive some radical incursion: volcanic eruption, meteor strike, alien invasion, nearby supernova, or the collapse of the "false vacuum." Whatever narrative we thought we were constructing, in this latter case, will be suddenly subverted. The new world will owe nothing—except perhaps some proverbs—to the old, since the records will have been wiped away—as of course they have often been in human and prehuman history.

> As were the days of Noah, so will be the coming of the Son of man. For as in those days before the flood they were eating and drinking, marrying and giving in marriage, until the day when Noah entered the ark, and they did not know until the flood came and swept them all away, so will be the coming of the Son of man.[42]

Dramatic unity, and laziness, and our own self-importance may lead us to prefer such futures as can be represented as extrapolations (even if those futures are very bleak). But it may well be just as likely, or yet more likely, that the future continues to be discontinuous. There may be a really virulent pandemic, or a radically new religion, or a strange new species. On the still larger scale, we may wonder if the Doom is heading towards us now—the nearby supernova has *already* happened, and the arrival of the attendant shockwave, wiping our world clean, would be predictable to a Galactic Survey Team, but not to us. Alternatively, the event is a quantum fluctuation in the vacuum, unpredictable on *any* theory, cancelling all futures, happy or unhappy. Or else the discontinuity is a completely human one: paradoxically a predictable effect of

---

41 Chesterton, *What's Wrong with the World*, 27.
42 Matthew 24.37-9.

the steady increase in computing power, and our understanding of both physical and biological reality, the Singularity. There will soon be entities as much cleverer than us—whatever quite that means—as we are than the earliest eukaryotes, and what they will want to do with us, who knows? The more like us they are, the less we can expect of them. Just possibly we can persuade them that the more powerful should care for the less, for the simple reason that they too can expect to be surpassed, and should treat us as they wish themselves to be treated, but our own history does not give us that much ground for hope. We seem to suspect that the Great Machines will destroy us—or else (and maybe this would be worse) will care for us in ways that we would, in our right minds, detest. What will it be like to be the subordinate species once again? Long ago in Babylonia it was supposed that the gods made human beings to do the drudgework. In northern Europe the gods merely discovered us, bred from the dead flesh of Ymir, and set us to work. In Greece, they were amused. Anyway, our purposes were not just our own, and perhaps won't be—unless the other possible world is real, the one that depends after all on something like humane being.

Maybe, if there are in the very distant future any sort of individuals to contest the world with the great machines, or the supercolonies, they will come back to examine how we cope, to get some sense of courage in uncertainty. Or perhaps the final generations, locked into merely virtual realities, will long to return to the days when there were *physical* selves, and *physical* sensations: hungry ghosts who seek to possess the living.

Or maybe the still more ancient theory is correct:

> Almost all gnostic writings start from a mythical view of reality, characterized by a sharp distinction between the invisible divine world and the earthly conditions in which we live. Various gnostic myths circulated, which are described in detail in some writings, and are casually touched upon in others.... The various myths have a common presupposition: the human inner self originates from the divine world, but has become alienated from it.[43]

---

[43] Van den Broek, *Gnostic Religion in Antiquity*, 25.

Maybe we already know, in our hearts, what that real and abiding world may be. Christians as well as Hermeticists have been very close to the Manichaean thought that this world here is in the hands of Ignorant Evil, that we are living (as it were) in territory occupied by thieves and rebels, apostates, and have not merely been given our own passports out, but a promise that there has already been an invasion, that the apostate has already been overthrown, though it may take centuries for the news to spread, and the effects of past apostasy to be reversed. Babylon's walls are breached. This is not entirely comfortable news for Babylonians like ourselves!

> Hail the day so long expected!
> Hail the year of full release!
> Zion's walls are now erected,
> And her watchmen publish peace:
> From the distant coasts of Shinar,
> The shrill trumpet loudly roars:
> Babylon is fallen! is fallen! is fallen!
> Babylon is fallen to rise no more.[44]

---

44 Richard McNamar (?), "Babylon is Fallen" [1813], after Revelation 18:2-3. See Williams, "Babylon is Fallen: Story of a North American Hymn"; for a summary, see http://bluegrassmessengers.com/babylons-falling-spiritual-version-2-stickles-.aspx.

11
New Beginnings

> And is it true? And is it true,
> This most tremendous tale of all,
> Seen in a stained-glass window's hue,
> A Baby in an ox's stall?[1]

STORIES OLD AND NEW

So to summarize: The oldest story of our beginnings is that Everything began from Nothing, and will in the end return. "Nothing" is often assigned a character, most probably a destructive one, so that Everything is at war with Chaos (originally only a Gap, but quickly conceived as Disorder). That original Nothing is given such character as it has by conceiving it as an Ocean without any distinctions, a sea (as it were) of virtual particles and undisciplined possibilities. The powers that crystalise from that unimaginable beginning manifest in the world are not our friends, and are often at odds themselves. Some may even, on the older story, be our enemies, and the gods'. A later, radical claim is that there are no *monsters* after all, no beings essentially alien to an originating Word. But either way it is possible to discern a sort of order to the world, and we may manage to live in it with some degree of comfort, always remembering that we are not "gods" ourselves. There is no original clear division between the many sorts of creature here: we're all in "this" together—except that conceit and jealousy create further divisions (including the notion that there are creatures wholly "evil").

Even if we suppose that our world is essentially "at war," we can still imagine an Otherworld, where things go otherwise, and we—maybe—will find long-lasting comfort there. Originally that Otherworld allows our many kinds to meet, but it comes to seem, to some, that *human* beings are special, both in the here-and-now

---
1 Betjeman, "Christmas," in Collected Poems, 153–54.

and in the Otherworld. That does not, at first, give any special regard to being "humane": even if (human) intelligence is somehow aligned with the order of Everything, so that we can conceive and even partly understand the whole world, rather than simply the world-as-it-is-for-creatures-of-our-kind, transcending our biological nature, it does not follow—nor do we feel it does—that the world will favour "humanity" or "the humane." The world, the All, that emerges somehow from Nothing, from the Void, has no concern for us, and its beauty—if it is really beautiful—is nothing for us to cherish, nor to be cherished by. The monsters that side, as it were, with Nothing, with Destruction, may be, probably will be, "winners," just because Nothing wins. Till then we only survive.

And yet we may also, somehow, go on living.

> I tell you naught for your comfort,
> Yea, naught for your desire,
> Save that the sky grows darker yet
> And the sea rises higher.
>
> Night shall be thrice night over you,
> And heaven an iron cope.
> Do you have joy without a cause,
> Yea, faith without a hope?[2]

Is there any escape from this world here, if something "from Outside" does not intervene, if it does not show itself to be, in the end, the Lord?

Consider the most obvious "fairytale" intrusion in orderly, secular history, as it has been described in Christian thinking. Egyptian stories, and cult-images, of Isis and her son Horus, are concerned with a time before our time, or else express timeless and abstract truths of the sort that Plutarch and others think important. Greek stories of the birth of gods, or demigods, or heroes, are simple messages, declaring those same heroes, demigods and gods a part of the Olympian system ruled by Zeus. Even the threat that some new Son of Zeus might follow Hellenic custom and overthrow his father is only a rebellion, not a real

---

2 Chesterton, "Ballad of the White Horse" [1911], in *Collected Poems*, 233. Chesterton's poem celebrates a time when there seemed indeed no rational hope of survival.

revolution: the new ruler of the heavens would still be bound by Fate, and everything would in the end lose all distinctions, whether in fire or flood. Further afield, the many avatars of Vishnu are devoted only to maintaining the proper existing order against unruly demons (and the breath of Brahman will someday be withdrawn from all).

Maintaining order and proper ranks is not an unworthy project: how else, we may reasonably ask, shall we avoid dissolution? Those who resent and vilify all "organised religion" have never fully considered what *disorganised* religion might be like: a world in which we all do exactly what we please, in the name of our own personal "truth," made "true" merely because we assert it.[3] Obviously, we shall all be better off if there are practical limits on what we each can do. And those limits can more profitably be created by shared stories than by unending violence. In ordinary civil life, we have internalized familiar figures from old stories, sculptures, paintings, dramas, and have also found some more-or-less coherent context for them all. Or better still, maybe: there is no rigid structure for the stories—each of us can emphasise one or another figure or happy fable about who we are to be. Better again: we must each learn to recognize those various figures. Once again:

> "Know Yourself" is said to those who because of their selves' multiplicity have the business of counting themselves up and learning that they do not know all the numbers and kinds of things they are, or do not know any one of them, nor what their ruling principle is, or by what they are themselves.[4]

Even (or especially) if there is no transcendent meaning to the world, nor any escape from worldly living, we will still divide our time by seasons and ceremonials, just as we also divide our space by familiar landmarks, monuments, and boundary lines. If there is no transcendent meaning we had better rely on the stories we tell about it. Tradition rules, even as it slowly changes, and we must learn neither to subvert all ceremonial, all past rules and divisions, nor yet to kill off change. "When ancient opinions and

---

3 Which is, so Plotinus and MacDonald agree, the Fall: *Ennead* V.1 [10].1; MacDonald, "Kingship," in *Unspoken Sermons*, 158.
4 *Ennead* VI 7 [38].41, 22-25.

rules of life are taken away, the loss cannot possibly be estimated. From that moment we have no compass to govern us; nor can we know distinctly to what port we steer."[5] Nor can we expect our successors to respect *our* aims, especially if we have taught them to disrespect tradition!

What can we learn from popular ceremonials? "Christmas" is now widely celebrated even by atheists, even by people from other than Abrahamic traditions. As a merely "secular" occasion it is a time for giving presents (especially to children), eating and drinking to excess, family parties (and quarrels), and singing carols with — sometimes — Christian themes: the midwinter festival of eating, drinking and gift-giving. Its chief god or demon or spirit is Santa Claus; its most notorious story is Charles Dickens's *Christmas Carol*. Even (or especially) atheists seem concerned that children should not be advised that there is no Santa Claus, nor any Ghosts of Christmases past or possibly-yet-to-come. Pratchett offers a rationale for this quaint practice: we are to believe the "little lies" so that we can come to believe the big ones: "Justice. Mercy. Duty. That sort of thing."

> Take the universe and grind it down to the finest powder and sieve it through the finest sieve and then show me one atom of justice, one molecule of mercy. And yet... and yet you act as if there is some ideal order in the world, as if there is some... some rightness in the universe by which it may be judged.[6]

Facing the real truth instead — or what is now imagined to be the truth — may drive us all to terminal depression, except that "cheerfulness is always breaking in."[7] How to conserve that cheerfulness is an ongoing project, which should not be left to the mere whim of individuals. Fortunately, we seem capable of inventing any number of distractions, and requiring selected

---

5 Burke, *Reflections on the Revolution in France*, 172; see also 129–31. "It is madness to countermand the gods" (that is, oracular instructions), according to Apollonius (Philostratus, *Life of Apollonius*, 2:161 [6.20.2]), whose defence of custom goes lamentably further than Burke, who recognized the need to judge and to reform past practice.
6 Pratchett, *Hogfather*, 408. That "rightness" cannot, logically, be simply part of the universe.
7 Cf. Boswell, *Life of Johnson*, April 17, 1778, p. 340.

individuals to perform for us: sportsmen, royalty, priests, novelists, musicians and, most absurdly of all, "celebrities."

Future historians, on the far side of catastrophe, may find it hard to rationalize our Christmas customs. Some may be satisfied to say that food and drink and music have always been our comforts, whatever excuse we imagine. It hardly matters whether the feasts are supposed to honour gods, heroes, or celebrities: the "residue,"[8] the instinctual impulses that remain when the excuses are stripped away, is what engaged our interest — and also the future historians', if they are still remotely human. The more cynical (or astute) will point to the commercial gains that depend on our pretences. Other and more imaginative critics may propose instead that the imaginings themselves are really what counted for us: food, drink and music themselves may have been the excuse for *fantasy*, and it was (and is) that fantasy which supported us in hard times. "Believing" or "putting our trust" in Santa Claus and his imaginary elves may be what we and our children need, and we are prepared to pay the cost of maintaining the illusion. Seeking to banish Christmas and the elves (or whatever other permutation of a Midwinter Festival) is not a programme likely to please the public: at any rate, it hasn't in the past.

But how will historians interpret the clash of Santa Claus and the Baby Jesus, let alone the Easter Bunny and the Crucified? The muddle will doubtless lead some to describe our age as illogical, as "prelogical" as the Egyptians were for the Frankforts. They may also follow precedent in describing the birth as a simple celebration of the Sun's return (as also the Resurrection), and point to the many other stories, round the world, of a hero's birth and later deification. They may also notice that worship is so often given to a Child rather than an imagined Father: a child that may perhaps replace the Father soon. In some ages worship or respect is also paid to the Mother of that Child, who is granted more or less personal agency in the stories told. At the simplest level of interpretation this is merely to acknowledge that we are programmed biologically to love young children, or else we would

---

8 See Pareto, *Mind and Society*. Pareto distinguished the "residue" of (e.g.) a feast, the instinctual enjoyment, from its "derivations," the rationales offered for it.

abandon the annoying brats.⁹ That programmed adoration needs social confirmation and support, as does the immediate amorous attraction between potential parents. Not all ages can afford to adore their children quite as much, nor can they all adore their fellow parents: children and adults die. And we had better continue half-believing that somehow they also live, in memory as well as graveyards and the skies.

But other readings are also possible, as they are for the older myths I have been addressing. What is invoked in both the Nativity stories and (to comic effect) "Father Christmas" or Santa Claus is the chance of a *personal* relationship to the Divine. The ceremonies are focused on *family*. Gift-giving is meant to be *personal*, chosen by gift-givers—including Santa Claus—as appropriate for particular (chiefly) children. Decorations are meant to combine inherited or customary ornaments and individual creation. Music must always be familiar—except for a few deliberately new songs of a still familiar sort. It is not merely the fact of children, of young life, that is here to be celebrated, but *these* young lives, *these* moments, which are at once themselves and images of what we might as well acknowledge as God, "like images of the sun in drops of water."¹⁰

There is ancient precedent for such a *personal* contact.

> A last aspect of the belief in the individual's personal god in Mesopotamia that should claim our attention is the inner form or image under which he was envisaged. Just as the center of the concept of the personal god, the caring and concern for an individual, stands apart in Mesopotamian religious literature as something quite special, so the "inner form," "image," or—to be precise—"metaphor" under which the personal god was seen is also quite unique: it is the image of the parent—divine father or mother—an image for the gods in their relation to man which we meet nowhere else. Normally, the image of the god in relation to his worshiper is quite a different one,

---

9 Boethius, *Consolation* 3.7 (*Tractates*, 257): "Someone invented children to be tormentors. There is no need to warn you—having experienced it before and even now being anxious—how, whatever their condition is, it gnaws at you with worry. In this matter I agree with the opinion of my Euripides, who said that one who lacks children is happy in his misfortune"!
10 After Plutarch, "Isis and Osiris" 74, in *Moralia*, 5:173.

that of master and slave. Even the most powerful king was a slave in relation to the god of his city and country; only in relation to his own personal god was he, to quote a standard phrase, "the man, son of his god."[11]

But the Christmas ceremonial offers an even stranger image: we are allowed to consider ourselves *God's parent*, either like Mary *Theotokos* (Mother of God), or at least like Joseph, as a willing adoptive father! We are to carry God as an infant in our hearts. Our God is the One to Come! Or in an older reading:

> *El* means grammatically and metaphysically the same, namely Thou art, in the sense of the timelessly unchangeable existence of God. *Eh'je asher eh'je*, on the other hand, places even at the threshold of the Yahweh phenomenon a god of the end of days, with *futurum* as an attribute of Being.[12]

And that "Future" is to be known in the direct and personal relationship of Love. As Wren-Lewis wrote in a fierce response to Julian Huxley's praise for the "evolutionary spirit,"

> When the prophets of the Bible raved about idolatry, they meant just this sort of mystical subordination of man to the great system of nature. Against this, those who have the religion of Jesus want to assert that people do *not* acquire significance by performing any sort of function, however lofty, in any larger system, however universal. They can have absolute significance *as individuals*, by the simple process of giving it to each other in ordinary personal relationships. The Christian believes this because he holds that the Absolute God, whose name is love, is present in personal relationships.[13]

---

11 Jacobsen, *Treasures*, 158.
12 Bloch, *The Principle of Hope*, 1235–36, speaking of the Name provided to Moses (Exodus 3.13–14) and contrasting this with the more common interpretation: God as the One who will be what He will, rather than simply the One that Is.
13 *Observer: Letter Page*, September 10, 1961. Huxley, said Wren-Lewis, had "described the universe as an 'all-embracing evolutionary process,' and the whole tone of his language shows that he gives mankind a religious significance because evolution has at this point 'strangely and wonderfully' acquired the power of conscious self-direction." It is a theme very common amongst moderns who wish to ease our appreciation of the natural world.

THE BIRTH OF THE SON OF GOD

Both Heracles (aka Hercules) and Jesus were reputed Sons of God, each born of a mortal mother, required to labor in the service of humanity although—or because—he was the rightful king. They were both tempted, and resisted the temptation, to take the easier, pleasanter path.[14] They perished through the treachery or folly of a trusted friend, but were raised up to Heaven and thereafter served as an ideal, an inspiration, even a supernatural aid. Heracles was identified with a Mesopotamian god, Nergal, as well as with the Tyrian Melqart.[15] Cornutus, a first century allegorist, identified him as "the Logos in all things, in accordance with which Nature is strong and powerful, since it is immovable and endlessly generative."[16] The Cynics especially took him as their patron, as one who had chosen the path of Virtue[17] and showed it was possible to live entirely by one's wits and courage, even in the face of celestial—that is, Hera's—malice.[18] In short, he was simultaneously mortal and divine—except that those two aspects were, as it seems, divided: the god may be on Olympus, but his shadow self is still among the dead.[19]

It is relatively easy to imagine alternate histories in which either it was Zeus and Heracles who were seen as the eternal "parents and originals" of mortal emperors, or else God and Christ together were remodelled on the very same pattern, as the emperors often wished.

> The imperial theology of the greatest of the persecutors [e.g. Diocletian (AD 244-311)] had important features in common with the religion which they persecuted. Jupiter is the supreme god. His son, Hercules, acts as his executive representative, and is a benefactor of man. The resemblance to Christian theology is obvious.[20]

---

14 Xenophon, *Memorabilia* 2.1.21-34; Matthew 4.1-11, Luke 4.1-13.
15 Kingsley, *Ancient Philosophy*, 274-75.
16 Cornutus, *Greek Theology* (C2/31), 123, as cited by Grant, *Gods and the One God*, 119.
17 Xenophon, *Memorabilia* 2.1.21-34.
18 Diodorus, *Library* 1.2.4: "It is generally agreed that during the whole time which Heracles spent among men he submitted to great and continuous labours and perils willingly, in order that he might confer benefits upon the race of men and thereby gain immortality."
19 *Odyssey* 11.601-2.
20 Liebeschuetz, *Continuity and Change*, 242-43.

New Beginnings

But the differences are also obvious.

> It should never be forgotten that Christianity entered human history not as a new creed or sapiential path or system of religious observances, but as apocalypse: the sudden unveiling of a mystery hidden in God before the foundation of the world in a historical event without any possible precedent or any conceivable sequel; an overturning of all the orders and hierarchies of the age, here on earth and in the archon-thronged heavens above; the overthrow of all the angelic and daemonic powers and principalities by a slave legally crucified at the behest of all the religious and political authorities of his time, but raised up by God as the one sole Lord over all the cosmos; the abolition of the partition of Law between peoples; the proclamation of an imminent arrival of the Kingdom and of a new age of creation; an urgent call to all persons to come out from the shelters of social, cultic, and political association into a condition of perilous and unprotected exposure, dwelling nowhere but in the singularity of this event—for the days are short.[21]

But that event must also, it seems, be prefigured. Christians interpreted the Hebrew Scriptures typologically: their own escape from civic and imperial authority, from slavery not just to "sin" but to the spiritual powers of wickedness, the rulers of this world who claimed (as it were) "the moral high ground,"[22] echoed the Hebrews' escape from Egypt, and also—from a still earlier date—the flight from Ur of the Chaldees. These departures were, symbolically, an escape from stellar determinism, from the control of destiny written in the skies.

> For the Chaldeans were especially active in the elaboration of astrology and ascribed everything to the movements of the stars. They supposed that the course of the phenomena of the world is guided by influences contained in numbers and numerical proportions. Thus they glorified visible existence, leaving out of consideration the intelligible and invisible. But while exploring numerical order as applied to the revolution of the sun,

---

21 Hart, *Tradition and Apocalypse*, 135.
22 Paul, Ephesians 6.12.

moon and other planets and fixed stars, and the changes of the yearly seasons and the interdependence of phenomena in heaven and on earth, they concluded that the world itself was God.[23]

Nowadays we may hope instead to be freed from *genetic* determinism, from the destiny written in our cells—as Heracles, according to Plotinus's reading, broke the chains on Prometheus.[24]

The early Christian church had many easy options in attempting to describe their experience, and prescribe their creeds. In Jewish circles Jesus could be simply a martyred teacher, even one raised from the dead, and even one born by special dispensation. Or else, in a wider realm, something like a Cynic preacher: Cynic aphorisms indeed are very close to the early Christian.[25] Or simply a "good man": "every man who is considered good is honored with the title of 'god.'"[26] Even when a grander status was granted, there were simple answers: Jesus was inspired by the Spirit of God, adopted at the Baptism as God's representative; or else maybe he was indeed "the First Born of Creation"—a grander creature than the usual, but still only a creature. He could even have been counted a demigod, like Heracles, or a new Olympian, like Dionysos, though these options would have made the break with his Jewish followers even more abrupt. Like Heracles again, he might have been divided between the immortal Christ and the fading memory, Jesus. All these possibilities had precedents; all were readily assimilable to contemporary speculation and moral reasoning. All were judged inadequate, even when the Emperor preferred some less inscrutable theory than the Nicene or Chalcedonian. The guiding principle of those who were reckoned later to be the "fathers of the church" was to insist that they were following something, Someone, at once both wholly human and wholly divine, and were likewise inspired or guided by a spirit that was also identically God.

---

23 Philo, *On Abraham* 15 (69), in *Collected Works*, 6:39–41.
24 *Ennead* IV.3 [27].14, 14–18.
25 See Downing, *Cynics, Paul and the Pauline Churches*.
26 Philostratus, *Life of Apollonius*, 2:321 [8.5.1]: Apollonius explains why he himself might be called "a god" (see also ibid., 1:261 [3.18]).

If (to use the familiar formula) "God became human that humans might become God," could it possibly be the case that the Son or the Spirit was a lesser expression of God or, even worse, merely a creature? It would seem to be a necessity of logic that only God is capable of joining creatures to God; any inferior intermediary, especially one like the created Logos of Arius, will always be infinitely remote from God himself. The Cappadocian arguments against the Eunomians were numerous, complex, and subtle, but at their heart lay a single simple intuition: If it is the Son who joins us to the Father, and only God can join us to God, then the Son must be "capable" of the Father, so to speak. The Son must be God not in an inferior and secondary sense, but in a wholly consubstantial sense. Moreover, as the argument would play out further at the Council of Constantinople and afterward, if in the sacraments of the church and the life of sanctification it is the Spirit who joins us to the Son, and only God can join us to God, then the Spirit too must be God in this wholly consubstantial sense.[27]

For the very same reason, Jesus could not be merely *influenced* by, even *possessed* by, God, but must—somehow—actually *be* both God and man. So the Galilean rabbi, they declared, was and is the uncreated Word of God: "uncreated" because it was only by that very Word that anything was created. "How can the Logos, being the Counsel and Will of the Father, come into being Himself by an act of will and purpose?"[28]

Might we then read the original stories of the birth simply as fictions, devised to convey a wonder? May we not simply allegorize them, as theologians both Hebrew and Hellenic have so often done with their stories? "When people read the theogonies of the Greeks and the stories about the twelve gods, they make them sacred by allegories. But if they want to ridicule our histories, they say that they are recounted simply to small children."[29]

What they allegorize is evident. So Philo, on Sandmel's account, read the story of Abraham and his descendants:

---

27 Hart, *Tradition and Apocalypse*, 123–24.
28 Prestige, *God in Patristic Thought*, 151, after St. Athanasius.
29 Origen, *Contra Celsum*, 218 [4.42].

> Each of us who is capable of learning is like Abraham. We too need to migrate from Chaldean pantheism, we too need to abandon the vices of our babyhood, Egypt, and our adolescence, Canaan, and then get us a college education, symbolized by mating with Hagar. At that stage we can father only the sophist Ishmael. When we go beyond the university education, we can mate with true philosophy, Sarah. Let me now interrupt to induct you into the mystic item, as I promised. Let me first state it simply. No man, no matter how wise he is, attains happiness by his own efforts. It is a gift to him of God, out of his genuine wisdom. Let me now state it in Philonic terms. Isaac, joy, is God's gift to Abraham, born to him out of his wisdom, Sarah. But Abraham is not the father of his joy, he is the recipient of it. The father is God who "visited" Sarah in her tent in *Genesis* 17, siring out of her the offspring, joy, which is then presented to the sage. Moreover, Sarah represents not individual virtues, but generic virtue, which is by assumption virgin. Sarah's ceasing after the manner of women means her restoration to virginity. Hence, allegorically, Isaac is the offspring of the virgin, Sarah, and God is his father.[30]

So also in John's Gospel:

> In the beginning was the Word, and the Word was with God, and the Word was God. The same was in the beginning with God. All things were made by him; and without him was not any thing made that was made. In him was life; and the life was the light of men. And the light shineth in darkness; and the darkness comprehended it not. There was a man sent from God, whose name was John. The same came for a witness, to bear witness of the Light, that all men through him might believe. He was not that Light, but was sent to bear witness of that Light. That was the true Light, which lighteth every man that cometh into the world. He was in the world, and the world was made by him, and the world knew him not. He came unto his own, and his own received him not.

---

30 Sandmel, "Philo's Environment and Philo's Exegesis," 252, drawing chiefly on Philo, *On Abraham*. Why Ishmael—who is very badly treated in the story, along with his mother, if the story be read "literally"—should be thus denigrated is obscure to me!

But as many as received him, to them gave he the power to become the sons of God, even to them that believe on his name: *Which were born, not of blood, nor of the will of the flesh, nor of the will of man, but of God.* And the Word was made flesh, and dwelt among us, (and we beheld his glory, the glory as of the only begotten of the Father), full of grace and truth...[31]

We may suppose that the Virgin Birth was a tale invented by believers to convey this thesis. Or else—perhaps—this was what really happened, precisely to convey the thesis. But the theological exegesis does not exhaust the story, any more than other allegorical readings wholly exhaust the meaning and effect of pagan myths, or the story of Abraham and his family. Lamberton's comment, cited earlier, could be aptly adjusted: "the whole emotional texture of the Gospel passages is lost," he might reasonably complain![32]

Strictly there are two Gospel stories of the Nativity: Matthew's and Luke's. These have been conflated and developed over centuries, so that it is now considered improper—even in secular circles—to bother to disentangle them. The story as we now tell it demands that Mary agreed to bear the coming King, despite being a virgin (*Luke*), that Joseph knew that the child wasn't his but was persuaded by an angel not to disown her (*Matthew*), the birth was attended both by shepherds alerted by angels (*Luke*), and by "wise men from the East" following a strangely mobile star (*Matthew*), that it occurred in Bethlehem because Joseph lived there (*Matthew*) or because he had to register himself and his family there for an imperial census, "being of the house of David" (*Luke*), and that "there was no room for them in the inn"[33]

---

[31] John 1.1-14 (my italics). It is commonly supposed that John's Gospel must be relatively late, as a meditation or commentary on what is more plainly recounted in the other gospels—but this is to assume both that such a meditation must take many years, and that there was no other source for the story than the written word. It seems to me as likely that at least the opening of the Gospel—which was perhaps a paschal hymn (see Behr, "The Prologue as a Paschal Hymn")—was already known before 'Matthew' and 'Luke' wrote their nativities.
[32] After Lamberton, *Homer the Theologian*, 229.
[33] Which last may be a copyist's misinterpretation simply of the child's being placed in a manger, which could easily serve as a cradle even if there *was* room in the inn. There is at least no need to invent a mean-spirited innkeeper with a bias against refugees (which Joseph and Mary, at that moment, weren't).

(*Luke*). It is sometimes also recounted that the family then fled to Egypt to avoid King Herod's soldiers, who killed all the other (male) children of Bethlehem two years old or less (*Matthew*). Alternatively, Joseph and Mary simply went to Jerusalem with the child to "present him to the Lord" (*Luke*), and then went back to their hometown Nazareth (*Luke*), or else took refuge there after their Egyptian exile (*Matthew*). The "wise men" have since become three kings, with appropriate ethnic backgrounds, and astronomical records are probed to identify "the Star."

The Gospel story—and especially the Nativity—is a real-life fairytale, as Tolkien and others have proposed.

> The Gospels contain a fairy-story, or a story of a larger kind which embraces all the essence of fairy-stories. They contain many marvels—peculiarly artistic, beautiful, and moving: "mythical" in their perfect, self-contained significance; and among the marvels is the greatest and most complete conceivable eucatastrophe. But this story has entered History and the primary world; the desire and aspiration of sub-creation has been raised to the fulfilment of Creation. The Birth of Christ is the eucatastrophe of Man's history. The Resurrection is the eucatastrophe of the story of the Incarnation. This story begins and ends in joy. It has pre-eminently the "inner consistency of reality." There is no tale ever told that men would rather find was true, and none which so many sceptical men have accepted as true on its own merits.[34]

Whether Tolkien's conviction, that the story at least *sounds* true, is now widely shared may be moot. In essence, the claim may be that the story is made really, historically, true because "we" have told it as true. It is true as a whole, despite being drawn from at least two differing and not easily reconciled sources, because it has come to *seem* true to those who have "received Him." Tradition, perhaps, rules, despite being poorly supported by the particular written texts that the early Church decided to take as canon. Many modern, would-be "humanistic" theologians and critics

---

34 Tolkien, "On Fairy Stories," in *Monsters and the Critics*, 155–56. Cf. Browning, "Bishop Blougram's Apology" [1855], in *Poems*, 435: "'What think ye of Christ,' friend? when all's done and said. Like you this Christianity or not? It may be false, but will you wish it true? Has it your vote to be so if it can?"

New Beginnings

would prefer to abandon the fairytale, and concentrate on the clearly "ethical" messages of the Gospel. Early believers—so those moderns say—*invented* the stories so as to give more depth and excitement to the tales of a wandering rabbi who may (or may not) have annoyed the Romans, or the Jerusalem establishment, or moneychangers and capitalistic traders enough for them to wish him dead. Like Socrates, perhaps, Jesus had insisted on forcing their hands (whoever "they" might be) and so ensured that *they* would be condemned at least in the eyes of the innocent, and perhaps in the eye of God. Both Resurrection and Virgin Birth were simple ways to emphasise his status as the appointed Judge over all the Earth, the one who had *already* found the world wanting. Clearly, the story echoes ancient expectations:

> Like Re, the king could emerge from the womb of the sky-goddess Nut in the morning: "because you are Re who came forth from Nut, who bears Re daily, and like Re you are born daily." The motif of the birth of life from the maternal womb continued into Christian times, as a prayer to Mary, which goes back at least to the Middle Ages, shows: "Blessed are you, for out of your womb a radiance emerged, shining all over the world announcing your praise... Be greeted, you, dawn of Salvation, you, origin of joy."[35]

And perhaps we might still wonder if it's true.

> And is it true? And is it true,
> This most tremendous tale of all,
> Seen in a stained-glass window's hue,
> A Baby in an ox's stall?
> The Maker of the stars and sea
> Become a Child on earth for me?
> And is it true? For if it is,
> No loving fingers tying strings
> Around those tissued fripperies,
> The sweet and silly Christmas things,
> Bath salts and inexpensive scent
> And hideous tie so kindly meant,

---

35 Schweizer, *Sungod's Journey through the Netherworld*, 6–7, quoting Faulkner, *Ancient Egyptian Pyramid Texts*, 1:250, § 1688.

No love that in a family dwells,
No carolling in frosty air,
Nor all the steeple-shaking bells
Can with this single Truth compare —
That God was Man in Palestine
And lives today in Bread and Wine.[36]

---

36 Betjeman, "Christmas," in *Collected Poems*, 153–54.

∽12∽
Conclusion

> Let not thy heart be puffed-up because of thy knowledge;
> be not confident because thou art a wise man. Take counsel with the ignorant as well as with the wise.[1]

IS THERE A FINAL MORAL TO THIS EXAMINAtion and evocation of ancient myths and fables, alongside a few new fantasies? The first is simple enough: our predecessors wondered how things came to be, how best to live, and where we should be going. Their thoughts and arguments are congruent, at least, with more familiar themes, both moral and cosmological. The second may suggest that we don't know what earlier cultures achieved, and whether myths and proverbs might not be, as Aristotle suggested, the remnants and mementos of earlier developed philosophies. The third moral, and the most significant, is that we can still work our way towards a better understanding of the world and our place in it by reimagining and reconstructing those old stories, and even by making new ones. "Philosophy," as the pursuit of understanding, is not confined to modern, "analytical," or "Western" minds. Nor is such understanding bound to be as neutral, secular, "objective" as is currently supposed. The stories we tell ourselves, the gods or ghosts or demons we invoke, may at least assist us to sustain a worthwhile life in a confused and confusing cosmos. Alternatively, it is those demons that surreptitiously create our torments, and our ignorance of their influence—perhaps especially in that delusion of "objectivity"—is itself "the first torment":

> The second [so Hermes continues] is grief. The third is intemperance. The fourth is lust. The fifth is injustice. The sixth is greed. The seventh is deceit. The eighth is envy.

---

[1] "Instructions of the Vizier Ptah-Hotep" (c. 2450 BC), in Pritchard, *Ancient Near Eastern Texts*, 234.

> The ninth is treachery. The tenth is anger. The eleventh is recklessness. The twelfth is corruption. These are twelve in number; but under them, child, others more numerous use the prison of the body to torment [lit. force to suffer] the inner person through his sense perceptions. But they depart, one after the other, from the one to whom God has shown mercy—and that is the manner and the meaning of rebirth.[2]

But it may be honest also to acknowledge a more personal and troubling aim. The story itself, after all, requires me to take seriously my own involvement in the enterprise, as merely the self or selves I am (and which I do not wholly or accurately know). My most common recurring dream involves an unsuccessful search for a lecture hall, my home, my car, a hotel room, a railway station, through some almost familiar urban wilderness. Sometimes I have a companion—who may change in the way of dreams from son to daughter to colleague or passing stranger. More often, I find myself without any support or halfway helpful advice: I cannot even program my smart phone to trace my route through Google Maps! So far, I have always woken up (as we suppose) before finding my destination—and even before collapsing in despair.

At one level, of course, my dream merely expresses a familiar fear: I have a poor sense of direction, and a bad memory even for roads I have walked or driven down before. I might as easily be dreaming that I hadn't read any of the scripts I was supposed to mark, just before an important examiners' meeting, or that I hadn't prepared a lecture, or dressed to welcome guests. And all such dreams may be merely literal imaginings of realistic possibilities for waking life. Maybe, at best, they might be warnings to wake early and mark the scripts, prepare the lecture, or get ready for whatever party. The dreams of searching for a mislaid destination are less literally helpful—except perhaps as suggestions that I should find someone to rely upon when navigating even a

---

[2] CH 13.7, in Hanegraaff, *Hermetic Spirituality*, 245 (see Copenhaver, *Hermetica*, 51). Hanegraaff (ibid., 250) goes on to suggest that "the dodecad of tormenting energies that reflect the twelve signs of the zodiac, manifesting themselves as harmful passions, is expelled by the overwhelming force of two clusters of healing energies that act in perfect unison and are ultimately one: a septenary of positive energies linked to seven chief virtues, and a supreme divine triad."

familiar town (as my most recent dream of that sort sarcastically provided). But perhaps the dreams have a deeper meaning: I am wandering without clear direction in search of a destination that may present itself, in the dream, as itself either a staging post—a station, a car parked in some forgotten side street—or somewhere that I am needed—a lecture hall, or a home. I am trying, somehow, to get back where I belong—and failing, lost not so much in a dark wood like Dante[3] as in a decaying city, and rather nearer the end than the middle of our accustomed life. They are also reminders, perhaps, that I so often fail to complete a project or an assignment properly: that I begin well, but lose the thread of the argument or mismanage the necessary steps towards completion. Or else maybe the dreams depict the same condition as Empedocles' confession (though less grandiloquently): "an exile from the gods, a wanderer, putting my trust in the insanities of strife."[4]

"If we mistakenly trust our private reasonings we shall construct and build the city of the mind that destroys the truth," so Philo tells us.[5] The notion that we should simply "think for ourselves" (and that this is what Socrates required of his fellow citizens[6]) is at least optimistic—as foolish indeed as supposing that I could easily find my own way through the urban desert, that I can trust "my truth"! Would we happily advise people to *calculate* for themselves, or rather to consult accountants, or to *self-diagnose*, rather than consult a medic? And even amateur calculation or self-diagnosis may be a safer enterprise than "thinking" (that is, most often, daydreaming, rationalizing or reciting half-remembered stories). Even or especially the Very Clever, or those who think that they are Very Clever, should perhaps be warned away from always relying on their own "reasoning" about what is or should be. As Chesterton remarked, "believing utterly in one's self is a hysterical and superstitious belief like believing in

---

3 Dante, *Inferno*, Canto 1.1–3.
4 Empedocles F35 [DK31B115], in Waterfield, *First Philosophers*, 153–54.
5 Philo, *Allegorical Interpretation* 3.81, in *Collected Works*, 1:457.
6 Cf. Xenophon, *Memorabilia* 2.1.20: "I wonder how the Athenians can have been persuaded that Socrates was a freethinker (*peri theous me sophronein*), when he never said or did anything contrary to sound religion, and his utterances about the gods and his behaviour towards them were the words and actions of a man who is truly religious and deserves to be thought so."

Joanna Southcote."[7] Notoriously, the Very Clever are very apt to rationalize their own desires. "Is my mind my own possession? That parent of false conjectures, that purveyor of delusion, the delirious, the fatuous, and in frenzy or senility proved to be the very negation of mind."[8]

Should I not therefore hang on to a tradition and a personal commitment, which at least may guide consistently (or almost so)?

> My second maxim [so Descartes said] was to be as firm and decisive in my actions as I could, and to follow even the most doubtful opinions, once I had adopted them, as constantly as if they had been quite certain. In this I would be imitating travellers who find themselves lost in a forest: rather than wandering about in all directions or (even worse) staying in one place, they should keep walking as straight as they can in one direction, not turning aside for slight reasons, even if their choice of direction was a matter of mere chance in the first place; for even if this doesn't bring them to where they want to go it will at least bring them to somewhere that is probably better for them than the middle of a forest.[9]

But sometimes we need Silence, if that were possible.

> It is a hard matter to bring to a standstill the soul's changing movements. Their irresistible stream is such that we could sooner stem the rush of a torrent, for thoughts after thoughts in countless numbers pour on like a huge breaker and drive and whirl and upset its whole being with their violence.... A man's thoughts are sometimes not due to himself but come without his will.[10]

Almost all our thoughts, indeed, owe nothing to our will. So the very first step should be to try and quieten our minds, to call a halt to the incessant monologue in which we almost all indulge, the constant stream of thoughts, hurt feelings, fancies. Ritual, whether overt or private, is a help with this, as is attention to our breathing in and out (which is what Palamas insists is the main

---

7 Chesterton, *Orthodoxy*, 14.
8 Philo, *On Cherubim*, 114f., in *Collected Works*, 2:77.
9 Descartes, *Discourse*, 11-12.
10 Philo, *On the Change of Names*, 239f., in *Collected Works*, 5:265ff.

point of hesychastic breathing practices).[11] It may even be a help, sometimes, to hold ourselves to rigorously connected arguments, cast in propositional form, simply to put aside distractions. But Plotinus is not unusual in insisting that "the vision is hard to put into words."[12] Breathing, or doing arithmetical or logical puzzles, or even practising "forms," may gradually suppress the noise, and so allow us to listen.

> As the soul returns to the body, the luminous vision will fade, and its place will be taken by the usual play of mental imagery with all its seductive potential. Thus having returned from a state of "astonishment" to normal consciousness, practitioners would still be faced with the daily challenge of living a life of reverence, of "giving birth in beauty, both in body and soul" instead of getting sucked back into limited awareness and negative patterns all the time. Was it at all possible, they must have asked themselves and their teachers, to really and permanently change one's consciousness — to actually become the *aiōn*? To this question the answer was "yes, that is possible — but you need to be reborn."[13]

On the one hand, we cannot profitably start again, or think we can make our own way in the world, without relying on unvoiced principles and unacknowledged desires and fears. On the other, we cannot plausibly or forever pretend that the customs of our time and place are always right. We may hope that something like Athena may tug us round, or something like Hermes intervene to save us from disaster. We may be led by something like a Star, or sometimes recognize an angel.[14] We may even, sometimes, be on the verge of waking, and decide instead to dream, for what seem to us good reasons. Consider another dream: the appearance of a golden opening, a door most truly into summer: light and warmth and welcome may be there if we only choose to step outside. And yet to do so is to abandon others, our dependants. The invitation

---

11 Palamas, *The 150 Chapters*, 45 [1.2.7], in Palmer et al., *Philokalia*, 337.
12 *Ennead* VI.9 [9].10, 19.
13 Hanegraaff, *Hermetic Spirituality*, 219; cf. John 3.1-5.
14 The ancient stories testify that angels, gods, or heroes may appear in dreams, and address the dreamer directly — though not always truthfully. Such an event may be life-changing, even if the apparition lies.

itself is a sort of reassurance: "summer" is not an illusion, and "Fairyland" is real. Andreas Schweizer reports:

> I remember a woman who came into my practice just before learning that she had a terminal illness. Shortly after receiving her diagnosis, she dreamed, "I am together with my friend in a marvellous, sunny landscape. There are fields of wheat, sun, blue sky, grass. We stand in front of a field with very tender ears, which were silently moved to and fro by the wind. My friend says: How nice is this! Everything is completely silent. We speak with very low voices. I wake up. The image was very beautiful." This dream had a very consoling effect on the dreamer. The tenderness of it seemed to annihilate the brutality of her approaching death.[15]

Maybe the dream is veridical. At least such dreams are the basis, as well as the expression, of a hope deferred. But our duties for the moment at least lie here.

---

15 Schweizer, *Sungod's Journey through the Netherworld*, 68–69.

RELATED WORKS BY STEPHEN R.L. CLARK

BOOKS

Aristotle's Man: Speculations on Aristotelian Anthropology. Oxford: Clarendon Press, 1975.

The Mysteries of Religion: An Introduction to Philosophy through Religion. Eugene, Oregon: Wipf and Stock, 2020 [1986].

How to Live Forever: Science Fiction and Immortality. London: Routledge, 1995.

G.K. Chesterton: Thinking Backwards, Looking Forwards. West Conshohocken, PA: Templeton Foundation Press, 2006.

Understanding Faith: Religious Belief and Its Place in Society. Exeter: Imprint Academic, 2009.

Philosophical Futures. Frankfurt: Peter Lang, 2011.

Ancient Mediterranean Philosophy. London: Continuum, 2013.

Plotinus: Myth, Metaphor, and Philosophical Practice. Chicago: University of Chicago Press, 2016.

Can We Believe in People: Human Significance in an Interconnected Cosmos. Brooklyn, NY: Angelico Press, 2020.

Cities and Thrones and Powers: Towards a Plotinian Politics. Brooklyn, NY: Angelico Press, 2022.

PAPERS

"Waking-up: A Neglected Model for the After-life." *Inquiry* 26 (1983): 209–30.

"Eradicating the Obvious." *Journal of Applied Philosophy*, 8.1 (1991): 121–25.

"Does the Burgess Shale Have Moral Implications?" *Inquiry* 36 (1993): 357–80.

"A Plotinian Account of Intellect." *American Catholic Philosophical Quarterly* 71 (1997): 421–32.

"The End of the Ages." In David Seed, ed., *Imagining Apocalypse: Studies in Cultural Crisis*, 27–44. London: Macmillan; New York: St Martin's Press, 2000. Reprinted with corrections in Clark, *Philosophical Futures*.

"Berkeley's Philosophy of Religion." In *Cambridge Companion to Berkeley*, edited by Kenneth Winckler, 369–404. New York: Cambridge University Press, 2005.

"Can Animals Be Our Friends?" *Philosophy Now* 67 (May/June 2008): 13–16.

"Elves, Hobbits, Trolls and Talking Beasts." In Celia Deane-Drummond and David Clough, eds., *Creaturely Theology*, 151–67. London: SCM Press, 2009.

"Therapy and Theory Reconstructed." In *Philosophy as Therapy*, edited by Clare Carlisle and Jonardon Ganeri, 83–102. Royal Institute of Philosophy Supplementary Volume 66. Cambridge: Cambridge University Press, 2010.

"The Mind Parasites: Wilson, Husserl, Plotinus." In *Around the Outsider: Essays Presented to Colin Wilson*, edited by Colin Stanley, 42–62. Alresford: O-Books, 2011.

"Folly to the Greeks: Good Reasons to Give up Reason." *European Journal for Philosophy of Religion* 4 (2012): 93–113.

"Personal Identity and Identity Disorders." In *Oxford Handbook of Philosophy and Psychiatry*, edited by K.W.M. Fulford, Martin Davies, George Graham, and John Z. Sadler, 911–28. Oxford: Oxford University Press, 2013.

"Living the Pyrrhonian Way." In *The Science, Politics, and Ontology of Life-Philosophy*, edited by Scott M. Campbell and Paul W. Bruno, 197–209. London: Bloomsbury, 2013.

"Atheism Considered as a Christian Sect." *Philosophy* 90 (2015): 277–303.

"Platonists and Participation." *Revista Portuguesa de Filosofia* 71 (2015): 249–66. Special volume: *Metaphysics: Historical Perspectives and its Actors*, edited by Ricardo Barroso Batista.

"Going beyond our Worlds." In *Animals: New Essays*, edited by Andreas Blank, 397–418. Munich: Philosophia Verlag, 2016.

"The Sphere with Many Faces." *Dionysius* 34 (2016): 8–26.

"Climbing up to Heaven: the Hermetic Option." In *Purgatory: Philosophical Dimensions*, edited by Kristof K.P. Vanhoutte and Benjamin W. McCraw, 151–74. London: Palgrave-Macmillan, 2017.

"Lovecraft and the Search for Meaning." In *Proceedings of the Colin Wilson Conference*, edited by Colin Stanley, 10–45. Cambridge: Cambridge Scholars, 2017.

"Souls, Stars and Shadows." In *Differences in Identity in Philosophy and Religion: A Cross-cultural Approach*, edited by Sarah Flavel and Russell Re Manning, 7–20. London: Bloomsbury, 2020.

"Selfless Civilizations: Robots, Zombies, and the World to Come." In *Minding the Future: Artificial Intelligence, Philosophical Visions and Science Fiction*, edited by Barry Dainton, Will Slocombe, and Attila Tanyi, 165–78. Bern: Springer, 2021.

"New Histories of the World: Spenglerian Optimism." *Philosophical Journal of Conflict and Violence* 22 (2022): 1–18.

BIBLIOGRAPHY

Adam, James, ed. *The Republic of Plato*. Cambridge: Cambridge University Press, 2010 [1902].

Al-Ghazali, Abu Hamid Muhammad Ibn Muhammad Ibn Ahmad al-Tusi. *Deliverance from Error and Mystical Union with the Almighty* (1106/7): *A Translation of al-Munqidh min al-Dalal* by Muhammad Abulaylah, ed. George F. McLean. Washington, DC: Council for Research in Values and Philosophy, 2002.

Allen, J. P. *Genesis in Egypt: the Philosophy of Ancient Egyptian Creation Accounts*. New Haven: Yale University Press, 1988.

Allen, James P. *Middle Egyptian: An Introduction to the Language and Culture of Hieroglyphs*. 3rd ed. Cambridge: Cambridge University Press, 2014.

Allione, Tsultrim. *Feeding Your Demons: Ancient Wisdom for Resolving Inner Conflict*. London: Hay House, 2008.

Allison, Ralph B. "Multiple Personality Disorder, Dissociative Identity Disorder, and Internalized Imaginary Companions." *Hypnos* 25.3 (1998): 125–33.

———. *Mind in Many Pieces: Revealing the Spiritual Side of Multiple Personality Disorder*. 2nd ed. Los Osos, CA: Cie Publishing, 1999.

Almond, Philip. "Adam, Pre-Adamites, and Extra-Terrestrial Beings in Early Modern Europe." *Journal of Religious History* 30.2 (2006): 163–74.

Amzallag, Nissim. "Was Yahweh Worshiped in the Aegean?" *Journal for the Study of the Old Testament* 35 (2011): 387–415.

Ando, Clifford. *The Matter of the Gods: Religion and the Roman Empire*. Berkeley: University of California Press, 2008.

Anscombe, G.E.M. *Faith in a Hard Ground: Essays on Religion, Philosophy and Ethics*. Edited by Mary Geach and Luke Gormally. Exeter: Imprint Academic, 2008.

Apollodorus. *The Library*. Translated by J.G. Frazer. Cambridge, MA: Loeb Classical Library, Harvard University Press, 2014.

Apuleius of Madaura. *The Golden Ass*. Translated by E.J. Kenney. Harmondsworth: Penguin, 1988.

Aristotle. *Posterior Analytics and Topica*. Translated by Hugh Tredennick and E.S. Forster. Cambridge, MA: Harvard University Press, 1960.

Armstrong, A.H. and Markus, R.A. *Christian Faith and Greek Philosophy*. London: Darton, Longman and Todd, 1960.

Armstrong, A.H., trans. *Plotinus' Enneads*. London: Loeb Classical Library, Heinemann, 1966–88.

Armstrong, A.H. "Some Advantages of Polytheism." *Dionysius* 5 (1981): 181–88.

Assmann, Jan. *From Akhenaten to Moses: Ancient Egypt and Religious Change.* New York: Oxford University Press, 2014.
———. *Moses the Egyptian.* Cambridge, MA: Harvard University Press, 1997.
———. *Of God and Gods: Egypt, Israel, and the Rise of Monotheism.* Madison: University of Wisconsin Press, 2008.
Athanasius. *On the Incarnation* [c. 318]. London: Bles, 1944.
Augustine. *City of God.* R.W. Dyson. Cambridge: Cambridge University Press, 1998.
———. *On Genesis.* Translated by E. Hill. New York: New City Press, 2002.
———. *On the Trinity.* Edited by Gareth B. Matthews. Translated by Stephen McKenna. Cambridge Texts in the History of Philosophy. Cambridge: Cambridge University Press, 2002.
Azize, Joseph. *The Phoenician Solar Theology: An Investigation into the Phoenician Opinion of the Sun Found in Julian's Hymn to King Helios.* Piscataway, NJ: Gorgias Press, 2005.
Baillie, Mike and Pat McCafferty. *Celtic Gods: Comets in Irish Mythology.* Cheltenham: History Press, 2005.
Baker, Gideon. "'Now We Have Been Delivered from the Law': Thoughts towards a Genealogy of Anarchism." *Griffith Law Review* 21 (2012): 369–91.
Ball, Philip. "Hawking Rewrites History." *Nature* (21 June 2006). www.nature.com/articles/news060619-6.
Barber, Elizabeth Wayland and Paul T. Barber. *When They Severed Earth from Sky: How the Human Mind Shapes Myth.* New Jersey: Princeton University Press, 2012.
Barfield, Raymond. *The Ancient Quarrel between Philosophy and Poetry.* Cambridge: Cambridge University Press, 2011.
Barker, Andrew, ed. *Greek Musical Writings,* vol. 2: *Harmonic and Acoustic Theory.* Cambridge: Cambridge University Press, 1989.
Barton, John. *A History of the Bible: The Book and Its Faiths.* London: Allen Lane, 2019.
Baumgarten, A.I. *The Phoenician History of Philo of Byblus.* Leiden: Brill, 1981.
Beahrs, John O. *Unity and Multiplicity: Multilevel Consciousness of Self in Hypnosis, Psychiatric Disorder and Mental Health.* New York: Brunner/Mazel, 1982.
Beard, Mary. "The Roman and the Foreign: The Cult of the 'Great Mother' in Imperial Rome." In *Shamanism, History and the State,* edited by Nicholas Thomas and Caroline Humphrey, 164–90. Ann Arbor: Michigan University Press, 1996.
Behr, John. "The Prologue as a Paschal Hymn." In idem, *John the Theologian and his Paschal Gospel: A Prologue to Theology,* 245–72. Oxford: Oxford University Press, 2019.
Berkeley, George. *Works.* Edited by A.A. Luce and T.E. Jessop. Edinburgh: Thomas Nelson, 1948–57.

Bibliography

Betegh, Gábor. *The Derveni Papyrus: Cosmology, Theology and Interpretation*. Cambridge: Cambridge University Press, 2004.

Betjeman, John. *Collected Poems*. London: John Murray, 2006.

Billigheimer, Rachel V. "Conflict and Conquest: Creation, Emanation and the Female in William Blake's Mythology." *Modern Language Studies* 30.1 (2000): 93–120.

Blake, William. *Complete Works*. Edited by Geoffrey Keynes. London: Oxford University Press, 1966.

Blish, James. *Black Easter*. London: Faber, 1969.

Bloch, Ernst. *The Principle of Hope*. Translated by N. Plaice, S. Plaice and P. Knight. Oxford: Blackwell, 1986.

Bodine, Joshua J. "The Shabaka Stone: An Introduction." *Studia Antiqua* 7.1 (2009): 1–21.

Boethius. *The Theological Tractates*. Translated by Hugh Fraser Stewart and S.J. Tester. Cambridge, MA: Loeb Classical Library, Harvard University Press, 2011.

Borges, J.L. "Avatars of the Tortoise" (1939). In *Labyrinths*, edited by D. A. Yates and J. E. Irby, 202–8. Harmondsworth: Penguin, 1970.

———. "Pascal's Sphere" (1951). In *Other Inquisitions, 1937–1952*, translated by Ruth L.C. Simms, 6–9. Austin: University of Texas Press, 1993.

Bos, A. P. "Aristotle on Myth and Philosophy." *Philosophia Reformata* 48.1 (1983): 1–18.

Bostrom, Nick. "Are You Living in a Computer Simulation?" *Philosophical Quarterly* 53 (2003): 243–55.

Boswell, James. *Life of Samuel Johnson*. Edited by Charles Grosvenor Osgood. Delhi: Delhi Open Books, 2021 [1917, 1791].

Bourguignon, Erika. "Multiple Personality, Possession Trance, and the Psychic Unity of Mankind." *Ethos* 17, no. 3 (1989): 371–84.

Boyle, Marjorie O'Rourke. "Pure of Heart: From Ancient Rites to Renaissance Plato." *Journal of the History of Ideas* 63 (2002): 41–62.

Boys-Stones, G.R. "The Stoics' Two Types of Allegory." In *Metaphor, Allegory, and the Classical Tradition: Ancient Thought and Modern Revisions*, edited by G.R. Boys-Stones, 189–216. Oxford: Oxford University Press, 2003.

Breasted, James Henry. *The Dawn of Conscience*. New York: Charles Scribner Sons, 1935.

Brisson, Luc. *How Philosophers Saved Myths: Allegorical Interpretation and Classical Mythology*. Translated by Catherine Tihanyi. Chicago: University of Chicago Press, 2004.

Brown, Christopher G. "Ares, Aphrodite, and the Laughter of the Gods." *Phoenix*, 43.4 (1989): 283–93.

Brown, David. *Mesopotamian Planetary Astronomy-Astrology*. Cuneiform Monographs 18. Groningen: Styx, 2000.

Browning, Robert. *Poems 1833–1865*. London: Cassell and Co., 1907.

Brunner, John. *Times without Number.* Morley, Yorkshire: Elmfield Press, 1974 [1962].
Buber, Martin. *I and Thou.* Translated by Walter Kaufmann. New York: Simon and Schuster, 1996 [1923].
Buchan, John. *The Moon Endureth.* Edinburgh: Thomas Nelson, 1923 [1912].
Burgess, Jonathan S. *The Death and Afterlife of Achilles.* Baltimore: Johns Hopkins Press, 2009.
Burke, Edmund. *Reflections on the Revolution in France.* Edited by Conor Cruise O'Brien. Harmondsworth: Penguin, 1968.
Burkert, Walter. "From Epiphany to Cult Statue: Early Greek Theos." In *What Is a God? Studies in the Nature of Greek Divinity,* edited by Alan B. Lloyd, 15–34. London: Duckworth, 1997.
Burnyeat, Myles, and Michael Frede. *The Pseudo-Platonic Seventh Letter.* Edited by Dominic Scott. Oxford: Oxford University Press, 2015.
Burnyeat, Myles. "Idealism and Greek Philosophy: What Descartes Saw and Berkeley Missed." *Philosophical Review* 91 (1982): 3–40.
Butcher, S.H. *Aristotle's Theory of Poetry and Fine Arts, with a Critical Text and Translation of the "Poetics."* London: Macmillan, 1907.
Butler, Samuel. *Erewhon.* London: Penguin, 2006 [1901: third edition].
Buxton, Richard. *Forms of Astonishment: Greek Myths of Metamorphosis.* Oxford: Oxford University Press, 2009.
Calderón de la Barca, Pedro. *Life's a Dream.* Boulder, Colorado: University Press of Colorado, 2004 [1635].
Card, Orson Scott. *Pastwatch: The Redemption of Christopher Columbus.* New York: Tor, 1996.
Carroll, Lewis. *"Alice's Adventures in Wonderland" and "Through the Looking-Glass."* London: Macmillan, 2016 [1865; 1871].
Carver, Ben, ed. *Alternate Histories and Nineteenth-Century Literature: Untimely Meditations in Britain, France, and America.* London: Palgrave Macmillan, 2017.
Caseau, Béatrice. "Sacred Landscapes." In *Late Antiquity: A Guide to the Post-classical World,* edited by G.W. Bowersock, Peter Brown, and Oleg Grabar, 21–59. Cambridge, MA: Harvard University Press, 1999.
Chesterton, G.K. *Autobiography.* London: Hutchinson and Co., 1936.
———. *The Ball and the Cross.* London: Darwen Finlayson, Ltd., 1963 [1910].
———. *Collected Poems.* London: Methuen, 1950.
———. *The Defendant.* London: J. M. Dent and Sons Ltd., 1914 [1902].
———. *The Everlasting Man.* London: Hodder and Stoughton, 1925.
———. *The Father Brown Stories.* London: Cassell, 1929.
———. *G.F. Watts.* London: Duckworth, 1904.
———. *Heretics.* Delhi: Lector House, 2019 [1905].
———. *A Miscellany of Men.* Scotts Valley, CA: CreateSpace, 2018 [1912].
———. *Orthodoxy.* London: Fontana 1961 [1908].
———. *The Poet and the Lunatics.* London: Darwen Finlayson, 1962 [1929].

———. *The Thing: Why I Am a Catholic*. London: Sheed and Ward, 1929.
———. *Tremendous Trifles*. London: Methuen, 1904.
———. *What's Wrong with the World*. London: Cassell and Co, 1910.
Chittick, William C. *Science of the Cosmos, Science of the Soul: The Pertinence of Islamic Cosmology in the Modern World*. Oxford: Oneworld, 2007.
Chuang Tzu. *Book of Chuang Tzu*. Translated by Martin Palmer and Elizabeth Breuilly. London: Penguin, 2006.
Ćirković, Milan M. *The Astrobiological Landscape: Philosophical Foundations of the Study of Cosmic Life*. Cambridge: Cambridge University Press, 2012.
Cohn, Norman. *Noah's Flood: The Genesis Story in Western Thought*. New Haven: Yale University Press, 1996.
Collins, Adela Yarbro. "The Seven Heavens in Jewish and Christian Apocalypses." In *Death, Esctasy, and Other Worldly Journeys*, edited by John J. Collins and Michael Fishbane, 59–93. Albany: SUNY Press, 1995.
Collins, John D. "The Zeal of Phinehas: The Bible and the Legitimation of Violence." In *Journal of Biblical Literature* 122 (2003): 3–21.
Connell, Sophia C. "'Nous alone enters from outside': Aristotelian Embryology and Early Christian Philosophy." *Journal of Ancient Philosophy* 2 (2021): 109–38.
Copenhaver, Brian P., trans. *Hermetica: The Greek Corpus Hermeticum and the Latin Asclepius*. Cambridge: Cambridge University Press, 1992.
Cornutus, L. Annaeus. *Greek Theology, Fragments, and Testimonia*. Edited by George Boys-Stones. Atlanta: SBL Press, 2018.
Coulter, James A. *The Literary Microcosm: Theories of Interpretation of the Later Neoplatonists*. Leiden: Brill, 1976.
Cox Miller, Patricia. "In Praise of Nonsense." In *Classical Mediterranean Spirituality: Egyptian, Greek, Roman*, edited by A.H. Armstrong, 481–505. New York: Crossroad, 1986.
Crabtree, Adam. *Multiple Man: Explorations in Possession and Multiple Personality*. Toronto: Somerville House, 1997.
Craig, William Lane. *The Kalam Cosmological Argument*. London: Macmillan, 1979.
Crowley, John. *Aegypt*. London: Gollancz, 1987.
Culianu, Ioan Petru. *Psychanodia I: A Survey of the Evidence Concerning the Ascension of the Soul and Its Relevance*. Leiden: Brill, 1983.
Dal Santo, Matthew. *Debating the Saints' Cult in the Age of Gregory the Great*. Oxford: Oxford University Press, 2012.
Dante Alighieri. *The Divine Comedy: Inferno, Purgatory, Paradise*. Translated by Robert M. Durling. Oxford: Oxford University Press, 2011.
Darnell, John Coleman and Colleen Manassa Darnell. *The Ancient Egyptian Netherworld Books*. Williston: Society of Biblical Literature, 2017.
Davis, Whitney M. "The Ascension Myth in the Pyramid Texts." *Journal of Near Eastern Studies* 36.3 (1977): 161–79.

Dawson, David. *Allegorical Readers and Cultural Revision in Ancient Alexandria*. Berkeley and Los Angeles: University of California Press, 1992.

De Castro, Eduardo Viveiros. "Cosmological Deixis and Amerindian Perspectivism." *Journal of the Royal Anthropological Institute* 4.3 (1998): 469-88.

De Lubac, Henri. *Medieval Exegesis, Volume 1: The Four Senses of Scripture*. Translated by Mark Sebanc. Grand Rapids: Eerdmans, 1998.

Dearmer, Percy, R. Vaughan Williams, and Martin Shaw, eds. *Oxford Book of Carols*. London: Oxford University Press, 1964 [1928].

Dennis, John. *The Critical Works of John Dennis*. Edited by Edward Niles Hooker. Baltimore: Johns Hopkins, 1939-1943.

Denyer, Nicholas. "The Seventh Letter: A Discussion of Myles Burnyeat and Michael Frede, *The Pseudo-Platonic Seventh Letter*." *Oxford Studies in Ancient Philosophy* 51 (2016): 283-92.

Descartes, René. *The Philosophical Writings of Descartes*. Translated by John Cottingham, Robert Stoothoff, and Dugald Murdoch. Cambridge: Cambridge University Press, 1985.

———. *Discourse on the Method of Rightly Conducting One's Reason and Seeking Truth in the Sciences*. Translated by Jonathan Bennett. www.earlymoderntexts.com/assets/pdfs/descartes1637.pdf (2017).

———. *Meditations on First Philosophy*. Translated by Jonathan Bennett. www.earlymoderntexts.com/assets/pdfs/descartes1641.pdf (2017).

Descola, Philippe. *Beyond Nature and Culture*. Translated by Janet Lloyd. Chicago: University of Chicago Press, 2013.

Deutsch, David. *The Fabric of Reality: Towards a Theory of Everything*. London: Allen Lane, 1997.

Dillon, John. "The Letters of Iamblichus: Popular Philosophy in a Neoplatonic Mode." In *Iamblichus and the Foundations of Late Platonism*, edited by Eugene Afonasin, John Dillon and John F. Finamore, 51-62. Leiden: Brill, 2012.

Dio Chrysostom, *Discourses*. Translated by J.H. Cohoon. London: Loeb Classical Library, Heinemann, 1939.

Diodorus Siculus, *Library of History*, vol. 1. Translated by C.H. Oldfather. Cambridge, MA: Loeb Classical Library, Harvard University Press, 1933.

Donne, John. *Complete Verse and Selected Prose*. Edited by J. Hayward. London: Nonesuch Press, 1929.

Downing, F. Gerard. *Cynics, Paul and the Pauline Churches*. London: Routledge, 1998.

Druon, Maurice. *Alexander the Great*. London: Rupert Hart-Davis, 1960 [1958].

Dunbar, Robin. *Grooming, Gossip and the Evolution of Language*. London: Faber, 1996.

Dunsany, Lord [Edward J.M.D. Plunkett]. *The King of Elfland's Daughter*. Berkeley: Mint Press, 2021 [1924].

Bibliography

Durkheim, Emile. *The Elementary Forms of the Religious Life: A Study in Religious Sociology*. Translated by J.W. Swain. London: Allen and Unwin, 1915.

Dyson, Freeman J. "The Darwinian Interlude." *Technology Review*, March 1, 2005. www.technologyreview.com/2005/03/01/274577/the-darwinian-interlude-2.

———. "Time without End: Physics and Biology in an Open Universe" (1979). In *Selected Papers of Freeman Dyson*, 529–42. Providence, Rhode Island: American Mathematical Society, 1996.

Edwards, Jonathan. *Works of Jonathan Edwards*. Volume 6, edited by Paul Ramsey. New Haven: Yale University Press, 1980 [1714].

Edwards, Anthony T. "Achilles in the Underworld: *Iliad, Odyssey*, and *Aethiopis*." *Greek, Roman, and Byzantine Studies* 26 (1985): 215–27.

Edwards, M. J. "Porphyry's 'Cave of the Nymphs' and the Gnostic Controversy." *Hermes* 124.1 (1996): 88–100.

Edwards, M.J., trans. *Neoplatonic Saints: The Lives of Plotinus and Proclus by Their Students*. Liverpool: Liverpool University Press, 2000.

Eliot, C.W., ed. *English Poetry I: From Chaucer to Gray*. Harvard Classics, volume 40. Whitefish, Montana: Kessinger Publishing, 2004 [1910].

Eliot, T.S. *Four Quartets*. Edited by Valerie Eliot. London: Faber and Faber, 1979 [1944].

Elliott, J.K., ed. *The Apocryphal New Testament*. Oxford: Clarendon Press, 2005 [revised version of M.R. James's 1924 translation and edition].

Eusebius of Caesarea. *Praeparatio Evangelica*. Translated by E.H. Gifford. Oxford: Clarendon Press, 1903.

Faulkner, R.O. *The Ancient Egyptian Pyramid Texts*. Oxford: Oxford University Press, 1969.

Feldman, Louis H. "The Portrayal of Phinehas by Philo, Pseudo-Philo, and Josephus." In *Jewish Quarterly Review* 92 (2002): 315–45.

Ficino, Marsilio. *Platonic Theology*. Volume 4: Books XII–XIV. Cambridge MA/London: The I Tatti Renaissance Library/Harvard University Press, 2004.

Finamore, John. *Iamblichus and the Theory of the Vehicle of the Soul*. American Philological Association. Chicago: Scholars Press, 1985.

Fishbane, Michael. *Biblical Myth and Rabbinic Mythmaking*. Oxford: Oxford University Press, 2003.

Foltz, Bruce V. *The Noetics of Nature: Environmental Philosophy and the Holy Beauty of the Visible*. New York: Fordham University Press, 2013.

Ford, Andrew. *The Origins of Criticism: Literary Culture and Poetic Theory in Classical Greece*. Princeton: Princeton University Press, 2002.

Fowden, Garth. *The Egyptian Hermes: A Historical Approach to the Late Pagan Mind*. Cambridge: Cambridge University Press, 1986.

Fowler, D.H. *The Mathematics of Plato's Academy: A New Reconstruction*. Oxford: Clarendon Press, 1999 [1987].

Frankfort, Henri, John A. Wilson, and Thorkild Jacobsen. *Before Philosophy: The Intellectual Adventure of Ancient Man*. Harmondsworth: Penguin, 1949 [1946].
Gammage, Bill. *The Biggest Estate on Earth: How Aborigines Made Australia*. Sydney: Allen and Unwin, 2011.
Gandhi, Ramchandra. *Sita's Kitchen: Testimony of Faith and Inquiry*. New York: SUNY Press, 1992.
Gardner, Helen. ed. *New Oxford Book of English Verse*. Oxford: Clarendon Press, 1972.
Gaskin, J.C.A., ed. *Hume's Dialogues Concerning Natural Religion, and The Natural History of Religion*. New York: Oxford University Press, 2008 [1993].
Gibson, William. "The Gernsback Continuum" (1981). In idem, *Burning Chrome*, 37–50. London: Grafton Books, 1988.
Gilhus, Ingvild Saelid. *Animals, Gods and Humans: Changing Attitudes to Animals in Greek, Roman and Early Christian Ideas*. London: Routledge, 2006.
Gill, Christopher. "Plato's Atlantis Story and the Birth of Fiction." *Philosophy and Literature* 3.1 (1979): 64–78.
Gould, Stephen Jay. *Wonderful Life: The Burgess Shale and the History of Nature*. London: Vintage Books, 2000 [1990].
Graeber, David and David Wengrow. *The Dawn of Everything: A New History of Humanity*. London: Allen Lane, 2021.
Grant, Robert M. *Gods and the One God*. Philadelphia: Westminster Press, 1986.
Graves, Robert. *The White Goddess*. Edited by Grevel Lindop. London: Faber, 1999 [1948].
Greene, Mott T. *Natural Knowledge in Preclassical Antiquity*. Baltimore: Johns Hopkins University Press, 1991.
Gregory of Nyssa *The Life of Moses*. Translated by Abraham J. Malherbe and Everett Ferguson. New Jersey: Paulist Press, 1978.
Gregory the Great. *Morals on the Book of Job*. Oxford: John Henry Parker, 1844.
Griffith, R. Drew. "Sailing to Elysium: Menelaus' Afterlife (*Odyssey* 4.561–569) and Egyptian Religion." *Phoenix* 55 (2001): 213–43.
Gruen, Erich S. *Rethinking the Other in Antiquity*. New Jersey: Princeton University Press, 2011.
Guthrie, W.K. *The Greeks and their Gods*. London: Methuen, 1950.
Hacking, Ian. *Rewriting the Soul: Multiple Personality and the Sciences of Memory*. Princeton: Princeton University Press, 1995.
Hadot, Pierre. "Ouranos, Kronos and Zeus in Plotinus's Treatise against the Gnostics." In *Neoplatonism and Early Christian Thought: Essays in Honour of A.H. Armstrong*, edited by H.J. Blumenthal and R.A. Markus, 124–52. London: Variorum, 1981.
Halpern, Paul. *The Quantum Labyrinth: How Richard Feynman and John Wheeler Revolutionized Time and Reality*. New York: Basic Books, 2018.
Halsberghe, Gaston H. *The Cult of Sol Invictus*. Leiden: Brill, 1972.

Hanegraaff, Wouter J. *Hermetic Spirituality and the Historical Imagination: Altered States of Knowledge in Late Antiquity.* Cambridge: Cambridge University Press, 2022.

Harré, Rom. *Personal Being: A Theory for Individual Psychology.* Cambridge, MA: Harvard University Press, 1984.

Hart, David Bentley. *Tradition and Apocalypse: An Essay on the Future of Christian Belief.* Grand Rapids: Baker, 2022.

Hawking, Stephen W. *A Brief History of Time.* London: Bantam, 1988.

Hawking, Stephen W. and Thomas Hertog. "Populating the Landscape: A Top-down Approach." *Physical Review D* 73, 123527 (2006). https://journals.aps.org/prd/pdf/10.1103/PhysRevD.73.123527.

Hawking, Stephen W. and Leonard Mlodinow. *The Grand Design.* London: Bantam Press, 2010.

Heath, John. "Blood for the Dead: Homeric Ghosts Speak Up." *Hermes* 133.4 (2005): 389–400.

Heath, Thomas. *Aristarchus of Samos, the Ancient Copernicus: A History of Greek Astronomy to Aristarchus, Together with Aristarchus's Treatise on the Sizes and Distances of the Sun and Moon.* Cambridge: Cambridge University Press, 2013.

Heinlein, Robert. *Orphans of the Sky.* New York: Baen Books, 2001 [1963].

Helle, Sophus. *Gilgamesh: A New Translation of the Ancient Epic.* New Haven: Yale University Press, 2021.

Herodotus of Rhodes. *Histories.* Translated by Aubrey de Selincourt. Edited by John Marincola. London: Penguin, 2003 [1954].

Heschel, Abraham Joshua. *God in Search of Man.* New York: Harper and Row, 1966.

Hesiod. *The Poems of Hesiod: Theogony, Works and Days, and The Shield of Herakles.* Translated by Barry B. Powell. Berkeley: University of California Press, 2017.

Hillman, James. *The Dream and the Underworld.* New York: Harper, 1979.

Hornung, Erik. *Conceptions of God in Ancient Egypt: The One and the Many.* Translated by John Baines. New York: Cornell University Press, 1982 [1971].

Hoyle, Fred. *The Black Cloud.* New York: Harper, 1957.

Hudry, Françoise, ed. *Liber Viginti Quattuor Philosophorum.* Paris: J. Vrin, 2009.

Hutton, F.W. *Darwinism and Lamarkism.* London: Duckworth, 1899.

Iamblichus of Chalcis. *Letters: Writings from the Greco-Roman World.* Translated by John M. Dillon and Wolfgang Pelleichtner. Atlanta: Society of Biblical Literature, 2009.

Jacobsen, Thorkild. *The Treasures of Darkness: A History of Mesopotamian Religion.* New Haven: Yale University Press, 1978.

Jaeger, Werner. *Aristotle: Fundamentals of the History of His Development.* Translated by Richard Robinson. Oxford: Clarendon Press, 1962 [1934].

Jaki, Stanley. *Science and Creation: From Eternal Cycles to an Oscillating Universe.* Edinburgh: Scottish Academic Press, 1974.
James, William. "Rationality, Activity and Faith." *Princeton Review* 2 (1882): 58–86. Reprinted as part of "The Sentiment of Rationality" in idem, *The Will to Believe,* 63–110. New York: Longmans, Green and Co., 1896.
———. *Pragmatism.* London: Longmans, Green, 1907.
———. *The Varieties of Religious Experience: A Study in Human Nature.* New York: Longmans, Green and Co., 1917.
Janowitz, Naomi. *Icons of Power: Ritual Practices in Late Antiquity.* University Park, PA: Pennsylvania State University Press, 2002.
Johnston, Sarah Iles. "Animating Statues: A Case Study in Ritual." *Arethusa* 41.3 (2008): 445–77.
Joshi, S.T. *A Subtler Magick: The Writings and Philosophy of H. P. Lovecraft.* New York: Hippocampus Press, 2016.
Julian. *Works.* Translated by W.C. Wright. London: Heinemann, Loeb Classical Library, 1913.
Kadowaki, J.K. *Zen and the Bible.* Translated by J. Rieck. London: Routledge and Kegan Paul, 1980.
Kaiser, D. "History: Shut Up and Calculate!" *Nature* 505 (2014): 153–55.
Kant, Immanuel. *Critique of Practical Reason.* Translated by Lewis White Beck. New York: Bobbs-Merrill, 1956.
Karhausen, Lucien. *The Bleeding of Mozart: A Medical Glance on His Life, Illness and Personality.* Dartford: Xlibris, 2011.
Kelly, Emily Williams, ed. *Science, the Self, and Survival after Death: Selected Writings of Ian Stevenson.* Blue Ridge Summit: Rowman and Littlefield Publishers, 2012.
Keyes, Daniel. *The Minds of Billy Milligan.* New York: Random House, 1981.
Kidd, I.G. *Poseidonius. Volume 3: Translation of the Fragments.* Cambridge: Cambridge University Press, 1999.
Kingsley, Peter. *Ancient Philosophy, Mystery and Magic: Empedocles and the Pythagorean Tradition.* Oxford: Clarendon Press, 1995.
———. *A Story Waiting to Pierce You: Mongolia, Tibet and the Destiny of the Western World.* Salisbury: Golden Sufi Centre, 2010.
———. *Reality.* London: Catafalque Press, 2020.
Kipling, Rudyard. *Complete Verse.* London: Hodder and Stoughton, 1940.
Klibansky, R., E. Panofsky, and F. Saxl. *Saturn and Melancholy.* Edinburgh: Nelson, 1964.
Kragh, Helge. "Big Bang: The Etymology of a Name." *Astronomy and Geophysics* 54.2 (2013): 2.28–2.30. https://doi.org/10.1093/astrogeo/att035.
Krauss, Lawrence M. *A Universe from Nothing: Why There Is Something Rather Than Nothing.* London: Simon and Schuster, 2012.
Kuzminski, Adrian. *Pyrrhonism: How the Ancient Greeks Reinvented Buddhism.* Plymouth: Lexington Books, 2008.
Lafferty, R.A. *Past Master.* New York: Ace Books, 1968.

Bibliography

Laks, André and Glenn W. Most. *Early Greek Philosophy. Volume 2: Beginnings and Early Ionian Thinkers, Part 1.* Cambridge, MA: Loeb Classical Library, Harvard University Press, 2016.
Lambert, W.G. *Babylonian Creation Myths.* Winona Lake, Indiana: Eisenbrauns, 2013.
———. *Babylonian Wisdom Literature.* Oxford: Clarendon Press, 1960.
Lamberton, Robert. *Homer the Theologian: Neoplatonist Allegorical Reading and the Growth of the Epic Tradition.* Los Angeles: University of California Press, 1989.
Larson, Jennifer. *Greek Nymphs: Myth, Cult, Lore.* New York: Oxford University Press, 2001.
Lasky, Richard. "The Psychoanalytic Treatment of a Case of Multiple Personality." *Psychoanalytic Review* 65 (1978): 355–80.
Layton, Bentley, ed. *The Gnostic Scriptures.* London: SCM Press, 1987.
Lehrer, Keith. "Why Not Scepticism?" *The Philosophical Forum* 5 (1971): 289–98. Reprinted in *The Theory of Knowledge: Classical and Contemporary Readings*, third edition, edited by Louis Pojman, 56–63. Belmont: Wadsworth, 2003.
Lem, Stanislaw. "The New Cosmology" (1971). In *A Perfect Vacuum*, ed. Stanislaw Lem and M. Kandel, 197–227. Evanston, Illinois: Northwestern University Press, 1993.
———. *Summa Technologiae.* Translated by Joanna Zylinska. Minneapolis: University of Minnesota Press, 2013 [1964].
Leslie, John. *The End of the World: The Science and Ethics of Human Extinction.* London: Routledge, 1996.
Levenson, Jon D. *Creation and the Persistence of Evil.* New Jersey: Princeton University Press, 1994.
Lewis, C.S. *The Abolition of Man.* London: Bles, 1943.
———. *The Discarded Image: An introduction to Medieval and Renaissance Literature.* Cambridge: Cambridge University Press, 1964.
———. *The Four Loves.* London: Bles, 1960.
———. *That Hideous Strength: A Modern Fairy-tale for Grown-ups.* London: Bodley Head, 1945.
———. *Letters to Malcolm, Chiefly on Prayer.* London: HarperCollins, 2020 [1964].
———. *Of Other Worlds.* London: Bles, 1966.
———. *Out of the Silent Planet.* London: Pan, 1952 [1938].
———. *Poems.* Edited by Walter Hooper. New York: Harcourt, Brace and World, 1964.
———. *The Silver Chair.* London: Bles, 1953.
Liebeschuetz, J.W.W.G. *Continuity and Change in Roman Religion.* Oxford: Clarendon Press, 1979.
Liu, Cixin. *The Three-Body Problem.* Translated by Ken Liu. London: Head of Zeus, 2014.

Loeb, Avi. *Extraterrestrial: The First Sign of Intelligent Life beyond Earth*. London: John Murray, 2021.
Long, A.A. and D.N. Sedley, eds. *The Hellenistic Philosophers*. Cambridge: Cambridge University Press, 1987.
Louth, Andrew. *Denys the Areopagite*. London: Continuum, 1989.
Lovecraft, H.P. *The Dreams in the Witch House and Other Weird Stories*. Edited by S.T. Joshi London: Penguin, 2005.
———. *Fungi from Yuggoth*. Edited by David E. Schultz. Illustrated by Jason C. Eckhardt. New York, NY: Hippocampus Press, 2017.
———. *Selected Letters V: 1934-37*. Edited by August Derleth and James Turner. Sauk City, Wisconsin: Arkham House, 1971.
———. *The Thing on the Doorstep and Other Weird Stories*. Edited by S.T. Joshi. London: Penguin, 2002.
Maccoby, Hyam. *The Philosophy of the Talmud*. London: Routledge, 2002.
MacCoull, L.S.B. "Plotinus the Egyptian?" *Mnemosyne* [4th series] 52 (1999): 330-33.
MacCulloch, Diarmaid. *A History of Christianity: The First Three Thousand Years*. London: Penguin, 2009.
MacDonald, George. *Unspoken Sermons, Series I, II and III*. Sioux Falls, South Dakota: Greenwood Publications, 2011 [1867, 1885, 1889].
MacIntyre, Alasdair. "Relativism, Power and Philosophy." *Proceedings and Addresses of the American Philosophical Association* 59.1 (1985): 5–22.
Mack, Katie. *The End of Everything (Astrophysically Speaking)*. London: Penguin, 2020.
MacLeod, Jeffrey J. and Anna Smol. "A Single Leaf: Tolkien's Visual Art and Fantasy." *Mythlore: A Journal of J.R.R. Tolkien, C.S. Lewis, Charles Williams, and Mythopoeic Literature* 27.1 (2008): 105-26.
Macrobius. *Commentary on the Dream of Scipio*. Translated by William Harris Stahl. New York and London: Columbia University Press, 1952.
Mahé, Jean-Pierre and Marvin Meyer. "Discourse on the Eighth and Ninth." In *The Nag Hammadi Scriptures: The Revised and Updated Translation of Sacred Gnostic Texts*, edited by Marvin Meyer, 409-18. New York: HarperCollins, 2007.
Maisel, Richard, David Epston, and Alisa Borden. *Biting the Hand That Starves You: Inspiring Resistance to Anorexia/Bulimia*. New York: W.W. Norton and Co, 2004.
Malin, Shimon. *Nature Loves to Hide*. New York: Oxford University Press, 2001.
Marx, Karl. "A Contribution to the Critique of Hegel's *Philosophy of Right*: Introduction." In *Marx: Early Political Writings*, edited by J. O'Malley, 57–70. Cambridge: Cambridge University Press, 1994.
Mathew, Gervase. *Byzantine Aesthetics*. London: John Murray, 1973.
Maycock, Alan., ed. *The Man Who Was Orthodox: A Selection from the Uncollected Writings of G.K. Chesterton*. London: Dobson, 1963.

Mead, G.R.S., trans. *Pistis Sophia: The Gnostic Tradition of Mary Magdalene, Jesus, and His Disciples*. London: Watkins, 1921.
Mendel, Arthur. "Spengler's Quarrel with the Methods of Music History." *The Musical Quarterly* 20.2 (1934): 131–71.
Merchant, Jo. "Ancient Astronomy: Mechanical Inspiration." *Nature* 468 (2010): 496–98.
——. *Decoding the Heavens: Solving the Mystery of the World's First Computer*. London: Windmill Books, 2009.
Mersini-Houghton, Laura. *Before the Big Bang: The Origin of our Universe from the Multiverse*. London: Bodley Head, 2022.
Meyer, Marvin. *The Unknown Sayings of Jesus*. Boston: Shambala, 1998.
Milne, A.A. *The House at Pooh Corner*. London: Egmont, 2016 [1928].
Minucius Felix, "Octavius." In the Loeb Classical Library No. 250, together with Tertullian's *Apology* and *De spectaculis*. Translated by Gerald H. Rendall. Cambridge, MA: Harvard University Press, 1931.
Montaigne, Michel de. *Apology for Raymond Sebond*. Translated by Roger Ariew and Marjorie Grene. Indianapolis: Hackett, 2003.
Moore, Ken. "Plato's Puppets of the Gods: Representing the Magical, the Mystical and the Metaphysical." *Arion: A Journal of Humanities and the Classics* 22.2 (2014): 37–72.
Morenz, Siegfried. *Egyptian Religion*. Translated by Ann E. Keep. New York: Cornell University Press, 1973 [1960].
Morgenstern, Julian. "On Gilgameš-Epic XI, 274–320. A Contribution to the Study of the Role of the Serpent in Semitic Mythology." *Zeitschrift für Assyriologie und Vorderasiatische Archäologie* 29.3–4 (1915): 284–300.
Muller, Richard A. *Nemesis: The Death Star—Story of a Scientific Revolution*. London: Heinemann, 1989.
Murray, C. D. and S.F. Dermott. *Solar System Dynamics*. Cambridge: Cambridge University Press, 1999.
Murray, Les. *Killing the Black Dog: A Memoir of Depression*. Collingwood, Australia: Schwartz Publishing Ltd., 2015 [2009].
Naddaf, Gerard. "Allegory and the Origins of Philosophy." In *Logos and Mythos: Philosophical Essays on Greek Literature*, edited by W. Wians, 99–131. Albany: SUNY Press, 2009.
Naess, Arne. *Scepticism*. London: Routledge and Kegan Paul, 1968.
Nagel, Thomas. "What Is It Like to Be a Bat?" *Philosophical Review* 83 (1974): 435–50.
Natali, Carlo. *Aristotle: His Life and School*. Edited by D.S. Hutchinson. Princeton, NJ: Princeton University Press, 2013.
Naydler, Jeremy. "Plato, Shamanism and Ancient Egypt." *Temenos Academy Review* 9 (2006): 67–92.
Neugebauer, Otto. "The Alleged Babylonian Discovery of the Precession of the Equinoxes." *Journal of the American Oriental Society* 70 (1950): 1–8.

Newman, John Henry. *The Grammar of Assent*. London: Burns, Oates and Co., 1870.
Norris, Ray P. and Norris, Barnaby R.M. "Why Are There Seven Sisters?" In *Advancing Cultural Astronomy*, edited by E. Boutsikas, S.C. McCluskey, and J. Steele, 223-36. Cham: Springer, 2021.
North, Claire. *The First Fifteen Lives of Harry August*. London: Orbit, 2014.
Nunn, Patrick D. and Nicholas J. Reid. "Aboriginal Memories of Inundation of the Australian Coast Dating from More than 7000 Years Ago." *Australian Geographer*, 47:1 (2016): 11-47.
O'Daly, Gerard. *Augustine's Philosophy of Mind*. London: Duckworth, 1987.
Ockinga, Boyo G. "The Memphite Theology — Its Purpose and Date." In *Egyptian Culture and Society: Studies in Honour of Naguib Kanawati*, ed. Alexandra Woods, Ann McFarlane, and Susanne Binder, 2:99-117. Cairo: Conseil Suprême des Antiquités, 2010.
O'Flaherty, Wendy Doniger. *Dreams, Illusions and Other Realities*. Chicago: Chicago University Press, 1984.
Origen. *Contra Celsum*. Translated by Henry Chadwick. Cambridge: Cambridge University Press, 1980.
Otto, W.F. *The Homeric Gods*. Translated by M. Hadas. London: Thames and Hudson, 1954.
Ouspensky, P.D. *Strange Life of Ivan Osokin*. London: Stourton Press, 1947.
Palamas, Gregory. *The 150 Chapters*. Translated by Robert E. Sinkewicz. Toronto: Pontifical Institute of Mediaeval Studies, 1988.
Palmer, G.E.H., P. Sherrard, and Kallistos Ware, eds. *The Philokalia*, volume 4. London: Faber, 1995.
Panofsky, E., ed. *Abbot Suger on the Abbey Church of St.-Denis*. New Jersey: Princeton University Press, 1979 [1946].
Papaioannou, Stratis. *Michael Psellus: Rhetoric and Authorship in Byzantium*. Cambridge: Cambridge University Press, 2013.
Pareto, Vilfredo. *The Mind and Society*. Edited by Arthur Livingston. Translated by Andrew Bongiorno, Arthur Livingston, and James Harvey Rogers. New York: Harcourt, Brace and Co., 1935.
Parker, Theodore. *Ten Sermons of Religion*. Boston: Crosby, Nichols and Company, 1853.
Paton, W.R., trans. *Greek Anthology*, Volume 1, Book 1: Christian Epigrams; Book 2: Description of the Statues in the Gymnasium of Zeuxippus; Book 3: Epigrams in the Temple of Apollonis at Cyzicus; Book 4: Prefaces to the Various Anthologies; Book 5: Erotic Epigrams. Revised by Michael A. Tueller. Loeb Classical Library 67. Cambridge, MA: Harvard University Press, 2014.
———, trans. *Greek Anthology*, Volume 5, Book 10: The Hortatory and Admonitory Epigrams; Book 11: The Convivial and Satirical Epigrams; Book 12: Strato's *Musa Puerilis*. Loeb Classical Library 86. Cambridge, MA: Harvard University Press, 1918.

Bibliography

Patrides, C.A., ed. *The Cambridge Platonists*. Cambridge: Cambridge University Press, 1980 [1969].
Peccorini, Francisco L. "Divinity and Immortality in Aristotle: A 'De-Mythologized Myth'?" *The Thomist: A Speculative Quarterly Review* 43 (1979): 217–56.
Pendergrast, Mark. *Mirror Mirror: A History of the Human Love Affair with Reflection*. New York: Basic Books, 2003.
Philo of Alexandria. *Collected Works*. Translated by F. H. Colson, G. H. Whitaker, et al. London: Loeb Classical Library, Heinemann, 1929.
Philostratus. *Apollonius of Tyana*. Volumes 1–3. Edited and translated by Christopher P. Jones. Loeb Classical Library 16. Cambridge, MA: Harvard University Press, 2005–2006.
Pike, Nelson. *Mystic Union: An Essay in the Phenomenology of Mysticism*. New York: Cornell University Press, 1992.
Plato. *The Republic*. Translated by Robin Waterfield. Oxford: Oxford University Press, 1993.
Plotinus. *Enneads*. Translated by A.H. Armstrong. Cambridge, MA: Loeb Classical Library, Harvard University Press, 1966–1988.
Plutarch. *Lives*. Translated by Bernadotte Perrin. London: Loeb Classical Library, William Heinemann Ltd., 1914.
———. *Moralia*, Volume V: *Isis and Osiris; The E at Delphi; The Oracles at Delphi; The Obsolescence of Oracles*. Translated by Frank Babbitt. Cambridge, MA: Loeb Classical Library, Harvard University Press, 1936.
———. *Moralia*. Translated by E.L. Minor, F.H. Sandbach and W.C. Helmbold. London: Loeb Classical Library, William Heinemann Ltd., 1961.
Polansky, R. *Aristotle's "De Anima."* Cambridge: Cambridge University Press, 2007.
Pratchett, Terry. *Hogfather*. London: Corgi, 2013 [1996].
Pressel, Esther. "Negative Spirit Possession in Experienced Brazilian Spirit Mediums." In *Case Studies in Spirit Possession*, edited by V. Crapanzano and V. Garrison. Hoboken, NJ: John Wiley and Sons. 1977.
Prestige, G.L. *God in Patristic Thought*. London: SPCK, 1952.
Prince, M. *The Dissociation of a Personality*. New York: Longmans, Greene and Co., 1908.
Pritchard, James B., ed. *Ancient Near Eastern Texts Relating to the Old Testament*. Third edition. New Jersey: Princeton University Press, 1969.
Proclus, *Commentary on Plato's Timaeus [In Tim.]*, Volume 2. Translated by David T. Runia and Michael Share. Cambridge: Cambridge University Press, 2008.
———. *The Elements of Theology*. Edited by E.R. Dodds. Oxford: Clarendon Press, 1963.
Pseudo-Dionysius. *Complete Works*. Translated by Colm Luibheid and Paul Rorem. London: SPCK, 1987.

Ptolemy. *Almagest*. Second edition. Translated by G.J. Toomer. New Jersey: Princeton University Press 1998.
Purves, Libby. *Holy Smoke: Religion and Roots*. London: Hodder and Stoughton, 1998.
Quirke, Stephen. *Exploring Religion in Ancient Egypt*. Chichester: Wiley Blackwell, 2015.
Radhakrishnan, S. and C. Moore, eds. *Sourcebook of Indian Philosophy*. New Jersey: Princeton University Press, 1957.
Raine, Kathleen. *Blake and the New Age*. London: Routledge, 2011.
Ramsey, F.P. "Epilogue" [1925]. In *Philosophical Papers*, edited by D.H. Mellor, 245–50. Cambridge: Cambridge University Press, 1990.
Ransome, Arthur. *Winter Holiday*. London: Jonathan Cape, 1933.
Rappe, Sara. *Reading Neoplatonism: Non-discursive Thinking in the Texts of Plotinus, Proclus, and Damascius*. Cambridge: Cambridge University Press, 2000.
Raup, D.M. and J.J. Sepkoski. "Periodicity of Extinctions in the Geologic Past." *Proceedings of the National Academy of Sciences* 1984.81 (3): 801–5.
Reckford, K. J. *Aristophanes' Old-and-New Comedy*. Volume 1: *Six Essays in Perspective*. Chapel Hill, NC: University of North Carolina Press, 1987.
Rhys-Davies, Thomas W. *Milinda Panha*. Augsburg: Jazzybee Verlag, 2017.
Rist, J.M. *Plotinus: The Road to Reality*. Cambridge: Cambridge University Press, 1967.
Ritchie, D.G. *Darwinism and Politics*. London: Swan Sonnenschein and Co., 1891.
Rochberg, Francesca. *The Heavenly Writing: Divination, Horoscopy, and Astronomy in Mesopotamian Culture*. Cambridge: Cambridge University Press, 2004.
Romer, John, ed. *The Egyptian Book of the Dead*. Collated and translated by E.A. Wallis-Budge in 1899. London: Penguin, 2008.
Rose, Valentin. *Aristoteles Pseudepigraphus*. Leipzig: Teubner, 1863.
Ross, Colin A. *Dissociative Identity Disorder: Diagnosis, Clinical Features and Treatment of Multiple Personality*. Second edition. Hoboken, NJ: John Wiley and Sons, 1996.
Ross, W.D., ed. *Works of Aristotle*. Volume 12: *Select Fragments*. London: Oxford University Press, 1952.
Rossi, Vincent. "Presence, Participation, Performance: The Remembrance of God in the Early Hesychast Fathers." In *Paths to the Heart: Sufism and the Christian East*, edited by James S. Cutsinger, 64–111. Bloomington, Indiana: World Wisdom Inc., 2004.
Rovelli, Carlo. *Anaximander: And the Nature of Science*. London: Allen Lane, 2023.
Rowland Smith, B.E. *Julian's Gods: Religion and Philosophy in the Thought and Action of Julian the Apostate*. London: Routledge, 1995.
Rubenstein, Mary-Jane. *Worlds Without End: The Many Lives of the Multiverse*. New York: Columbia University Press, 2014.

Russell, Eric Frank. *Sentinels from Space*. New York: Bouregy and Curl Inc., 1952.
Russell, Bertrand. *Mysticism and Logic*. London: Allen and Unwin, 1918.
Sabo, Theodore. "The Nous: A Globe of Faces." *Journal for Late Antique Religion and Culture* 9 (2015): 1–12.
Sacks, Oliver. *Anthropologist on Mars: Seven Paradoxical Tales*. New York: Alfred A. Knopf, 1995.
——. *Musicophilia: Tales of Music and the Brain*. Second edition. New York: Vintage Books, 2008.
Sallustius. *Concerning the Gods and the Universe*. Edited by Arthur Darby Nock. Cambridge: Cambridge University Press, 1926.
Sandmel, Samuel. "Philo's Environment and Philo's Exegesis." *Journal of Bible and Religion* 22.4 (1954): 248–53.
Santillana, Giorgio de and Hertha von Dechend. *Hamlet's Mill: An Essay Investigating the Origins of Human Knowledge and its Transmission Through Myth*. Boston: Nonpareil/Godine, 1969/1977.
Sayers, Dorothy L. *Unpopular Opinions: Twenty-one Essays*. London: Gollancz, 1946.
Schaefer, Jenni and Thom Rutledge. *Life without Ed: How One Woman Declared Independence from Her Eating Disorder and How You Can Too*. New York: McGraw Hill, 2004.
Scharf, Caleb. "Is Physical Law an Alien Intelligence? Alien Life Could Be So Advanced It Becomes Indistinguishable from Physics." *Nautilus Cosmos*, November 2016. http://cosmos.nautil.us/feature/55/is-physical-law-an-alien-intelligence.
Schibli, Hermann. *Pherekydes of Syros*. Oxford: Clarendon Press, 1990.
Schmidt, Gavin A. and Adam Frank. "The Silurian Hypothesis: Would It Be Possible to Detect an Industrial Civilization in the Geological Record?" *International Journal of Astrobiology*, 10 April 2018, doi: 10.1017/S1473550418000095.
Schultz, David E. and S. T. Joshi., eds. *Essential Solitude: The Letters of H. P. Lovecraft and August Derleth 1926–37*. New York: Hippocampus Press, 2013.
Schweizer, Andreas. *The Sungod's Journey through the Netherworld: Reading the Ancient Egyptian Amduat*. Edited by David Lorton. Foreword by Erik Hornung. Ithaca, NY: Cornell University Press, 2010 [1994].
Scott, Alan. *Origen and the Life of the Stars*. Oxford: Clarendon Press, 1991.
Segal, Alan F. *Life After Death: A History of the Afterlife*. New York: Doubleday, 2004.
Segev, Mor. *Aristotle on Religion*. Cambridge: Cambridge University Press, 2017.
Sextus Empiricus. *Against the Ethicists*. Translated by R.G. Bury. Loeb Classical Library. London: Heinemann, 1936.
——. *Outlines of Scepticism*. Translated by Julia Annas and Jonathan Barnes. Cambridge: Cambridge University Press, 1994.

Shelley, Percy Bysshe. *Poetical Works*. Edited by Mrs. Shelley. London: E. Moxon, 1839.
Sherwood, Polycarp. *The Earlier Ambigua of Saint Maximus the Confessor and his Refutation of Origenism*. Rome: Herder, 1955.
Shoval, Ilan. *King John's Delegation to the Almohad Court (1212): Medieval Interreligious Interactions and Modern Historiography*. Turnhout: Brepols, 2016.
Shuve, Karl. *The Song of Songs and the Fashioning of Identity in Early Latin Christianity*. Oxford: Oxford University Press, 2016.
Skinner, Martyn. *The Return of Arthur*. London: Chapman and Hall, 1966.
Slater, Philip E. *The Glory of Hera: Greek Mythology and the Greek Family*. New Jersey: Princeton University Press, 1968.
Smith, Logan Pearsall. *All Trivia*. London: Constable and Co., 1933.
Smolin, Lee. *The Life of the Cosmos*. Second edition. London: Phoenix, 1998.
Sorensen, Roy A. "Philosophical Implications of Logical Paradoxes." In *A Companion to Philosophical Logic*, edited by Dale Jacquette, 131–42. Oxford: Blackwell, 2002.
Spanos, Nicholas P. *Multiple Identities and False Memories: A Sociocognitive Perspective*. Washington: American Psychological Association, 1996.
Spengler, Oswald. *The Decline of the West*. Translated by Charles Francis Atkinson. Budapest: Arktos Media, 2021 [vol. 1, *Form and Actuality*, 1919; vol. 2, *Perspectives on World History*, 1922].
Sprat, Thomas. *History of the Royal Society*. Third edition. New York: Elibron, 2005 [1722].
Sprigge, Timothy. "Final Causes." *Aristotelian Society Supplementary Volume* 45 (1971): 149–70.
Stamatellos, Giannis. "Plotinus on Transmigration: A Reconsideration." *Journal of Ancient Philosophy* 7 (2013): 49–64.
Stanley, Colin, ed. *Proceedings of the Colin Wilson Conference*. Cambridge: Cambridge Scholars, 2017.
Stapledon, Olaf. *Darkness and Light*. London: Methuen, 1942.
———. *Last and First Men*. London: Methuen, 1930.
———. *Last Men in London*. London: Methuen, 1934.
———. *The Opening of the Eyes*. Edited by Agnes Stapledon. London: Methuen, 1954.
———. *Star Maker*. London: Methuen, 1937.
Stern, Philip D. *The Biblical Herem: A Window on Israel's Religious Experience*. Atlanta: Scholars Press, 1991.
Stevenson, Ian. *Twenty Cases Suggestive of Reincarnation*. Second revised edition. Charlottesville: University Press of Virginia, 1974 [1966].
Stoneman, Richard. *Palmyra and Its Empire*. Ann Arbor: University of Michigan Press, 1992.
Strickland, Edward. "John Dennis and Blake's Guinea Sun." *Blake* 14.1 (1980): 36.

Sturluson, Snorri. *The Prose Edda*. Translated by Arthur Gilchrist Brodeur. New York: American-Scandinavian Foundation, 1916.
Swerdlow, N.M. *The Babylonian Theory of the Planets*. Princeton, NJ: Princeton University Press, 1998.
Tate, J. "On the History of Allegorism." *Classical Quarterly* 28 (1934): 105–14.
Taubes, Jacob. *The Political Theology of Paul*. Redwood City, CA: Stanford University Press, 2004.
Taylor, Thomas, et al. *Select Works of Porphyry: Containing His Four Books on Abstinence from Animal Food; His Treatise on the Homeric Cave of the Nymphs; and His Auxiliaries to the Perception of Intelligible Natures*. London: T. Rodd, 1823.
Tegmark, Max. *Our Mathematical Universe: My Quest for the Ultimate Nature of Reality*. London: Penguin, 2014.
Tehrani, Jamshid J. "Descent with Imagination: Oral Traditions as Evolutionary Lineages." In *Evolutionary Perspectives on Imaginative Culture*, edited by J. Carroll, M. Clasen, and E. Jonsson, 273–89. Cham: Springer, 2020.
Tester, S.J. *A History of Western Astrology*. Woodbridge: Boydell Press, 1997.
Thompson, Francis. *Works of Francis Thompson*. Edited by Wilfrid Meynell. London: Burns and Oates, 1913.
Tilby, Angela. *The Seven Deadly Sins: Their Origin in the Teaching of Evagrius the Hermit*. London: SPCK, 2009.
Tipler, Frank J. *The Physics of Immortality: Modern Cosmology, God and the Resurrection*. New York: Doubleday, 1994.
Tolkien, J.R.R. *Letters*. Edited by Humphrey Carpenter. London: Allen and Unwin, 1981.
———. *The Lord of the Rings*. Second edition. London: Allen and Unwin, 1966.
———. *The Monsters and the Critics*. Edited by Christopher Tolkien. London: HarperCollins, 2006 [1983].
———. *Tree and Leaf*. Edited by Christopher Tolkien. London: HarperCollins, 2001 [1964].
Toynbee, Arnold. *A Study of History*. Volume 10. Oxford: Oxford University Press, 1954.
Trzaskoma, Stephen, Stephen Brunet, R. Scott Smith, Stephen Brunet, Thomas G Palaima, R. Scott Smith, and Stephen Trzaskoma. *Anthology of Classical Myth: Primary Sources in Translation*. Indianapolis, IN: Hackett Publishing, 2004.
Tyldesley, Joyce. *The Penguin Book of Myths and Legends of Ancient Egypt*. London: Penguin Books, 2010.
Ulansey, David. *The Origins of the Mithraic Mysteries: Cosmology and Salvation in the Ancient World*. New York: Oxford University Press, 1991.
Uzdavinys, Algis. "Animation of Statues in Ancient Civilizations and Neoplatonism." In *Late Antique Epistemology: Other Ways to Truth*, edited by Panayiota Vassilopoulou and Stephen R.L. Clark, 118–40. Basingstoke: Palgrave Macmillan, 2009.

———. *Ascent to Heaven in Islamic and Jewish Mysticism*. London: Matheson Trust, 2011.

Van den Broek, Roelof. *Gnostic Religion in Antiquity*. Cambridge: Cambridge University Press, 2013.

Van Dusen, Wilson. *The Presence of Other Worlds: The Psychological/spiritual Findings of Swedenborg*. West Chester, PA: Swedenborg Foundation Publishers, 2004 [1971].

Vaughan, Henry. *Silex Scintillans*. Charleston: Bibliobazaar, 2008 [1650].

Von Balthasar, Hans Urs. *Cosmic Liturgy: The Universe according to Maximus the Confessor*. Translated by A.M. Allchin. San Francisco: Ignatius Press, 2003.

Von Rad, Gerhard. *Old Testament Theology. Volume One: The Theology of Israel's Historical Traditions*. Translated by D.M.G. Stalker. Introduced by Walter Brueggemann. Louisville, Kentucky: Westminster John Knox Press, 2001 [1967].

Waddell, Helen, trans. *Medieval Latin Lyrics*. Harmondsworth: Penguin, 1952 [1929].

Wagner, Jenny and Ron Brooks. *The Bunyip of Berkeley's Creek*. London: Puffin, 1975.

Wakoff, Michael. "Awaiting the Sun: A Plotinian Form of Contemplative Prayer." In *Platonic Theories of Prayer*, edited by Andrei Timotin and John Dillon, 73–87. Leiden: Brill, 2015.

Wallis-Budge, E.A. *The Egyptian Book of the Dead*. Edited by John Romer. London: Penguin, 2008 [1809].

Wardlaw Scott, David. *Terra Firma: The Earth not a Planet*. London: Simpkin, Marshall and Co., 1901.

Waterfield, Robin. *The First Philosophers: The Presocratics and Sophists*. Oxford: Oxford University Press, 2000.

Watts, Peter. *Blindsight*. New York: Tor Books, 2006.

Wells, H.G. *The World Set Free*. Frankfurt: Outlook, 2018 [1914].

Whitman, Cedric H. "Hera's Anvils." *Harvard Studies in Classical Philology* 74 (1970): 37–42.

Wigner, E.P. "The Unreasonable Effectiveness of Mathematics in the Natural Sciences." *Communications on Pure and Applied Mathematics* 13 (1960): 1–14.

Williams, Charles. *The Chapel of the Thorn: A Dramatic Poem*. Edited by Sørina Higgins. Berkeley, CA: Apocryphile Press, 2014.

Williams, G.F. "Babylon is Fallen: The Story of a North American Hymn." *The Hymn* 44 (April 1993): 31–35.

Wilson, Colin. *The Mind Parasites*. London: Barker, 1967.

———. *Religion and the Rebel*. London: Gollancz, 1957.

Wilson, Jake. "Hebrew Cosmology—A Plea for a Geocentric Terrestrial Plane." www.researchgate.net/publication/336512368_HEBREW_COSMOLOGY_-_A_PLEA_FOR_A_GEOCENTRIC_TERRESTRIAL_PLANE.

Wilson, Robert Anton. "My Debt to H. P. Lovecraft." *Crypt of Cthulhu* 12 (1983): 3-4, 16.
Wittgenstein, Ludwig von. *Tractatus Logico-Philosophicus*. Translated by D.F. Pears and Brian McGuinness. London: Routledge and Kegan Paul, 1971.
Woese, Carl. "A New Biology for a New Century." *Microbiology and Molecular Biology Reviews* 68.2 (2004): 173-86.
Wren-Lewis, John. "What I Believe." In *What I Believe*, ed. G. Unwin, 221-36. London: Allen and Unwin, 1966.
———. *What Shall We Tell the Children?* London: Constable: London, 1971.
Yannaras, Christos. *On the Absence and Unknowability of God: Heidegger and the Areopagite*. Translated by Andrew Louth. London: T. & T. Clark, 2005 [1986].
Yeats, W.B. *Collected Poems*. Edited by Cedric Watts. Ware, Herefordshire: Wordsworth, 2008.
Zimmer, H.R. *The King and the Corpse: Tales of the Soul's Conquest of Evil*. Edited by Joseph Campbell. Princeton: Princeton University Press, 1975 [1948].
———. *Myths and Symbols in Indian Art and Civilization*. Edited by Joseph Campbell. New York: Pantheon Books 1946.
———. *Philosophies of India*. Edited by Joseph Campbell. London: Routledge and Kegan Paul, 1967 [1952].
Zuntz, Günter. *Persephone: Three Essays on Religion and Thought in Magna Graecia*. Oxford: Clarendon Press, 1971.

INDEX

Abraham, 52, 111-13, 132, 198, 282-84
accidie, 264; see Depression
Achilles, 107, 125, 165, 238, 300, 303
Adam, James, 55, 297
Adam and Eve, 140-43
Agathias, 147
Akhenaten, 35, 192-98, 209; see 153-54
Al-Ghazali, 142, 165, 297
Allen, James P., 9-10, 21, 24-25, 34, 38, 92, 119, 193, 197, 297
Allione, Tsultrim, 102, 297
Allison, Ralph, 105-7, 297
Almond, Philip, 135, 297
Amun, 27, 36, 38, 81, 193
Amzallag, Nissim, 34, 187, 297
Anaxagoras, 21, 38, 243
Anaximander, 29, 312
angels, 6, 51, 69, 71-72, 98-99, 105, 109, 111, 147, 150, 152, 171, 263, 285, 293
animating statues, 40, 147, 306
Anscombe, G.E.M., 38, 297
Antikythera mechanism, 94; see Merchant
Apocryphal New Testament, 82, 217, 303
Apollo, 43, 55, 57, 64, 83, 86, 117-18, 134, 156, 167-68, 172, 185, 223, 235, 241
Apollodorus, 141, 224, 297
Apollonius of Tyana, 78, 96-97, 122-23, 134, 137, 171, 184, 210, 229, 234-35, 276, 282, 311
Apopis/Apophis, 22, 81, 124, 181
Apuleius, 194-95, 297
Aristarchus of Samos, 55, 305

Aristotle, ix, 10, 19, 26, 37-38, 46, 51-53, 71, 90, 98-99, 107, 110-11, 116, 142, 150, 156, 164, 170-71, 192, 209-10, 214-16, 225, 243, 297
Aristotle, *De Anima*, 150, 210, 215, 311
Aristotle, *De Motu Animalium*, 116
Aristotle, *De Partibus Animalium*, 46, 142
Aristotle, *Fragments*, 26, 192, 243, 312
Aristotle, *Generation of Animals*, 215
Aristotle, *Metaphysics*, ix, 10, 37-38, 51-52, 98, 111
Aristotle, *Nicomachean Ethics*, 37, 71, 90, 111, 164, 170, 215, 225, 243
Aristotle, *On Interpretation*, 156
Aristotle, *Politics*, 26, 170
Aristotle, *Posterior Analytics*, 214, 297
Aristotle, *Topics*, 107
Armstrong, A.H., ix, 40, 89, 189, 297, 301, 304, 311
Asclepius, 4, 42, 59, 78, 146-47, 149, 152-53, 168, 171, 301
Assmann, Jan, 1, 77, 86, 153, 187, 193, 195, 298
Athanasius, 5-6, 283, 298
atheists, 11-12, 15, 40, 82, 84-85, 175-77, 182, 195, 234, 253, 276, 296
Athena, 1, 83, 109, 165, 225, 235, 293
Atlantis, 20, 33, 208-9, 212, 220, 304
Atum, 21-22, 24-25, 27, 29, 33-35, 81, 139, 181-82, 196-97, 251
Augustine of Dacia, 17
Augustine of Hippo, 14, 24, 99-100, 119, 136, 142-44, 197, 298
Azize, Joseph, 78, 298

Index

Babylon, 43, 53, 56–57, 68, 73, 100, 129, 138, 198–99, 208, 267, 271–72, 307, 309, 315
Babylon is Fallen, 272, 316
Baker, Gideon, 232, 298
Barber & Barber, 17, 55, 57, 298
Barfield, Raymond, 98, 298
Barker, Andrew, 172, 298
Barton, John, 12, 298
Baumgarten, A.I., 28, 298
Beahrs, John O., 107, 298
Beard, Mary, 188, 298
Beguiling of Gylfi; see Sturluson
Behr, John, 285, 298
Benedict XVI, 175
Berkeley, George, 133, 207, 295, 298
Betjeman, John, 273, 288, 299
Big Bang, 21, 24–25, 30, 32, 35, 48, 127, 155, 157, 250, 306, 309
Billigheimer, Rachel, 187, 299
Blake, William, 74–75, 79, 122, 167, 185, 187, 189, 257, 299, 312, 314
Blish, James, 264, 299
Bloch, Ernst, 279, 299
Blue Cliff Record, 97
Boethius, 110, 162, 204, 268, 278, 299
Book of the Dead, 21–22, 24, 44, 209, 219, 245, 312, 316
Borges, Jorge Luis, 33, 251, 299
Bostrom, Nick, 250, 299
Boswell, James, 276, 299
Bourguignon, Erika, 103–4, 299
Boyle, Marjorie, 65, 299
Boys-Stones, George, 82, 299, 301
Brisson, Luc, 18, 98–99, 299
Brown, Christopher, 117, 299
Brown, David, 68, 299
Browning, Robert, 85, 286, 299
Brunner, John, 158, 299
Buber, Martin, 120, 184, 300; see 9
Buchan, John, 162–63, 300
Buddhism, 85, 191, 205, 208, 306
Bunyip, 19, 31, 316

Burgess, Jonathan, 238, 300
Burke, Edmund, 276, 300
Burkert, Walter, 36, 300
Burnyeat, Myles, 179, 247, 300, 302
Butcher, S.H., 170, 300
Butler, Samuel, 99, 300
butterflies, 243, 251
Buxton, Richard, 45, 148, 225, 229, 235–36, 310

Calderón de la Barca, 252, 300
Caliphate, 268–69
Card, Orson Scott, 158, 300
Carneades, 156
Carroll, Lewis, 170, 300
Caseau, Béatrice, 188, 300
catastrophes, 14, 19, 26–27, 45–50, 87, 124, 151–53, 262, 277; cf. 286
Catechism of the Catholic Church, 136–37
Cave of the Nymphs, 221, 223, 303, 315
Celsus, 15–16, 62; see Origen
changing the past, 157–58
Chaos, 27–29, 41, 100, 113, 124, 128–31, 181–82, 192, 202, 257, 273
Chesterton, G.K., 3–4, 11, 33–34, 86–87, 122, 144, 156, 160, 184, 230, 246–47, 252, 259, 266, 269–70, 274, 291–92, 300, 308
children, 27, 59, 80–81, 85, 91, 166, 171, 199, 201, 204, 210, 229, 276–78, 286
Chittick, William C., 11, 301
Christmas, 273, 276–78, 288
Chrysippus of Soli, 123, 136
Chrysostom, John, 137
Chuang Tzu, 240, 251, 301
Cicero, 74, 82, 136, 156, 236, 268
Ćirković, Milan, 30, 155, 263, 301
Clark, Stephen R.L., 17, 46, 58, 60, 85, 94, 98, 102, 133, 136, 159, 160, 174, 189, 208, 237, 240, 242, 250, 295–96

Coffin Texts, 22, 25, 44, 198
Collins, Adela Yarbro, 63, 301
Collins, John D, 199–200, 301
common sense, 36, 75, 100, 109, 157, 247, 265
Connell, Sophia, 215–16, 301
consciousness, hard problem, 7–8, 120; see 65, 109, 176–77, 182, 239
Copenhaver, 22, 39, 42, 55, 59, 61, 66–67, 78, 139, 152, 168, 171, 178, 252, 266, 290, 301
Corinthians (I) (Epistle), 245
Cornutus, 82, 280, 301
Corpus Hermeticum, 39, 139, 236; see Copenhaver
Coulter, James, 90, 301
Cox Miller, Patricia, 168, 301
Crabtree, Adam, 102–3, 301
Craig, William Lane, 26, 301
Crowley, John, 73, 301
Crum, John M.C., 86
Culianu, Ioan Petru, 241, 301
Cybele, 188
cycles, 24–25, 48, 51–60, 73, 81, 118, 203, 210, 306

daimones, 5–6, 105, 168, 243; see angels, demons
Dal Santo, Matthew, 69, 301
dancing, 34, 43, 55, 74, 85, 97, 228, 245, 258, 267
Dante Alighieri, 68–71, 224–25, 291, 301
Darnell & Darnell, 219, 301
Darwinism, 102, 165, 175, 214, 220, 230, 233, 255; see 210–11
Davies, John, 74
Davis, Whitney, 66, 301
Dawson, David, 12, 18, 82, 301
De Castro, Eduardo Viveiros, 120, 227, 302
Demetrius, 168
Democritus, 150, 239

demons, 6, 66–67, 69, 72, 76, 99–102, 105, 107, 109, 111, 124, 132, 134, 168, 200–201, 275, 289
Denis (saint), 42, 310; see Ps-Dionysius
Dennis, John, 39, 79, 302, 314
Denyer, Nicholas, 179, 302
depression, 37, 72, 165, 264, 276, 309
Descartes, René, 2, 161, 162, 292, 300, 302
Descola, Philippe, 118, 120, 302
Deuteronomy, 141, 201
Deutsch, David, 155, 302
Dillon, John, 167, 302
Dio Chrysostom, 43, 172, 232, 236, 302
Diodorus Siculus, 46–47, 280, 302
Diogenes Laertius, 38, 87, 90, 161, 166, 241–42
Dionysos, 34, 187, 238, 282
Dissociative Identity Disorder (DID), 102–7; see Multiple Personality Disorder
Donne, John, 45, 302
Downing, F. Gerard, 282, 302
Dream of Scipio, 74, 268, 308
Druon, Maurice, 56, 302
Dunbar, Robin, 144, 302
Dunsany (Lord), 219, 302
Durkheim, Emile, 177–78, 303
Dyson, Freeman, 233, 303

Ecclesiastes, 26, 209, 256
Ecclesiasticus, 69, 200
Edwards, Anthony, 238, 303
Edwards, Jonathan, 21–23, 181, 303
Edwards, Mark, 78, 221, 223, 238, 246
egoism, 105, 143, 261
Egyptian souls, 245
Eliot, C.W., 227, 303
Eliot, T.S., 40, 303

Index

Elysium, 238-39, 244, 304
Empedocles, 118, 240-42, 290-91
Enuma Elish, 28-29, 129-30, 139
Ephesians (Epistle), 281
Epicureans, 155, 208
eternity, 24, 47, 54, 87, 110, 156, 167, 203, 268
eucatastrophe, 286
Euripides, 85, 134, 278
Eusebius, 28, 77, 303
Evagrius of Pontus, 70, 72, 315
evolution, 128, 166, 175-76, 211, 220, 227, 229-30, 233, 248, 255, 279
Exodus, book of, 36, 201, 236, 279; see 140
Ezekiel, 8, 132

fairies/fairyland, 6, 16, 76, 217-27, 247
faith, 3-4, 13, 85, 133, 137, 160, 166, 174, 177-78, 189, 252, 274
father-beating, 27, 90-91, 114, 130, 190, 224, 274; see 266, 277
Faulkner, R.O., 287, 303
Feynman, Richard, 110, 157, 304
Finamore, John, 244, 303
Fishbane, Michael, 28, 119, 129, 140, 303
flat earth, 33, 75, 316
Flecker, James Elroy, 262
flood, 8-9, 14-15, 46, 140, 220, 270, 301
Foltz, Bruce V., 41, 303
Fowden, Garth, 27, 39, 61, 65-66, 168, 303
Fowler, D.H., 214, 303
Frankfort & Frankfort, 92, 277, 304
Friends (sitcom), 125

Galatians (Epistle), 144
Galileo Galilei, 73-74
Gammage, Bill, 20, 304

Gandhi, Ramchandra, 145, 304
Genesis, book of, 13-15, 52, 112, 119, 131, 135-44, 262, 284
Gilgamesh, 219-20, 305, 309
Gilhus, Ingvild, 234, 304
Gill, Christopher, 209, 304
Giordano Bruno, 73
Gould, Stephen Jay, 159, 304
Graeber & Wengrow, 47, 304
Grant, Robert, 280, 304
Graves, Robert, 56, 304
Greek Anthology, 147, 310
Gregory (Pope), 69-70, 304
Gregory of Nyssa, 189, 304
Griffith, R. Drew, 239, 304
Gruen, Erich S., 28, 304

Hacking, Ian, 103, 304
Hadot, Pierre, 91, 254
Hagia Sophia, 41
Halpern, Paul, 110, 304
Halsberghe, Gaston, 78, 304
Hanegraaff, Wouter J., 39-40, 42, 66-67, 72, 78, 96, 139, 147, 150, 153, 169-71, 178, 195, 217, 236, 252, 290, 293, 305
Harré, Rom, 107, 305
Hart, David Bentley, 281, 283, 305
Hawking, Stephen, 24, 32, 157, 298, 305
Heath, John, 237, 305
Heath, Thomas, 55, 305
Hebrews (nation), 111, 113, 131, 151, 188, 208, 236, 281
Hebrews (Epistle), 197
Heinlein, Robert, 265, 305
Heliopolitan theology, 21, 25, 27, 80
Hera, 83, 90, 115-17, 123, 187, 280
Heracles/Hercules, 115, 237-38, 244-45, 280, 282
Heraclitus/Heracleitos, 12, 72, 99, 166

Hermes, 23, 34, 37, 57, 62, 83, 117–18, 146–47, 149, 152, 167, 178–79, 239, 289, 293; see Fowden, Mercury
Herodotus, 36, 149, 208, 267, 305
Hesiod, 12, 27, 29, 31, 52, 58, 82, 87, 113–14, 142, 235, 238, 240, 305
Hildegard of Bingen, 71
Hillman, John, 237, 305
Hipparchus, 55
Holmes, Sherlock, 86, 134, 144, 153
Homer, 12, 36, 45, 57, 82–83, 99, 107, 115–16, 118, 126, 165, 221, 235, 237–39, 243
hope, 10, 24, 67, 85, 99, 106–9, 131, 133, 139, 165, 171, 191, 203, 210, 239, 242, 244, 254, 262, 267–68, 274, 279, 294
Hornung, Erik, 4, 21, 22, 25, 34, 36, 37, 39, 40, 44, 59, 60, 67, 77, 149, 151, 192–196, 198, 203, 205, 305
Hoyle, Fred, 26, 305
Hume, David, 174, 182, 304
Huxley, Julian, 279

Iamblichus of Chalcis, 23, 167–68, 170, 241, 244, 302, 303, 305
Ibn Arabi, 11
icons, 84, 148, 169
identity, 23, 100, 102, 108, 145, 191–92, 210, 225, 239, 242
Inanna, 126–27
intolerance, 153, 186, 188, 201
Isaiah, book of, 128, 132, 140, 149–50
Isis, 1, 34, 59, 67, 124, 190, 194–96, 274

Jacobsen, Thorkild, 29, 35, 41, 44–45, 76, 100, 126–27, 130, 138–39, 188, 190, 201, 204, 220, 226, 279, 305
Jaeger, Werner, 10, 305
Jaki, Stanley, 26, 306

James, William, 109, 151, 163, 180, 306
Janowitz, Naomi, 64, 168, 170, 306
Jeremiah, book of, 132, 201
Jesus, 6, 141–42, 167, 189, 277, 279–80, 282–83, 287
Job, book of, 203–4; see 70
John of Damascus, 148
John, Gospel of, 8, 284–85, 293
Johnston, S.I., 40, 306
Jones, Steven, 175–76
Joshi, S.T., 162, 174, 211, 213, 218, 248, 306, 308, 313
Judas Maccabaeus, 200
Judges, book of, 199
Julian (Emperor), 14, 78, 123, 298, 306
jumping the shark, 125

Kaiser, D., 173, 306
Kant, Immanuel, 54, 306
Karhausen, Lucien, 107, 306
Keyes, Daniel, 102, 306
King, Martin Luther, 255
Kings (I) (book), 36, 149
Kings (II) (book), 148
Kingsley, Peter, 118, 167, 280, 306
Kipling, Rudyard, 154, 306
know yourself, 101, 275
Koran, 230
Kragh, Helge, 26, 306; see Big Bang
Krauss, Lawrence, 31, 306
Kronos, 27, 62, 89–91, 114, 125, 190, 266, 304; see Saturn
Kuzminsky, Adrian, 166, 306

Lafferty, R.M., 7, 306
Laks & Most, 87–88, 307
Lambert, W.G., 100, 129, 307
Lamberton, Robert, 117–19, 224, 285, 307
Larson, Jennifer, 223, 225, 307

Index

Lasky, Richard, 103-4, 307
Lawrence of Arabia, 165
Laws, 18, 31-32, 152, 155, 160, 162, 189, 218, 259, 265
Layton, Bentley, 61, 307
Lehrer, Keith, 161-62, 307
Lem, Stanislaw, 182, 263, 307
Leslie, John, 251, 307
Levenson, Jon D., 37, 198, 202, 307
Leviathan, 128, 140, 203
Leviticus, book of, 199
Lewis, C. S., 5-7, 62, 65, 102, 166, 218, 249, 254-55, 307
Liebeschutz, J.W.W.G., 280, 307
Liu, Cixin, 178, 307
Loeb, Avi, 49, 308
Logos, 112, 176, 183, 197, 280, 283
Long & Sedley, 22, 136, 156, 181, 308
Louth, Andrew, 72, 308, 317
Lovecraft, H. P., 162-63, 174, 185, 210-13, 218, 233-34, 248, 253-54, 257-58, 260, 296, 308, 313, 317
Luke, Gospel of, 6, 8, 280, 285-86

Maccabees (I) (book), 200
Maccoby, Hyam, 22, 308
MacCoull, L. S. B., 23, 308
MacCulloch, Diarmaid, 112, 308
MacDonald, George, 143, 275, 308
MacIntyre, Alasdair, 145, 308
Mack, Katie, 97, 129, 308
Macleod & Smol, 26, 308
Macrobius, 61-62, 72, 74, 308
Mahé & Meyer, 170, 308
Maisel, Richard, 102, 105, 308
Malin, Shimon, 162, 308
Manilius, 56
Marcus Aurelius, 252
Marduk, 128-30, 138-39, 190
Markandeya, 109
Marx, Karl, 132-33, 308
Mathew, Gervase, 147, 308

Matthew, Gospel of, 15, 141-42, 186, 199, 252, 270, 280, 285-86
Maximus the Confessor, 12, 206, 314
Maycock, Alan, 3, 160, 308
McKinnon, Susie, 246
Mead, G. R. S., 69, 309
memory, 33, 93-94, 184, 208, 215, 226, 237-38, 242-46
Memphite theology, 21, 27, 194, 196-97, 310
Mendel, Arthur, 172, 309
mental microbes, 1, 102, 105, 176
Merchant, Jo, 94, 309
Merchant of Venice, 15
Mercury, 57, 61-62, 72-73, 77, 99, 169; see Hermes
Mersini-Houghton, Laura, 24, 127-28, 155-56, 309
Meyer, Marvin, 142, 309
Micah, 201
Midsummer Night's Dream, 4, 247, 248
Milne, A. A., 78, 160, 309
Minucius Felix, 188, 309
Moabites, 198-200
Montaigne, 163-64, 166, 309
Moore, Ken, 150, 309
Morenz, Siegfried, 239, 309
Morgenstern, Julian, 220, 309
Mozart, 107, 306
Muller, Richard, 48, 309
Multiple Personality Disorder (MPD), 101-6, 297, 301, 304; see 64, 185, 275
multiverse, 27, 127, 154-55, 309, 312
Murray, Les, 72, 103, 309

Naddaf, Gerard, 12, 83, 88, 99, 309
Naess, Arne, 163, 309
Nagel, Thomas, 34, 314
narrative, 19, 23, 61, 137, 154, 225, 270

Natali, Carlo, 10, 309
Naydler, Jeremy, 66, 309
Neugebauer, Otto, 57, 309
Newman, John Henry, 75, 310
Nilus Scholasticus, 147
Norris & Norris, 53, 310
North, Claire, 159, 310
nothing, 2, 19–25, 28, 31–32, 124, 128–29, 151, 181–82, 202, 262, 273–74; see Apophis, Chaos
nous, 32, 38, 71, 96, 142, 147, 178, 191, 215, 236, 313
Numa, 148, 236
numbers, 54, 94–95, 215, 281–82
Numbers, book of, 199
Nunn & Reid, 53, 310

Ockinga, Boyo G., 194, 310
O'Daly, Gerard, 197, 310
O'Flaherty, Wendy, 165, 247, 310
Odin, 195–96, 253, 255
Odysseus, 144, 201, 219–25, 238
Ogdoad Reveals the Ennead, 169, 257; see Mahé & Meyer
Only One Electron, 110
Origen, 6, 10, 16, 39, 61–63, 102, 107, 119, 123, 143, 283, 310
Orion, 53–54, 67, 239
Osiris, 22, 29, 34, 59, 66–67, 81, 86, 124, 196, 239
Ouspensky, P. D., 159, 310

Palamas, Gregory, 69, 135–36, 292–93, 310
Panofsky, E., 42, 71, 306, 310
Papaioannou, Stratis, 148, 310
Pareto, Vilfredo, 277, 310
Parker, Theodore, 255–57, 310
Parmenides, 12, 21, 88
Patrides, C. A., 263, 311
Patrologia Graeca, 12, 137
Patrologia Latina, 70
Peccorini, Francisco, 92–93, 311

Pendergrast, Mark, 73, 311
Pherekydes/Pherecydes, 12, 87–88, 313
Philo of Alexandria, 8, 22, 49, 52, 101, 111–13, 119, 168, 199, 252, 282–84, 291–92, 303, 311
Philo of Byblos, 28, 78, 298
Philokalia, 69, 101, 293, 310
Philostratus; see Apollonius
Phinehas, 199–200, 301, 303
Pike, Nelson, 13, 311
Pindar, 36, 171
Plato, *Apology*, 244
Plato, *Cratylus*, 91
Plato, *Euthyphro*, 91, 151
Plato, *Gorgias*, 91, 244
Plato, *Laws*, 115
Plato, *Meno*, 168, 215
Plato, *Phaedrus*, 71, 83–84, 89, 115, 190
Plato, *Republic*, 43, 55, 71, 93, 168, 170, 181, 213–14, 216, 241, 244, 311; see 84, Proclus
Plato, *Seventh Letter*, 179, 183, 300, 302
Plato, *Sophist*, 65, 88
Plato, *Symposium*, 38, 166, 179
Plato, *Theaetetus*, 10, 95, 99, 247
Plato, *Timaeus*, 46, 52, 54–55, 60, 205–6, 209
Plato's birth, 225
Plato's Cave, 93
Platonic Year, 55
Pleiades, 53, 145
Pliny the Elder, 150, 241
Plotinus, *Ennead* I.1 [53], 71, 237
Plotinus, *Ennead* I.4 [46], 176
Plotinus, *Ennead* I.6 [1], 61, 98, 116, 179, 182, 244
Plotinus, *Ennead* I.7 [54], 78
Plotinus, *Ennead* I.8 [51], 23, 116, 182
Plotinus, *Ennead* II.2 [14], 206
Plotinus, *Ennead* II.3 [52], 53, 60, 62–63, 181, 244

Plotinus, *Ennead* II.9 [33], 50, 59, 61–62, 64, 168, 206
Plotinus, *Ennead* III.2 [47], 24, 60, 204, 213, 242
Plotinus, *Ennead* III.4 [15], 63, 106, 245
Plotinus, *Ennead* III.5 [50], 24, 89, 154, 187
Plotinus, *Ennead* III.6 [26], 98
Plotinus, *Ennead* III.8 [30], 25, 116, 180
Plotinus, *Ennead* IV.3 [27], 4, 20, 23, 29, 38, 40, 96, 166, 181, 237, 242–44, 282
Plotinus, *Ennead* IV.4 [28], 64, 78, 142
Plotinus, *Ennead* IV.8 [6], 72, 81, 92, 108, 118, 181, 243, 245
Plotinus, *Ennead* V.1 [10], 23, 29, 95, 143, 257, 275
Plotinus, *Ennead* V.3 [49], 180, 183
Plotinus, *Ennead* V.5 [32], 64, 78, 98, 109, 185, 250
Plotinus, *Ennead* V.7 [18], 243
Plotinus, *Ennead* V.8 [31], 4, 38, 64, 96, 166, 181, 236, 266
Plotinus, *Ennead* VI.4 [22], 181, 244
Plotinus, *Ennead* VI.5 [23], 109, 165, 243, 245
Plotinus, *Ennead* VI.7 [38], 97, 149, 182–83, 194, 275
Plotinus, *Ennead* VI.9 [9], 10, 64, 89, 160, 183, 203, 293
Plutarch, 34, 148, 168–69, 187, 214, 216, 225, 236, 245, 274, 311
Plutarch, *Isis and Osiris*, 1, 12, 25, 72, 124, 195, 231, 234, 278, 311
Poimandres, 61–62, 72, 139, 252
Polansky, R., 215, 311
Porphyry of Tyre, 77–78, 82, 109, 116, 170, 197, 221, 223–24, 244–45, 303
Porphyry, *Life of Plotinus*, 78, 109, 224, 244–45

possession, 66, 72, 99–109, 301, 311; see 292
Pratchett, Terry, 134, 276, 311
prayer, 64, 76, 116, 147, 172, 219, 263, 287, 307, 316
Pressel, Esther, 103–4, 311
Prestige, G. L., 283, 311
Prince, Morton, 106, 109, 311
Pritchard, James B., 29, 44, 129–30, 139, 196, 198, 200, 289, 311
Proclus, 23, 56, 61, 64, 78, 90, 98, 114, 117–19, 210, 244, 246, 303, 311–12
Psalms, 36, 128, 198–200, 202–3
Ps-Dionysius, 71–72, 107, 206, 311; see Denis
Psyche, 150, 237, 243
Ptah, 21, 27, 32, 59, 193, 196–97
Ptah-Hotep, 289
Ptolemy, 55, 172, 311; see 94
Purves, Libby, 171, 312
Pyrrhonism, 160–66, 173, 186, 296, 306
Pythagoras, 95, 148, 172, 184, 241–43

Questions of King Milinda, 191
Quirke, Stephen, 24, 312

Radhakrishnan & Moore, 191, 240, 312
Raine, Kathleen, 185, 312
Ramsey, Frank, 207, 312
Ransome, Arthur, 207, 312
Rappe, Sara, 249, 312
Raup & Sepkoski, 48, 312
Reckford, K. J., 229, 312
refutation, 65, 70, 167–68
Rhys-Davies, Thomas William, 191, 312
Rist, J. M., 244, 312
Ritchie, D. G., 102, 312
Rochberg, Francesca, 53, 56, 68, 312
Ross, Colin, 106, 312

Ross, W.D., 26, 65, 192, 243
Rossi, Vincent, 121, 312
Rovelli, Carlo, 29, 312
Rowland Smith, 78, 312
Rubenstein, Mary-Jane, 155, 312
Russell, Bertrand, 259, 312
Russell, Eric Frank, 243, 312
Ruth, book of, 199

Sabo, Theodore, 97, 313
Sacks, Oliver, 246, 313
Samuel (I) (book), 198
Sanchuniathon of Berytus, 27–28
Sandmel, Samuel, 283–84, 312
Santillana & Von Dechend, 17, 56–57, 313
Saturn, 56, 61–62, 72, 77, 126, 169, 306; see Kronos
Sayers, Dorothy, 134, 264, 313
Schaefer & Rutledge, 103, 313
Scharf, Caleb, 49, 314
Schmidt & Frank, 47, 313
Schultz & Joshi, 211, 218
Schweizer, Andreas, 23, 41, 66, 81, 124, 130, 196, 217, 219, 287, 294, 313
Scott, Alan, 61, 313
Segal, Alan, 245, 313
Segev, Mor, 116, 313
Seneca, 22, 181
serpents, 22, 128–29, 140–41, 143, 181, 220, 253, 268, 309; see snakes
Sextus Empiricus, 161, 163, 173, 313
Shelley, P.B., 58, 314
Sherwood, Philip, 51, 314
Shoval, Ilan, 269, 314
"Shut up and calculate!," 173, 306
Shuve, Karl, 13, 314
silence, 4, 109, 148, 173, 182–84, 247, 292
Sirius, 52–53, 67
Skinner, Martyn, 68, 314

Slater, Philip, 90, 314
Slaves, 43, 86–87, 144–45, 164, 201, 205, 215, 255, 259, 279, 281
Smith, Logan Pearsall, 259, 314
Smolin, Lee, 48, 314
snakes, 58, 87, 124, 142, 167, 219, 253; see serpents
Socrates, 83, 89–91, 111–13, 151, 179, 214–15, 243–45, 247, 249, 287, 291
Sodom, 8, 112, 132
Song of Songs, 13, 314
Sorensen, Roy, 2, 314
Spanos, Nicholas, 103, 314
Spengler, Oswald, 171–72, 191, 208–9, 296, 309, 314
Sprat, Thomas, 5–6, 146, 227, 314
Sprigge, Timothy, 34, 314
Stapledon, Olaf, 46, 76, 154–55, 211, 213, 258, 260–63, 314
statues, 39–40, 64, 85, 99, 145–51, 171, 188, 306, 310, 315
Stern, Philip, 200, 315
Stevenson, Ian, 242, 306, 314
Stamatellos, Giannis, 241, 314
Stoneman, Richard, 78, 314
Strickland, Edward, 79, 314
Sturluson, Snorri, 28, 59, 131–32, 196, 253, 314
substances, 38, 52, 99, 109–10, 240, 257
Suger (Abbot), 41–42, 310
Swerdlow, N.M., 73, 315

Tacitus, 34–35
Taliban, 85
Tate, J., 12, 315
Taubes, Jacob, 232, 315
Tegmark, Max, 95, 175, 315
Tehrani, Jamshid, 53, 220, 315
Terah, 111–13
Tertullian, 232, 308
Tester, S.J., 61, 315

Thales, 87, 208
The Place (*hamaqom*), 22, 266
Theophrastus, 29
theoria, 37, 111
Thessalonians (I) (Epistle), 245
Thompson, Francis, 109, 315
Thoth, 27, 34, 58–59, 205
Thucydides, 201, 208
Tiamat, 28–29, 129–30
Tilby, Angela, 70, 72, 315
Tipler, Frank, 250, 315
Titus (Epistle), 142
Tolkien, J.R.R., 18, 26, 121, 146, 153, 159, 181, 184, 217, 225–26, 228, 247, 249, 253–54, 260–61, 286, 308, 315
tolma, 143, 261, 275; see egoism
Toynbee, Arnold, 213, 315
tradition, 4, 12, 15, 30, 53, 85, 91, 131, 138, 140, 152–53, 162–63, 193–94, 210, 246, 259, 275–76, 286, 291–92
transmigration, 208, 240–42, 314
Tyldesley, Joyce, 22, 80–81, 124–25, 209, 219, 315
Typhon, 84, 141

Ulansey, David, 55, 315
Uzdavinys, Algis, 40, 51, 66, 315–16

Van den Broek, Roelof, 271, 316
Van Dusen, Wilson, 108, 316
Vaughan, Henry, 185, 316
Virgil, 45, 56, 58, 61, 225, 232, 250
Virgin Birth, 56, 284–85, 287
virtual reality, 96, 161, 207, 250–51, 268, 271
von Balthasar, Hans Urs, 12, 316
von Rad, Gerhard, 151–52, 316
vowels, 168–69, 257

Waddell, Helen, 162, 315
waking up, 3, 76, 82, 106, 108–9, 245, 247–48, 251–52, 290, 292–93, 295
Wakoff, Michael, 78, 316
Waterfield, Robin, 21, 118, 167, 236, 239, 240, 242, 291, 316
Watts, Peter, 7, 316
Wells, H.G., 230, 249–50, 316
Wheeler, John, 110, 304
Whitman, Cedric, 116, 316
Wigner, E., 30–31, 175, 215, 316
Williams, Charles, 267, 316
Wilson, Colin, 102, 212–13, 316
Wilson, Jake, 75, 316
Wilson, Robert Anton, 258, 317
Wisdom of Solomon, 141, 149, 154, 234
Wittgenstein, Ludwig, 31, 265, 317
Woese, Carl, 233, 317
Wren-Lewis, John, 137, 259, 279, 317

Xenophanes of Colophon, 46, 88, 236, 242
Xenophon, 90–91, 280, 291

Yannaras, Christos, 184–85, 317
Yeats, W.B., 246, 267, 317
YHWH, 34, 36, 140, 185, 187, 279
Ymir, 130–31, 271

Zeus, 29, 34, 36, 52–53, 57, 62, 83, 87–89, 91, 99, 115–17, 123, 125–26, 131, 142, 167, 172, 181, 187, 190–91, 235–36, 238, 266, 274, 280, 304
Zieliński, Tadeusz, 62
Zimmer, H.R., 58, 109, 168, 216, 317
Zodiac, 56, 68, 77, 290
Zuntz, Günther, 240, 317

STEPHEN R. L. CLARK is Emeritus Professor of Philosophy at the University of Liverpool, and an Honorary Research Fellow in the Department of Theology at the University of Bristol. His books include *The Mysteries of Religion: An Introduction to Philosophy Through Religion* (1986), *How to Live Forever: Science Fiction and Philosophy* (1995), *G. K. Chesterton: Thinking Backwards, Looking Forwards* (2006), *Plotinus: Myth, Metaphor and Philosophical Practice* (2016), *Can We Believe in People: Human Significance in an Interconnected Cosmos* (2020), and *Cities and Thrones and Powers: Towards a Plotinian Politics* (2022). His chief current interests are in the philosophy of Plotinus, the understanding and treatment of non-human animals, neurodiversity, and science fiction.

www.ingramcontent.com/pod-product-compliance
Lightning Source LLC
Chambersburg PA
CBHW020324170426
43200CB00006B/259